Very Special Ships

The *Manxman* at speed on 7 July 1941. (Imperial War Museum FL 4435)

VERY SPECIAL SHIPS

Abdiel Class Fast Minelayers of World War Two

Arthur Nicholson

Seaforth
PUBLISHING
NAVAL INSTITUTE PRESS

DEDICATION

To F N 'Norman' Goodwin, author of *Midshipman RNR*,
who encouraged me to write about the fast minelayers,
and
To all the Men Who Served in the Fast Minelayers
and to their Fast Minelayers Association

Copyright © Arthur Nicholson 2015
Credited drawings copyright © Eric Leon 2015

First published in Great Britain in 2015 by
Seaforth Publishing,
Pen & Sword Books Ltd,
47 Church Street,
Barnsley S70 2AS

www.seaforthpublishing.com

Published and distributed in the
United States of America and Canada by the
Naval Institute Press,
291 Wood Road, Annapolis,
Maryland 21402-5034

www.nip.org

British Library Cataloguing in Publication Data
A catalogue record for this book is available from the British Library

Library of Congress Control Number: 2015946697

ISBN 978 1 84832 235 6

Drawings by Eric Leon
Typeset and designed by Mousemat Design Limited
Printed and bound in China by Imago

CONTENTS

Colour plate section between pages 64 and 65

ACKNOWLEDGEMENTS

IN this task, the author has received the generous help of many, many people. I would like to specifically mention the fine detective work of Sue Savidge of Winchester, a relation of the Author's wife Sandy. At the risk of leaving someone out, he wishes to acknowledge the generous assistance of the following people: Richard Alcock; Douglas Austin; Commander Erminio Bagnasco; Jo Bailey; Gertrude Barrett; Alec Bateson; Maurizio Brescia; Jane (née Friedberger) and Michael Bretherton; Jim Calcraft; Peter Cannon, Petty Officer, Royal Australian Navy, HMAS *Canberra*; Christian Carpenter; Joseph Caruana; Ron Checketts; Andrew Choong, National Maritime Museum, Woolwich; Julie Cochrane; David Davies; Elizabeth K Dickson; Michael Eisenstadt; Meredith Elsik; Contrammiraglio Maurizio Ertreo; Angela Evennett; Robert Ferry; Hans Frank; Mark Friedberger; Frederick Galea; Jock Gardner, Naval Historical Branch; Edward Barry Gibson, 4th Lord Ashbourne; Rachel Gill, Tyne & Wear Archives; Ian Goodwin; Norman Goodwin, RIP, & son Tim Goodwin; Jeremy Grindle; Catherine Hamilton née Robertson; Jean Hannant née Cowie; Brian Hargreaves, World Ship Society and *Warships*; Detlef Hartwig; Dolores Ho; Harley and Peta Hodges; Heather Johnson, National Museum of the Royal Navy; Mark Johnston; Alexander Kasterine; Christopher Langtree; Eric Leon; Ken Maher, RIP; L O Maurer; Helen Mavin, Imperial War Museum; Michael McAloon, Naval Historical Branch; Alison Metcalfe, National Library of Scotland; Jeremy Michell, National Maritime Museum, Woolwich; John Mizzi; Ray Moore, Fast Minelayers Association; Victoria Northridge, Imperial War Museum; Charles Orr Ewing; Trevor Piper; Francesca Pitaro, Associated Press Corporate Archives; Robin and Flickie Pleydell-Bouverie; Diana Porter; Anthony Price; Steven Prince, Naval Historical Branch; Bill Pye; George Robbert; Jane Rosen, Imperial War Museum; Sue and Mark Savidge; Randy Short; Peter C Smith; Sue Sullivan, *Navy News*; Bob Swartz; Leanne Tamaki, 28maoribattalion.org; Ronald Thake; Jack Tully-Jackson; Lt. Cmdr. Ben Warlow, RN; Corinna Westwood, Isle of Wight Heritage Service; Jacqueline Whiting née Ferry; Alastair Wilson; Jennifer Wraight, Admiralty Library.

To anyone he has inadvertently left out, and there is surely someone, the author sincerely apologises. The author of course takes full responsibility for any and all errors in this work.

PREFACE

THE fast minelayers of the *Abdiel* class have fascinated me since I was in my teens and somehow ran across Tom Burton's *Warship Profile No. 38*. They still do, more than forty years later. They truly were 'very special ships', a title admittedly inspired by Patrick Beesly's books *Very Special Intelligence* and *Very Special Admiral*.

I still revere that *Warship Profile*, but a 48-page booklet could not tell all the many amazing stories about these ships and the men who served in them. I have tried to include as many as I could find and I have no doubt missed some, but it is in the grand scheme of things that some stories are recorded and some are not and some are more easily found than others.

The story of six ships operating in many different places at once does not lend itself to purely linear storytelling and the organisation of the book's chapters reflects that. The alternative was to tell each ship's story one after the other and the book's first draft was actually so organised, but fortunately Julian Mannering of Seaforth Publishing thought this form of organisation better. The author is very pleased to have Seaforth publish this book.

Part of the magic of the fast minelayers is their handsome appearance. The choice of photographs, some of which have been published before but many have not, and the superlative if not stunning artwork of Eric Leon, are designed to celebrate their appearance as well as to help tell their story. The photographs include most of the wartime commanding officers of the fast minelayers and some of their officers and crew.

Making no claim to be the best or the only one able to tell the story of the fast minelayers – though I am a step-relation to Captain John S Cowie, a figure in the story – the author nevertheless hopes to have done them and the men who served in them justice.

My main regret is that this project has taken so long to come to fruition. There are now very few men of the fast minelayers left. May we remember them, as well as the men who served in them but who are no longer with us.

Arthur Nicholson
San Antonio, Texas USA
May 2015

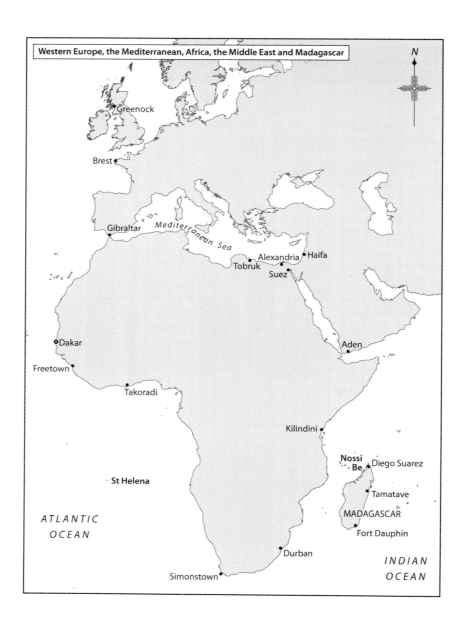

INTRODUCTION

ON 13 August 1940, as the Luftwaffe was unleashing the Blitz on Britain, Captain Edward Pleydell-Bouverie RN sat down to write a letter to his wife Pearl to tell her of his appointment to HMS *Abdiel*, the name ship of a new class of warship that was then fitting out at J S Stephens & Co at Cowes on the Isle of Wight. Unable to contain himself, he wrote in part:[1]

> All well. I've been very busy here . . . I go to a ship, it is signed + sealed. Name is '*Abdiel*' and she is brand new, won't be ready for a little while in fact. More than that I can't say but she's of a new type and can (or will) go like the very devil. I've very pleased I must say to get things settled a bit and . . . this outfit will, I think, be a most independent command in many ways and with every chance of a bit of excitement. You must contain yourself for the rest until Friday.

The Captain had his new ship and his new command perfectly pegged. The *Abdiel* would indeed 'go like the very devil', he was often to have a 'most independent command' and he and the crew of the new *Abdiel* were to experience much more than a 'bit of excitement'. The very same things could well be said of the other ships of the *Abdiel* class.

To many, the term 'minelayer' is hardly exciting and to some the term 'fast minelayer' might sound like an oxymoron. Certainly Norman Goodwin was not expecting much when in March of 1941, as a sixteen-year-old midshipman, he was ordered to report to a new ship, the *Abdiel*. Having no idea what sort of ship she might be, he was sent to look for her at Gourock on the River Clyde. Upon his arrival there, he was told that she was a fast minelayer, but only the 'minelayer' part of the name registered with him. Surveying the ships, he later recalled, 'There was nothing that looked anything like my conception of a minelayer. I imagined that she would look more like a merchant ship than a warship. I felt a little disappointed. Mine-laying sounded rather a dull occupation.' All the way in the launch out to the ship, 'I kept wondering which ship we were going to. It was something of a shock when I realised we were going alongside a grey three-funnelled ship, too big for a destroyer and too small for a cruiser.' Once aboard, he quickly realised that she was a unique ship and that he had joined an exclusive and elite club that was manned almost completely by regular Royal Navy personnel.[2]

The fast minelayers were indeed unique, and in that way alone theirs was a bold design. No other ship in any other navy combined their high speed with their capacity to carry not only a useful mine load but much, much more. In the heat of battle and arduous service, their captains and crews turned out to be extraordinary. And, contrary to what Midshipman Goodwin had assumed, minelaying did not turn out to be such a dull occupation, at least not in the fast minelayers.

The Admiralty had high hopes for the fast minelayers and their hopes would be more than fulfilled. The *Abdiel*s were not only fully capable of fulfilling the mission they were designed for, offensive minelaying, but they could also perform many other tasks their designers could have scarcely imagined, such as blockade running, transporting VIPs and more, tasks that mining expert Captain John Cowie would refer to as 'extraneous'. They would carry out the arduous tasks assigned to them in every ocean and in many of the seas, at storied places like Crete, Tobruk and Malta, in the English Channel, off Normandy and Norway and in the Pacific. In short, the *Abdiel* class fast minelayers were a brilliant success.

This is their story and the story of the men who sailed in them.

CHAPTER 1

MINES, MINELAYING AND MINELAYERS
Origins to the Eve of the Second World War

THE *Abdiel* class fast minelayers were extraordinarily versatile ships, which could do much more than lay mines, but it is safe to say they would not have been built if not for the existence of the naval mine. Like its cousin the landmine and unlike its cousin, the torpedo, the naval mine has never been considered a glamorous weapon. At times, some powers have even thought of the naval mine as a downright ungentlemanly or wicked way of waging war. Others, however, embraced it immediately and those who at first despised it then came to embrace it.

Although the popular image of a naval mine as a sphere with deadly horns is sometimes accurate, the subject is much more complicated than that and can be extremely technical. The terminology of naval mines can be rather involved. A naval mine is a 'submarine mine', an underwater explosive device set off by a ship that touches it (in the case of a contact mine) or that activates it by the ship's magnetic field (in the case of a magnetic mine), the noise of the ship (in the case of an acoustic mine) or the pressure created by a passing ship (a pressure mine). Magnetic, acoustic and pressure mines are 'influence' mines, as opposed to 'contact' ones. 'Moored mines' are connected by a 'sinker' to the seabed, while 'ground mines' lie themselves on the seabed and 'drifting mines' – well – drift on or just below the surface of the water. 'Controlled mines' are set off by someone on dry land, as opposed to 'independent mines' which explode when they receive the necessary stimulus (such as contact, noise, magnetic signature or pressure) from a passing ship. For the sake of completeness, explosive devices attached by someone to or placed on the seabed under the hull of a ship are sometimes called 'mines', such as the devices used by the Italians and the limpet mines by the British.

To make matters even more confusing, mines were once called 'torpedoes', but what is now called a torpedo or more properly a 'locomotive' torpedo, is a device that is launched from a surface ship, aircraft, submarine or shore battery and that uses steam, electricity or oxygen to propel itself against a ship (with a contact exploder) or under a ship (in the case of a magnetic exploder).

As it involves British fast minelayers, the terminology is not quite so complicated. The *Abdiel*s laid 'mines', as in independent, submarine mines, both of the contact and the influence (magnetic and acoustic) variety and of the moored (contact or magnetic) and ground (magnetic or acoustic) variety.

Whatever it is called, the naval mine is a relatively recent development in naval warfare. Putting aside explosives placed on the surface of the water and pointed in the direction of a ship, which date back to the Dutch in 1585, and concentrating just on those designed to attack a ship below the waterline, the first real pioneer in naval mining was an American, David Bushnell. Bushnell designed a one-man submarine with an explosive charge to be placed against the underwater hull of a warship. On 7 September 1776 Bushnell's *American Turtle*, manned by a Sergeant Ezra Lee, attacked the frigate HMS *Eagle* off New York. The submarine's drill was unable to penetrate the ship's copper bottom to attach the explosive and Lee had to give up the attempt, but the explosion of the charge caused some excitement among the British observers. For purposes of contemporary naval mining, Bushnell's main contribution was to be the first to set off gunpowder underwater.[1]

The first real moored contact mine was designed by another American, the inventor Robert Fulton, in about 1810, after he had tried to peddle various mine-like devices first to Napoleon and then to the British, both of whom were horrified by the weapons, and then to the Americans. Fulton's intentions were pure enough – he wanted to make war too horrible to pursue – but he only succeeded in furthering the development of a weapon that just made it worse. He may have coined an early name for the mine – the 'torpedo'.

Enter yet another American inventor, Colonel Samuel Colt, who was born in 1814 and as early as 1829 conceived an idea for a system of controlled mining called a 'harbor defense battery' while he was studying in a laboratory in Massachusetts. After patenting his revolver, Colt returned to his 'torpedo' idea, one of his favourites. In spite of the vehement opposition of ex-President John Quincy Adams, Colt eventually obtained US Government funding for a series of mine demonstrations on a series of unfortunate vessels. The first one took place on 4 July 1842 and the fourth and last one, on 13 April 1844, shattered a 500-ton ship under full sail. All of the demonstrations were successful and were well attended by dignitaries. Colonel Colt thus proved his mining idea, but by 1844 the US Government had little need of the weapon and did not adopt it. Colt instead made a fortune from his revolvers and passed away in 1862.[2]

Other nations, however, began to take some interest in the weapon, notably Imperial Russia. During the Crimean War of 1854–5, the Russians employed mines developed by a Professor Jacobi and by the Nobel family to defend the

ports of Kronstadt in the Baltic and Sevastopol in the Black Sea. While nosing around the defences off Kronstadt on 9 June 1855, the British paddle warship *Merlin* struck first one and then another mine, giving her the dubious distinction of being the first warship damaged by enemy mines. HMS *Firefly* came to her assistance after the first explosion, only to strike a mine herself. The *Merlin*'s only leak came from a fractured drainpipe, but eight sheets of copper were blown off her hull and inside she suffered considerable shock damage, with 'almost everything moveable in the ship displaced'. The *Firefly*'s hull was undamaged, but inside bulkheads were 'thrown down' or displaced and every bit of crockery broken. When HMS *Vulcan* struck a mine on 20 June, the Royal Navy had had enough, and the next day began carrying out the first minesweeping operation in history, recovering thirty-three 'infernal machines,' the standard British term of the day for sea mines.[3]

It was their use in the American Civil War that provided the real spur to the development of

Colonel Samuel Colt, a pioneer of the naval submarine mine. (Robert Swartz)

An engraving depicting the mining of the *Merlin* and *Firefly* off Kronstadt in 1855. (Author's collection)

mines as a viable weapon of naval war. The Confederates used mines in great numbers to defend their harbours against the Union blockade. Confederate mines were called 'torpedoes' and when Admiral David Farragut shouted, 'Damn the torpedoes, full speed ahead!' during the battle of Mobile Bay, he was referring to Confederate naval mines. In December 1862, Confederate mines accounted for the first warship to be sunk by such weapons, the Union ironclad *Cairo*. In all, thirty-seven Union and Confederate ships were sunk or disabled by mines during the war.

The successful use of naval mines by the Russians and the Confederacy led to increased international interest in the weapon, but the United States lost the lead in the field to other nations. Advances in mine design were greatly assisted by the introduction of guncotton in 1870, long after its invention by a Swiss chemist in 1846.[4]

This new form of warfare was not at first welcomed by the Royal Navy, as it threatened its freedom of movement and its command of the seas. Nevertheless, in 1876 the Royal Navy commissioned its Naval Torpedo School at the old HMS *Vernon*, where, despite British aversion to the very idea of mines, the Royal Navy began to develop its own mines. In an important innovation, the Royal Navy invented the 'plummet' version of the 'automatic sinker', which allowed mines to be laid in varying depths of water but to rest at a pre-set distance under the water.

The Royal Navy's bias against mines changed considerably with the Russo-Japanese war of 1904–5, which marked the first use of independent mines as offensive tactical weapons.[5] On April 13, 1904, Japanese mines laid near Port Arthur by the 745-ton *Koryo Maru*[6] sank the Russian battleship *Petropavlovsk*, with 652 dead, including the Russians' best naval commander Admiral Makarov. Just a month later, on 15 May, mines from the Russian minelayer *Amur* accounted for two Japanese battleships, the *Hatsuse* and the *Yashima*, also off Port Arthur, with the loss of 493 lives in the *Hatsuse*.[7] The 15,000-ton *Hatsuse* was a serious loss; built by Armstrong in Britain, she was armed with four 12in and sixteen 6in guns and was one of the newest battleships in the Japanese fleet.[8] Before the war ended in 1905, enough Russian and Japanese warships had been sunk or damaged by mines to impress every naval power, including Great Britain.

The naval mine had truly arrived, but its success also led to efforts to regulate this abhorrent (to some) weapon. Questions about the employment of this relatively new weapon

The Japanese battleship *Hatsuse*, sunk by a Russian mine in May 1904. (IWM Q 41327)

caused the major maritime powers to attend a Hague Conference on the subject in 1907, but the resulting 'Convention Relative to the Laying of Automatic Submarine Contact Mines (No. VIII)'[9] was not strong enough or well enough observed, to stem the use of the weapon.

The Royal Navy finally began taking steps toward a minelaying capability. Beginning in 1907, it converted to minelayers seven old *Apollo* class cruisers, two of which were named the *Apollo* and the *Latona*. They could make about 20 knots, were armed with 4.7in guns and could carry 100 mines. They constituted the 'Minelaying Squadron' commanded by a 'Captain-in-Charge Minelayers' and operated directly under the orders of the Admiralty. The Navy also developed a 'Service' type mine with a charge of 325lbs.[10]

At the beginning of the First World War, the Royal Navy was galvanised into action by almost immediate use of offensive minelaying by the Imperial Germany Navy, which had enthusiastically embraced the relatively new form of warfare. Shortly after a state of war broke out between Britain and Germany, the Germans wasted no time and sent the former pleasure steamer *Königin Luise* across the Channel into waters off the English coast to lay her 200 mines. On the morning of 5 August, she was sighted by HMS *Amphion*, a scout cruiser of 3440 tons armed with 4in guns,[11] and the 2nd Destroyer Flotilla. She hurriedly laid her mines 30 miles off the coast of Suffolk before her pursuers opened fire.

The *Königin Luise* fled at her maximum speed of 21 knots and fought back gamely with her light guns, as her 3.4in guns had not yet been fitted. A truly fast minelayer might have escaped, but this one was pounded to pieces after Captain Biermann refused to strike her colours. She finally sank, with much of her crew still aboard and the survivors were picked up by her British pursuers. The next morning, the same British ships unwittingly sailed over part of the minefield and the *Amphion* struck a mine. After another massive explosion, she foundered in just minutes, taking with her more than 150 of her officers and men and many of the German survivors aboard.

The naval mining war was on. The first British minelaying operation was carried out on the night of 2 October in the Channel to the north of Ostende by the old minelayers *Apollo*, *Intrepid*, *Andromache* and *Iphegenia*, who were escorted by destroyers. Two more fields were laid on succeeding nights, with a total of 1064 mines laid. As it turned out, the field interfered with the route to Zeebrugge and part of the first minefield had to be swept.[12] It was a learning experience.

The cruiser *Amphion* after hitting a German mine, 6 August 1914. (IWM Q 57066)

The battleship *Audacious* sinking after hitting a German mine, 27 October 1914. (IWM Q 48342)

The first major victim of German minelaying after the *Amphion* was the British dreadnought battleship *Audacious*. On 27 October 1914, she was sailing off the coast of Ireland for a gunnery exercise when she struck a single mine laid by the former passenger liner *Berlin*. After a twelve-hour battle to keep her afloat and tow her to safety, she finally sank by the stern, her magazines exploding as she went down. Unlike the *Königin Luise*, the *Berlin* evaded notice for some time, until she finally entered Norwegian waters to evade British ships and was interned.[13]

Shortly afterwards, naval mines achieved one of their greatest successes. During the Gallipoli campaign, a Turkish steamer named the *Nousret* laid a mere twenty mines in the path of an Anglo-French naval effort to force the Narrows on 18 March 1915. This seemingly meagre minefield was cleverly laid and caused the sinking of the French pre-dreadnought battleship *Bouvet* and the British pre-dreadnoughts *Irresistible* and *Ocean*. The mines caused the attempt to force the Narrows with warships alone to be abandoned.[14] As a result, Allied and Anzac troops had to be sent in and in the end the campaign in Gallipoli eventually failed miserably. Revenge for the destruction wrought by the humble *Nousret* was a long time coming, but it did come. In January 1918, mines laid by the *Latona* sank the once-German-then-Turkish light cruiser *Breslau* and severely damaged the battlecruiser *Goeben* in the Aegean.

The Royal Navy was encouraged by the possible use of mines against the emerging threat from German U-boats. During the War, the Royal Navy did not design or build any new minelayers, but employed a number of ships converted into minelayers. The most unusual conversion took shape when a 'Clapham Junction' maze of mine rails was fitted to the quarterdeck of the 'large light cruiser'

The minelayer *Latona* in 1916. (Imperial War Museum SP 333)

Courageous, a white-elephant project of First Sea Lord 'Jacky' Fisher. At 18,600 tons, she was the largest minelayer ever, with her four 15in guns, she was certainly the most heavily-armed minelayer ever and with a speed of 32 knots, she was one the fastest of any era.[15] Unfortunately, perhaps, she never laid a mine operationally. A few years after the end of the First World War, she and her sister *Glorious* were converted into aircraft carriers and served as such into the Second World War until their untimely ends.

The most prodigious minelayers in the Royal Navy in the Great War were converted merchant ships, which laid many thousands of mines in defensive minefields designed to entrap U-boats venturing out to attack merchant shipping. Of course, they were too slow for offensive minelaying. The Royal Navy eventually found a different sort of ship for that.

In 1916 the Royal Navy began to convert destroyers into minelayers and by far the best known and most successful was undoubtedly the *Abdiel*, a *Marksman* class flotilla leader. Ordered as part of the 1914 war programme, she was laid down in 1915 and was converted before her completion in 1916 to carry eighty mines. Essentially a large destroyer for her day, she was 324ft overall and displaced about 1600 tons and was armed with 4in guns. She had four funnels and her turbines could generate 36,000 horsepower. She could make 34 knots, much faster than any other minelayer conversion up to that time.[16] She did not have an enclosed mining deck and when carrying mines on the rails on her deck she would erect a screen to hide them, painted to depict the torpedo tubes

The large light cruiser-minelayer *Courageous*. (Constance Keogh via Hermione Alcock)

she would otherwise have been carrying.

Shortly after her completion, the *Abdiel* was attached to the Fleet. On 4 May 1916, she laid one offensive minefield off the Vyl lightship. Under Commander Berwick Curtis, she then played a unique part in the battle of Jutland on 31 May and 1 June. After the rival battlecruiser squadrons and then the two rival battle fleets encountered each other on the afternoon and evening of the 31st, the German High Seas Fleet turned away and the fleets lost contact with each other in the fading light. Admiral Jellicoe sought to cut off the escape routes of the High Seas Fleet and, as one precaution, at 21.32 he ordered the *Abdiel* to lay a minefield 15 miles off the Vyl lightship,[17] an area through which the German High Seas Fleet would have to pass if it attempted to escape via the Horns Reef.

It had been intended for the *Abdiel* to lay this minefield anyway, even before the British knew the High Seas Fleet was at sea and the *Abdiel* duly laid the new minefield, in two lines of forty mines each, between 01.24 and 02.04 the morning of 1 June. As it turned out, the High Seas Fleet did use that route for its retirement.

The destroyer-minelayer *Abdiel*, which was with the Grand Fleet at Jutland. (IWM SP 3155)

German minesweepers sent out to meet the returning ships failed to discover the *Abdiel*'s minefields,[18] and at 05.30 the German dreadnought battleship *Ostfriesland* hit a mine laid by the *Abdiel*, though it was likely one from the field she had laid on 4 May. Like other German dreadnought battleships, the *Ostfriesland* was tough. While she lost one man killed and ten wounded, her torpedo bulkhead held and she only shipped 400 tons of water,[19] and she was able to keep up with the rest of the High Seas Fleet. The incident did create some alarm in the High Seas Fleet and at least one ship started firing its guns at imagined submarines. The *Ostfriesland* was able to reach port, was repaired and ready for sea again by 29 July.[20] She survived the war, only to be transferred to the United States, which sank her in July 1921 in trials with Colonel Billy Mitchell's bombers. That the *Ostfriesland*'s sister dreadnoughts did not strike more mines laid by the *Abdiel* was perhaps due to the limited size of the minefield that could be laid by a minelayer carrying only eighty mines. This was a shortcoming of the first *Abdiel*'s design that the British would later remedy in a second *Abdiel*.

With the German High Seas Fleet rarely venturing out again before the end of the war, the *Abdiel* continued her minelaying duties, but did not have another opportunity to ply her offensive minelaying skills as she had at Jutland. Her sister *Gabriel* was similarly converted and a number of other destroyers were converted to minelaying duties before the end of the war. In 1918 the *Abdiel* was the leader of the 20th Flotilla, based at Immingham, She survived the war and was not sold for scrap until 1936.

Most importantly for the future of British

offensive minelaying, the Grand Fleet's Admiral Jellicoe was very impressed by the *Abdiel*'s role in the battle of Jutland. Writing after the war, he referred to her as 'this most useful little vessel' and because one of the British submarines Stationed near Horn's Reef on the morning of 1 June heard several underwater explosions between 02.15 and 05.30, 'it was judged that several enemy ships had struck mines'. Finally, he noted that she had 'carried out her duties with the success which has always characterised her work',[21] praise that boded well for her unique type of ship.

The Imperial German Navy engaged in minelaying from the first days of the Great War and to it goes the distinction of building the first fast minelayers designed and built as such, the *Brummer* and *Bremse*, the former completing just before the battle of Jutland in 1916 and the latter just after. Using turbines ordered for the Russian battlecruiser *Navarin*, they could develop 33,000 horsepower from coal and oil-fired boilers and were rated at a maximum speed of 28 knots, though 34 knots has been claimed for them. Rated as cruiser-minelayers, their normal displacement was 4385 tons, they were lightly armoured and were armed with 5.9in guns and 88mm anti-aircraft guns. It has been claimed they could carry from 360 to 450 mines, an astounding feat for ships of their size without an enclosed mining deck, but it was probably more like 120.[22] With their three funnels and raked bow, the two ships were built to resemble the British *Arethusa* class light cruisers.

The *Bremse* and *Brummer* did carry out some minelaying operations, without spectacular results, but are best known for attacking and nearly annihilating a British-escorted convoy sailing between Scotland and Norway in October 1917. Their designed appearance worked well; at first mistaken by the convoy escorts for British cruisers, they got in the first shots and quickly sank the British destroyers *Strongbow* and *Mary Rose* and then most of the ships in the convoy. Both ships were interned at the end of the war and were scuttled with most of the rest of the High Seas Fleet at Scapa Flow in June 1919.[23]

While the *Abdiel* was the first fast destroyer-minelayer, the *Brummer* and *Bremse* were the first fast cruiser-minelayers, though not blindingly fast or fitted with an enclosed mine

The German cruiser-minelayer *Brummer*. (Author's collection)

deck. The Germans revived their names for ships that served in the Second World War and were equipped for minelaying, but Germany never built anything like a fast minelayer again, instead relying on destroyers and S-boats for that function.

At the Admiralty, on the other hand, the idea of a fast offensive minelayer had definitely caught on and doggedly hung on. According to a detailed study of the subject, in July 1918 the Admiralty Controller requested a specially-built fast minelayer, based on two cruiser designs then under construction, the large *Hawkins* class with 7.5in guns or the smaller 'E' class with 6in guns (completed after the war as the *Emerald* and *Enterprise*). So close to the end of the war, the idea lapsed, but was revived in earnest in 1920.[24]

The Admiralty studied various options between the wars and the result was the 6740-ton minelayer HMS *Adventure*. Laid down in 1922 and not completed until 1927, she was armed with 4.7in guns for anti-aircraft defence and carried 280 mines in an enclosed mining deck. She was designed to make 28 knots, but was too large and slow for offensive minelaying.[25] A follow-on design to the *Adventure* was considered, but in the end did not materialise. The idea lapsed for the time being, but did not quite die.

Instead, after the *Adventure* was built the need for offensive minelayers was addressed in other ways. Several classes of standard destroyers were outfitted as minelayers, much as the *Abdiel* had been in the First World War. In the event, the destroyers so fitted were two of the 'E' class, the *Express* and *Esk*, later followed by four destroyers of the 'I' class, the *Icarus*, *Impulsive*, *Ivanhoe* and *Intrepid*.

The minelayer *Adventure* early in her career. (Constance Keogh via Hermione Alcock)

Submarine minelaying was introduced. In the early 1930s six members of the *Grampus* class were built.[26] Of the six, the *Seal* was damaged and captured by the Germans in 1940, but the *Rorqual* would make quite a name for herself in the Second World War.

The Royal Navy actually did construct one purpose-built minelayer in the 1930s, but the 805-ton coastal minelayer *Plover*, completed in 1937, could make only 14.75 knots and was thus the antithesis of a fast, offensive minelayer,[27] though she later impersonated one in a wartime propaganda film called *HM Minelayer*.[28]

These expedients were not sufficient for real offensive minelaying. In 1935, the Admiralty was presented with a memorandum urging the construction of 'a number of specially designed vessels to form the permanent nucleus of an offensive mine force'.[29] In 1936, the Admiralty became interested in a replacement for the *Adventure* and explored the design of a single large minelayer of about 9000 tons, with 5.25in guns, 360 mines, cruiser-like armour and a speed of 38 knots.[30] At least in November of 1936, it was giving serious consideration to an 8000-ton minelayer with a speed of 34–38 knots.[31] Those designs never saw the light of day; something more suitable was needed.

The minelayer *Adventure* in camouflage on 30 June 1942. (Author's collection)

CHAPTER 2

GETTING IT JUST RIGHT
Designing the *Abdiel* Class

There is nothing like a threat to focus the mind and, as Britain rearmed in response to the threat from Nazi Germany in the 1930s, the Admiralty finally decided what it really needed was a small fast minelayer. In January 1937, the Controller of the Admiralty gave verbal instructions that a sketch design of such a ship should be prepared. They were to be known as 'fast minelayers', *not* 'cruiser-minelayers', though they have been frequently referred to as such, even by the enemy. For administrative purposes, they were rated as 'cruisers and above'.[1]

For a completely unprecedented type of ship, their design moved along relatively quickly, especially since the Construction Department of the Admiralty was very busy with many other designs at a time of fevered rearmament. At that time, the Director of Naval Construction was Sir Stanley Goodall and his very able assistant was Sir Charles Lillicrap. The Chief of the Naval Staff (the First Sea Lord) approved a sketch design on 19 July 1938 and Goodall submitted specifics of the design and drawings for the approval of the Board of Admiralty on 18 November. The Board approved the design's legend and drawings on 1 December 1938. In the meantime, tenders from prospective builders were to be invited so that orders might be placed before the end of the year.

During the design process, there were many choices to be made as the design of the fast minelayers began to take shape. At first, the design called for just two twin 4in gun mounts, but this was increased to three. It was proposed at one time to fit two of them aft and one forward and somewhat detailed plans were drawn up,[2] sufficient to inspire an artist's impression of the design. In the end, however, two ('A' and 'B') were to be fitted forward, one superfiring over the other and one ('Y') aft.

During the design process, some bad ideas were rejected. The idea of replacing the 4in dual-purpose guns – which could be used against aircraft or surface targets – with two heavy weather-proof, power-operated 4.7in twin mountings with only 50° of elevation (which were to be fitted in the 'L' class destroyers then under development) was fortunately rejected, as they would have been of little use against aircraft. One of the worst ideas, the provision of quadruple 21in torpedo tubes, was also rejected. During the design process, it had to be pointed out that the 'offensive' in the term 'offensive minelayer' meant the minefield they were to lay rather than the ship itself and the emphasis on maintaining high speed had to be pointed out in connection with additional fittings that would decrease their speed.

The result was a class of ships that was larger than any British destroyer and smaller than any British cruiser and plenty faster than any of them. Specifically, at 2650 tons standard displacement, the *Abdiel*s were larger than the largest British destroyers of the day, the 1850-ton 'Tribal' class, an example of which was the legendary HMS *Cossack*, and were smaller than the smallest modern British light cruisers of the day, the 5419-ton[3] *Arethusa* class, an example of which was the similarly legendary HMS *Penelope*. The *Abdiel*s' displacement was 3780 tons in deep condition, their length overall was 417ft 11in, their maximum beam was 40ft, their draught forward was 10ft and 12ft aft.[4]

Many regarded the *Abdiel*s as very attractive ships. Rear Admiral Sir Morgan Morgan-Giles, who as a veteran of the war in the Mediterranean when they were operating there likely had plenty of opportunities to observe them, said it best: 'What lovely ships those *Abdiel*s were.'[5] Captain John S Cowie, who had a hand in the 1935 memorandum that eventually led to their construction, referred to them as 'these beautiful little ships'. Samuel Elliot Morison, the official American naval historian of the Second World War, described the *Ariadne* as 'handsome'.[6]

Sir Stanley Goodall, Director of Naval Construction during the design of the *Abdiel* class. (NPG x 89436, undated portrait by Elliott & Fry, © National Portrait Gallery, London)

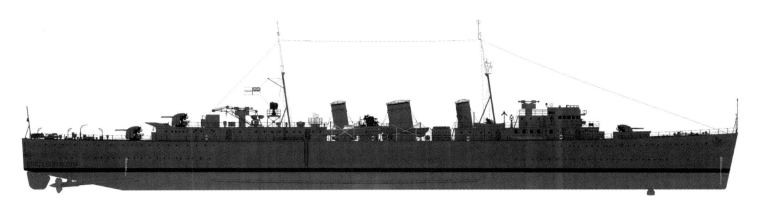

The *Abdiels* had a raked stem and a cruiser stern and were flush-decked, with the sheer line of the upper deck running straight most of their length but then rising gently from the bridge to the stem. Their bridge was much more like a destroyer's than a cruiser's. They shipped a tripod foremast aft of the bridge and forward of the first funnel and a shorter tripod mainmast aft of the third funnel, with both masts upright, not raked. The two twin 4in gun mounts forward and the single one aft gave their appearance a certain balance and a look of truculence.

One of the most distinctive features of the class was their three funnels, of almost equal height, the middle one larger in cross-section than the first and third ones. The fore funnel was 46ft 8in above the waterline. In having three funnels, they were unique among warships built during the Second World War.

The *Abdiels'* twin 4in (102mm) Mk XVI guns were in shielded Mk XIX mounts. They fired a 67lb fixed round with a firing cycle of five seconds. The guns were 45 calibres long, i.e. 45 x 4in, and could elevate to 80° and could depress to 10° below the horizontal.[7] The *Abdiels* were to carry 250 rounds per gun for their 4in guns.[8] In spite of reports to the contrary, which began at least as early as the 1941 edition of *Jane's Fighting Ships* and persisted for decades, the *Abdiels* never, ever, carried 4.7in guns.

The disposition of the 4in guns enabled the *Abdiels* to ship a Mk M (or Mk VII) four-barrel, 2pdr (40mm) pom-pom mount to be placed on a bandstand aft of the third funnel with excellent arcs of fire, instead of between the second and third funnels with much poorer ones. The pom-poms had barrels 39 calibres long, with elevation of 80° and a rate of fire of about 100 rounds per minute per gun. The projectile weighed 1.684lb.

– not 2lb – and the entire fixed round weighed 3lb. The *Abdiels* were to carry 1800 rounds per barrel. The ships were designed so that the four-barrel pom-pom could later be replaced by an eight-barrel pom-pom, but this was never done.

The *Abdiels'* gun armament also included two quadruple Mk III .5in (12.7mm) Vickers machine guns, which were fitted in the port and starboard bridge wings and for which the *Abdiels* carried 2500 rounds per barrel. The Vickers machine guns were soon replaced or at least supplemented by up to seven single-mounted, Swiss-designed 20mm Oerlikon cannon, a much better weapon with a slower rate of fire (465–480rpm vs. 650–700rpm) but a much heavier HE shell, weighing 0.272lb (vs. 1.326 oz. for the .5in gun). The Vickers machine gun was 62.2 calibres in length and the Oerlikon cannon was 70 calibres in length, which resulted in a higher muzzle velocity.[9] The *Abdiels* were to carry 2400 rounds per gun for the Oerlikons.

As for fire control and 'sensors', the *Abdiels'* 4in guns were controlled by a Mk III director, or High Angle Control System (HACS), sited aft of the bridge, which was equipped with a rangefinder and a Type 285 radar aerial. The pom-pom was controlled by a Mk III director that was sited just forward of the mount. Neither director was optimal. The Vickers machine guns and later the Oerlikons had to make do with local control. The initial four ships sported a Type 286 radar aerial on the foremast, and were equipped with a Type 128 Asdic – now called sonar – for detecting submarines and a DF coil forward of the wheelhouse.

Last but surely not least, the *Abdiels'* armament naturally included an outfit of mines. At first, they were designed to carry 100 mines, but the number was fortunately increased to 150

A profile of the 1938 Fast Minelayer design. (Eric Leon)

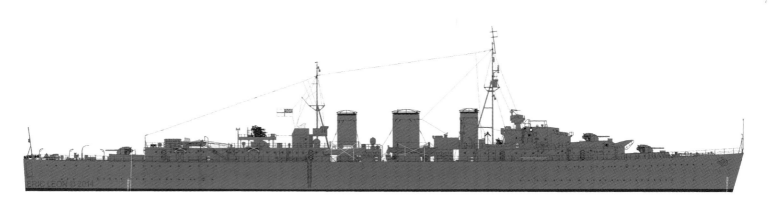

A profile of the final design of the *Abdiel* class. (Eric Leon)

and in practice they could carry a maximum of 160. The mines were loaded through four hatches in the upper deck and were stowed on tracks in a completely enclosed mining deck that ran much of their length. The mines were disgorged through two mining doors at the stern. The fast minelayers were fitted with the 'chain conveyor' system for moving the mines around and laying them, with the older 'wire and bogie' system as a backup.

To facilitate their minelaying operations, the *Abdiel*s were equipped with taut wire measuring gear, which fulfilled the very important function of allowing the positions of their minefields to be assessed with greater accuracy. The gear was first designed for ships laying submarine telegraph cables and consisted of 'in simple terms a long length of piano wire paid out astern of the minelayer, the amount of wire run off being measured with a high degree of accuracy and recorded on a form of cyclometer'.[10] It would prove to be a vital tool for the fast minelayers, when it worked.

The *Abdiel*s' capacious mining deck was a salient feature of the ships, designed for mines weighing $1^{1}/_{4}$ tons to run on a 'Clapham Junction' network of rails. The ships were equipped with two large cranes, one to port and another to starboard. A post-war history of the Navy's Construction Department recognised that the fast minelayers were often used for carrying stores and naively claimed that the stores carried on the mining deck were limited to 200 tons.[11] That may have been the official policy, but someone must have neglected to tell the Construction Department that in practice the *Abdiel*s carried at much as 373 tons of stores and equipment on the mining deck.[12]

The ships were unarmoured, with only 10lb protective plating on the bridge. Their hulls were too small for any special protection against torpedoes, other than their normal compartmentation, which unfortunately featured fairly large machinery spaces prone to flooding over a large area with a single torpedo. In hindsight, the bigger problem was their large, undivided mining deck, which did not improve their chances of survival in the event of flooding.

The *Abdiel*s' accommodation was to be that of a cruiser or above and their designed complement was twelve officers and 224 men; in practice they accommodated more, by one count 260.[13] They were also capable of carrying many passengers and sometimes carried 'special' ones, such as brass hats, wounded men and POWs. Their designed complement of boats included a 25ft motor cutter and a 14ft sailing dinghy to port, a 27ft whaler and a 25ft motor boat to starboard, and a 16ft planing dinghy atop the after deckhouse.

The heart of the design of the fast minelayers was, naturally, their machinery. The design provided for four boilers with a working pressure of 300lb/sq. in. at 200° F superheat, divided between two boiler rooms, No 1 forward of No 2, with one boiler in each compartment trunked into the middle funnel. They sported two sets of single-reduction geared turbines – high-power, low-power and cruising turbines – in a single engine room, with the associated gearing in a gearing room immediately aft of the engine room. The turbines drove two shafts and two propellers, each of which had a diameter of $11^{1}/_{2}$ft. Each boiler was designed to develop 18,000 SHP at 350 revolutions per minute, for a total of 72,000 SHP, exactly double that of the

Abdiel of the First World War and more than any destroyer in the Royal Navy at the time; the 'Tribal' class destroyers developed 44,000 SHP.[14] The *Abdiels*' designed maximum speed was 39.5 knots at 350 revolutions.

However, the *Abdiels*' true maximum speed soon became the stuff of exaggeration, if not legend. One former crewman claimed with complete earnestness and sincerity to have been shown his ship was making 50 knots. The controversy over their true speed has persisted at least as late as 2012, in the pages of the *Navy News*, where a claimed speed of 44 knots prompted some spirited debate. The fact is that while the *Abdiels* were very fast ships, they could not defy the laws of physics. Their design was original but not obviously innovative, especially since they lacked a secret such as superheated boilers; they simply packed very powerful machinery into a small hull with just two shafts and propellers. If there was secret to their speed, it was that they packed more power on each shaft (36,000 SHP) than any other British warship[15] besides the battlecruiser *Hood*, which was also designed to develop 36,000 horsepower on each of her (four) shafts.[16]

In any case, they were without a doubt the fastest ships in the Royal Navy and may have made just over 40 knots. The *Welshman* made 37.6 knots on trials,[17] and on her trials the *Manxman* made 35.6 knots while developing 73,000 SHP.[18] After her refit in 1942, the *Abdiel* made 38.6 knots, according to her Navigator, Lieutenant Alastair Robertson, who took great care to measure her speed. For the sake of comparison, the highest speed a major British warship ever made on trials was the 39.4 knots made by the Yarrow 'S' class destroyer HMS *Tyrian* in 1919, though she was in a light condition and with 'very highly stressed machinery'. In service, she could probably make 36 knots with a clean bottom.[19]

More importantly, again and again the *Abdiels* proved that they could maintain high speed in real sea conditions. Almost as important, they could do so without excessive vibration, which would have hindered their effectiveness. A downside to great speed was that, at least early in the *Abdiel*'s first commission, it led to cavitation, erosion of the base of the propellers. The propellers had to be replaced, but for a time she had to limit her speed to 25 knots.[20]

The *Abdiels* were faster than any ship in the US Navy and were equalled or outstripped by very few ships of other navies. For speed, the *Abdiels*' competitors were the six French super-destroyers of the *Fantasque* class (2569 tons, up to 45.02 knots on trials), the French super-destroyers *Volta* and *Mogador* (2994 tons, up to 43.78 knots on trials),[21] the Italian-built Soviet destroyer leader *Tashkent* (2893 tons, rated at 110,000 SHP and 42 knots),[22] the three Italian small light cruisers of the 'Capitani Romani' class (3747 tons, up to more than 43 knots),[23] and the Japanese large destroyer *Shimakaze*, which was about the size of an *Abdiel*, at 2567 tons, and made as much as 40.7 knots at 79,240 SHP during her short life, but she also sported boilers that operated at an extremely high temperature (400° C) and pressure (571 psi).[24] Not to take away anything from these ships, but they were not nearly as versatile as an *Abdiel*, though the *Tashkent* was used a fast transport during the siege of Sevastopol in 1942[25] before she was damaged at sea and then sunk at the quayside by German dive bombers.

The speed of the *Abdiels* was one thing, but their endurance was a very different matter. The *Abdiels* were designed to store 591 tons of oil fuel and 58 tons of diesel fuel, which was primarily for their generators but could be used in the boilers as well. They were to have an endurance of 5300 to 5500 miles at 15 knots when six months out of dock (and with a correspondingly barnacled bottom), but it was estimated from their sea trials that their endurance was only 4680 miles under those conditions. With a clean bottom, their endurance was estimated at 5810 miles.[26] In 1942, based on experience with the *Manxman*, the Admiralty estimated their endurance as 3300 miles at 20 knots, 2070 miles at 25 knots, 1450 miles at 30 knots, 1060 miles at 35 knots and only 845 miles at their maximum speed of 38 knots.[27]

The *Abdiels*' limited endurance was to become a real concern and was the Achilles' heel of the design. This unfortunate trait was to some extent rectified in the Repeat *Abdiels*. In not living up to their designed endurance, the *Abdiels* were hardly unique among British warships of the Second World War; according to a Royal Navy study, British warships entered the war with machinery that was 25 per cent less economical than that used in the US Navy.[28]

Another class that disappointed in this regard was no less than the *King George V* class battleships. Their fuel consumption under trials conditions was 2.4tons/hr at 10 knots, but in practice it was 6.5 tons/hr, due to heavy consumption by auxiliaries and steam leaks. In 1942, it was found that the true endurance of the new American battleship *Washington* was double that of a *KGV*.[29] During the *Bismarck* chase, both the *King George V* and the *Prince of Wales* barely made port after playing their parts. That the *Abdiel*s were not unique in their disappointing endurance would have been little comfort.

When the *Abdiel*s were designed, there was nothing like them. And there was never anything like them. Before and during the Second World War, a number of navies constructed purpose-built minelayers with enclosed mine decks, but none of them could exceed 21 knots. The US Navy's sole representative was the USS *Terror*, which on a displacement of 5875 tons was armed with four 5in guns and could carry a whopping 900 mines, but could not make more than 18 knots.[30] Similarly, the Imperial Japanese Navy built the *Tsuguru*, *Itsukushima* and *Okinoshima*,[31] the Polish Navy the *Gryf*, the Royal Norwegian Navy the *Olav Tryggvason*, the Spanish Navy the *Jupiter*, *Marte*, *Neptuno* and *Vulcano* and the Soviet Navy the *Marti,* actually the former Imperial Russian yacht *Shtandart*.[32] The Royal Netherlands Navy built a number of small, slow minelayers, the newest being the *Jan van Brakel* and the *Willem Van de Zaan*.

The originators of the fast cruiser-minelayer, the Germans built two minelayers before the war, the *Brummer* and the *Bremse*. The *Bremse* could even make 27 knots, but they were not the equal of their Great War namesakes. Just before the war broke out, the Germans did design a class of purpose–built minelayers, the first being known to history as just 'Minenschiff A'. The design provided for a ship of 5800 tons, 4.1in and 37mm guns and enclosed minedecks with a capacity of 400 mines. With a speed of only 28 knots, however, they did not quite qualify as fast minelayers and in any event their construction was not pursued.[33]

The closest analogue to the *Abdiel*s was the French cruiser-minelayer *Pluton*, later renamed *La Tour d'Auvergne*, which was launched in 1929. She carried four 5.5in guns and 290 mines on a semi-enclosed mine deck and was rated at 30 knots. She was lost to an accidental explosion of her mines at Casablanca on 13 September 1939,[34] and so never had the chance to prove her worth.

Not that an effective offensive minelayer had to have an enclosed mine deck or carry many mines. The Italian *Regia Marina* employed light cruisers and destroyers for minelaying and on 3 June 1941, a force of five light cruisers and seven destroyers laid two fields northeast of Tripoli.[35] The effort bore fruit more than six months later, on 19 December, when the Royal Navy's Force K ran across one of the fields and lost the light cruiser *Neptune* and the destroyer *Kandahar*. The German *Kriegsmarine* used destroyers to carry out a daring and highly effective offensive minelaying campaign off the British coast in the winter of 1939–40. In this effort, German destroyers undertook eleven missions, all undetected by the British and laid 1800 mines, which resulted in the sinking of three British destroyers, sixty-seven merchant ships totalling 238,467 tons and other vessels.[36]

While some other navies employed fast cruisers or destroyers for offensive minelaying duties, none of them was as fast in real conditions, none of them had an enclosed mine deck, none could carry the mineload of the *Abdiel*s and none was as versatile. The *Abdiel*s were not the only game in town in offensive minelaying, but they were truly unique and were no doubt the best.

Once the design of the *Abdiel*s was finalised, the first three fast minelayers, the *Abdiel*, *Latona* and *Manxman*, were ordered in December 1938 as part of the 1938 shipbuilding programme. A fourth ship, the *Welshman*, was approved at the November 1938 Cabinet meeting as part of the 1939 programme, but she was not actually ordered until March 1939.[37] The first two fast minelayers were named after minelayers that served in the First World War,[38] but the *Manxman* and the *Welshman* would be exceptions to the rule.

CHAPTER 3

THE ROYAL NAVY READIES FOR MINE WARFARE IN THE SECOND WORLD WAR

While in practice the *Abdiel*s performed many functions, they were first and foremost designed for minelaying operations and obviously required suitable mines. The Royal Navy had developed magnetic and acoustic mines by the end of the First World War and continued development of contact mines between the wars with the Mk XIV mine with the traditional Herz horns and the Mk XV with 'switch horns'. The end result was that a new type of moored contact mine, the Mk XVII, was developed in time to be used by the fast minelayers. More suited for quantity production in wartime, the new mine used a broader gauge than previous mines, had eleven 'switch' horns, had a detachable case for two different sizes of charges, 500lbs and 320lbs, and could be laid in

500 fathoms of water. With an eye to the future, the Royal Navy started production before the war started of a moored magnetic mine designated the M Mk I.[1] Any of these types of mine could be laid with a Mk XVII sinker.

The *Abdiel*s were to need mine depots to load their mines from in various locations, including Frater, Wrabness and Immingham, but the most important for them was the one at Milford Haven on the south coast of Wales. There were also mining depots in such far-flung places as Malta, Haifa, Trincomalee, Hong Kong and Singapore. The *Abdiel*s would use many different ports for their minelaying operations, but the most important one in home waters was located at the Kyle of Lochalsh, also known as 'Port ZA', on the north-west coast of Scotland by the Isle of Skye.[2]

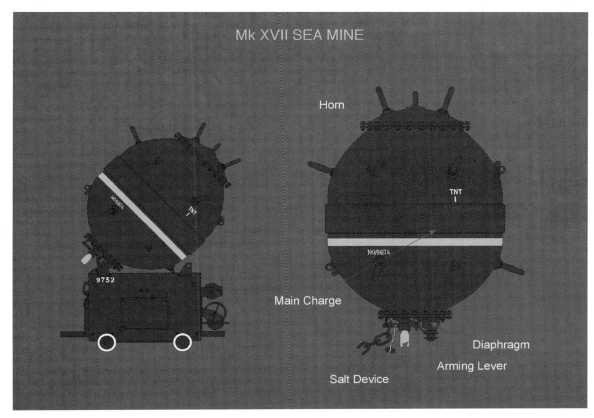

Mk XVII moored contact mine. (Eric Leon)

When war broke out in 1939, the Royal Navy was not as ready for mine warfare as it might have been, but, even though the first fast minelayer did not complete until March 1941, it was much more ready for mine warfare in 1939 than in 1914. Four merchant ships were converted for minelaying, the *Agamemnon*, *Menestheus*, *Southern Prince* and *Port Napier*, of which the fastest could make 17 knots.[3] Some of the pre-war destroyers built to be used as minelayers were also employed, as were the submarines of the *Grampus* class. The Royal Navy soon began using small coastal craft such as motor launches and motor torpedo boats as well. Later in the war, destroyers of the War Emergency 'O' class were used for minelaying. As in the previous war, the Royal Navy began laying minefields with thousands of mines to counter the U-boat threat.

For much of the war, the 1st Minelaying Squadron was based at the Kyle of Lochalsh, 'Port ZA' or HMS *Trelawney*, commanded by a RA(M), Rear Admiral Mines or a Commodore(M). The Royal Navy was blessed with officers who could and would lead the mine warfare effort and were experts in the field. Two of the most important ones were Captain R H De Salis, OBE, DSC and Captain John S Cowie, later CBE, LM. In his book, *Mines, Minelayers and Minelaying*, Captain Cowie gave De Salis credit for inspiring his interest in mining and for teaching him everything he knew.[4]

John Stewart Cowie was born in Mildura, Victoria, Australia, on 23 June 1898, to James Eden Cowie, who was born in Britain, and Maud Brown Cowie, who was born in Tasmania. He and his parents travelled to Britain when he was ten to continue his education. According to Admiral Sir Robert L Burnett's foreword to Captain Cowie's book, in his youth John Cowie 'was a really fine athlete and an excellent exponent of the game of Rugby football'. Upon graduation from Dartmouth as a midshipman he was assigned to the dreadnought battleship *Monarch* and during the Great War he fought at Jutland, Zeebrugge and Ostende. After the war, he served in the cruiser *Exeter* during her South American tour and also the aircraft carrier *Courageous*.

According to Admiral Burnett, Cowie was a brilliant officer, passing his sub-lieutenant's courses with many 'firsts' and qualifying as a torpedo officer in 1923 as 'best of the year'. Again according to Admiral Burnett, Cowie's athleticism, allied with his love of the stage and his 'very considerable ability as a producer and writer, assisted him in maintaining his sense of proportion and very considerable sense of humour'. Both were essential in the minelaying business, Burnett wrote, 'because there is nothing inherently amusing in steaming in foul weather, attacked at times by aircraft and submarines, with some 560 primed mines on board and laying them with great accuracy in the close proximity to fields which may or may not have drifted'.[5] During part of the war, Captain Cowie served as the Deputy Director, Operations Division (Mining) (DDOD[M]), and his comments and his signature can be seen on many of the papers on the fast minelayers at the National Archives at Kew. In 1946, the King made him a CBE, Companion of the British Empire, and the President of the United States awarded him the Legion of Merit for distinguished service to the Allied cause during the war.

Captain Cowie married Mary Keogh, the daughter of a Surgeon Commander, whom he met at a tea party in Malta given by an admiral and his wife. They had two daughters, Jean Hannant and Anne Rowan (to whom the author was related by step-marriage). In addition to being an accomplished thespian, Captain Cowie was an avid shipmodeller. His great love was actually the law and, after retiring from the Royal Navy in 1948, he not only studied law, but became the Acting Solicitor-General in Bermuda.

HMS *Vernon*, the Royal Navy's torpedo and mine shore establishment, founded in 1876.
(Constance Keogh via Hermione Alcock)

He passed the final bar in 1981.

The Royal Navy needed experts like De Salis and Cowie, because the *Abdiel*s became operational at a time when minelaying and minesweeping were becoming an extraordinarily complex cat-and-mouse game, at least between the British and the Germans. The Italian *Regia Marina* was very active in minelaying operations, primarily using light cruisers and destroyers, but was far less proficient in – or interested in – minesweeping. The Japanese and Americans had little interest or proficiency in either, at least at the beginning of the war in the Pacific.

In one of the first moves of the naval war, the Germans introduced the magnetic mine in 1939 and one of the first victims was the new heavy cruiser *Belfast*, which had her back broken and took several years to repair. The British began to employ their own magnetic mine, which was based on a different principle than the German mine.[6] Other types of mines were introduced, such as the acoustic mine, equipped with a microphone and actuated by the sound of an approaching ship. Mines could be set with time delays or set to explode after a certain number of 'actuations', such as a certain number of ships passing before the mine detonated. Mines could also be set to deactivate or sink after a set period of time. In 1944, the Germans were the first to introduce the pressure mine.

Protection against mines and minesweeping became part of the game. The days when mines could be swept just by cutting their mooring cables were gone. Minesweeping had to be adapted to meet their threat of each new type of mine. With magnetic mines, each side developed special 'degaussing gear' for their ships to deactivate a ship's magnetic field and render magnetic mines harmless. Each side also developed mines with diabolical defences against minesweeping, such as 'sprockets' and 'grapnels', and even special floats called 'obstructors'.

Another important development in the Second World War was the aerial mine, allowing mines to be laid not just by surface ships and submarines, but, for the first time, by aircraft, beginning with the Germans and the British. The British first obtained a sample of the new German magnetic mine when the Luftwaffe

Captain John S Cowie, CB, LM, RN, in 1922. (Jean Hannant née Cowie)

generously deposited one in a tidal area. Aerial minelaying would very quickly become an important part of mining operations during the war, the United States taking up aerial minelaying in a big way, to the great detriment of Japanese merchant shipping. At least in European and Mediterranean waters, aerial minelaying supplemented rather than replaced minelaying by surface ships.

In the Second World War, naval mining would play a very important part in the war at sea and the British fast minelayers would play no small part in that war. The first to do so was the name ship of the class, the *Abdiel*.

CHAPTER 4

THE *ABDIEL* COMPLETES AND PROVES HER WORTH
Home Waters and the Mediterranean, 1941

IT was only fitting that the name ship of the class would be named after the *Abdiel* of First World War fame, which was named after the faithful seraph in Milton's *Paradise Lost* who withstood Satan when he urged the angels to revolt.[1]

The *Abdiel* was built by the venerable J Samuel White & Company, on the River Medina at Cowes on the Isle of Wight. She had the distinction of being the longest and largest ship ever built there. Ordered in December 1938, the *Abdiel*'s keel was laid on 29 March 1939, just as Hitler was moving into what was left of Czechoslovakia after Munich, making the Second World War inevitable. She was launched on 23 April 1940 and was supposedly commissioned on 7 March 1941,[2] but was not fully completed until 15 April 1941.[3]

Her crew was from Devonport,[4] and 50 per cent of them had never been to sea before.[5] She was painted up in a medium gray and was given the pennant number M 39. Her motto was *Semper Fidelis* – 'Always Faithful'[6] – and her crest was decidedly not classical, featuring a silver mine with golden wings.

The *Abdiel*'s first commanding officer was the aforementioned Captain Edward Pleydell-Bouverie, MVO, who had already been with her for months during her fitting-out. He was born on 10 September 1899, the second son of the sixth Earl of Radnor and grew up at Longford Castle in Salisbury. At home with his wife Pearl – Lady Montagu – in Beaulieu in the New Forest of Hampshire, he liked to hunt pheasant and duck.

The Captain had already been to sea under the most trying circumstances early in his career. While still a cadet at Britannia Royal

The *Abdiel* after completion. (Lt Cmdr Ben Warlow, RN)

Naval College at Dartmouth, he was sent to sea on the old armoured cruiser *Hogue* almost immediately after the declaration of war against Germany in August 1914. With a number of reservists, he and his fellow cadets, soon promoted to midshipmen, formed the complements of the sisters *Aboukir, Hogue* and *Cressy*, which were patrolling off the coast of Holland when the three were sunk in quick succession on 22 September 1914, by the German U-boat *U-9*, commanded by Lieutenant Otto Weddigen.[7] The heavy loss of life, especially among the young midshipmen, shocked Britain. Ned Pleydell-Bouverie survived because, as he later said, his father had insisted he learn how to swim in the River Avon by the castle where he grew up. At first interned in Holland, he and his fellow survivors were quickly repatriated to Britain.

From that point on, young Pleydell-Bouverie's career was for the time being less exciting. He experienced the battle of Jutland aboard the battleship *Orion* and after the war served afloat and ashore. One of his last appointments before the war was as a Commander on the royal yacht *Victoria and Albert*. Once the Second World War broke out, he was sent to France as a liaison officer to the French admiralty, finally becoming the Naval Attaché. Leaving Paris just ahead of the Germans in June 1940, he made it to Bordeaux and then escaped to Britain in a fishing boat and then a submarine. He was posted to the battlecruiser *Hood* just before she took part in the tragic attack on the French fleet at Mers-el-Kebir on 3 July 1940, to keep it out of the hands of the Germans.

About 5ft 10in tall, the Captain was a heavy smoker and was at times in less than perfect health, being prone to stomach ailments. Lieutenant N H G Austen found him a 'most charming and friendly man' and the two got on right away. The *Abdiel*'s young midshipman, Norman Goodwin, held the Captain in awe and remembered him as a strict disciplinarian by observation and personal experience, though on the whole he thought the Captain treated him well.

The *Abdiel*'s First Lieutenant was Lieutenant Nigel Hubert George Austen, better known to some as 'Bunny'. He was the son of a vicar and was born in 1910 at Thirsk, Yorkshire. The ship's first Torpedo (electrical) and Mine Officer was

Captain The Hon Edward Pleydell-Bouverie, MVO, RN. (Robin Pleydell-Bouverie)

Lieutenant-Commander Paul Morrison Bushe Chavasse. He had just been awarded a Distinguished Service Cross and had commanded the minelayer *Princess Victoria* when she was mined and sunk off the Humber in May of 1940. In spite of his bruises, he had been bitten by the 'minelaying bug'. When he applied for more of it, the Admiralty sent him to the *Abdiel*.[8]

Midshipman Goodwin was born in 1923 in Franche, near Kidderminster in Worcestershire. His father was from a line of millers and his mother ran a school from their house. After attending a prep school he decided on a career at sea and at the age of fourteen he joined the officer training ship *Conway*, an old sailing ship moored off Birkenhead. He did well, attaining the rank of Junior Cadet Captain and upon graduating at the age of seventeen he joined the Royal Navy. He was first posted to the armed merchant cruiser *Canton*, formerly a P&O liner and his next posting was the *Abdiel*.

Officers and men began joining the *Abdiel* while the ship was at Cowes fitting out. Lieutenant Austen joined at the end of July and found the *Abdiel* 'the usual depressing sight of a ship in that state, a mass of rusty plates with

The *Abdiel* fitting out at Cowes. (Carisbrooke Castle Museum)

dockyard gear of all imaginable sorts as well as dockyard workers. It all looked too dreary for words'. He and the other officers had all the plans of the ship and 'each of us spent our time chasing up the first representatives in an effort to get things heaving around and ensuring that the parts of the ship for which we were responsible were as they should be'.

As fitting out progressed, the Battle of Britain was at its height, but in spite of frequent air-raid warnings the Luftwaffe did not hinder the work. The weather was wonderful and the Isle of Wight provided a grandstand seat. Lieutenant Austen was almost ashamed to admit that that in the evenings they were able to sit in a garden 'with a drink in our hands and watch the war in the air go on as almost as though watching a film'.

As the months passed, the *Abdiel* looked less and less dreary as she neared completion. Finally, she was sufficiently finished to go to sea, first at Spithead. She carried out a full-power trial during which, according to Lieutenant Austen, she exceeded 40 knots. Then on 20 March she sailed to Greenock, where preparations were made for builder's trials. There ended the best-laid plans.

On 21 March 1941, the German battlecruisers *Scharnhorst* and *Gneisenau* were sighted near the French port of Brest, at the end of their raiding operations in the Atlantic and they arrived at Brest the next day.[9] The two sisters were a menace that had to be contained. On 22 March, he Admiralty ordered the *Abdiel* to the mine depot at Milford Haven in Wales to pick up mines. She left Greenock at 05.00 and proceeded at 35.5 knots to Millford Haven, dumping her dummy mines on the way. On the voyage she also carried out her first gunnery practice, on a raft with a flag on it, to unimpressive reviews.

After arriving at 14.30, she embarked as many mines as she could from the wooden mining jetty there and sailed to Plymouth. On the way, she was 'given a welcome' by an aircraft that announced it was not friendly by dropping its bombs in her wake. The *Abdiel* did not fire at the aircraft, which Lieutenant Austen thought was 'not creditable'.

The ship then departed Plymouth to carry out her first minelaying operation, on the night of 23/24 March, off the Little Sole Bank. The destroyers *Kipling* and *Kashmir* escorted her as far as the Bishop Rock and then she was on her own, for the first time, in enemy waters. The visibility was good and as the ship approached the laying position, Lieutenant Austen thought 'we could vaguely see the French coast and we felt remarkably visible ourselves!'[10] For the first time in a fast minelayer, the order to 'lay mines' was given and she began to lay her 141 mines.

The *Abdiel* at speed on trials. (Imperial War Museum FL 18)

Once the first one went out, 'it seemed to us tense souls on the bridge to make a great splash and noise and one almost felt we could be heard ashore!' The lay could not proceed quickly enough for those souls on the bridge, but eventually they heard 'All mines laid' and sped back to Plymouth. For this work, the *Abdiel* received a 'well done' signal from the First Sea Lord.[11]

Their Lordships were not quite done with her. The *Abdiel* was ordered to perform the same feat on the night of 28/29 March, this time in company with destroyers commanded by Captain Lord Louis Mountbatten. Lieutenant Austen 'had a nasty feeling Lord Louis was spoiling for a fight', which was not at all what the *Abdiel* was looking for. After sailing, Lieutenant Austen and the ship's navigator thought they should try to use the taut wire measuring gear. Once the wire parted two or three times, they gave up on it. The *Abdiel* slipped her escort 25 miles off Brest and proceeded to lay her 150 mines without incident. Upon rejoining the destroyers, Lord Mountbatten signalled to the still-uncommissioned *Abdiel* that Samuel White & Co. was to be congratulated on their minefield.[12] On this operation, the ship first fired her guns in action, at an enemy aircraft overhead.[13]

The *Abdiel* was finally formally commissioned on 15 April. She was ordered to proceed to the Tail o' the Bank on the Clyde to

have workmen put right some nagging defects and to carry out her much-anticipated first-of-class trials. The trials were, once again, not to be. As the Captain was conducting a church service on a Sunday morning, two tugs approached the ship and informed her officers that they were to park her at a berth 'as they were wanted in a hurry'. The church service ended prematurely and off went the *Abdiel* to the Princess Dock in Glasgow to have her defects corrected, to load equipment and to receive secret orders.

Those orders required the *Abdiel* to sail off to the Mediterranean bound for Malta and Alexandria carrying urgently needed aerial mines, 2pdr anti-tank guns and other military equipment, as well as some service passengers.[14] She would be in company with the light cruiser *Dido* and the 5th Destroyer Flotilla, commanded by Captain Lord Mountbatten in the *Kelly*, with her sister-ships *Kipling*, *Kelvin*, *Kashmir*, *Jackal* and *Jersey*.[15]

The *Abdiel* set sail for Gibraltar on 20 April. On the way, the weather was good, but an enormous swell was running and each wave was of great length. The heavily-laden ship's hull hogged and sagged as she reached the crest of a wave, resulting in a nasty tear in deck plates on the forecastle. In spite of her damage, the *Abdiel* got a chance to show what she could do. As Midshipman Goodwin wrote,

Being so new, the rest of the fleet knew little of the capabilities of the *Abdiel* class. This was demonstrated when, in calm weather, we approached the western entrance to the Straits of Gibraltar. Captain D [Mountbatten], wishing to get into harbour as quickly as possible ordered his destroyers to form line ahead formation and increase speed to 30 knots. *Abdiel* was told to act independently, presumably on the assumption that she would soon be left behind. I was fortunate to be on the bridge at the time to see and hear what transpired. As soon as the signal was received, the Captain called the Chief Engineer to him. After a brief discussion concerning the state of the engines and the remaining fuel, speed was increased. As we steamed past the Flotilla Leader we sent the signal 'Will this do?' We were already tied up and taking in fuel by the time the destroyers came in.[16]

With that incident, word of the *Abdiel*'s capabilities no doubt started getting around the fleet.

The *Abdiel* and her consorts arrived on the 24th and enjoyed a brief stay in Gibraltar. Orders were received forbidding anyone but naval personnel on deck, but, as the Captain recalled, a 'considerable addition was made to the Officers

and Ship's Company', as the 'passengers entered into the spirit of the game' and 'moustaches were shaved off and so on'. The Captain recalled with satisfaction that the ruse was a success, such that when Admiral Somerville came aboard he asked where the passengers had been put.

The ships departed Gibraltar that evening, with Malta as the next port of call. The passage through the Sicilian Channel was delayed for one day due to bad weather and then was made on a brilliant, starlit night. The Captain was surprised that the enemy was silent, as the force, passing within four miles of the island of Pantelleria in line ahead and at 30 knots, presented a wonderful target for shore batteries.

Malta was reached on 28 April. At the time, the island was under heavy bombing and aerial mine attacks and ships were sometimes trapped in the harbour by mines. The *Abdiel* and the *Dido* unloaded 'certain important stores',[17] and then sailed for Alexandria the day they arrived, just as an air raid on Malta developed, giving the *Abdiel* 'a wonderful view of what the Malta A/A barrage could produce'. The same day the supply ship *Breconshire* and the 14th Destroyer Flotilla sailed for the same destination and Mountbatten's 5th Flotilla was left at Malta.

On the voyage to Alexandria, the force was attacked by Ju 88 twin-engined bombers, which made shallow diving attacks. One plane put a stick of bombs about 150 yards off the *Abdiel*'s bow and another missed everyone by at least a

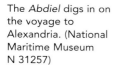

The *Abdiel* digs in on the voyage to Alexandria. (National Maritime Museum N 31257)

The *Abdiel* arrives at Alexandria, 30 April 1941. (National Maritime Museum N 31262)

half a mile. After dark, the *Abdiel* and *Dido* were detached to proceed at high speed for Alexandria.[18] At 16.00 on 30 April, they reached Alexandria,[19] joining the Mediterranean Fleet at a critical moment, shortly after it completed the evacuation of British and Dominion troops from Greece just ahead of the invading Germans and just before start of the battle for Crete. The *Abdiel* was quickly put to work and on 2 May was sent to Haifa in British-ruled Palestine to load mines.

The C-in-C of the Mediterranean Fleet, Vice Admiral Andrew Browne Cunningham, quickly detected the ship's Achilles heel. On 3 May, he wrote to the First Sea Lord;

> I don't know if you have realised the low endurance of the *Abdiel*. She can't lay mines off Lampedusa [an island between Malta and Tunisia] from Alexandria and must refuel at Malta. So our minelaying there also depends on Malta being open. I suggest, if it's not too late, that the question of fitting extra fuel tanks in the others be studied and, if successful, one of them be sent to replace her in due course.[20]

Admiral Cunningham could nevertheless see the *Abdiel*'s worth; just ten days later, in a meeting that discussed the likely invasion of Crete, he pointed out that he had 'a fast ship, the *Abdiel*,

which could be used to run guns and other urgent equipment into Crete'.[21] Cunningham was so enamoured of her speed that one day he signalled her to pass close by at speed, which she did at 35 knots, to have her picture taken. In the coming weeks and months, Admiral Cunningham was able to find some very useful employment for the speedy *Abdiel* that did not require her to traverse the Mediterranean without refuelling.

On 6 May, the *Abdiel* went to sea with the Mediterranean Fleet and took station as part of the destroyer screen.[22] The Fleet's sortie was but one part of Operation 'MD.4', a complex movement of convoys to Malta and Suda Bay, as well as the running from Gibraltar to Alexandria of the vital 'Tiger' convoy of merchant ships to reinforce the British Army in Egypt and warships to reinforce the Mediterranean Fleet.[23] On several occasions, the Fleet was heavily bombed and on board the *Abdiel* it seemed that she was the only target. She had a load of mines on board at the time and everyone on board 'felt their position somewhat acutely'. One stick of bombs fell right across her bows, but caused her no damage.[24] While the Fleet returned to Alexandria, the *Abdiel* disembarked her mines at Haifa and then made her way to Alexandria. It had been planned to have her lay mines off Lampedusa the night of 10/11 May, but the operation was cancelled due to the uncertainly of her being able to fuel at Malta.[25]

The *Abdiel*'s unique minelaying abilities were nevertheless soon put to work. On 17 May, she once again sailed from Alexandria to Haifa to embark mines,[26] and received orders to sail from Alexandria to lay two lines of mines inside and at the entrance to the Gulf of Patras between the islands of Levkas and Cephalonia off the western coast of Greece. On the evening of 19 May she departed Alexandria[27] to begin Operation 'Mat One' and proceeded to the target area at high speed.

On the outbound voyage, two enemy reconnaissance planes sighted the *Abdiel*, but by the use of diversionary courses she was able to shake them off. To the Captain, the lay was 'a most eerie performance', as the entrance to the Gulf of Patras was very hard to find at night and the first mines had to be laid just a quarter of a mile offshore. As the mine doors were opened, the mining party could be heard to mutter, 'Lord! The Owners almost put us on the _____ beach'. Lieutenant Austen recalled it as a calm, clear night and 'one had the feeling that even if those ashore did not see us they must hear the plop as the mines were dropped' and 'it seemed impossible that we could not be spotted'. No

alarm was raised and beginning at 03.28 on 21 May the *Abdiel* proceeded to lay her 158 mines.

Once the minelaying was completed, the *Abdiel* made tracks to the south at full speed and was out of sight of land by dawn. It was intended that she would rendezvous with the Mediterranean Fleet to the southwest of Crete, but the fleet was not at the appointed position and the *Abdiel* continued on her way alone. Once she turned to the east, she became the object of three air attacks, one of them by thirty bombers that dropped everything they had but missed by a mile and a half. On 22 May she returned safely to Alexandria.[28]

As it turned out, the waters off Cape Dukato were rich with targets for the *Abdiel*'s mines. At 05.40, a little more than two hours after the first mine hit the water, they claimed their first victim, the old Italian gunboat *Pellegrino Matteucci,* which was proceeding alone from Brindisi to Patras at a leisurely 7 knots. Of only 630 tons and armed with 76mm guns,[29] she sank immediately, her demise marked by a column of smoke. She went down with forty-one of her crew.

The *Matteuci*'s smoke was soon sighted by a convoy of three Italian tankers, which was escorted by the armed merchant cruiser *Brindisi* and the old 1811-ton destroyer *Carlo Mirabello*, armed with eight 4in guns.[30] At 06.30, the *Mirabello* hit another of the *Abdiel*'s mines, with more flames and smoke the result. The more substantial *Mirabello* stayed afloat for a time, but her captain decided to abandon her at 11.20 and she finally foundered at 12.00, about two miles south of the lighthouse at Cape Dukato. She took with her forty-four of her crew.

More pickings were on their way. A small but important convoy consisting of two large German transports, the *Kybfels* of 7764 tons and the *Marburg* of 7564 tons. They were carrying elements of the Wehrmacht's 2nd Panzer Division, which had taken part in the invasion of Greece and was on its way from Patras in Greece to Taranto in Italy *en route* to Germany.[31] On board the *Marburg* there was a young Panzergrenadier named Zaloudek, who wrote an account of the day's events in his diary.[32]

The *Marburg* and *Kybfels* had left Patras at 09.00 the morning of the 21st. The ships were escorted by two Italian aircraft, which seemed a bit weak to some of the men aboard, but they trusted in their commanders' judgement. It was a sunny day and soldiers were allowed to sunbathe up on deck as long as they had their life jackets with them. Only a few soldiers were below deck. On the horizon, ships could be seen, with smoke rising from one of them. One of those ships, the *Brindisi*, sighted the *Marburg* and *Kybfels* and made ready to send a signal, 'You're heading into danger'.

It was too late. At 14.15 observers in the *Marburg* saw a huge fountain of water rising next to the *Kybfels*. She and the *Marburg* veered to port. An alarm was sounded in *Marburg* and then there was another explosion. All men were ordered up on deck and told to don their life jackets. In total, there were four explosions. From the *Marburg*, the *Kybfels* could be seen slowly disappearing, with men jumping from her deck. The captain of the *Marburg* soon ordered all men aboard her to jump into the water. Zaloudek jumped and was pleasantly surprised to find the water was warmer than he thought it would be. While she still could, the *Marburg* lowered at least one boat. As its occupants rowed away, they could see the

The steamer *Marburg* sinking after hitting an *Abdiel* mine. (Franz Steinzer, *Die 2. Panzer-Division 1935-1945* [Friedburg: Podzun Pallas Verlag, 1977])

Marburg down by the bow, with smoke streaming from her fires. Both ships went down, with a total of 121 men.[33] Most who survived the sinkings came ashore on the island of Cephalonia and those who had drowned were buried in Argustoli.

The authors of the German Naval War Diary was not pleased that the ships had not been warned about the mines and described the sinkings as a particularly severe blow. The ships went down with all the 2nd Panzer's cargo, including sixty-six artillery pieces, ninety-three artillery tractors, fifteen armoured cars and 136 motor vehicles.[34] The Wehrmacht high command was at first informed that 122 tanks had been lost in the ships, but soon learned that they had already been transported to Taranto in an earlier convoy.[35] The Germans at first believed a British submarine was responsible for the sinking of their ships,[36] but they soon realised that mines were the cause.

Much of the lost materiel was not easy to replace, particularly the artillery and their prime movers.[37] Perhaps as a result of that, the 2nd Panzer Division missed the opening of Operation 'Barbarossa', the invasion of the Soviet Union, on 22 June 1941. Instead, in July the division was sent from Germany to Galicia in Poland and then in August to France. It did not reach the Eastern Front until October of that year, when it joined Army Group Centre. Arriving in time for the onset of the Russian winter, the division participated in the Wehrmacht's final drive on Moscow. On 5 December, it was stopped just 25 kilometres from Moscow's defensive perimeter, almost within sight of the Kremlin, and was forced to retreat for the first time in the war.[38] The 2nd Panzer Division's losses to the *Abdiel*'s mines probably delayed its arrival on the Eastern

Front and that delay may have made a difference in the outcome of the offensive against Moscow, if not the war on the Eastern Front. The Royal Navy had not only designed a ship capable of such an operation, but had boldly ordered and executed the operation and was amply awarded for it.

Not many ships can take credit for 'sinking' a Panzer Division or rather much of it, but the men of the *Abdiel* could have if they had known the extent of her success. Lieutenant Austen never learned of the *Abdiel*'s success, but Lieutenant-Commander Chavasse later heard from the Director of Naval Intelligence that the minefield 'had been most successful. A German coastal convoy had gone into it and been decimated'.[39] It was not a bad payoff for the ship's first minelay in the Mediterranean.

By the time the *Abdiel* returned to Alexandria, the battle for Crete had begun and her latent talents would soon become useful. The Germans had launched an airborne invasion of the island on 20 May and the fighting was fierce. At first, Crete's defenders inflicted severe casualties on the Germans paratroopers and their Ju 52 transport planes took heavy losses. Then the surviving paratroopers captured the vital Maleme airfield and the Germans began to bring in reinforcements by air.

While the fighting took place ashore, the Mediterranean Fleet turned back efforts to bring in reinforcements by sea and escorted reinforcement to the island. Almost completely unprotected by the RAF, the Royal Navy had to operate in waters close to Luftwaffe bases. As its ships endured long hours of bombing attacks, they often ran low on anti-aircraft ammunition and losses mounted. On 22 May the battleship *Warspite* was badly damaged by a bomb and the light cruisers *Gloucester* and *Fiji* were sunk. On 23 May bombers sank the *Kelly* and *Kashmir* from Lord Mountbatten's 5th Destroyer Flotilla. The Mediterranean Fleet was in the fight of its life.

On the evening of 23 May, the *Abdiel* sailed from Alexandria for Suda Bay in Crete with 50 tons of ammunition and stores and 195 men from 'A' Battalion of 'Layforce', which consisted of two battalions of 'Special Service' or commando troops commanded by Colonel Robert Laycock.[40] The next day, she passed through the Kaso Strait in the evening in a thick fog, during which the ship was sighted by one enemy aircraft, which immediately made off on being fired at. A BBC report that 'massive reinforcements were on their way to Crete' caused some amusement on the *Abdiel*.[41]

No further incident occurred until arrival at Suda Bay at 23.30 on the 24th. The bay contained many beached and burning wrecks and there was also quite a lot of bombing and gunfire in the surrounding district. Troops and stores were disembarked alongside the small pier and a number of evacuees embarked, including four Greek cabinet ministers, sixty walking wounded and several POWs, including a young Luftwaffe pilot.

At 02.00 on the 25th the *Abdiel* sailed from Suda Bay at 34 knots to rendezvous with a cruiser squadron to the west of Crete. After sailing, a signal was received informing her that the cruisers would not be there and that the ship would have to make her way home by herself. The POWs were aboard were very nervous, knowing that the ship would be passing very close to German bomber bases, and were convinced the ship would be sunk.

The *Abdiel* experienced heavy weather passing through the Kithera Channel and speed had to be reduced to a mere 28 knots. As a result, the ship was far from being out of sight of land by dawn. A reconnaissance plane sighted her, leading the Captain to expect a heavy air attack. Instead, she was only attacked by four aircraft, which went after her one after the other. The POWs could have relaxed, as the ship was not hit, but she was near-missed, such that the men in the Transmitting Station below decks could hear bomb splinters striking the hull. The *Abdiel* safely reached Alexandria that same evening.

There would be no rest for the weary. Orders were immediately received to take on another load for Suda Bay, in this case troops and stores that destroyers had been unable to land in Crete because of bad weather. The *Abdiel* sailed from Alexandria at 06.00 on the 26th in company with the destroyers *Hero* and *Nizam*, with the remaining 750 men of Layforce,[42] including Colonel Laycock, his intelligence officer and famous novelist Captain Evelyn Waugh,[43] and about 50 tons of stores. The ships were warned to expect a large number of wounded for evacuation and suitable arrangements had to be made.

The passage to Suda Bay on a brilliant day

with maximum visibility was, surprisingly, made without incident. Captain Waugh wrote in his diary that 'we were shown no hospitality; the ship's officers were tired out', but he got a large cabin to himself 'and spent the day in great comfort and contentment'.[44] At about 18.00, the ship's crew all blew up their life belts somewhat tightly on receiving a signal from the Commander-in-Chief saying that intercepted enemy messages indicated that the heaviest scale of dive-bombing and torpedo attacks could be expected just before dusk.

On arrival in Suda Bay at about 23.00 on the night of 26/27 May, it became apparent that a very confused situation existed. Instead of empty lighters for the commandos and full ones with wounded, nothing but ones full of the whole of the Naval Base came alongside and even they were slow to do so. While Laycock and his staff were waiting in the Captain's cabin to disembark, a terrified naval officer in a greatcoat and shorts came in to tell them how horrible things were ashore. It was reported that the Germans were about a mile and a half up the road from the town.

According to Evelyn Waugh, 'No light could be shown on deck and there was confusion between the wounded and runaways and our troops waiting in the dusk to disembark'. Somehow, in all the chaos the three ships disembarked the commandos but only some of their stores. In the haste of the moment, some items, such as valuable wireless sets, had to be thrown overboard. The ships embarked 930 walking wounded and other unneeded men,[45] about 500 of them in the *Abdiel*, all in the space of an hour and then the three ships sailed at full speed for Alexandria.

At dawn on 27 May, when the *Abdiel* was just turning the northeastern corner of Crete, the first enemy aircraft appeared, in the form of three large bombers. From this time on until about 10.30 to 11.00, the three ships were under almost continuing bombing attack by a variety of aircraft, including one large-scale dive-bombing attack that was concentrated on the *Hero*. No hull damage was done to any ship, but the *Hero* had her main circulators put out of action, with the result that she could only steam at full speed and keep herself going by the scoop effect through the circulator inlets. Alexandria was finally reached at 19.00 the same day.

The *Abdiel* had landed the last reinforcements to be sent in to Crete.[46] On the 26th the Germans had broken though the main defensive line and the defence of the island had begun to collapse. General Freyberg had to convince General Wavell in Cairo and Wavell had to convince a reluctant Winston Churchill that the battle was lost and that evacuation was necessary. The order to evacuate troops from Crete was finally given and began to proceed. Evacuation would be difficult, as the port at Suda Bay had been lost, leaving only Heraklion and the small port at Sphakia on the south coast of Crete. The *Abdiel* was kept at short notice until she could play her part.

On 30 May the *Abdiel* received orders to sail with the light cruiser *Phoebe*, flying the flag of Admiral King, on the 31st for one last evacuation, this one from Sphakia. The two ships, to which were added three destroyers, the *Kimberley*, *Jackal* and *Hotspur*,[47] sailed at 06.00 on the 31st. The passage to Sphakia was made mostly without incident, save for three air attacks between 18.25 and 19.05 in which none of the bombs fell very close and one Ju 88 may have been damaged.[48]

The ships reached Sphakia shortly before midnight. The *Abdiel* was at full Action Stations because it was not known if it was still in British hands until English voices were heard coming over the water.[49] In moments, the first landing craft came alongside. The evacuation continued from about 11.20 until about 02.30 on 1 June, at which time the force had to sail in order to obtain the benefit of the fighter protection that had been ordered.

The ships together had embarked 4050 men, including just twenty-seven men from Layforce.[50] The *Abdiel* alone had embarked 1200 men. Many of the passengers were New Zealanders, including a number of Maori soldiers of 28 Battalion, whose mood was one of resentment at having to give up the fight. Midshipman Goodwin noticed that some of the Maoris had strange things attached to their belts, which on closer examination turned out to be the ears of the enemy they had killed in combat, according to Maori custom.[51] Lieutenant-Commander Chavasse greatly admired one Maori officer who had had both his arms broken, but had gotten himself from Suda Bay over the hills to Sphakia.[52]

One of the *Abdiel*'s Maori evacuees was Second Lieutenant Rangi France Logan. Born in Hastings on the North Island on 3 July 1916, he held the rank of Command Sergeant Major in D Company when the Battalion was sent to England in 1940 to defend Britain from a German invasion. While in Britain, he was one of the first two Maoris to be sent to Sandhurst for training and passed out with an 'A Outstanding'.[53] After hard fighting in the Maleme sector in the opening days of the battle for Crete, Lieutenant Logan and his men began an exhausting retreat, over the White Mountains and along the Askifou Plain until they reached the high ground above Sphakia. There, they could finally rest and find something to eat and drink for the first time in days. Armed with just a captured Luger, Lieutenant Logan helped form the rearguard at Sphakia, barring the way to the Germans as well as to Allied stragglers. At nightfall on the 31st, the order came for Logan and his men to move

to the beach to be embarked. Lieutenant Logan recalled, 'I suppose every man had the urge to get ahead and make sure he got into a boat, but there was no such move from any of the men. If anyone felt the urge to do so, the urge for self-preservation, he kept in under control.'

Finally, after all of his men had boarded a boat, it was Lieutenant Logan's turn to leave.

In time I came to the water's edge and this was the last boat, loaded deeper into the water, the dark shape of the boat getting nearer; I reached out my hands, stifling a little feeling of panic – if the boat should move out now – and then my hands were on it. I grasped the gunwale, nothing could make me let go now; I pulled myself out of the water and my boys pulled me into the boat – oh, the relief and then the boat was grounded because of the excessive load,

Lieutenant-Commander Paul Chavasse, a chief petty officer and a rating examine the taut wire measuring gear. (Robin Pleydell-Bouverie)

so several of us got into the water again to push. It didn't take much effort and the boat was clear and we hastened to clamber aboard again. As the boat moved quietly away from the shore to the waiting ships, the evacuation of Crete was almost over; I was the last NZ'er to leave Crete in the official evacuation.

'In no time at all', he recalled, he and his men had boarded the *Abdiel* via the stern doors. Once in the bowels of the ship, Logan and his men 'gathered around huge chests containing cheese and biscuits; we just ate and ate, nothing to say, but thankful to be there'.[54]

Other New Zealanders aboard the ship were just as grateful for the ride. Lieutenant Alex Atchison of the 2nd New Zealand Division's Cavalry Regiment wrote, 'The ship's crew gave us biscuits and hot cocoa. It seemed the best meal we had ever had. Afterwards the Officers brought us whiskey and offered us their beds. Everyone was so tired that I am sure that those who slept on the floor [sic: deck] were just as happy as the ones with beds'.[55] Private Charles Pankhurst of 23 Battalion wrote, 'The sailors fed us and treated us very well' and 'We were in the space where mines were usually kept and, as we were very crowded, it was a hot as a furnace. But it would not have mattered to us if the ship had been a slave trader so glad were we to be off Crete'.[56] Some of the famished passengers got a bit carried away and helped themselves to store crates containing tomato puree. The result was predictable. With so many passengers, the ship's sanitary arrangements were overwhelmed and she would later need a considerable hosing-down.

On the voyage, Rangi Logan observed that the *Abdiel* was tucked in behind the two destroyers; being faster, she would zig-zag and settle in behind one destroyer and then zig-zag and settle in behind the other. 'Anxious eyes would scan the skies behind us, looking for sign of enemy bombers' and the passage back to Alexandria was made under almost continuous red warning. Nevertheless, except for one 'half-hearted attempt at intervention' that hit nothing but got a hot reception from the anti-aircraft gunners, the passage was without incident.

Unfortunately, it was not so for two venerable anti-aircraft cruisers, *Coventry* and *Calcutta*, that Admiral Cunningham sent from Alexandria to shepherd them in. Ignoring the *Abdiel*'s troop-laden band, a Ju 88 attacked up-sun at 09.45 and put two bombs into the *Calcutta*'s engineering spaces. She sank in just five minutes, with two officers and 116 ratings,[57] the Royal Navy's last loss in the painful battle for Crete.

As Alexandria came into sight, Major Dyer of 28 Battalion told his men, 'Let's tidy ourselves as best we can, smarten ourselves up and march off the ship like the good soldiers we are.' His men went to work with a will and did what they could. The force arrived at Alexandria at 17.00 and Midshipman Goodwin recalled the *Abdiel*'s arrival. 'Once we knew which side we were going to at the landing wharf, all troops were cleared to the other side. This gave us quite a list, which quickly prompted an anxious signal from the C-in-C, Admiral Cunningham, asking if we had suffered any damage', but he was assured there was none.[58] Once the men had disembarked, waiting trucks took them away to camps.

Admiral Cunningham signalled, 'I congratulate you all on a very successful effort on the night of 31/5'.[59] The evacuation of Crete was finally over. By this time, the *Abdiel* was one of only five or six ships in the Mediterranean Fleet left unscathed. In the previous forty-two days, she had been at sea for thirty-six of them and had sailed about 17,000 miles.[60] The *Abdiel* had played a vital part in the battle for Crete, though certainly not in a role she was designed for.

The month of June was relatively quiet for the *Abdiel*, as she was not needed in the Syrian Campaign and all that came her way was working-up, drills and exercises, a boiler clean and various odd jobs. Perhaps at this point she was repainted into an unusual scheme of light gray overall with very dark gray or black geometric shapes on her funnels and superstructure and on her hull extending from the waterline to the uppermost row of scuttles.

On 21 June, the *Abdiel* was joined by her sister-ship *Latona*, so she finally had a companion that could keep up with her. The *Latona* had sailed from England all the way around the Cape of Good Hope, an adventure in itself. More adventures would follow for both ships.

CHAPTER 5

THE *LATONA* TAKES TO THE WATER AND SAILS AROUND THE CAPE, 1941

THE second ship of the class to complete, the *Latona,* had the shortest career of all the fast minelayers, but it was in no way an unexciting one. She was built by Thornycroft & Co. Ltd. at Southampton and was the largest ship ever built by that firm.[1] She was laid down on 4 April 1939, was launched on 20 August 1940 and was completed on 4 May 1941.[2]

The *Latona* was manned out of Portsmouth,[3] and was assigned the pennant number M 76. Her motto was *Vestigia Nostra Cavete*, which translates as 'Beware our tracks'.[4] She seems to

have had two crests, an official one with a gold sun eclipsed by a white crescent moon and another – which adorned the Captain's stationery – featuring a bird on an island.

When new, the *Latona* was painted up in a layer-cake camouflage scheme of three tones, with the darkest one lowest and the lightest one highest in the ship. She was the fourth Royal Navy warship to bear this name, the Latin version of the Greek 'Leto', the mother of the god Apollo and the goddess Artemis. The *Latona* was also named after the small, old protected cruiser

The launch of the *Latona* on 20 August 1940. (National Maritime Museum N 14035)

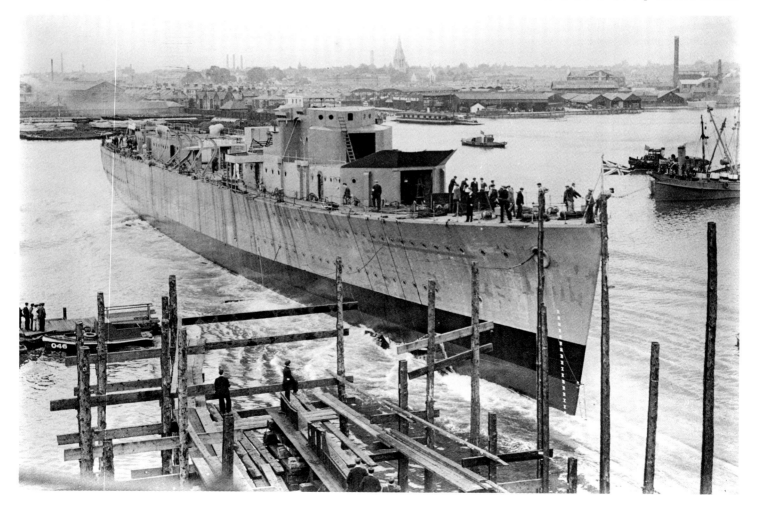

that was converted to a minelayer in 1908 and served in the First World War,[5] during which she supposedly laid the mines that sank the German light cruiser *Breslau* and badly damaged the battlecruiser *Goeben* off Imbros in the Aegean Sea on 18 January 1918.[6]

The *Latona*'s first and only commandeering officer was Captain Stuart Latham Bateson, who took command on 15 January 1941, when she was still fitting out. Wanting to know more about this Latona woman, he wrote to his sixteen-year-old son Alec, who was then pursuing a classical education at Rugby School. Alec told him that Latona 'was a Roman mythological figure derived from a Greek one called Leto, one of the Titans, who had been punished for – or had escaped from – an "affair" with Zeus (Jupiter) the King of the Gods and helped by Poseidon (Neptune) the God of the Sea, against the angry vengeance of Hera (Juno) the Queen of the Gods, into becoming a quail, alighting as a fugitive on an island (Ortygia/Delos) floating in the sea, which was then anchored for her comfort and where in due course she became the mother of Apollo and Artemis (Diana) the twin deities of sun and moon'. The *Latona* would also have an exciting life, but not quite as colourful as that of her namesake.

Captain Bateson and his twin brother were born in 1898, their father being a High Court judge. He attended Rugby School and the Royal Naval College Keyham and then entered the Royal Navy as a special entry cadet in 1916. In 1923, he qualified as a 'Torpedo Officer', when the Torpedo Branch was responsible for maintaining ships' electrical equipment. Also in 1923, he married Marie Elphinstone Fleming Cullen and they had two children, Alec and Isobel. Stuart Bateson was promoted to Captain in 1939.[7]

After Admiral Bateson's death in 1980, Marie Bateson received a letter from the *Latona*'s Cook-Baker, a Charles Simmons, who offered a glowing tribute to her husband, a 'Real Gentleman' whom he greatly respected. He reported that the 'bond of friendship we had aboard HMS *Latona* was created by our Wonderful Skipper who always had time to listen to what one said to him'. After his signature, he added, 'The Baker who used to make the cakes your husband did so enjoy'.

As the *Latona* completed in Southampton,

Captain Stuart Latham Bateson. (NPG x 163947, portrait of 25 January 1949 by Walter Stoneman, © National Portrait Gallery, London)

the rest of her crew joined her. One was a Telegraphist Sidney Albert Banner, who was born in the Aston district of Birmingham. Once the war began, he tired of life in the barracks and volunteered to go to sea and was informed he was on draft to a ship called the *Latona*. No one seemed to have heard of her, though some, confusing her with *Laconia*, thought she was a liner converted to an armed merchant cruiser. Telegraphist Banner recalled later that 'it was something of a shock to us when, having been trucked to the appropriate dock, we were confronted by a sleek, three-funnelled warship like a small cruiser in appearance'.[8] Once again, an *Abdiel* had fooled someone.

On completion, the *Latona*, as Job No. 1198, ran a four-hour full-power trial. Maddeningly, Thornycroft's one-page record of the trial did not record the speed attained, but did record the shaft horsepower (72,860, higher on the starboard shaft than the port one), fuel consumption (24.5 tons per hour), steam pressures, draught and other information. A few slight defects were found, but a handwritten note at the bottom of the record declared, 'A very fine performance + shows care in design + construction'.[9]

The *Latona* was allowed no time to dawdle

The *Latona* fitting out in Southampton. (National Maritime Museum N 499983)

about. She was sent straight to Milford Haven to have her minelaying equipment checked, which was done by dropping dummy mines out the mine doors and onto a lighter.[10] She then proceeded to the King George V Dock at Glasgow to load cargo and personnel. On her way, she performed a speed trial and is unofficially said to have achieved 40.3 knots in an unladen condition.

On 15 May, the *Latona* loaded a number of 2pdr anti-tank guns, ammunition and stores needed for the army in North Africa, as well as 20mm Oerlikon cannon for the Mediterranean Fleet at Alexandria. As the cargo was loaded, the temperature on the mining deck was said to be 100° F. The *Latona* also took on a number of Royal Air Force and Royal Navy passengers, one of whom was a Signalman named Harold Osborne, who was surprised to find himself on the *Latona* instead of a troopship and kept a journal during the upcoming voyage. There was not enough space for every passenger to sling a hammock and some had to sleep – rather uncomfortably – on the mess tables. During the

long voyage ahead the men in the *Latona* began to form opinions of the other men aboard, not always favourable ones, such as the Regular Service ratings' opinions of the Hostilities Only men and vice versa.

As the *Latona* completed loading, Acting Sub-Lieutenant William Barrett, RNR, noticed that the ship's masts were sloping toward opposite sides of the ship, which indicated that the ship was twisting. He reported his observation to the First Lieutenant and the Captain ordered the cargo discharged and reloaded so it would be properly balanced.[11]

Sub-Lieutenant Barrett was Horace William Augustin ('Bill') Barrett, who was born in 1920 in Wellington, New Zealand, to British parents. His family returned to Britain when he was five or six years old and he attended St Joseph's College in Beulah Hill in London. Barrett then entered the Merchant Navy before transferring to the Royal Naval Reserve.

Barrett shared a cabin in the *Latona* with Acting Sub-Lieutenant Paddy Donovan from Weymouth, Dorset. Both were a bit wet behind the ears and when the ship's First Lieutenant wanted both of them he bellowed, 'Stupids!' When he wanted Dovovan, he bellowed 'Stupid Mk I' and when he wanted Barrett he bellowed 'Stupid Mk II', names the two men used to address each other for years afterwards.

On Friday 16 May, the *Latona* cast off from the King George V Dock and set sail for Greenock. She was quickly recalled to load more cargo and then sailed for Greenock for good. As she sailed down the Clyde, Signalman Osborne opined that:

> the sight of the shipbuilding yards at full blast was an amazing sight; ships nearly completed, half built, keels newly laid, all shapes and sizes, it was marvellous. We saw the sister-ship of the *Latona* nearly finished and named *Manxman* and also the new battleship *Duke of York*, sister-ship to K.G.5 [*King George V*] practically ready for sea.[12]

The *Latona* reached Greenock at 20.00 and dropped anchor to refuel from an oiler. At 23.00 she weighed anchor and proceeded down the Clyde to the open sea. It was a sad goodbye. Signalman Osborne wrote:

> All of us passengers and crew were on the upper deck, as the nights were short and we could see the riversides until about 11.30 p.m., mainly, though, we were all taking the last glimpse of our homeland and wondering when we should be able to return to the pleasant shores once again; these thoughts animated all of us and there were certainly some very sad faces there. I wouldn't like to picture mine; I'm sure it was terrible. There we all stood until the grey mist changed to black of night and enveloped our dear land and the only thing left was our thoughts and dreams of those we left behind.

As the *Latona* headed out to sea, many of the men who had never been to sea before discovered seasickness, sometimes alleviated by being up on deck in the open air.

The day the *Latona* left, Captain Bateson addressed the crew, saying that, while many of the crew had never been at sea before, they would pull together as a team.[13] The next day, Captain Bateson went on the loudspeaker and informed the crew and passengers they were bound for Gibraltar. The *Latona* ploughed steadily along at 22 knots and was soon well out into the Atlantic. That day she spotted a convoy heading for home.

On the third day out there were new wonders to behold, flying fish that spread their wings and skimmed over the water as the *Latona*'s bow-wave disturbed them and then porpoises appeared jumping and diving and playing about the ship.

On the voyage there was often not a lot for many of the crew and passengers to do, but there

The *Latona* as completed. (National Maritime Museum N 49991)

were exercises to be carried out and there was usually something to be painted, such as the flag deck (several times on the voyage). There were usually plenty of signals for the signalmen to decode and distribute and the *Latona* had begun receiving signals warning her of the presence of U-boats in her path. Each time she skirted the dangerous areas and avoided them.

There was still plenty of boredom, leading to thoughts of home and random thoughts such as wondering 'why with all this water one nation would want to rule it'. In addition to the boredom there was also sometimes 'chokker', the feeling of being fed up with life, with fellow sailors, with the Navy or with a long voyage.

On 20 May, land was sighted as the coasts of Spain and Portugal came into view, including miles of sandy Spanish beaches. Seagulls began following the ship as she neared the Straits of Gibraltar and sighted Africa on the starboard side. Then the Rock of Gibraltar itself was sighted, described by travel guide Osborne as 'a stupendous sight – I can see why it's never been taken off us'. The *Latona* docked in the harbour that afternoon, but there would be no run ashore for the passengers and crew; instead the ship refuelled and loaded stores and provisions, more Oerlikons and mail for the Middle East. That morning, the German airborne invasion of Crete began.

The next day the *Latona* sailed from Gibraltar at 06.00, but not for the Malta and the eastern Mediterranean, as some aboard assumed. Instead she sailed back through the Straits and into the Atlantic, bound for Freetown. As she headed south, the heat became terrific. She passed the Azores, zig-zagging all the while to avoid German raiders or U-boats.

On 24 May – the day the *Bismarck* sank the *Hood* far to the north – the *Latona* was passing the French port of Dakar in Senegal when 'the Skipper seemed to think something was up', sounded Action Stations and increased speed to a reported 39 knots. At least the passengers were duly impressed; Signalman Osborne wrote, 'Oh! Boy did we go, like an express train as though a million devils were after us'. The British and Free French had made an unsuccessful attack on Dakar the previous September, but the French let the *Latona* pass without retribution.

On Sunday the 25th, the men of the *Latona* could see the greenery of the land getting closer and closer and at midday the ship anchored at Freetown, only to see many ships already there, including the battleship *Nelson* and the aircraft carrier *Eagle*. The ship tied up alongside the giant *Nelson*, whose bulk deprived the *Latona* of any breeze there might have been and worsened the already hot climate. Apart from inspecting the *Nelson*, the men spent time trading clothes for souvenirs with the locals in their boats. The locals were well used to carrying on this business and were even ready with old English variety songs to entertain their prospective customers. The stay was not a long one and at 19.00 the *Latona* weighed anchor and set sail for the island of St Helena, Napoleon's final home.

On 27 May – the day the *Bismarck* was sunk off France – the *Latona* was within eighteen hours of St Helena when she was given orders to return to Freetown. Apparently she had missed an Admiralty signal she should have received at Gibraltar and had to turn back. On the return voyage, she was very short on fuel and had to reduce speed to a crawl. The buzz aboard was that they would refuel at Freetown and would continue to Gibraltar and through the Mediterranean. An albatross began to follow her on the way to Freetown.

On 29 May, on her way back to Freetown, the *Latona* held her first 'crossing the line' ceremony, complete with a bath of seawater, King Neptune and his queen, the police and a dunking chair. Captain Bateson welcomed Neptune as he 'appeared' on the foc'sle, having come up the hawse pipe. The novices were thoroughly soaped by Neptune's barber before being chucked into a canvas tank manned by 'Bears'. This exercise took an entire afternoon and no one was spared, least of all the ship's First Lieutenant.[14]

The next day the *Latona* arrived back in Freetown, only to be sent back in the direction of St Helena and the Cape the same day. A prospective voyage through the Mediterranean was supposedly not in the offing due to the battle then raging in Crete.

On 2 June, the *Latona* arrived at St Helena, anchoring at 08.00. This green island reminded Signalman Osborne of an English village with its English-style homes, English-speaking inhabitants and modern motorcars. Their stay there was a brief one, however, and the *Latona* sailed at 14.00 for Simonstown in South Africa.

During the next few days of the voyage, news arrived of the fall of Crete and of the severe losses and damage suffered by the ships of the Mediterranean Fleet in the battle. Some on board the *Latona* were glad to have missed sailing through the Mediterranean.

As the ship sailed farther south, Telegraphist Banner enjoyed some 'magical nights under the huge stars of the Southern Hemisphere', as the ship 'drove along in velvety darkness with a phosphorescent wake streaming out astern'. The heat was such that it was much more comfortable for men to sleep on deck, as long as the men were up before morning cleaning stations. Looking up from the deck, one could see 'the masts and funnels outlined against an amazing backdrop of stars, swaying gently to and fro'.[15]

The *Latona* passed Capetown during the night and arrived at Simonstown at 08.00 on 6 June. On arrival leave was piped and some made up for bypassing Capetown by taking a train there. After a trip along a beautiful sea front and by lovely villages and towns, they arrived at Capetown, with Table Mountain in the background. 'Jack' was welcome everywhere; he rode everywhere free, had free drinks, enjoyed large meals for very little cash and generally received royal treatment.

Signalman Osborne wanted to live there, which may have been the point of the royal treatment and wrote that he could understand why eighty men from the battleship *Nelson* had deserted there. As Osborne concluded, 'All good things end', and the men returned to Simonstown and the *Latona*. Or most of them did, anyway; a Leading Telegraphist did not return and was rumoured to have been picked up later in Johannesburg.[16] His absence would increase the workload of the remainder of the W/T staff, which sometimes had to double up to cover an inexperienced 'Hostilities Only' rating, Barham.

On 8 June the *Latona* sailed at high speed from Simonstown for Durban, but was battered on the way by heavy seas. Durban was reputed to idolise 'Jack', but the *Latona* only stayed long enough to refuel and her men were largely denied the hospitality of Durban. On Friday the 13th the *Latona* arrived at Mombasa in Kenya in time for the rainy season and on cue rain came down in buckets the whole time she was there.

A *Latona* 'Crossing the Line' certificate. (Author's collection)

In the harbour, the battleship *Barham* was repairing damage suffered during the battle for Crete. The *Latona* left early the next day for Aden. On Thursday, 17 June, the *Latona* arrived at Aden, dubbed by some on board as 'the hottest place on Earth'. She departed that day and sailed into the Red Sea, with Arabia on one side and Africa on the other and reached Port Tewfik on the southern edge of the Suez Canal on 19 June. Her voyage was finally nearing its end.

At dawn on the 20th, the *Latona* started a slow passage through the Suez Canal, passing

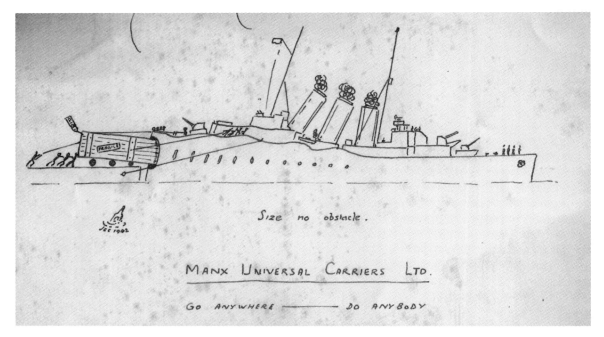

Size no obstacle.

MANX UNIVERSAL CARRIERS LTD.

GO ANYWHERE ——— DO ANYBODY

wrecks, fortifications and airfields along the way. She passed through the canal and arrived at Port Said the same day and unloaded her cargo, after a journey of thirty-six days.[17] During the voyage, according to Captain Bateson, 'We arrived before we were expected everywhere we called'.

At Port Said, the passengers and crew were allowed a swim and ice cream could be purchased from an Egyptian boat. That night the *Latona* sailed into the Mediterranean, bound for Alexandria. She was supposed to arrive at dawn, but because of an air raid that night the approaches had to be swept for mines first. The *Latona* finally arrived at Alexandria at midday on 21 June.

At Alexandria, she joined the Mediterranean Fleet and almost immediately came a signal from Admiral Cunningham's flagship to paint ship, supposedly in 'Mediterranean gray' with only her funnels a 'duck-egg green'. The *Latona*'s slightly older sister, the *Abdiel*, was already a veteran member of the fleet and soon they were carrying out exercises together. The *Latona* carried out a minelay with dummy mines to try her hand at the art she was designed for. During nightly air raids on Alexandria, the *Latona* lent her 4in guns and sometimes her pom-pom to the cacophony.[18] The *Abdiel* had shown the way at Crete, but the *Abdiel* and *Latona* were about to demonstrate the fast minelayers' versatility and usefulness in an even bigger way, paving the way for further demonstrations by their sisters.

CHAPTER 6

PAWNS OF COALITION WAR
The *Abdiel* and *Latona* on the Tobruk Run, 1941

THE *Latona*'s cargo had been badly needed in Egypt. In early 1941, General Erwin Rommel's Afrika Korps launched its first offensive in North Africa and quickly drove back the British forces, depleted by the campaign in Greece. On 11 April, Rommel cut off the port city of Tobruk in Cyrenaica, eastern Libya. The Afrika Korps launched assaults on the perimeter around the city in April and May, but it ran up against a stout defence and failed. In June, the British Army launched an offensive, Operation 'Battleaxe', which failed to relieve Tobruk. The result was a protracted siege, which would eventually involve the *Abdiel* and *Latona*.

Meanwhile, the British began the long process of building up enough forces and supplies to launch a major offensive to drive back the Afrika Korps and to relieve Tobruk. General Claude Auchinleck replaced General Archibald Wavell as Commander-in-Chief, Middle East Forces, on 5 July 1941 and the date for the offensive was initially set for 1 November. In London, Prime Minister Churchill waited impatiently for Auchinleck to launch the offensive. Meanwhile, General Rommel waited for the supplies and the opportunity to launch his own offensive, to take Tobruk once and for all and then to move east to Cairo and beyond.

The *Abdiel* at a dockside somewhere in the Mediterranean. (Robin Pleydell-Bouverie)

The garrison defending the 'fortress' was made up of Australian, British and Indian units and were under the overall command of Australian Major-General Leslie Morshead, also the commander of the Australian 9th Division. Ably led by General Morshead, they heroically and actively defended the fortress. Indeed, General Morshead's motto was, 'We are not here to take it. We're here to give it.'[1]

The troops defending Tobruk had to be supplied from Alexandria in Egypt by Royal Navy and the Royal Australian Navy units of the 'Inshore Squadron' and the 10th Destroyer Flotilla, also known as the 'Scrap Iron Flotilla'. All sorts of craft were used, from destroyers to sloops to lighters and to small sailing ships. To their great credit and glory, the ships making the runs to Tobruk had to endure all sorts of hazards, including air attacks and later U-boat torpedoes and suffered heavy losses, but they kept the men of Tobruk supplied.

The *Abdiel* and *Latona* were not part of the effort to supply Tobruk. Instead the sisters went to sea to engage in minelaying exercises together. On 18 July both went to sea with the Mediterranean Fleet's battleships and five destroyers for exercises.[2] On 1 July the *Abdiel* made a trip to Famagusta in Cyprus with a load of sandbags and torpedoes for an MTB depot ship.

Perhaps inevitably, the *Abdiel* and the *Latona* were tried out on the run to Tobruk. The *Abdiel* and the destroyer *Decoy* made a trial run on the night of 19/20 July,[3] while in the early hours of the 21st, the *Latona* and the Australian destroyer *Stuart* made a trial run to Tobruk with personnel and supplies.[4] There was a delay in unloading at Tobruk due to constant shelling and air raids and neither minelayer was able to discharge more than half her cargo in the time allowed. As a result, the powers-that-be decided that there was little to be gained by employing a fast minelayer instead of another destroyer and the experiment in using fast minelayers on the run to Tobruk was abandoned[5] – for the time being.

Later in July, the *Latona* and the *Abdiel* took part in Operation 'Guillotine', the movement of the 50th Division and RAF personnel from Port Said in Egypt to Cyprus[6] to guard against another Crete. In each run, troops and stores were embarked at Port Said and were landed at Famagusta. The operation began in July and was completed on 29 August,[7] freeing the *Latona* and the *Abdiel* for more exciting duties.

* * *

As the *Abdiel* and *Latona* soldiered on in the Mediterranean, discussions that would affect their fate were taking place between Cairo, London and Canberra, Australia. That summer of 1941, the Australian Government began to insist on the withdrawal of all Australian troops from Tobruk. General Auchinleck's deputy in Cairo was Australian Lieutenant-General Thomas Blamey, who was also the Commander, Australian Imperial Forces (AIF).

The opening salvos were fired on 18 July, when Blamey sent Auchinleck a letter urging the relief of the garrison from Tobruk, on the grounds that there had been signs of a definite decline in 'the health resistance' of the troops. He also argued that the relief of the Australian portion of the garrison would fulfil the agreement between the British and the Australian governments that all Australian troops in the Middle East should operate as a single force, asserted that this was particularly desirable 'in view of the readiness the Australian Government has so far shown to meet special conditions as they arose' and closed, 'I can see no adequate reason why the conditions agreed as between the Australian and United Kingdom Governments should not now be fulfilled'.[8]

On the same date, Blamey sent a personal note to Australian Prime Minister Robert Menzies with a copy of the letter to Auchinleck. In the note, Blamey asserted that the 'only obstacle' to providing fresh troops for Tobruk or to reassembling the AIF in Palestine was 'the unwillingness of the Middle East Command to do so',[9] suggesting that he had already proposed the relief to Auchinleck and had been rebuffed. If he had not, General Morshead may have done so in a meeting the week before, on 10 July.[10] In his note to Menzies, General Blamey also suggested that Menzies 'take strong action to ensure the collection of the AIF as a single force'. Blamey does not seem to have cleared his letter to Auchinleck with the Australian Government before sending it off, even though Auchinleck said in his despatch that Blamey wrote to him 'at the instance of the Australian government'.[11]

From there, the telegrams flew. Menzies took up Blamey's challenge and cabled Prime Minister Churchill on 20 July, stating in part, 'We regard it as of first class importance that, now the Syrian Campaign has concluded, Australian Troops in Middle East should be aggregated into one force', that having all Australian soldiers in one zone would give 'immense satisfaction to Australian people' and was a principle agreed to by the British and Australian governments when the troops were dispatched to the Middle East. 'I would be glad if you could direct British High Command in Middle East along these lines'. In case the addressees had not already caught his drift, he closed by referring to the move 'to which we attach real and indeed urgent importance'.[12]

On 23 July, Auchinleck received a telegram from the War Office in London repeating the message from Menzies and urging him to give full and sympathetic consideration to its views, but also saying, 'At the same time we realise, as no doubt does the Australian Government, that the grouping and distribution of divisions must be subject to strategical and tactical requirements and to what is administratively practicable.'[13]

Churchill did not reply immediately to Menzies' telegram of 20 July and on 7 August Menzies requested an early reply, stating that the War Cabinet was 'considerably perturbed' over Blamey's report on the condition of their troops.[14] Two days later, a reply was made for Churchill by Lord Cranborne, the Secretary of State for Dominion Affairs, who informed Menzies that his telegram had been referred immediately to Auchinleck and that, 'We entirely agree in principle that the Australian Imperial Forces should be concentrated into one force as soon as possible and General Auchinleck has undertaken to see to this immediately on his return [from London]. He does not anticipate any difficulty except in regard to the garrison of Tobruk. He is as anxious as you in this connection to relieve the garrison.'[15] Lord Cranbrooke's reply did not have a particularly mollifying effect, since the whole point of the exchange was the relief of Australian troops from Tobruk.

Thus ended the first round of a difficult and painful political and military dispute between Britain and Australia, one that Churchill later described as 'this unhappy episode'.[16] The dispute was not over and would play out over the next several months and would have repercussions not only for the course of the war in North Africa, but also for the fate of the *Abdiel* and *Latona*.

In spite of the disagreement, some common ground was found. Plans were drawn up to replace the Australian 18th Infantry Brigade and the 18th (King Edward VII's Own) Cavalry of the Indian Army with the Polish Carpathian Brigade during the moonless period in August and for the 9th Division to be replaced by the British 70th Division during the two succeeding moonless periods.[17] The Carpathian Brigade had been formed in April 1940 in Syria from Polish soldiers who had escaped the German occupation and had marched to Palestine to join the British after the fall of France.[18]

The person whose opinion on the matter was either not sought or not heeded was General Morshead, who believed the Australian 18th Brigade was the best brigade at Tobruk and should have been the last to be withdrawn. He wrote to Blamey, 'I trust you that you will approve of this',[19] but evidently Blamey did not or at that stage could not and plans stayed in place to withdraw the 18th Brigade.

It fell to the *Abdiel* and the *Latona* to spearhead Operation 'Treacle' to take out the Australian troops and to ferry in replacement troops and stores for the fortress garrison. The Tobruk runs would put the *Abdiel* and *Latona* at great risk, but it also kept them occupied when their minelaying abilities were not being utilized. In fact, on 15 August, just before the Tobruk runs began in earnest, Admiral Cunningham wrote to First Sea Lord Dudley Pound, 'If you are badly in need of *Abdiel* or *Latona* or both I can do without them. They are most useful running troops but I have at the moment no use for them as minelayers.'[20] Perhaps the time and place were not right for their minelaying abilities, but in hindsight it is very hard to see how Admiral Cunningham and the Mediterranean Fleet could have done without them and still undertaken the Tobruk runs.

Before the *Latona*'s first trip to Tobruk to take out Australian troops, Captain Bateson cleared the lower deck to explain what was involved. He said that to reduce the chances of detection, the voyages would only be made during periods of reduced moonlight. Stores would be packed so that they could be carried on the mining deck and then passed aft by hand to the mining doors onto Army lighters. That meant that the lower deck would have to be cleared to do the job of moving some 150 tons of stores in two hours, the length of time they could stay in Tobruk.[21]

Operation 'Treacle' was executed in the second half of August and involved seven runs by the fast minelayers on alternate nights during the 'moon down' part of the month, with the ships leaving Alexandria during the day and reaching Tobruk that night. A fighter escort was arranged for the ships, but they would undergo high-level bombing and sometimes low-level bombing as well. Lieutenant-Commander Chavasse ran a sweepstakes on the time the first bomb would fall, but he never won. The ships would start out in line abreast to carry out an Asdic sweep for submarines and then would adopt a diamond formation. The men would be at first-degree readiness for action from about 16.00 to about 09.00 the next day.

The *Latona* had the honour of participating in the first run, on 20 August, with the destroyers *Kipling*, *Nizam* and *Kingston* and with cover provided by the light cruisers *Ajax* and *Neptune*.[22] The *Latona* also made the last run by a fast minelayer, leaving Tobruk the morning of the 29th. The destroyers *Griffin* and *Havock* actually made the final run of Operation 'Treacle', returning to Alexandria on the 30th.

A British general hitching a ride to Tobruk in the *Abdiel* wrote about the voyage, but neglected to supply his name.[23] 'The weather was gorgeous – a cloudless sky and a sea as blue as only the Mediterranean can be. A light breeze made it pleasant on deck in spite of the hot sun, as we raced along; the decks all crowded with soldiers going to Tobruk'. He described the ships, 'A number of warships close together rushing through the water gives an impression of smooth, swift and relentless determination it is hard to describe.'

The nameless General continued to wax lyrical about the voyage. 'The Captain was kind and hospitable. Besides putting his cabin at my disposal (he, of course, never left the bridge), he let me spend as much time as I liked on the bridge and of this I took full advantage. It was my first experience of a warship at sea in wartime conditions – a most inspiring experience.' Towards evening, they passed a British ship steaming eastwards and later friendly fighters appeared high above them, 'so we were being well cared for'.

Darkness finally fell on the ships. The General wrote, 'still we sped along completely blacked out. It was a wonderful starlight night with no moon. Looking ahead or astern one could just make out the faintly deeper blackness of another ship'. As they neared Tobruk, 'a dark coast line could be distinguished quite close and we slowed again until we were just moving and so we crept into the harbour'.

The *Abdiel* in camouflage at Alexandria in 1941. (Australian War Memorial P00090.104)

Entering the harbour at Tobruk presented its own challenges. According to the *Abdiel*'s Captain,

Tobruk was reached usually by about 22.00 to 23.30 . . . Tobruk was a filthy harbour to find with no features to guide the Navigator. The only light was what came to be called 'the green light of Tobruk' which no one would have recognised as such unless he knew what to look for.

To make the entrance to Tobruk in a ship as large as the *Abdiel* class, full wheel had to be used on the turn from the swept channel through the double boom and full wheel again when in the middle of the double boom to get round and avoid a variety of wrecks just inside it. Once inside, troubles were not over for the Harbour was full of mines and wrecks and in the darkness the latter were almost indistinguishable from the many lighters which used to be sent out to take our stores.[24]

As the *Abdiel* entered the harbour, the General recognised one wreck as a ship he had once travelled in from Karachi to Bombay.

That famous 'green light of Tobruk', a ship's starboard light, was always shown in the sunken ship alongside of which ships were to unload. Some time later, that light would rest on the grave of Captain Frank Montem Smith, DSO, RD, RNR. Captain Smith was the long-serving Naval Officer-in-Charge at Tobruk and was described by Admiral Cunningham as 'outstanding among gallant men'.[25]

'Presently the engines stopped and with a loud rattle our anchor chain ran out', recalled the General. Watching the disembarkation and the embarkation, the General commented, 'There was scarcely a sound as all this went on rapidly and smoothly in complete darkness'. There were no jetties in Tobruk, so the *Abdiel*'s cargo had to be unloaded onto lighters or wrecks. The ship's crew had to go 'flat out' to get her stores unloaded in time. Once the ship's Surgeon Lieutenant pitched in to help, specially outfitted in his rugby kit.

One night the same British general was ferried out to the *Abdiel* for the homeward voyage. While waiting to depart, 'I heard the noise of aircraft. Suddenly a large parachute flare was dropped immediately above us, which lighted the harbour as light as day. Tin hats were put on and work continued smoothly without a check. The captain turned to me and said, "That makes one feel very naked, doesn't it?" Indeed it did!' No attack was forthcoming and 'after what seemed like a very long time the flare burnt out'. The ship had to be underway by 02.00 and, if the stores were not unloaded by then, they were to be dumped overboard for collection by the Army.[26] The General recalled, 'As soon as all was ready up came the anchor and we crept out of the harbour'.

The *Latona*'s Telegraphist Banner later wrote about her voyages into Tobruk, 'How our Captain avoided the wrecks I shall never know'. Once a clear spot was found, lighters

The *Latona* at Alexandria. (Australian War Memorial 020452)

approached and supplies were pitched over or, in the case of ammunition, carefully lowered. Everyone pitched in, including the Captain and the officers, except the communications ratings. Then, any troops to be taken back to Alexandria were brought aboard. The *Latona* would thread her way out of the harbour and she and her escorting destroyers would then head for Alexandria. On the way, they might pass the *Abdiel* and would exchange signals 'in the form of cricket scores, the tonnage transferred being the runs and the number of troops the bowling'.[27]

During the runs to Tobruk, sailors in the *Abdiel* and *Latona* became acquainted with the traits of the various nationalities of the troops they were transporting. The men of the *Abdiel* found that the strict discipline of the Polish troops made them excellent passengers. Individually the Australians were thought excellent and good company, but en masse they appeared truculent and slow to respond to orders and with their very large packs took up much more room than any other soldier.[28]

During their voyages out of Tobruk, the men of the *Latona* learned the unique and special ways of Australian infantrymen. They were ferried out to the ship in barges and were quite invisible in the darkness until they were within a few feet of the ship's side. Their language was 'frightful' and if there was a hitch that caused them to stand off, they would amuse themselves by giving a 'detailed and stentorian history of the Captain's ancestry and physical defects', much to the embarrassment of the men on the *Latona*. Once on board, they were good-natured enough and the crew soon made friends with them by taking around mess kettles with hot, sweet tea 'liberally laced with rum'.[29]

The Australians could be grateful passengers. Somehow G J Dunning, a sailor on the *Abdiel*, acquired a paper stating, 'This voucher entitles you to one bottle of Australian beer at the Alexandria Fleet Club, Being a token of appreciation from the A.I.F., No. 10017'. The voucher was not redeemed.[30]

Mr Dunning also acquired two undated newspaper cuttings of unknown origin, each with a photograph taken on board a fast minelayer. The caption under each reads in part, 'On board a fast ship taking supplies to Tobruk. The journey is undertaken by the Navy and is probably the most dangerous trip in the world'.[31] Indeed it was.

Bombing was one hazard. On one occasion, an enemy plane took the *Latona* by surprise, 'flashing across the ship at low altitude and dropping a salvo of bombs in line from port to starboard'.[32] The bombs missed, however, and the *Latona* sailed on. On 21 August, a Ju 88 damaged the Australian destroyer *Nizam* with a near miss north of Bardia as she was returning from Tobruk. Her fuel pumps were put out of action and the destroyer *Kingston* had to take her in tow until she could proceed under her own power to Alexandria.[33]

Bombs were not the only danger. At dusk on 25 August, torpedo bombers unsuccessfully attacked the cruisers that were covering the *Abdiel* and her destroyers. Torpedo bombers tried again on the 27th against the ships making the run on that night, the *Abdiel*, the light cruisers *Galatea*, *Naiad* and *Phoebe* and the destroyers *Kingston*, *Kipling* and *Hotspur*. The force was being stalked by two Savoia-Marchetti S.79 torpedo bombers of the 279a *Squadriglia* A.S.

After sunset, at 19.45, a ship's radar detected aircraft. At about 21.16, the *Phoebe* altered course and opened fire on one aircraft and saw a torpedo pass astern. Then, at 21.20, as she altered course to join the rest of the force, she was hit on the starboard side forward by a torpedo that blew a 28ft by 18ft hole in her hull. Her speed was reduced to 12 knots and the *Galatea* and *Naiad* accompanied her back to Alexandria while the *Abdiel* and the three destroyers continued on to Tobruk[34] without further incident. The *Phoebe* lost eight men in this action. She travelled to the United States for repairs and would be out of action for eight months.[35] One of the Italian pilots claimed a probable hit on a light cruiser,[36] a good call.

In spite of the obstacles and the damage to the *Phoebe*, Operation 'Treacle' was a success. The Australian 18th Brigade and other units, including the Indian 18th Cavalry Regiment, were successfully pulled out and replaced by the Polish Carpathian Brigade. In the operation, 6116 men and 1297 tons of stores were disembarked from the fast minelayers and the destroyers and 4432 able-bodied men and 610 invalids were brought out of Tobruk.[37]

* * *

After the end of Operation 'Treacle', as General Auchinleck noted, 'It was then necessary to consider whether further relief of the garrison was desirable or feasible'. The easy part of the dispute over the relief of Australian troops at Tobruk was over and the hard part of the matter, whether to relieve the 9th Division, had to be squarely faced. To make matters more interesting, on 28 August, as Operation 'Treacle' was ending, Prime Minister Menzies resigned and was replaced by his deputy, Arthur Fadden, on the 29th.[38]

On 30 August Auchinleck consulted with his fellow service Commanders-in-Chief, Admiral Cunningham and Air Marshal Tedder. Together they were unanimous in recommending that it was undesirable to continue the relief.[39] Blamey evidently got wind of this and on 4 September he wrote to Fadden, 'Relief of the garrison strongly opposed here . . . Further, should the force be attacked with strength and determination after one or two months' further decline, it will not be fit to withstand such attack and catastrophe is possible'. He closed with, 'Unless you take the firmest stand, feel convinced the 9th Division will be left in Tobruk indefinitely, in spite of my efforts . . .'.[40]

Fadden took the hint and sent Churchill a telegram on 5 September, reiterating his predecessor's request. Picking up on Blamey's use of the 'c' word, Fadden wrote that 'This is a vital national question here and should any catastrophe occur to Tobruk garrison through further decline and inability to withstand a determined attack there would be grave repercussions'.[41] Churchill did not reply at once, but waited for further word from Auchinleck.

After the meeting with Cunningham and Tedder and further consultations, Auchinleck sent a telegram to London setting out many arguments against the relief and recommending that the relief be suspended and that the garrison be reinforced with a company of infantry tanks. One of the arguments was that the naval risks were appreciable, as nearly all the ships engaged in the relief of the 18th Brigade had been attacked from the air.[42] On 11 September, Churchill transmitted the entire Auchinleck telegram to Fadden and pointed out that it was the result of prolonged consultations with Naval and Air Commanders in the Middle East. Churchill made it clear that if Fadden insisted that Australian troops must be relieved orders would be issued accordingly 'irrespective of the cost entailed and the injury to future prospects'. He then appealed, 'I trust, however, that you will weigh very carefully the immense responsibility which you would assume before history by depriving Australia of holding Tobruk till victory was won, which otherwise by God's help with be theirs for ever.'[43]

Churchill's plea was to no avail. The appeal to future glory might have worked on him, but it did not work on Fadden. On 15 September, Fadden replied and set out a number of comments on the points made in Auchinleck's telegram. For example, as for the naval risks, he wrote, 'These are noted but in the absence of effective naval opposition in the Mediterranean or any contemplated naval operations this does not appear to be a sufficiently weighty reason', thus completely missing or avoiding Auchinleck's point about the danger to the ships from air attack. Fadden informed Churchill that he was bound to request that the withdrawal of the 9th Division and the reconcentration of the AIF be proceeded with. He also warned that, in the light of the reports and requests over many months, 'any reverse suffered by the Tobruk garrison . . . would have far-reaching effects'.[44]

The same day, Churchill informed Fadden, 'Orders will at once be given in accordance with your decision'.[45] On 15 September, London notified Auchinleck that 'after careful consideration of the opinions of the Commanders in Chief, the Australian Government felt compelled to request the withdrawal of the 9th Australian Division and the reconcentration of the Australian Imperial Force'.[46] Churchill had promised to abide by the Australian decision and at least for the moment he did. Plans were made to replace the 9th Australian Division with the British 70th Division during the next two moonless periods, during Operations 'Supercharge' in September and 'Cultivate' in October.

Churchill did not, however, take the Australian decision well. During a trip to Moscow, he 'began to abuse everyone and everything' and said that they were at war with almost every country, 'including Australia'.[47] In a note, he said, 'I was astounded by the Australian Government's decision, being sure it would be repudiated by Australia if the facts could be made known', but added that 'personal feelings must be subordinated to appearance of unity'.[48] Churchill told General Auchinleck on 17 September that he was much 'grieved' at the Australian attitude, but he also realised that the fault was not all Australia's. He continued, 'I have long feared the dangerous reactions on Australian and world opinion of our seeming to fight all our battles in the Middle East only with Dominion troops. For this reason, apart from the desire to reinforce you, I have constantly pressed sending out some British infantry divisions.'[49]

The British military chiefs in the Middle East did not take the Australian decision well either. General Auchinleck drafted a letter offering his resignation, on the grounds that he did not command the confidence of the Australian Government,[50] but was talked out of it by Minister of State Oliver Lyttleton in Cairo. On 17 September, Air Marshal Tedder wrote to his superior, Air Chief Marshal Portal, 'from the Middle East's view the decision appeared to be most dangerous'. What disturbed him most was what he called 'the devastating diversion of fighter effort just at the period when our air campaign should be working to the climax to ensure air superiority when the land operations begin'.[51] On the 18th, Admiral Cunningham wrote to First Sea Lord Dudley Pound, 'The relief of the Australians from Tobruk comes at a very bad time and may have serious repercussions. It may mean that the Western Desert offensive may have to be postponed 2-4 weeks'.[52] However,

A fast minelayer carrying stores on the Tobruk Run, 25 October 1941. (IWM E 6199)

what they thought mattered not, at least for the moment. The argument was over and the runs to Tobruk would have to continue.

And continue they did. Operation 'Supercharge' commenced on 17 September with a run by the *Abdiel* and the destroyers *Jervis*, *Jaguar* and *Hasty*. They returned the next day, when the *Latona* and the destroyers *Nizam* and *Napier* began the next run. The operation was completed by the 27th with the return of the *Abdiel* and the destroyers *Kandahar*, *Jaguar* and *Griffin*.[53]

The operation required nine runs by the two fast minelayers and destroyers, but succeeded in evacuating elements of the Australian 9th Division and replacing them with troops from the British 70th Division. The ships encountered little interference and the Royal Navy suffered no losses in the runs. When all was said and done, the Royal Navy had evacuated 5444 officers and men and 544 wounded and had taken in 6308 officers and men and 2100 tons of stores.[54]

Before the next operation could be executed to complete the relief of Australian troops, the British decided to make another run at the Australian Government to put off the relief. Admiral Cunningham expressed himself strongly against the relief and showed General Blamey the long list of ships sunk and damaged on the Tobruk run.[55] From London, Churchill sent Prime Minister Fadden a telegram on 30 September resuming his appeal, relying mainly on how continuing the relief would handicap the RAF. He also mentioned that Auchinleck had almost resigned on the grounds that the Australian Government had no confidence in his military judgment. Later he wrote, 'We have been greatly pained here by the suggestion, not made by you, but implied, that we have thrown an undue burden on the Australian troops. The debt to them is immense but the Imperial forces have suffered more casualties actually and relatively.' He closed with, 'Therefore we feel that we are entitled to count of Australia to make every sacrifice necessary for the comradeship of the Empire. But please understand that at whatever cost your orders about your own troops will be obeyed.'[56]

Churchill's telegram was received the day Fadden's government fell.[57] After discussing the matter with his successor, John Curtin, on 4 October Fadden sent a reply that Churchill described as 'obdurate'.[58] Fadden denied any want of confidence in Auchinleck and denied intending to convey that an undue burden had been thrown on Australian troops. He continued and closed, 'I and my Government have given most full and careful consideration to the request made in my cablegram . . . of 14th September and while assuring you that, as in past, we are prepared to make every sacrifice [in] common with the rest of the Empire we cannot see our way for the reasons fully set out in my cablegram to depart from this conclusion.'[59]

The next day, Churchill informed Auchinleck, 'I am sorry I could get no helpful response from the late Australian Government about avoiding a further SUPERCHARGE and I have not made contact with the new Government'. Then he got to the point. 'I trust however there will be no postponement of CRUSADER'. Auchinleck replied that he was very grateful 'for your efforts to help us and quite understand situation which cannot be helped' and answered Churchill's concern with, 'continuance Supercharge . . . will not be allowed to interfere with plans' and added, with some prescience, 'though sudden change in enemy air activity compared with that in (last?) phase might produce difficult situation'.[60]

On 13 October, Churchill addressed a final appeal, this time to Prime Minister Curtin, stating, 'I have heard again from General Auchinleck that he would be very greatly helped and convenienced if the remaining two Australian brigades could stay in Tobruk until the result of the approaching battle is decided.' He went on to say, 'I will not repeat the arguments I have already used, but I will only add that if you felt able to consent it would not expose your troops to any undue or invidious risks.' He closed by stating that consent would 'at the same time be taken very kindly as an act of comradeship in the present struggle'.[61] Obdurate once again, Curtin answered on the 16th that the 'War Cabinet has considered your request but it is regretted that it does not feel disposed to vary the previous Government's decision which was apparently reached after the fullest review of all the considerations involved'.[62] Churchill, apparently ignorant of recent events on the Tobruk run, did not reply until 26 October at 12.20, when he shot back, 'Relief is being carried

A musical interlude aboard a fast minelayer on the Tobruk Run. (IWM E 6195)

out in accordance with your decision which I greatly regret.'[63]

The die having been cast, Operation 'Cultivate' had to be executed. In it the last elements of the 9th Division were to be exchanged for the last elements of the 70th Division. The first run by a fast minelayer and accompanying destroyers was made on the night of 12/13 October,[64] and, after a delay of several days, the runs resumed on the night of the 17th/18th. They then continued almost every night of the moonless period of the month and were for a time uneventful. The destroyer *Encounter* made two of the runs and one of her Sub-Lieutenants later recalled that 'it was a great

joy to take 350 gallant Aussies on board each time, fill them with beer and take them back to Alex'.[65]

The pleasure was more than mutual. Three Australian soldiers from the 2/43rd Battalion who were evacuated by the *Latona* on 17 October well remembered their passage out of Tobruk, that 'hell-hole'. After boarding the ship, Lance-Corporal Allan Jones heard an authoritative voice order, 'Settle down as quick as you can, wherever you can.' Private William Mitchell, who incidentally thought Churchill a 'superman', recalled being glad to be out of Tobruk and of the *Latona* – 'the fastest ship in the British navy' – he remembered that the sailors fed them 'beautiful' fresh bread and corned beef (not that Private Mitchell was starving, having actually gained weight during the siege). Corporal John Lovegrove also remembered the bread, as well as hot coffee served in pannikins. All three men recalled falling asleep once on board, one of them thereby avoiding seasickness.

When Lance Corporal Jones awoke he was alarmed by the ship's vibration, but realised the ship was not in trouble but proceeding at maximum speed. Corporal Lovegrove thought the crew were marvellous and, after a proper breakfast, which for some included bully beef sandwiches with warm Australian butter and a shave and shower in the crew's quarters, thought it 'unbelievable luxury after the privations of the past eight months' and contrasted the 'unhygienic condition they had become accustomed to' to the 'superb cleanliness of the ship and its officers and crew'.

The men of the 2/43rd began to line the rails to watch the beautiful autumn day unfold, with 'the Mediterranean as clean and as blue as the sky, the atmosphere like mountain air'. Lance-Corporal Jones admired the graceful display of ship handling by the Australian destroyer *Nizam* and also noted the main armament manned and exercising and that the crew serious as they watched out for enemy aircraft through binoculars, telescopes or pieces of smoked glass. As the *Latona* sped eastwards, the soldiers became happier and more relaxed and entered a state of almost euphoria.

The *Latona* and her Australian passengers finally reached Alexandria, which was full of warships, and disembarked at 13.15. One soldier recalled being told after landing that the Australian people had been informed through the press of their relief from Tobruk, with headlines such as 'Our besieged heroes evacuated'.[66] The men 'believed that we had saved Egypt and the Suez Canal and showed the way to win eventual victory and could now look forward to some relaxation, because our part in the Siege of Tobruk was over'.

While the October runs to Tobruk were in progress, the British Major-General Ronald Scobie relieved General Morshead as commander of the Tobruk garrison. The change was surely a natural one, since Morshead was also the commander of the outgoing 9th Division

and Scobie was the commander of the incoming 70th Division, but the Australian insistence on the withdrawal of the 9th Division had deprived Australia of the honour of commanding the garrison of Tobruk. While General Morshead 'received many congratulatory messages during the siege . . . no plaudits hailed the 9th Division . . . as it left the battleground of its hard striving. If there had been some generous impulse to acclaim, perhaps the bitterness engendered by the controversy about the relief had quelled it . . .'.[67] The 9th Division surely deserved better, as the controversy over its relief was not of its making, even though it was the primary object of it.

The last run of Operation 'Cultivate' fell to the *Latona*. It was set for 25/26 October, after the *Abdiel* completed a run on the 25th accompanied by the destroyers *Kandahar*, *Griffin* and *Kingston*.[68] This would be the *Latona*'s 13th run to Tobruk.[69] On this one, she was carrying stores, ammunition and only thirty-eight extra personnel and was accompanied by the destroyers *Hero, Encounter and Hotspur*. Captain Bateson was the senior officer of the little flotilla, which was to take off the last remaining battalion of the 9th Division, the 2/13th and some smaller Australian units, in all about 1000 men.[70] On 25 November, the 2/13th was pulled out of the line in preparation for the embarkation.

About 30 miles north of Bardia and east of Tobruk, an enemy aircraft detected the force at 14.32 off the starboard bow and the ships went to Action Stations. The first attack was delivered at 14.33 from 12,000ft, when one aircraft dropped bombs. The *Latona* went to full speed and starboard wheel was put on and all six bombs missed, three to starboard and three to port. The *Latona* fired four salvos with her 4in guns before the aircraft were out of range. At 17.00, the four ships increased their speed to 26.5 knots. At 17.30, the ships closed to five cables apart. The weather was calm, with a clear sky, a smooth sea and no swell and visibility was at least 30 miles.

As darkness approached, the *Latona* and her consorts would be bereft of any fighter cover. Admiral Cunningham had tried to arrange fighter cover for ships making the run to Tobruk and often succeeded, but, as he later wrote, the problem of providing fighter protection at dawn, dusk and in moonlight was never satisfactorily

The after 4in mount on a
fast minelayer the
Tobruk Run. (Imperial
War Museum E 6204)

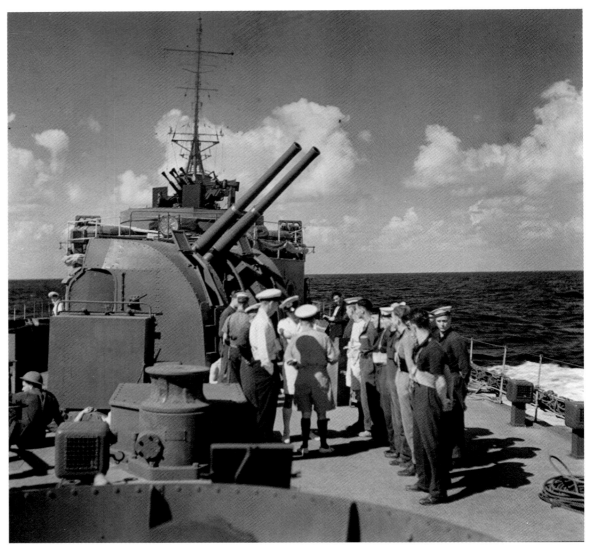

solved. Night-fighting Fairey Fulmar fighters had been trained, but without fighter direction, which Cunningham thought to be impossible from small ships, they were not successful.[71] That night, the *Latona* and her companions would be on their own.

The night deprived the force of fighter protection, but would be of little comfort or protection. As Sub-Lieutenant Sam Falle in the *Encounter* would later put it, 'some crass idiot decided we should make the trip by moonlight'.[72] The supposed 'moonless period' was ending and the moon was actually almost in its first quarter. As the moon rose, 'the sea and ship were lit with a radiance almost a bright as sunlight,' and the men in the *Latona* felt like 'mice in the middle of a white-washed floor, waiting for the cat to

pounce'. The moon would not set that night until 22.27,[73] much too late for the ships and men of the little force heading for Tobruk.

At 18.30, the ships took advantage of the lull to have supper and to shift into night clothing, but the lull did not last long. At 18.55, the *Latona*'s radar detected aircraft eight miles on the port bow. All hands were sent to Action Stations. When the alarm came, Captain Bateson was changing from his Whites into something warmer. He later related, 'I hustled into my gray flannel trousers and uniform jacket, grabbed my binoculars and tin hat and was on the bridge in time to take action . . . but I had to leave my cigarettes, lighter, pen, pencil and money on the desk'.

The *Latona* was about to become the target

of a series of attacks by ten Ju 87 Stuka dive bombers from I.St.G.3, the first Gruppe of SturzkampfGeschwader (Stuka Squadron) 3,[74] commanded by Captain Walter Sigel, and by three Italian Savoia-Marchetti S.79 trimotor torpedo bombers from Derna, commanded by Capitano Giulio Marini of the *279a Squadriglia A.S.*,[75] the same unit and the pilot[76] responsible for putting a torpedo into the cruiser *Phoebe* the previous August.

The first of the new wave of attacks was delivered at 18.59. The *Latona* and her mates attempted to counter the attacks by turning through 90 degrees and firing a 'whirling spray barrage' and then turning back to their proper course. A whirling spray barrage consisted of setting the three 4in mounts 120° relative to each other and at a fixed elevation, with the shells set to burst at 5000ft.[77] In that attack it was believed a torpedo fell close on the starboard quarter. At 19.05 a green Very light was sighted, perhaps to guide in more attackers. More attacks were delivered at 19.09, at 19.25, when a bomb or a torpedo fell near the *Hero*, at 19.30 and at 19.47. Each time the *Latona* opened fire with a whirling spray barrage.

The attackers were using one aircraft to shadow the *Latona* and when an attacking aircraft was in in the best position to attack the shadower fired a green Very light. When the attacking aircraft finished its attack, it fired a red Very light, to show the shadowing aircraft and the next attacker that the way was clear.

After the fifth attack, the radar operator reported the scan clear. Captain Bateson was beginning to hope that they had no more to expect, but there was to be more. The lull only lasted until 20.00, when there appeared to be a number of aircraft circling the ships at ranges from five to seven miles.

The sixth attack was delivered at 20.08, when the *Latona* was in position 32° 14' N, 25° 0' E. The *Latona* signal initiating a whirling spray barrage was suddenly cut short by an explosion and the failure of all electric power. In the Communications Office, a 'resounding thump' was felt, but to Captain Bateson 'there was hardly any sensation' on the bridge and it was not immediately clear what had happened. Soon a voice from the bridge roared down the voicepipe to the Communications Office, 'Send: Have been hit by aerial torpedo', as the Captain ordered the

Encounter to inform the C-in-C of the Mediterranean Fleet that she had been torpedoed.

Two of the three Italian S.79s in the area had actually dropped torpedoes on the *Latona* and Sub-lieutenant Aligi Strani claimed a hit, but he was mistaken. In fact, Stuka pilot Major Karl-Heinz Sorge had hit the *Latona* with a single 500kg bomb.[78] Almost immediately after releasing his bomb, Sorge witnessed the fireball from the explosion.[79] There was evidently a dispute among the Axis allies over who had hit the *Latona*; the German Naval War Diary noted that the Italians had reported that they had hit the ship before the Germans, but also noted that a Stuka observer placed the ship at full speed after the Italian attack.

The Stuka's bomb passed through the side of the ship just under the upper deck and burst in the engine room[80] immediately under the Engineer's Office, between Frames 115 and 126, aft of the third funnel. The resulting blast rose as high as the mainmast head, followed by falling debris. No doubt everyone in the engine room and in the Engineer's Office had been killed instantly.

The damage wrought by the bomb was devastating. The explosion cut the starboard main steam pipe and the fire main. The turbine-driven dynamos came off the board and the fire and bilge pump stopped. To make matters worse, the flash from the explosion started a fire among the cargo on the starboard side of the mining deck, which included some landmines,[81] and in the starboard side of the engine room. The blast had unseated the aftermost ('Y') 4in gun mount, the pom-pom mount and two of the Oerlikon 20mm guns from their mountings and blew off the mining hatches fore and aft.

The general result of all this was that the ship was still moving ahead, for the moment, but all electric lights and power were cut off. Steam was escaping rapidly from holes in the deck over a fierce fire on the mining deck. Communication had been cut off to the engine room, the emergency conning station and the after guns and messengers could not get down to the engine room. Unfortunately, the Engineer's Office was also the ship's Damage Control Headquarters. To make matters worse, the largest foam firefighting machine was stowed immediately outside it.

Nevertheless, damage-control efforts began, as the *Latona*'s men tried to save her. The ship's executive officer, Lieutenant-Commander John Waterhouse, was aft in the Emergency Conning Position when the bomb hit and tried to lead damage control efforts from the after end of the ship. Sub-Lieutenant Barrett reported to him that he was rigging up fire hoses and expected to have the fire under control in a minute, but he would soon find that the fire main was giving no water and he suffered burns for his efforts. Once the ship's fire extinguishers ran out, men resorted to buckets of water, sand and flour to put out the fires. To avoid more explosions, the magazines for the after 4in gun and the pom-pom were ordered flooded.

When the steam stopped escaping and the intensity of the fire became obvious to Captain Bateson on the bridge, the ammunition cargo started exploding and the ship finally stopped. Bateson later wrote,

> The fire spread to the mining deck, where all the Army stores were stowed. These included spare gun barrels, phosphorus, anti-tank mines, flour and

sugar. The crew worked hard to control the fire but with only buckets and fire extinguishers it was impossible. We managed to get all the phosphorus overboard but the anti-tank mines were stowed all along the mining deck on top of the other stores. When they got hot enough they exploded, making holes in the upper deck.

The Captain ordered the *Encounter* alongside the port bow to take off the soldiers aboard. Another air attack developed and the *Latona* opened fire with her forward 4in guns and her 0.5in machine guns. When the attack was over, the *Encounter*, commanded by Lieutenant-Commander E V St J 'Rattler' Morgan, berthed alongside and took off about 130 officers and men, including the soldiers and the wounded. Those transferred also included about half the ship's company, in spite of the shouts from the ship's First Lieutenant, 'Stand by your ship, Latonas'.

While the *Encounter* was alongside, there was another explosion from the cargo and the fire spread further. Below decks, the men in the Transmitting Station still stood around the fire-control table, speaking into microphones in flat, level voices, but next door in the Communications Office the atmosphere deteriorated. Smoke entered the compartment via the ventilation system and after Telegraphist Banner 'bawled up the voice pipe to report this' to the bridge, permission was given to abandon the Office. And so it was, with Telegraphist Banner little delayed by an obstructed hatch, eventually reaching the 'blessed night air'.

Captain Bateson ordered 'Emergency Stations' so the boats, rafts and floater nets could be got over the side and the ship prepared to tow forward. Hands not required for manning the guns and fighting the fire were ordered to get out all boats and rafts to be ready in case the crew should need to abandon ship. All were got out and the motor cutter collected them in tow, charts, deck log and navigation instruments being put in the power boat.

In passing astern of the ship, the motor cutter found a man unconscious in the water, having been blown overboard and he was rescued. He turned out to be a newspaper reporter who, with others had been ordered below when the attack began, but had disobeyed

Sub-Lieutenant William Barrett, DSC. (Gertrude Barrett)

orders and remained on deck – as it happened in the way of the blast from the bomb that did the damage. His luck was in, for no one knew that he had gone overboard and it was a very fortunate chance that the cutter passed close enough to spot him in the water.

The *Hotspur* was ordered to play a hose on the fire if she was able, but she was not. After the *Encounter* left, Captain Bateson decided it was useless to keep the crew on board any longer. As air attacks were continuing, the ammunition supply to the forward guns was running low and the fire could not be controlled, he decided that remaining on board would involve wanton loss of life and danger to the destroyers and gave the order to stand by to abandon ship.

As the *Hero* came alongside, the Captain finally gave the order to Abandon Ship, as yet another attack developed. The *Latona*'s forward guns opened fire one last time and a bomb dropped by a Lieutenant Steinhagen[82] near-missed the *Hero* on her starboard side, causing some damage to her steering gear. The *Hero* informed the *Hotspur* and *Encounter* that she had been damaged and could not steer and that she was proceeding at six knots. From Alexandria, Admiral Cunningham ordered the *Latona*'s destroyers to leave her to the destroyers from the 14th Destroyer Flotilla, but they were in no position to comply and the order was eventually cancelled.

The process of abandoning a burning ship in darkness could not have been easy, especially with wounded men to transfer. The NAAFI canteen boy had had both kneecaps blown off when a gas bottle under the counter exploded. Unable to move, he was put in a Cam Jacket and placed on the upper deck. The boy would have to be thrown across to the destroyer alongside. Leading Seaman Dusty Miller called to another seaman, 'Let's throw him over', but the boy called out, 'Don't try it! Let me go down with the ship'. The seamen yelled back, 'No way, off you go on the count of three' and away he went, to be caught on the other side.[83] The *Latona* was cleared as quickly as possible and Captain Bateson left her at 20.50, confident there was no one left aboard.

Captain Bateson still had hopes that the fire would burn itself out and the ship could be taken in tow after the moon set, but once aboard the *Hero* he saw there was no hope. He ordered the

Encounter to search for survivors in the water and then to torpedo the *Latona*. The *Hotspur* was to escort the *Hero*. The *Encounter* attempted to deliver the *coup de grâce* at 21.15 with a single torpedo, but the torpedo missed its mark, as the *Latona* lifted up her bows and slid stern-first into the sea. When she was gone, in Captain Bateson's words, 'that ghastly light went out'. To Telegraphist Banner, 'Darkness closed in on us once more' and the night felt suddenly chill.

The *Latona*'s three destroyers were crowded with survivors, but they did not have to make their way home alone. At 00.17 on the 26th, they were joined by the destroyers *Jervis, Jaguar, Jupiter* and *Kimberley* of Captain P J Mack's 14th Flotilla. This not-so-merry band arrived back at Alexandria with the *Latona*'s survivors at 14.00 on 26 October.[84] The *Hero* had not sustained any casualties, but her damage was structural and electrical and it was estimated she would need three weeks in dock for repairs.[85]

At least the *Latona* had not been crowded with troops on their way to Tobruk. As it was, there were fifty-two casualties: twenty-eight men were missing, including four officers, sixteen ratings and eight Army personnel, and twenty-four men were wounded, including eighteen crewmen and six Army personnel, including a Polish captain.[86]

Less importantly, the *Latona*'s survivors had lost everything they had on board. No one was exempt. This caused Captain Bateson reflect that 'the experience of finding oneself without possessions of any sort; no money, no washing or shaving kit, no clothes except the old things I had on and no ship was, I think, very good for me and released me from the burden of caring for material things'.

The *Abdiel* and *Latona* each had a midshipman, Norman Goodwin and Colin Wiltshire, who had had an arrangement whereby the one making the run to Tobruk that night would leave a suitcase with his best possessions with the midshipman remaining behind. Unfortunately, the system was not observed on the *Latona*'s last run and her midshipman lost everything but his life and the clothes on his back. The *Latona* actually had two midshipmen, and the other lost his life in the sinking.[87]

Back in Tobruk, no one at first had any idea of the *Latona*'s travails. The arrival of the *Latona* and her consorts was keenly anticipated by the

Australian 2/13th Infantry Battalion, which was to be taken out of Tobruk that night. Their day had begun early.

In the early hours of the morning of the 25th, they had handed over their positions on the perimeter to the 2nd Battalion of the Yorks and Lancs Infantry. By half past five that evening the Diggers had seen their last hot meal and downed their last tot of rum on the perimeter and were clambering into their transports. All were wearing desert boots or sand shoes and field service uniform for the first time for many months.

As the sun tipped the horizon, the Stukas came over and dropped a few bombs and then hurried off for home. The Diggers merely jeered at them. At the outskirts of the town, the convoy was held up for a while, in case the Stukas returned in the moonlight to bomb the wharf area and it was not until 11.30 that they reached their embarkation points.

Then, they settled down to wait. Unable to smoke, the troops just sat in the dark, forever glancing at their watches, talking in whispers and peering into the night to catch the first sound of the ships . . .

Midnight came and passed and there was still no sign of the ships. If they did not show up soon, the know-alls said, there would not be time to clear 'bomb alley' before daylight. If they did not show up soon, the pessimists foretold, they would not come at all.

'_____, the Navy always comes!'

By half past twelve, the waiting men were getting restive and the rumour started that the ships had been attacked *en route* and as it spread through the ranks of anxious soldiers it gathered credence.

The Battalion had been in Tobruk since the beginning of the siege and there was not a man who did not know how long it took for ships such as the *Latona* and the three destroyers to make the passage from Alexandria. So now, as

the minutes ticked by, they knew that something must have gone wrong, seriously wrong, for nothing short of disaster could have prevented the Navy from keeping its appointment.

At 1.15 the order came to collect kit and move back to the waiting transport. The ships would definitely not be arriving.

Silently, the Diggers shouldered their rifles and gathered up their kit-bags and turned their backs on the harbour.[88]

Their disappointment can well be imagined. The Navy had done its best, but it just couldn't come. Later, the Diggers of the 2/13th learned that something had indeed gone seriously wrong. As a result of that something, further relief was postponed for the moment and the 2/13th remained in Tobruk. The 2/13th was not 'relieved' until 9 December, when the Eighth Army finally lifted the 242-day siege of Tobruk and Rommel retreated to the west. A year later, under General Morshead the 9th Division would play an important part in the battle of El Alamein.

Churchill informed Prime Minister Curtin of the situation, telegraphing that

Our new fast minelayer, *Latona*, was sunk and the destroyer *Hero* damaged by air attack last night in going to fetch the last 1200 Australians remaining in Tobruk. Providentially, your men were not on board. I do not yet know our casualties. Admiral Cunningham reports that it will not be possible to move these 1200 men till the next dark period in November. Everything in human power has been done to comply with your wishes.[89]

The next day Churchill followed up with a message to Curtin about casualties incurred in the incident.

Fortunately, H.M.S. *Latona* was only carrying thirty-eight other ranks to Tobruk; remainder, to number of about 1000 were in three accompanying destroyers. About fifteen low bombing attacks between 19.00 and 22.30.

Casualties: H.M.S. *Latona* – Naval officers, 4 missing, 1 wounded; ratings, 25 missing, 17 wounded. Army officers, 6 wounded; other ranks, 7 missing, 1 wounded. H.M.S. *Hero* – No casualties. We must be thankful these air attacks did not start in the earlier stages of the relief.[90]

The Australian Prime Minister's reply, received on 28 October, started out sympathetically, 'I have learned with great regret from your telegrams of the unfortunate happenings which have befallen those who were assisting in relieving the Australians in Tobruk'. The message then turned to concern for the Australians still to be relieved. 'We can ill afford to lose any men and we hope that when the final effort is made to relieve our soldiers the venture will not be exposed to risks which have had to be faced up to the present.'[91] The Australian Government still wanted its men out, but at no risk, an impossible task.

In case Mr Churchill did not understand that the Australian Government still wanted its men out, on 30 October Curtin wrote:

> You may be interested to know that Inspector-General Medical Services who recently returned from a visit to the Middle East and who saw first units of 9th Division to be relieved reported they had suffered a considerable decline in their physical powers. As condition remainder would have deteriorated further we are naturally anxious that those remaining should be brought away during the next dark period as intended.[92]

Churchill was probably not very interested in the Inspector-General's report and with studied brevity he replied, 'Every effort will be made to carry out your wishes during the next dark period'.[93]

For the moment, though, the runs to Tobruk had to be suspended, except by schooners, owing to the state of the moon,[94] i.e., the full moon period at the end of October and the beginning of November. The *Abdiel* was instead detailed to take part in Operation 'Glencoe', the lift of the 5th Division from Alexandria to Cyprus and of the 50th Division from Cyprus to Palestine.

The *Abdiel* embarked Rear Admiral I G Glennie for the operation, marking the first if not the last use of an *Abdiel* as a flagship. The operation was conducted by *Abdiel* and ten destroyers and was successfully completed without enemy interference on 8 November.[95] A difficulty occurred when an Indian light infantry unit appeared on the jetty with a number of goats to be slaughtered aboard ship for the men's dinner. For Lieutenant Austen, that would not do and discussions ensued. Diplomacy prevailed and it was agreed that the goats would be slaughtered on the jetty and not on the ship.

At the end of the operation, as the ships were to sail from Haifa to Alexandria, the men, having gotten a bit fed up with the 'troop carrying game', had an idea for a bit of fun. Accounts differ on the origin of the idea, but it was somehow agreed that each of the three groups of ships would make a flag with the name of a famous moving company and would hoist the flag as they entered harbour. This they did, with the *Abdiel*'s group flying a 'Pickford's' flag, second group flying 'Carter Paterson & Company' and the third, made up of Australian ships, flying a flag with five Australian stars and 'Messrs. Gieves Limited, Universal Providers'. As they entered the harbour at Alexandria on a Sunday morning, to their surprise there stood the 'daunting figure' of Admiral Cunningham at Colours on the quarterdeck of the battleship *Queen Elizabeth* as they sailed past, 'in this somewhat unsuitably decorated manner'. Fortunately, there were no repercussions.[96]

During this time, the *Abdiel* experienced her first important change of personnel. To his great surprise, Lieutenant Austen was nominated to command the destroyer *Hasty*, whose captain had been killed. Ironically, while Captain Pleydell-Bouverie and Lieutenant Austen had gotten on very well and usually dined together when in harbour. By then Austen had realised how lonely the life of a captain could be, often on his own and living in 'the cuddy' with his own staff, not being a part of the wardroom mess.

The *Abdiel*'s officers threw Lieutenant Austen quite a going-away party, but he made it off the ship the next day anyway, to be cheered over the side by both officers and men. Lieutenant-Commander Chavasse replaced him as the ship's First Lieutenant and remained her

Mine Officer. He would be tested quickly, with four runs into Tobruk while the Captain recuperated from an illness. In gratitude, the Captain recommended him for a Mention in Despatches.

Even though the ships in Operation 'Cultivate' had taken 7138 troops into Tobruk and brought out 7234 (including 727 wounded), a fourth operation, this one codenamed 'Approach', was necessary. The relief resumed on 13 November and the *Abdiel* made three more runs. Her fourteenth[97] and last Tobruk run was on 15 November, when she embarked General Sikorsky, who had been visiting the Polish troops in the fortress,[98] and most of the remaining Australian units, save, once again, the 2/13th Battalion. Shortly afterwards, the *Abdiel* was allowed a much-needed docking.[99]

* * *

The *Abdiel* had to carry on alone without *Latona*, which had been lost while engaging for months in a very hazardous endeavour and the odds finally caught up with her. One may further wonder what took the Germans and Italians so long. They made the *Latona* the target of a sustained series of attacks in the afternoon and the evening and then into a moonlit night, with no fighter opposition. A number of bombs were aimed at her and two of the three Italian torpedo bombers dropped their torpedoes on her.[100] Finally, a particularly skilful Stuka pilot landed a single, fatal hit. The *Latona*'s crew fought very hard to save her, but they never really had a chance.

The men of the *Latona* would have had no idea at the time that their ship's loss was the result of the insistence of General Blamey and successive Australian governments that their troops be withdrawn over the protestations of the British Prime Minister and his service chiefs in the Middle East. To resolve the question of who was right, should one want to do so, the British desire that nothing should prejudice the long-awaited offensive against Rommel and specifically that too great a burden not be placed on the Royal Air Force or the Royal Navy as the time for the offensive neared, should be weighed against the Australian concerns for the health of their troops in Tobruk, the fulfilment of the agreement to concentrate Australian forces in

the Middle East and, implied though not explicitly stated to the British, the desire to avoid a catastrophe along the lines of the debacles of recent memory in Greece and Crete.

The British placed all their hopes in 'Crusader' and were anxious for it to be launched as soon as possible and for it to succeed, before the Germans succeeded in their invasion of the Soviet Union, which looked like a distinct possibility. The relief doubtless made preparations for the offensive more difficult, an offensive whose success could mean so much to winning not only the campaign in North Africa but the war, not only for Britain but also for Australia and the other Dominions. While the British did not much emphasise the point, the relief also endangered the ships and men conducting it.

As for the health of the troops defending Tobruk, the siege 'was not, like some famous sieges, a struggle for survival in the face of dire shortages of food or water or munitions. Shortages there were at times but never so acute that men were starving or guns without rounds to fire'.[101] The defence of Tobruk was a very active one, which made the lives of the besiegers somewhat miserable, but demanded much of the defenders. Sieges are typically not designed to improve the health of the besieged garrison and the health of the garrison in Tobruk should naturally have suffered to some degree over time, but not to a great degree and not because of dire shortages of food or water.

While the Australians had some legitimate concern about the future health of their men in Tobruk as the siege wore on, there is no reason to think their men were then any worse off than the Indian or British troops in the fortress. As for that, after Operation 'Treacle' was completed, Oliver Lyttleton wrote to Churchill, 'By all accounts the Indian Cavalry were fit to fight immediately after they arrived in the Delta [from Tobruk] and their powers of resistance to a long drawn out siege are notoriously less than those of white troops. Description of the state of the Australian brigade which has been relieved is also encouraging'.[102]

After the war, the Australian Government and General Blamey were afforded the chance to respond to General Auchinleck's despatch and the Government claimed that General Blamey's observations about the health of the troops were confirmed by the Inspector General of Medical Services of the Australian Army, who wrote, 'The first AIF troops transferred from Tobruk had suffered a considerable decline in their physical powers. The men did not think they were tired but few of them would be able to march eight miles . . .'. In other words, the men did not even think themselves tired, but their Army and their Government was telling them, 'Oh, yes you are'.

Moreover, though, it is not necessary to speculate on the health of the Australian troops; one need only look at the performance of the men who were not relieved. On 11 November, General Blamey told the Australian Advisory War Council that 'the Commander-in-Chief wished to keep [Australian troops at Tobruk] to make sorties in connection with the offensive', but in his view 'they were not fit to do this and his opinion had been confirmed by subsequent reports as to their physical condition'.[103] In fact, however, during Operation 'Crusader' the 2/13th Battalion did make a sortie from Tobruk, to Ed Duda and played an important, if not vital, part in the battle.[104]

As for the agreement between the British and the Australian governments, this was a political issue, involving an agreement between the British and Australian governments, not a military one.[105] It is no answer that the Australian Government was merely relying on military advice from General Blamey. There was no military reason to have an Australian corps of two or even all three divisions; it was not as if Australian troops did not play well with other Imperial forces; on the contrary. The British never argued that the Australian Government did not have the right to insist on the concentration of its forces or, for that matter, on the relief of the forces in Tobruk. A concentration of Australian formations would have soothed the Australian people, but that would hardly outweigh the military arguments against the relief.

Lastly, there is the fear of Australian politicians and General Blamey of a catastrophe – their word – in which their troops in Tobruk would be lost. It is true that Australia did not have unlimited manpower and could have ill afforded another Greece or Crete, much less a worse debacle in Tobruk. Churchill himself wrote that 'the Australian Governments had

little reason to feel confidence at this time in British direction of the war and that the risks their troops had run when the desert flank was broken and also in the Greek campaign, weighed heavily upon them'. When dealing with Rommel nothing was certain, but Tobruk had already withstood him once. On the other hand, what the future would hold was anyone's guess.

Understandably, in the end the Australian Governments put little store in the pleas of Churchill and the Middle East service chiefs and put the health and preservation of their troops in Tobruk above the Commonwealth goals of ousting the Germans and Italians from North Africa and winning the war. Of them, Oliver Lyttleton wrote, 'I think there is little doubt that the Government of the Commonwealth [*sic*] is anxious to take out a political insurance policy but the premium to be paid for it namely, grave risks of splitting the vital operations, seems to me to be too high'.[106]

In fairness to the Australian Governments of the day, there were several factors that made the situation more difficult. First, the dispute was surely not made any easier by the awkward circumstance that General Blamey was General Auchinleck's deputy, but was actively supporting, if he had not actually instigated, a position taken by the Australian Government that directly conflicted with Auchinleck's position. By writing to Auchinleck directly on the matter, Blamey made the dispute very much 'about him' and surely affected relations with Auchinleck, perhaps contributing to his intention to resign. Blamey's open support for the relief also made it very difficult for the Australian Governments to accede to Churchill's requests without repudiating him. Blamey forced the issue to begin with and then never wavered, writing at one point, 'I am pressing this issue again because I am convinced I am right'.[107]

Second, the dispute was likely not made any easier by its occurrence during an unstable period in Australian domestic politics. The instability manifested itself out in multiple changes in prime ministers during the dispute, though Churchill strongly implied, incorrectly, that the 'one sharp divergence harmful to our war effort' occurred under Fadden and Curtin after Menzies had resigned.[108] Churchill wrote at one point that 'Allowances must be made for a Government with a majority only of one faced by a bitter Opposition, parts of which at least are isolationist in outlook'.[109] It has been denied that the Australian political situation had any effect on the dispute, in that each prime minister was in agreement with General Blamey.[110] Be that as it may, surely it would have taken a very strong prime minister and government to overrule Blamey and to give in to the blandishments of a British prime minister on a matter of such great national importance.

That Australian political realities were a real factor was revealed by a note by the Australian High Commissioner to the UK, Stanley Bruce, of his lively conversation with Churchill on 31 March 1942. When Churchill brought up the 'unhelpfulness' of the Government in regards to Tobruk, Bruce told him 'that is was unfair to blame the present Government for this as the decision had been taken by their predecessors and it would have been politically impossible for the new Government immediately on coming into office to reverse the decision previously taken . . . in the face of requests for reconsideration'.[111]

Third and last, the dispute was with a Dominion and an important consideration for the British was unity with the Dominions or at least the appearance of unity. Even aside from the issue of operational security, Churchill could not take his case to the Australian public. A breach, much less an open breach, was not an option. Accordingly, Mr Churchill concealed the dispute from the public at the time, which he pointed out to Curtin on 28 November. 'We have not said a word in public about Australian Government's insistence upon the withdrawal of all troops from Tobruk', adding that the withdrawal 'cost us life and ships'.[112]

Churchill did not keep quiet forever. As his correspondence and memoirs suggest, he was bitter about the Australian attitude. Churchill let it all out – or most of it, anyway – in a chapter of *The Grand Alliance*, Volume III of his memoirs of the Second World War. After relating many of the details of the dispute, Churchill sounded a magnanimous note. After comments about Australia's 'rigid' party system and its understandable lack of confidence in British direction of the war, he said 'We can never forget the noble impulse which led Australia to send her only three complete divisions, the flower of her manhood, to fight in the Middle East or the valiant part they played in all its battles'.[113] At the end of the chapter, he confided, 'It has given me pain to relate this incident. To suppress it indefinitely would be impossible. Besides, the Australian people have a right to know and why'. One might speculate that, rather than pain, his being able to relate the incident actually gave Mr Churchill a delicious dish of revenge served cold.

No doubt the Australians also had hard feelings about the dispute. Australian politicians must have resented the repeated British requests that they reconsider their position after agreeing to go forward with the relief. For his part, General Blamey resented the British attitude toward the relief and towards him. In a note to Sir Percy Spender, the Minister for the Army, he shared his opinion that 'the Englishman is a born casuist' and revealed that he [Blamey] was 'becoming personally the most unpopular man in the Middle East over the matter . . .'.[114]

In the end, while who was right and who was wrong may still be disputed. What cannot be disputed is that, as a result of the evacuation, twenty-eight men lost their lives and the Royal Navy lost a very valuable ship but also that many a grateful Australian soldier was evacuated from a battlefield where he had served for months with distinction. The Admiralty announced the loss of the *Latona* on 20 November 1941.[115]

HMS *Abdiel*
As designed

Profile view with internal machinery

Plan view, upper deck

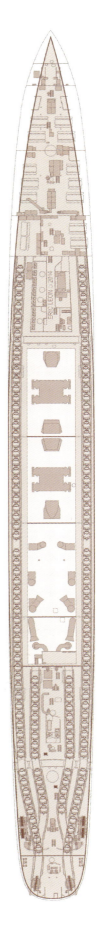

Plan view, mine and main deck

HMS *Abdiel*
1941–2

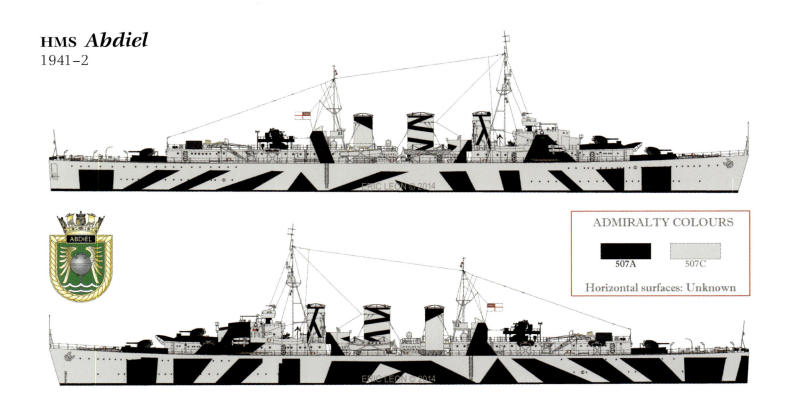

ADMIRALTY COLOURS

507A   507C

Horizontal surfaces: Unknown

HMS *Welshman*
1941

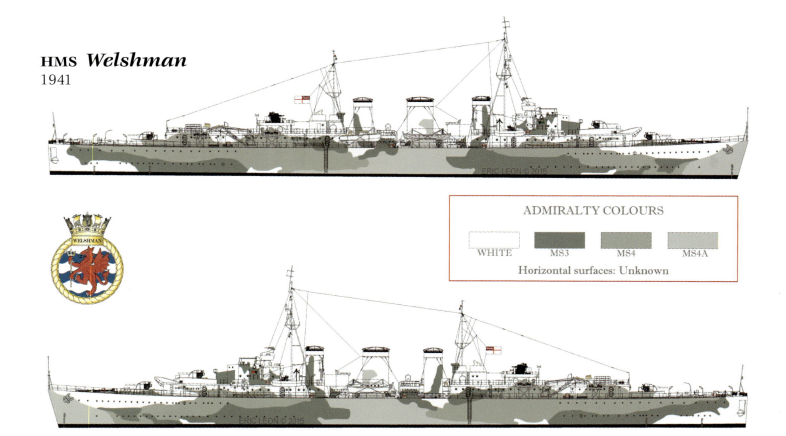

ADMIRALTY COLOURS

WHITE   MS3   MS4   MS4A

Horizontal surfaces: Unknown

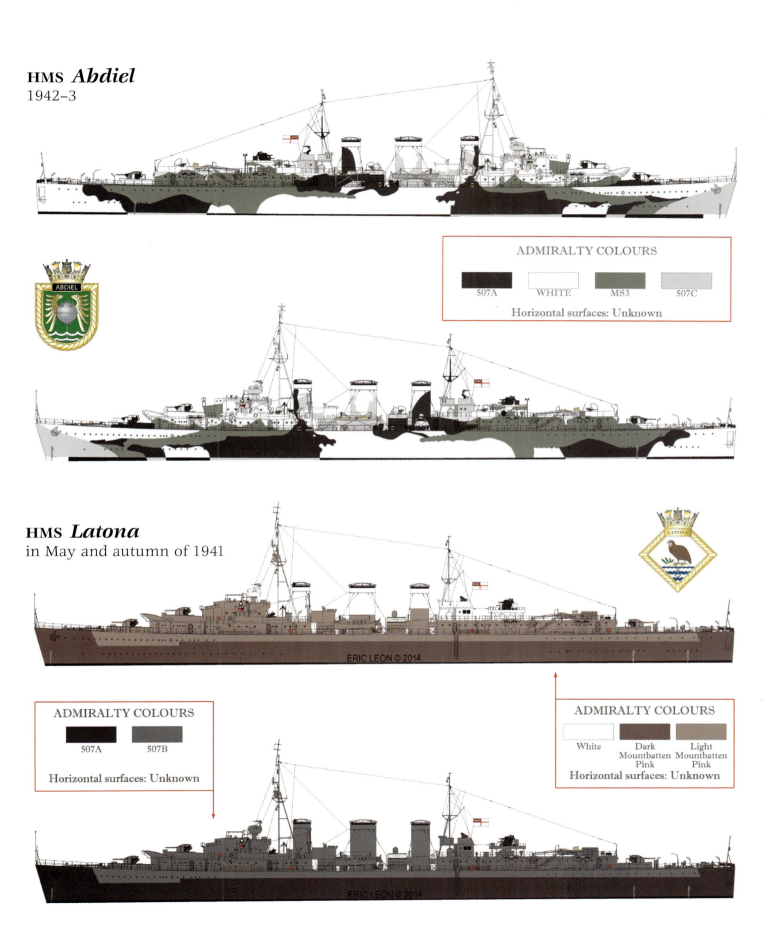

HMS *Abdiel*
1942–3

ADMIRALTY COLOURS

| 507A | WHITE | MS3 | 507C |

Horizontal surfaces: Unknown

HMS *Latona*
in May and autumn of 1941

ADMIRALTY COLOURS

| 507A | 507B |

Horizontal surfaces: Unknown

ADMIRALTY COLOURS

| White | Dark Mountbatten Pink | Light Mountbatten Pink |

Horizontal surfaces: Unknown

ERIC LEON © 2014

ERIC LEON © 2014

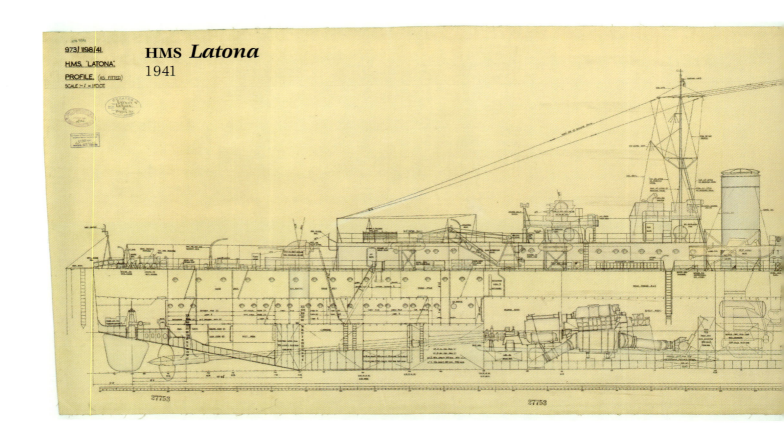

HMS *Latona*
1941

27753

27753

HMS *Manxman*
in 1941 and 1945

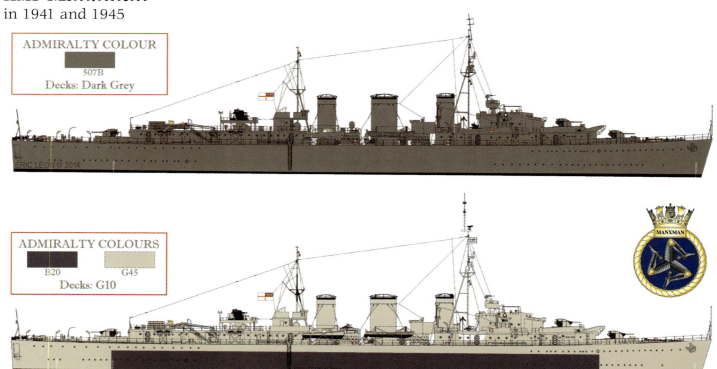

ADMIRALTY COLOUR

507B

Decks: Dark Grey

ERIC LEON © 2014

ADMIRALTY COLOURS

B20   G45

Decks: G10

MANXMAN

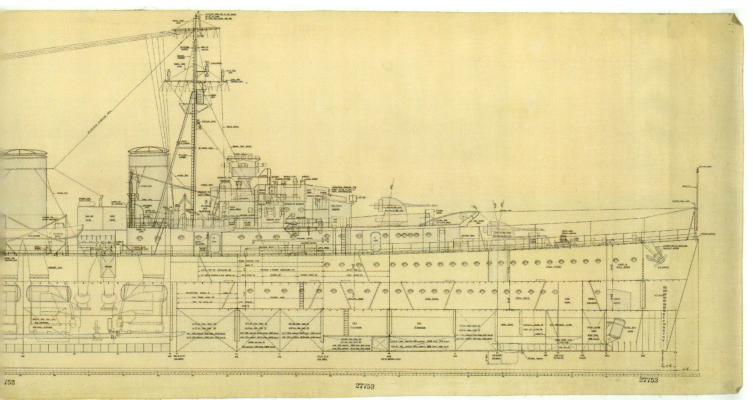

HMS *Welshman*
May–June 1942 and July 1942

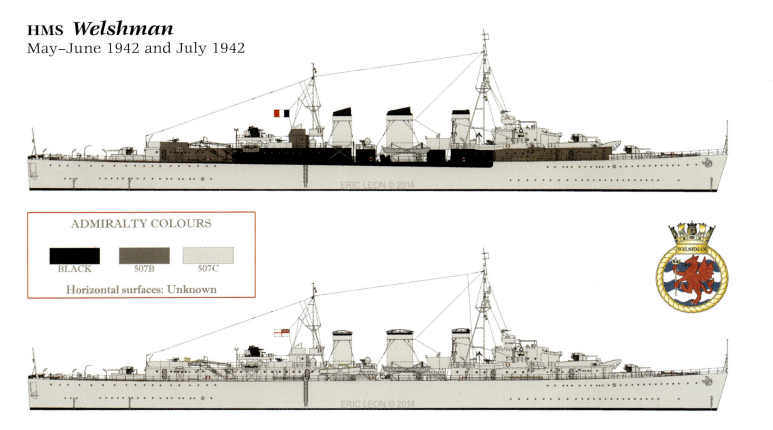

ADMIRALTY COLOURS

BLACK	507B	507C

Horizontal surfaces: Unknown

ERIC LEON © 2014

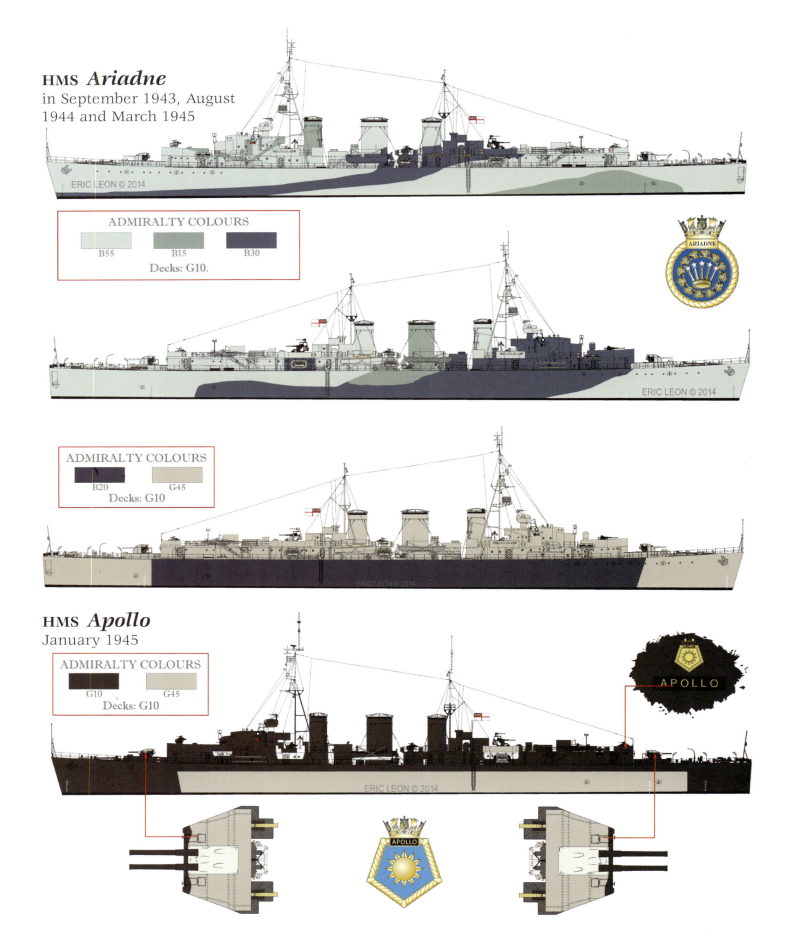

HMS *Ariadne*
in September 1943, August
1944 and March 1945

ADMIRALTY COLOURS
B55   B15   B30
Decks: G10.

ADMIRALTY COLOURS
B20   G45
Decks: G10

HMS *Apollo*
January 1945

ADMIRALTY COLOURS
G10   G45
Decks: G10

APOLLO

ERIC LEON © 2014

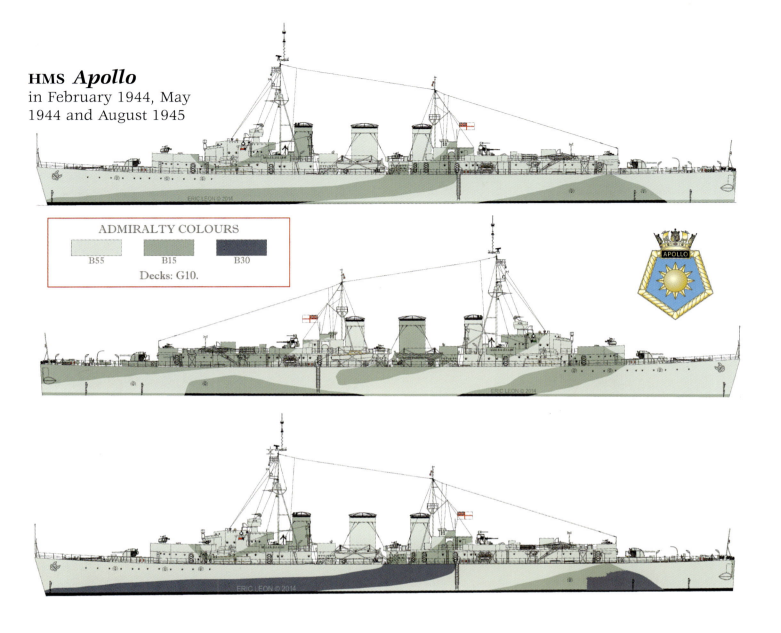

HMS *Apollo*
in February 1944, May
1944 and August 1945

ADMIRALTY COLOURS

B55   B15   B30
Decks: G10.

HMS *Apollo*
August 1945

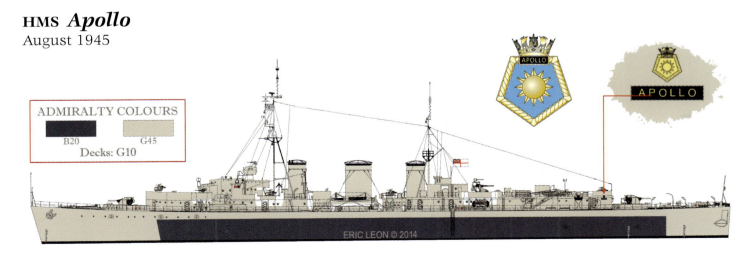

ADMIRALTY COLOURS

B20   G45
Decks: G10

APOLLO

H.M.S. LATONA

GREENOCK TO SUEZ ~ 16ᵀᴴ MAY 1941 — 19ᵀᴴ JUNE 1941

Duration of entire passage ... 811 hrs.
Total number of steaming hours .. 692 hrs
Distance along tracks followed ... 14955 miles
Total distance (incl. allowance for zigzagging. 15258 miles
Average sp. of adv. (entire passage) .. 21·6 kn (steaming hrs. only) .. 18·4 kn (incl. time in
Average speed (incl. allowance for zigzagging) .. 22·0 ~ 18·8 kn (incl. time in

Note: all the above figures include the false start from Freetown. Figures along
-side the tracks indicate the average speed of advance over the ground between points of call. Tha
brackets include an allowance for zigzagging where applicable. All times shewn are Gr. M

GREENOCK
dep 2115 16ᵀᴴ May

21·3
(23·6)

GIBRALTAR
arr 1500 20ᵀᴴ May. dep 0700 21ˢᵗ May

ALEXANDRIA
(arr. p.m. 21ˢᵗ June)

SUEZ
arr 1600 19ᵀᴴ June

25·1

20·9
(21·6)

ADEN
arr 0400 17ᵀᴴ June. dep 1100 17ᵀᴴ June

22·4

FREETOWN
arr 0800 25ᵀᴴ May. dep 1700 25ᵀᴴ May.   arr 0630 30ᵀᴴ May. dep 1145 30ᵀᴴ May

KILINDINI
arr 1545 13ᵀᴴ June
dep 0345 14ᵀᴴ June

15·7
(16·2)   24·0

22·8
(23·0)

22·1

Sᵀ HELENA
arr 0845 2ᴺᴰ June. dep 1220 2ᴺᴰ June

19·4

DURBAN
arr 2030 9ᵀᴴ June
dep 0330 10ᵀᴴ June

SIMONSTOWN
arr 0600 6ᵀᴴ June. dep 1600 8ᵀᴴ June

25·1

CHAPTER 7

THE *MANXMAN* ENTERS THE FRAY
Malta Runs and a Disguise, 1941

THE third ship of the *Abdiel* class to complete, the *Manxman*, had an extraordinarily varied career and became very well known to the Germans and Italians, who sometimes used her as the name ship of the class. She was built by Alexander Stephen & Sons, at Govan on the River Clyde. She was laid down on 24 March 1939, launched on 5 September 1940 and completed on 20 June 1941.[1] She was manned out of Chatham Barracks and took the pennant number M 70. Her crest and motto were from the coat of arms of the Isle of Man, the crest containing three legs conjoined and the ship's motto being *Stabit quocumque jeteris* or 'It will stand however it is thrown'.[2]

The *Manxman* was the second Royal Navy warship to bear the name, signifying someone from the Isle of Man, the first ship being an Isle of Man packet steamer that was converted to a seaplane carrier in 1916. The first *Manxman* was used at one time to support minelaying operations in the North Sea,[3] but in fact the second *Manxman* departed from the admittedly recent custom of naming fast minelayers after minelayers in the First World War.

There was a reason for this departure. In May 1938, the Lieutenant-Governor of the Isle of Man requested that the Secretary of State approach the Lords Commissioners of the Admiralty with a request that one of His Majesty's ships bear a name associated with the Isle of Man and suggested that either 'Manxman' or 'Isle of Man' might be considered as suitable. The request came well armed with facts and figures.

The Secretary of State will be aware of the record of the Isle of Man during the Great War – how it sent proportionately more men to the fighting forces than any other district of the British Isles except one, took over liability for £750,000 of the War debt and made a contribution

immediately on the outbreak of the war of £10,000, constructed and maintained prisoner of war camps for 26,000 prisoners and how practically all of the ships of the Isle of Man Steam Packet Company were engaged in the service of the Admiralty.

By October 1938 their Lordships had been persuaded and the Lieutenant-Governor of the island had been notified that they had approved of the name 'Manxman' for one of the three fast minelayers in the 1938 New Construction Programme.[4] It evidently didn't hurt to ask!

The *Manxman*'s first commanding officer, Captain Robert Kirk Dickson, was appointed to the ship in October 1940 when she was fitting out. On the day she was commissioned, 7 June 1941, he sent a signal to the Admiralty. That day he also began keeping a diary, which would eventually cover three volumes and which would not end until the day he left the ship.[5]

Known to family and friends as 'Bertie', Captain Dickson was born on 18 February 1898, in Edinburgh. His father was the Librarian of the National Library of Scotland and a great-great-grandfather was wounded at the battle of Bunker Hill in 1775. He entered the Royal Navy in 1911 via Osborne and Dartmouth. As a midshipman, in December 1914 he was present at the battle of the Falklands in the old battleship *Canopus*, which fired the first shots of the battle and later commanded boats in the landing at Anzac Beach in Gallipoli in 1915. He survived the battle of Jutland in 1916 unscathed in the battleship *Benbow*, but his only brother, Archie, was killed when the battlecruiser *Queen Mary* blew up and sank. After the Great War, he specialised in navigation and some of his inter-war posts were as First Lieutenant and Navigating Officer of HMS *Warspite* and as Naval Assistant to the First Sea Lord. When the Second World War broke out, he was the Commander of the Royal Naval College,

Captain Robert Kirk
Dickson, DSC, RN, in his
cabin aboard the
Manxman in Ceylon, in
1942. (Elizabeth K
Dickson)

Captain Robert Kirk Dickson, DSC, RN, in his cabin aboard the *Manxman* in Ceylon, in 1942. (Elizabeth K Dickson)

Greenwich and was immediately transferred to the War Room at the Admiralty, where he was promoted to Captain at the end of 1939.[6]

Captain Dickson's Executive Officer and also his Mining Officer was Lieutenant-Commander Robert Sydney Hopper, RN and his Navigator was Lieutenant Francis Price Brayne-Nicholls, RN. Dickson stuck with Brayne-Nicholls and later recommended him for an award and more seniority, in spite of learning that he had been court-martialled while in the battleship *Nelson* for 'indiscreet talk about a cipher signal'. Dickson wrote that Brayne-Nicholls was an efficient navigator and an exceptionally efficient general service officer and that he had come to the *Manxman* with the intention of living down the past and had done so.[7] The Captain's confidence was evidently well placed, as Brayne-Nicholls was awarded a Distinguished Service Cross for his service in the *Manxman*, would command the fast minelayer *Apollo* after the war and would be promoted to Rear Admiral.

Unlike the *Abdiel* and *Latona*, the *Manxman* was able to run a full series of trials. She was put through her paces in the Firth of Clyde on three separate days, 16, 18 and 20 June 1941.[8] The weather was ideal and no water was shipped at any time. In general, there was no serious vibration at any speed, but some parts of the

ship experienced noticeable vibration at certain speeds. Speed trials were held at 3000, 10,000, 55,000 and 72,000 SHP on the measured Arran course. At 72,000 SHP, the designed maximum, the ship made up to 35.821 knots on a displacement of 3520 tons. In turning trials, the ship's tactical diameter was found to be 1680 yards. The ship's pitching period was found to be six seconds and the rolling period was between 10 and 14 seconds. The ship's guns were fired, her radar was tested and she laid twenty sand-filled mines. During the trials, very few defects, omissions and areas of possible improvements were noted.

At the conclusion of the trials, Captain Dickson expressed complete satisfaction with the construction and behaviour of the ship and all officers present at the trials commented on the steadiness at full power and the general handiness of the ship. The report of her trials concluded, 'In general this ship is very well finished and there are very few deficiencies taking into consideration somewhat adverse conditions at the Shipyard during the finishing months'.

After completion of trials, the *Manxman* was ready to sail for Scapa Flow. Just before sailing, she was joined by Lieutenant Brayne-Nicholls, whom the Captain described as a gentleman. Of the voyage to Scapa Flow, Captain Dickson wrote in his diary, 'It's grand to be on the bridge of a ship again. I'm happier there than any other place in the world'.

The ship enjoyed a quiet work-up period for several weeks at Scapa Flow. Captain Dickson kept the crew busy with seamanship drills, night shoots, anti-aircraft shoots, practice anti-submarine attacks with a real submarine, the *P.31*, running paravanes, putting on the ship's first proper Church service and everything else it took to become battle-ready. There were of course mistakes to learn from, such as nearly shooting down an aircraft towing a target sleeve. At the end of the period, Captain Dickson met the C-in-C of the Home Fleet, Admiral Tovey.

On 10 July 1941, the *Manxman* left Scapa Flow for Greenock, to join up with a convoy bound for the Mediterranean. While there, the Captain had his wife Titia aboard for dinner and afterwards took her for a run around the harbour in the ship's motorbout. The rest of the time there was spent loading troops and stores and

The *Manxman* in July 1941. (Imperial War Museum FL4446)

fitting six 20mm Oerlikon guns, which Captain Dickson fired himself and called 'grand toys'.

On 13 July *Manxman* sailed at 20.45 to catch up with the convoy bound for Gibraltar. On the 15th she did so and was stationed as the lead ship of the starboard wing column, the ship's first chance at station-keeping. At 21.00 on the 16th the ship was detached to sail independently to Gibraltar. The weather became noticeably warmer on the way and the *Manxman* secured alongside at Gibraltar at 06.30 on the 19th. She was joined there by 460 soldiers and tons of their gear.

The ship was to take part in Operation 'Substance', a convoy carrying troops and stores from Gibraltar to Malta.[9] The six storeships of the convoy entered the Mediterranean the night of 20/21 July, escorted by the *Manxman* and other ships. The rest of the convoy escort joined up from Gibraltar, but before the convoy could get far, the troopship *Leinster* went aground in fog and could not accompany the convoy to Malta. The plan was for the convoy to be escorted part of the way by Admiral James Somerville's Force H, whose heavy ships included the aircraft carrier *Ark Royal*, the battleship *Nelson*, the battlecruiser *Renown* and then escorted by the cruisers and destroyers of Admiral Syfret's Force X, including the *Manxman*, all the way to Malta.

On the 23rd the convoy had to weather fierce attacks from Italian high-level and torpedo bombers. The destroyer *Fearless* was torpedoed and had to be scuttled, while the light cruiser *Manchester* was also torpedoed but was escorted back to Gibraltar. The *Manxman* shot down one bomber 'in small pieces' with the pom-pom and one Oerlikon. She hoisted a silk White Ensign that was presented to her at commissioning.

Force H turned back for Gibraltar at 17.13 on 23 July and the convoy reformed into two columns. The port column of the convoy was led by Admiral Syfret's flagship, the light cruiser *Edinburgh* and the starboard column was led by the *Manxman*. So reformed, the convoy sailed on, but had to contend with more air attacks, during which the destroyer *Firedrake* was damaged by near misses.

On the night of 23/24 July, the convoy had to contend with attacks by Italian MAS motor torpedo boats, whose engines could be heard in the distance. Beginning at 02.53 a fierce night action ensued, with British searchlights capturing the MAS boats and the convoy – including the *Manxman* – engaging them with every type of weapon that could be brought to bear. Captain Dickson saw one boat caught in searchlight beams hit repeatedly by the *Manxman*'s guns. The freighter *Sydney Star* was hit by one torpedo and badly damaged, but all of the ships of the convoy

The *Manxman* in action during Operation 'Substance'. Bomb splashes can be seen behind her. (Elizabeth K Dickson)

and the escort got through to Malta. The *Manxman* led the cruisers into Malta at midday on 24 July, followed by the destroyers and the merchant ships about four hours later.

The 'Substance' convoy brought 65,000 tons of supplies and stores, including food, spare Hawker Hurricane engines, ammunition and torpedoes for the 10th Submarine Flotilla.[10] Also brought in were Royal Artillery anti-aircraft units such as the 4th High Angle Artillery Regiment, the unit of a keen diarist, Gunner Stan Fraser,[11] who arrived on the merchant ship *Port Chalmers*. The new anti-aircraft units would become vital to Malta's survival in the coming months.

The cruisers and the *Manxman* that escorted 'Substance' sailed for Gibraltar soon after 16.00 on the 24th, followed by five of the destroyers. At dawn on 26 July, small surface and underwater assault craft of the Italian Navy's Xª Flottiglia MAS,[12] which had been launched from the sloop *Diana,* mounted a brave attack on Grand Harbour. The attack was met by heavy fire from batteries of the Royal Malta Artillery and the Royal Artillery and was repulsed with heavy losses in personnel and assault craft. The merchant ships of the 'Substance' convoy that were inside the harbour were undamaged, the only Allied casualty being the St Elmo Viaduct. One of the MAS boats was captured and the British later commissioned it as a tender and renamed it 'XMAS'.[13]

The *Manxman* returned safely to Gibraltar at 06.00 on the 27th with the rest of the force. Her labours for Malta were not yet done, though. She was to take part in Operation 'Style', a suitable name to succeed Operation 'Substance' (and the sort of thing that might have been dreamed up by Admiral Somerville). The operation has been described as a 'scalded cat' run,[14] and was designed to make up for the grounding of the

Leinster and the damage that caused the *Manchester* to turn back before reaching Malta. In 'Style', a total of ninety-two officers, 1714 men and 130 tons of stores[15] were to be transported to Malta in Force X, which consisted of the *Manxman*, the light cruisers *Arethusa* and *Hermione* (whose Captain Oliver was the Senior Officer of Force X) and the destroyers *Sikh* and *Lightning*.[16] The Admiralty turned down an alternate plan for everything to be carried by the *Manxman* alone in two trips.

Force X left Gibraltar at 01.00 on 31 July. The *Manxman* was crammed with 646 soldiers and RAF personnel and 22 tons of baggage. The rumour on the *Hermione* was that she and the *Arethusa* were expendable as long as the *Manxman* got through.[17] Fortunately, it didn't come to that and the only casualty of the operation was an Italian submarine. Early in the morning of 2 August, Force X was sailing at 28 knots in line ahead, with the *Hermione* leading the *Manxman* and *Arethusa*, when the *Hermione* sighted the Italian submarine *Tambien* on the surface off Tunis. The cruiser's captain shouted, 'Stand by to ram' and that she did, hitting the *Tambien* just abaft the conning tower. The *Tambien* sank and the damage to the *Hermione* was a 20ft gash in her bow.[18]

The rest of the voyage was uneventful, and Force X arrived at Malta at 10.00 on 2 August.[19] Its mission completed, the force sailed at 16.00 that afternoon and joined up with Force H along the way to Gibraltar. On the afternoon of the 4th a single torpedo plane launched an abortive attack on the *Hermione*,[20] and Force X returned safely to Gibraltar later that day.[21] The *Manxman*'s crew was exhausted, so much so that when Admiral Somerville came aboard to confer with Captain Dickson, he had to manoeuvre around bodies dozing on her deck, to mutual apologies.[22]

It was time for commendations. The Prime Minister sent his personal congratulations to Forces H and X. Captain Dickson commended one officer, the ship's cook, who had had many extra mouths to feed and the gunlayer of S.1 Oerlikon, who during a torpedo bomber attack stood by his gun even though badly burned from the blast from No. 1 4in mount. The *Manxman* would have no public glory, though. Film and photographs of 'Substance' were published, but the *Manxman* was deliberately cut out because of her secret nature and appearance.

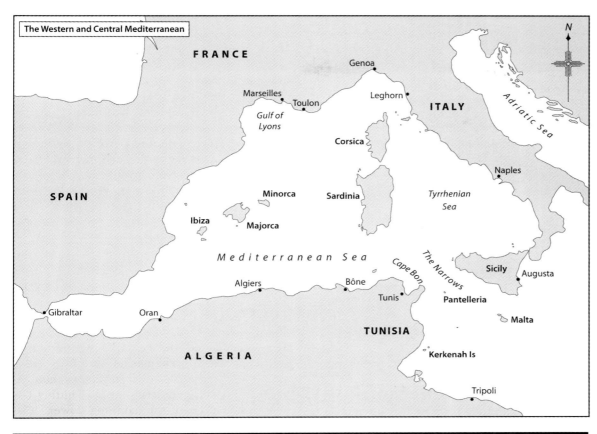

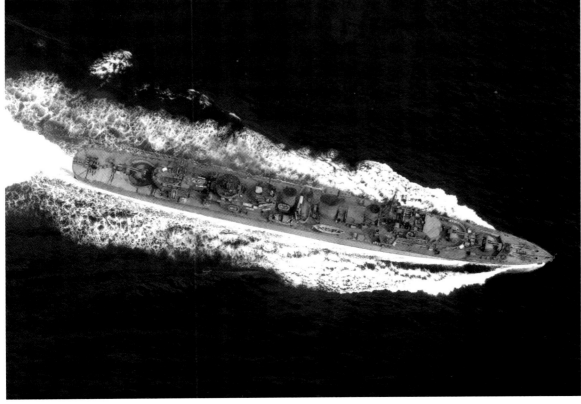

An overhead view of the
Manxman. (Imperial War
Museum FL 4434)

When the *Manxman* sailed from Malta for Gibraltar, she carried with her all eighteen Italian prisoners from the attack on Grand Harbour of 26 July. One was an officer, whom Captain Dickson ordered to be treated as such. The *Manxman* sailed from Gibraltar with the *Arethusa* at 22.30 on 5 August and transported the prisoners all the way to Britain, after which they ended up in a PoW camp on the Isle of Skye.[23] On 10 August the *Manxman* then returned to her base at the Kyle of Lochalsh,[24] Port ZA, which was, coincidentally, next-door to Skye.

Captain Dickson brought with him a proposal from Admiral Somerville for an operation in which, covered by Force H, the *Manxman* would disguise herself as the French super-destroyer *Léopard* and lay a minefield off the west coast of Italy. After the Captain's arrival at Port ZA, he was sent to the Admiralty by car to report on 'Substance' and 'Style' and to pitch the proposal, which met with general approval, especially from Captain De Salis, 'the minelaying king'. The Captain even met with the Vice Chief of the Naval Staff, Admiral Tom Phillips and the First Lord, A V Alexander, with whom he did not discuss the proposal. Captain Dickson returned to Port ZA by train.

The operation was to be called 'Mincemeat', which is not to be confused with a subsequent, more famous operation, carried out in 1943, involving a corpse and bogus papers. Of this Operation 'Mincemeat', Captain Dickson later said, 'I've never discovered whether he [Somerville] meant that code name to indicate the intended condition of Italian shipping after the operation or the certain condition of the minelayer if this fearsome gamble did not come off'. With Admiral Somerville, one never knew.

Admiral Somerville's proposal was approved and on 14 August the Admiralty ordered the *Manxman* to convert herself to resemble the *Léopard* 'in so far as reasonably practical'.[25] It would be a challenge. While the ships were not too different in size – at a robust 2126 tons, the *Léopard* was sometimes referred to as a light cruiser – there were a number of differences. The *Léopard* had three funnels, but they were, unlike the *Manxman*'s, unevenly spaced and had prominent black caps. Rather than having the *Manxman*'s three twin mounts for her main guns, she sported superimposed single 5.1in guns in shields, two forward and two aft. She also had raked masts, a more curved stem, a different stern shape and, worst of all, instead of being flush-decked like the *Manxman*, had a break in the foc's'le.

The challenge was taken up, not only by Captain Dickson, but also by Rear Admiral Robert Burnett, who commanded the 1st Minelaying Squadron at the Kyle of Lochalsh and who had been well known in his earlier years as a producer of naval theatricals. Another conspirator in the job was Captain Cowie,[26] who had plenty of theatrical experience himself and who served as Captain Dickson's 'Chief of Staff' for the project. Admiral Burnett gave his full support to the effort and 120 'extras' to help with the work. The 'histrionic talent' of the *Manxman*'s Chatham crew was 'fully aroused' and there were plenty of ideas. There was also plenty of paint, canvas, iron and steel.

Guided by much enthusiasm and the 1940 edition of *Jane's Fighting Ships*, the disguise was completed in nineteen hours, much of it overnight. As part of the disguise, a false bow and stern were rigged, the ship's funnels and masts were given a rake and painting altered the

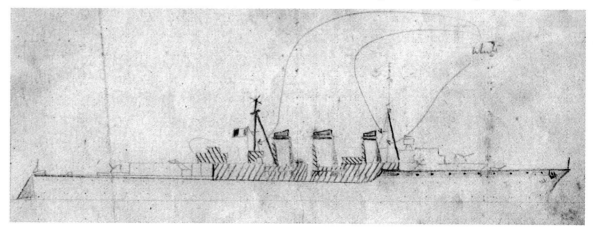

Captain Dickson's sketch of the *Manxman* disguised as the *Léopard*. (Elizabeth K Dickson)

lines of the ship[27] to make it look like she had a break in the foc'sle instead of a flush deck. To complete the disguise, 100 French navy uniforms were fabricated, plus a tricolour jacket and a cockade for the ship's cat.

At 11.30 the next day, the Admiral came to inspect the *Manxman*. As he came over the side, he addressed Captain Dickson as 'Ah, mon Capitaine'. Dickson replied, 'Ah, cher Amiral', embraced him and invited him to inspect the 'extremely' French guard that had fallen in on the quarterdeck.[28] Burnett was satisfied with the disguise and the signal notifying the Admiralty of the completion of the appointed task closed with, 'Vive la France'.[29]

The *Manxman* departed the Kyle of Lochalsh on 15 August for Milford Haven to embark 156 mines or 'rudenesses', as the Captain called them. She then sailed to Gibraltar, where she refuelled from the *Brown Ranger* in the bay in the darkness and picked up her orders. The *Manxman* cast off at 02.10 on the 22nd and after sunrise hoisted the French ensign. She sailed between the Spanish coast and the Balearic Islands and then headed for Toulon. She sighted a flying boat about eight miles away, but it showed no interest. The *Manxman* then turned east and then headed for Corsica. At 18.45 the uncomfortably bright sunshine gave way to a very fortunate patch of fog.

When the sun finally set, the French Tricolor was replaced by the White Ensign, French uniforms were taken off and the false bow dismantled. Speed was increased to 30 knots and she headed for the laying area. At 02.08 on 24 August, she began laying 140 mines and sixteen obstructors (floats equipped with devices designed to thwart minesweeping) off Leghorn (Livorno). The lay completed, at 04.14 Captain Dickson rang down 'Full Speed Ahead' and the *Manxman* 'just leapt forward. In little over half an hour we had worked up to 37 knots, the fans roaring and the whole ship quivering with life'. The plan was to clear the Gulf of Genoa before sunrise. She 're-Gallicised herself', but met no ships or aircraft – other than sighting a possible French cruiser hull-down on the horizon – before making her escape. She resumed her British identity at 12.00 on 25 August and arrived at Gibraltar at 23.00 on that night. No doubt relieved, she refuelled, picked up her confidential books and sailed for her base at the Kyle of Lochalsh.[30]

'French' sailors and the ship's cat aboard the *Manxman* for Operation 'Mincemeat'. (R K Dickson, *Naval Broadcasts*)

As Captain Dickson wrote in his diary, 'And so ended our awfully big adventure'.

While the *Manxman* was engaging in her cloak-and-dagger activities, Admiral Somerville's Force H from Gibraltar was doing its part to create a diversion. Just as the *Manxman* was laying her mines on the morning of the 24th, the *Ark Royal* flew off ten Swordfish to attack a factory in Sardinia and to set fire to the cork woods near Tempio. Force H then chased a reported Italian battle fleet, which was not where it was supposed to be, and then cruised along the Spanish coast with the *Ark Royal*'s aircraft overhead to attract attention. By then, the *Manxman* was out of dangerous waters.

Operation 'Mincemeat' seemed a complete success, but, alas, it was not so. No less than twenty-two of the 140 mines laid by the *Manxman* malfunctioned and came to the surface. The Italians sighted the floating mines and swept most of them on 26 August, their only casualty being the 109-ton minesweeper *Carmelo Noli*. To add insult to injury, the Italians recovered a British magnetic mine intact.[31] Such a daring and otherwise flawlessly executed operation deserved better results. Nevertheless, the *Manxman* did demonstrate that a fast minelayer could be disguised to look like the *Léopard*, and essentially the same disguise would later be put to a vitally important use by another fast minelayer.

The *Manxman* would soon be put to use on more conventional minelaying operations and would be joined in her endeavours by the fourth fast minelayer, the *Welshman*.

CHAPTER 8

THE *WELSHMAN* JOINS THE *MANXMAN*
Laying Mines for the *Scharnhorst* and *Gneisenau*, 1941–1942

THE *Manxman*'s return to the Kyle of Lochalsh was quickly followed by the completion of the fourth fast minelayer, the *Welshman*. Built by Hawthorn Leslie & Co. on the River Tyne, she was laid down on 8 June 1939, launched on 4 September 1940, during the Battle of Britain, and completed on 25 August 1941.[1] She was manned out of Chatham Barracks and took the pennant number M 84. Appropriately, the *Welshman*'s crest featured a red Welsh dragon, waves and a trident. If she had a motto, Latin or otherwise, it is unrecorded. The *Welshman* was adopted by the town of Wrexham in northeast Wales, which presented her with a Red Banner and sent 'comforts' to the ship.

The *Welshman* was probably the first Royal Navy warship to bear the name. There was, however, a 92-ton tug by that name on the Navy List from 1901 to 1904, which prompted an inquiry from Hawthorn Leslie to the Admiralty

Librarian the month the fast minelayer was launched.[2] Like the *Manxman* before her, the *Welshman* departed from the custom of naming fast minelayers after minelayers in the First World War and she was named to honour the people of Wales.

Like the *Manxman*, the *Welshman* was able to run an uninterrupted series of trials,[3] though they were a bit abbreviated. She was put through her paces from Tynemouth and Methil on three separate days, 22, 24 and 25 August 1941.[4] The ship was very steady in the moderate sea conditions encountered on the third day and no water was shipped except for a small amount over the stern during astern speed trials. In general, there was no serious vibration at any speed and only minor vibration in several locations and the ship was, if anything, even steadier than the *Manxman*. On full power trials, the ship made up to 36.62 knots on a

The *Welshman* as completed, starboard beam. (Tyne & Wear Archive)

The *Welshman* as completed, showing her mine doors. (IWM FL 4478)

displacement of 3300 tons. The ship's pitching period was found to be six seconds and the rolling period was $10^1/2$ seconds. Gun trials were successfully carried out, but no mines were laid. A few defects and problems were noted in the report.

The report on her trials concluded that the general finish of the ship was very satisfactory and no serious defects or omissions were noticed. The ship's Commanding Officer expressed great satisfaction with the ship in every way and put forward no complaints. He would have omitted some fittings for the sake of simplicity and reduction in weight, but in general he considered that he had 'a perfect ship'.

The *Welshman*'s first and only commanding officer was Captain William Howard Dennis Friedberger, DSO, RN. He was about 5ft 10in, slim and good looking in a Germanic sort of way. To those who knew him well, he went by 'Dennis'. He attended Gibbs, a London day preparatory school and entered the Royal Naval College, Osborne, at the age of 12. He then attended Britannia Naval College Dartmouth as a cadet and passed out second in his class. His seamanship skills came early at Dartmouth, where he spent a lot of time in small boats up and down the Dart River, as he was no good at games such as cricket.

As Midshipman Friedberger, he joined the battleship *Temeraire* in 1914. His seamanship and confidence in boats stood him in good stead in his first job as picket-boat midshipman and he quickly earned the respect of the crew. He was in the *Temeraire* at the battle of Jutland in 1916.

His family having immigrated to Britain from Germany, he was sensitive about his background and had overcome prejudice because of his name. His father was a stockbroker in peacetime, but when the First World War came, he served with the 3rd Royal Fusiliers and was killed in action at the 2nd battle of Ypres on 24 May 1915. His body was never found, but his name is listed on the Menin Gate in Ypres. Midshipman Friedberger was the first man on his ship to suffer a family member killed in the war.

After the battle of Jutland, Captain Friedberger's service during and after the First World War included several stints in submarines, including command of the *Odin* from 1929 to 1931, which must have prepared him well for the *Welshman*'s solitary service in the Mediterranean. His appointments between the wars also included the battleship *Iron Duke* and the light cruiser *Delhi*.

While not much at games, he was a life-long walker from when his father took his boys on long walks in England and the Continent when they went on holidays. He also learned to ride and in the late 1920s he met his future wife, Eleanor Renton, on a foxhunt and married her in Hong Kong in 1930 when in command of the *Odin*. They had two daughters and a son.

At the outbreak of the Second World War, he was in the Plans Division of the Admiralty. In December 1939, he was promoted to Captain. In 1940, he took command of the First Mine-laying Squadron in the converted minelayer *Menestheus,* which was rated at all of 15.5 knots. The speed of the *Welshman* must have come as a pleasant surprise to him.

Captain Friedberger was well liked and respected by the crew of the *Welshman*. His death notice in the *Daily Telegraph* prompted a

Captain Dennis Friedberger, DSC, RN. (Jane Bretherton née Friedberger)

letter to his widow from Able Seaman John Owen, who wrote that he was a 'lovely fella'.[5] He had a temper, but he could control it. As Able Seaman Jim Taylor recalled,

During her sea trials and dummy battle runs at Scapa, I made my first contact with our Skipper . . . As captain of the right hand gun on 'A' turret, I was ordered to take my own crew to extinguish a supposed fire on the bridge. Having connected the hose to the fire hydrant, I made as if to put out the imaginary fire. The Skipper howled out, 'What the bloody hell are you doing, Able Seaman?' to which I replied, 'Putting out a fire'. 'You can't put out a fire without water, man, turn it on!' which I promptly did. It wasn't my fault that he happened to be standing in the place where I thought the fire was and he received a short, sharp douche of water, much to my delight and to his dismay. He gave me a sly grin and said, 'Fires extinguished, return to gun quarters'. I knew from that moment on that he was a man who could see us through any future adversity.

So he was and so he did.

*   *   *

Shortly after her commissioning in August, the *Welshman* joined her sister-ship *Manxman*, which had just returned from Operation 'Mincemeat'. From September to March, they would be kept busy with minelaying operations from Home Waters. Together or alone, they would lay mines in the Northwestern Approaches, in the Bay of Biscay, off the Butt of Lewis, in the East Coast Mine Barrage and off the French coast in the English Channel.[6]

Before joining this effort, the *Manxman* had a special task, to lay mines off the coast of Norway near Statlandet. Sailing from Scapa Flow on 3 September, she was accompanied part of the way by the light cruiser *Kenya* and the destroyer *Lightning* under Rear Admiral Burrough. She had to lay her mines off a rocky coast in gale force winds, beginning at 02.17 on the 4th.[7] On the way back, her paravanes cut a

German mine, which bobbed alongside, causing those who saw it to hold their breath until it was clear of the stern.

Once back at the Kyle of Lochalsh, the *Manxman* had occasion to haul Admiral Burnett to Scapa Flow. During the stay, Captain Dickson entertained Admiral Sir John Tovey, C-in-C of the Home Fleet, Admiral Curteis and Rear Admiral Burnett in his cabin. The Captain's cook was sick, but the dinner was a success anyway.

The *Welshman* joined the *Manxman* at the Kyle of Lochalsh on 14 September. On the 18th the *Manxman* finally began the new minelaying operations with a lay west of St Malo and on the 22nd the *Welshman* carried out her first operational minelay, which turned out to be an uneventful one.

This period marked the first time the Admiralty had two fast minelayers to carry out operations from one base. The two ships were usually based in the northwest of Scotland at the Kyle of Lochalsh, 'Port ZA', to which much of the *Welshman*'s company took exception, saying 'Give me civilisation'.[8] The *Welshman* also had occasion to anchor at Scapa Flow, where she endured a severe gale and dragged her anchors on two occasions. Captain Friedberger wrote that 'the consequences might have been embarrassing, only few ships were in the anchorage and sea room was ample'.

A few years later, when Captain Dickson was Admiral Dickson and Director of Naval Information, he gave a radio war commentary called, in part, 'Adventures of a Fast Minelayer'. A country stationmaster friend had told him to talk about what the Navy actually did and to stick to a subject he really knew about himself. And so he did, on 28 February 1945, in one of the commentaries he published in a book called *Naval Broadcasts* after the war.[9]

After recounting the stationmaster's advice, Dickson said that what the Navy did could be summed up in one word – control – and chose to talk about one form of control – minelaying – and about one class – the 'Fast Minelayers' – and, finally, about the one he had had the honour to command, the *Manxman*. Of the fast minelayers, he said, 'Early in the war the British Admiralty built a class of ship entirely new in any Navy'.

Of offensive minelaying in a fast minelayer, he said two things were necessary to succeed.

> Firstly, the minefield in exactly the predetermined place and this required a very high standard of navigation . . . Secondly, we *had* to get there and back unseen and unheard. When we were with Force H in the Mediterranean, Admiral Somerville used to call us his 'Little Rat' – and if ever we'd allowed the enemy to suspect that the 'Little Rat' had been about the place, he could just have told his ships to avoid that neighbourhood until he had searched for the minefield and swept it up.

The *Welshman* at speed in 1941. (US Navy via Grand Valley State University)

Dickson then described in great detail a night minelaying run off the enemy's coast, presumably based on one of the *Manxman*'s runs from the Kyle of Lochalsh in 1941–2. 'The one thing we prayed for in those ships was a dark night – a really dark night. The moon was the devil.' Of the taut wire measuring gear, he said, 'It was worth a guinea a minute when it worked, but when it didn't it was a curse and an abomination'. The gear's dynamometer had an electric repeater on the bridge, 'where we kept absolute silence' and he remembered that the thing 'used to make a very sinister ticking noise'.

Of the run in to lay the mines, Dickson recalled, 'We did many of those operations, but we never lost the thrill of rushing toward the enemy's blacked-out coast in a fast ship crowded with high explosive'. Once the report 'All mines gone, sir' was heard, a number of things had to happen and 'the executive order for them all to happen at once was "Home, John". The great mining doors in the stern would be closed, the engine room telegraphs put to full speed and then you could just *feel* the acceleration as she worked up to it'. On the return leg, if they were in luck there would be Land's End on the right

bearing at the right distance and there would be friendly fighters overhead. In peacetime, he had thought Land's End 'a pretty grim sort of hole', but 'I've got a more friendly feeling for it now'.

The *Manxman* and *Welshman* carried out many such operations between September 1941 and February 1942, each very similar but each a little different, as reflected in the reports of their commanding officers. Of the operation commencing on 3 February, Captain Dickson wrote[10] that the ship sailed from Milford Haven at noon and that a departure was from the Wolf Rock at 18.31 with a course of 182° and a speed of 28 knots. The flyer arm of the taut wire measuring gear fractured soon after that, forcing the *Manxman* to rely on dead reckoning, but the Germans 'kindly arranged for the Ushant light to be burning just when it was wanted on the return run'. The sky cleared completely during the lay itself, which lasted from 02.02 to 02.53 on the 4th and which was carried out 'in brilliant moonlight'. On the return leg, the *Manxman* passed the Wolf at 0.908 and reached Milford Haven at 14.30 the same day. The weather was good enough on that operation, but Captain Dickson wrote of the operation commencing on

An aerial view of the *Welshman* from off the port quarter. (Imperial War Museum FL 4481)

The *Welshman* in October 1941. (Imperial War Museum A 6043)

5 February that during the lay there was a strong wind and a beam sea, causing the ship to roll 15° and for ice to form on the upper deck.

On most but not all runs, the ships were unobserved. On 20 December, the *Welshman* had her baptism of fire when a German twin-engined bomber approached undetected from astern and dropped two bombs, which fortunately missed astern by half a mile. The miscreant then turned away before the *Welshman* could open fire.[11]

For a change of pace, between 11 and 20 December the *Manxman* was sent on a run from Milford Haven to Gibraltar with a volatile cargo of 800 depth charges, twenty torpedoes and other explosives. She returned with a decidedly mixed cargo that included survivors from the aircraft carrier *Ark Royal*, bank securities and diamonds taken from German agents attempting to reach South America.[12] After her return, she underwent docking and repairs at Liverpool that lasted from Christmas Eve to 28 January,[13] after which she arrived at Port ZA on the 30th.[14]

Then it was the *Welshman*'s turn for a change of pace. On 6 January 1942, she sailed for Gibraltar, Freetown and Tokoradi in the Gold Coast, West Africa with essential stores, depth charges and personnel. She arrived at Gibraltar on the 10th and departed the next day for Freetown.[15] The dockyard maties she carried were intended for an urgent repair job and they enjoyed their time on the ship, when not sick, with cigarettes at 6d for twenty. They also received a free rum ration every day, but it was

too strong for some of them and the *Welshman*'s crew benefitted from the extra tots.[16] The ship arrived back at Gibraltar on 27 January and sailed the next day for the United Kingdom,[17] where she arrived on 1 February with a cargo of gold bullion from Freetown.[18] The gold had been stored in the after magazine for safekeeping, prompting Able Seaman L A Francis to recall, 'We thought of better places to stow it, but unfortunately, we didn't have much say in the matter'.[19] The *Welshman* was the first, but not the last, of her class to carry such a valuable cargo.

At the beginning of February, the *Manxman* was assigned to the Plymouth Command and the *Welshman* was placed at Dover under Admiral Bertram Ramsay. Both were to lay minefields in preparation for a possible breakout by German heavy units at Brest, the battlecruisers *Scharnhorst* and *Gneisenau* as well as the heavy cruiser *Prinz Eugen*,[20] which had joined them at the beginning of June after the end of her sortie with the *Bismarck*. As part of the same effort, bombers from the RAF's Bomber Command and the small minelayer *Plover* laid mines intended to catch the German ships.

The *Manxman* and *Welshman* went to work and worked hard. Between the 4th and the 9th, the two carried out six operations designed to catch the German squadron on its way up the Channel.[21] The Admiralty realised how hard the ships were working, but on 10 February signalled, 'The existing situation has necessitated MANXMAN and WELSHMAN carrying out numerous operations at high pressure. The strain involved is fully realised, but these two ships must persist in their efforts during the coming dark night period.'[22] And persist they did.

The Germans were indeed planning a breakout from Brest, codenamed Operation 'Cerberus', and were well aware of the danger from British mines. During the preparations for the squadron's run up the Channel, the Germans carried out extensive minesweeping operations, especially after the destroyer *Bruno Heineman* hit one of the *Plover*'s mines and sank on 25 January on her way to join the squadron. One of the *Welshman*'s mines sank the German auxiliary minesweeper *M 1208* on the night of 9/10 February, the captain and twenty-five men going down with the ship,[23] causing the Germans to alter the squadron's route.[24] By then, however, the attention of the *Manxman* and *Welshman* had been turned to laying mines in the Bay of Biscay to catch German U-boats. The *Manxman* laid the first minefield in that series the night of 10/11 February.[25]

The German squadron left Brest at 22.45 the very next day, on 11 February,[26] and then turned up the English Channel. The Admiralty did not become aware of the presence of the German ships in the Channel until about 11.25 the next day, when life at the Admiralty became decidedly more exciting. Upon his arrival at the War Room, Captain Cowie was informed that the ships had passed through one of *his* minefields. He had by then become inured to the theory that an unsuccessful minefield was his personal property, while a successful one belonged to the Admiralty.[27]

On their journey up the Channel and on the way to Germany, both battlecruisers did in fact hit mines, which were most likely laid by Royal Air Force aircraft on 6 February off Terschelling Island. At 21.34 on the 12th, the *Gneisenau* detonated a mine off Terschelling and lay dead in the water for about an hour. She finally got underway and limped into Wilhelmshaven the next morning, preceded to Germany by the *Prinz Eugen* and the *Scharnhorst*.

The *Gneisenau* was not badly damaged by the mine she hit, but because of that damage and some damage incurred in harbour, she had to be docked at Kiel for repairs before sailing for Norway. She would never make it. Before she

could leave Kiel, RAF bombers located her on the night of 26/27 February. A 1000lb bomb struck by 'Anton' turret, the forward triple 11in turret, and set off some powder charges that destroyed the turret and much of the structure around it, killing ten men.[28] Due to the severe damage she had suffered and the desire to replace her 11in guns with 15in guns, the *Gneisenau* was slated for reconstruction instead of just repair. That proved impossible and she never returned to service. For her, the war was over.

While the *Manxman* and *Welshman* did not lay the mines that damaged the *Scharnhorst* or the *Gneisenau*, they still played an instrumental part in the scheme of mining operations that was designed to catch them. And mines were the only weapon that damaged the German ships;[29] shore batteries, destroyers, bombers and torpedo planes all failed, no matter how bravely they pressed home their attacks.

The chickens at Brest having flown the coop, on 18 February the *Welshman* left the Kyle of Lochalsh for a refit on the River Tyne, which began on the 20th. On 2 April, she left the Tyne for Scapa Flow, where she arrived the next day and commenced working up practices. Having evidently worked up sufficiently, the *Welshman* left Scapa Flow on 9 April and arrived at the Kyle of Lochalsh later that day, the same day the *Manxman* departed. On the 11th she arrived at Milford Haven and in the coming weeks she carried out minelays in the Bay of Biscay, off Ile de Bas and, finally, off Ile Vierge, which she completed on 20 April.[30] She returned to Port ZA on 21 April, but stayed only a few days. On the 23rd, she sailed for Plymouth, arriving the next day.[31] The Admiralty had big plans for her, which did not include any more overnight minelaying runs to the shores of occupied Europe.

In March, while the *Welshman* refitted, the *Manxman* was still attached to the Rear Admiral (Minelayers) at Port ZA. Her comings and goings that month are of record, but what she was actually doing is not obvious. On 6 March, she sailed for Operation 'SN.18A' and Rosyth. On the 9th, she arrived back at Port ZA, embarked mines and sailed for Scapa Flow, arriving on the 12th. She did not return there until 27 March, but did not stay long, sailing for Tobermory, the main town on the Isle of Mull, on the 30th. She quit Tobermory on 6 April and arrived at Port ZA the same day.[32] She would not be there long; the Admiralty had other plans for her as well.

The *Manxman* and *Welshman* in October 1941. (Imperial War Museum A 6042)

CHAPTER 9

THE *ABDIEL* AND THEN THE *MANXMAN* TO THE INDIAN OCEAN, 1941–1942

After the end of the Tobruk runs in November 1941, the *Abdiel*'s time in the Mediterranean drew to a close. War was clearly about to come to the Far East and the Pacific. In October, the War Cabinet had made the decision to dispatch the battleship *Prince of Wales* to Cape Town and in November she sailed from there for Singapore, joining up with the battlecruiser *Repulse* in the Indian Ocean. The situation in the Mediterranean seemed to be in hand: Force K at Malta was busily decimating Axis convoys to North Africa and Operation 'Crusader' had finally been launched. Ominously, though, German U-boats had entered the fray and in November they sank the *Ark Royal* off Gibraltar and then the *Barham* in the eastern Mediterranean.

As Christmas approached, the men of the Mediterranean Fleet were allowed to send special Christmas notes to their families. The *Abdiel*'s commanding officer sent one off to his son Robin, who received it in due course with great delight. The *Abdiel* had already been away from Home Waters for seven months and would not return for many more.

In the second week of December, an unnamed person in the *Abdiel* found the time to publish a second edition of the *Abdiel News*, the first having been hobbled by a problem with the 'duplicator'. Besides erudite essays on China and on Japan, it included a number of features. The advice column, 'Auntie Nellie's Corner', refused multiple requests for financial assistance to purchase rubbers. In 'The Stars Foretell', one helpful horoscope read, 'You will receive a sum of money which you should spend at once because by the end of the week you will have none left'. In the 'Exchange & Mart', two items read, 'Will exchange my job in the Navy for a quiet executive position in the Home Guard' and 'Wanted: a female secretary for typing and odd jobs in the office. Salary . . . Apply editor'.

The *Abdiel News* also contained a column called 'A Loss'. It read, 'It was with much regret we learned we were losing our 'Jimmy', Lieut. Austen. In the few months we served under him we found him friend and mentor. Amongst other things we gratefully remember his efforts towards our concerts and his unfailing humour'. In closing, 'We offer our congratulations on his promotion. May his rings multiply and near misses his only worries.'

The *Abdiel* was to prove useful to the Mediterranean Fleet one last time. In the middle of December 1941, the Italians and the British ran convoy operations in the Central Mediterranean at the same time. Force K from Malta was sent to sea and the Mediterranean Fleet sent a force of cruisers and destroyers to sea to intercept the Italians, but the Fleet had insufficient destroyers to send its battleships to sea, an especially important consideration since the battleship *Barham* had been sunk by a U-boat. Admiral Cunningham's solution was to order the *Abdiel* to sea from Alexandria to Haifa to create a radio diversion to give the impression that a British battle squadron was at sea.[1] That she did and the ruse was successful, the Italian convoys being recalled on 13 December.[2] The *Abdiel* sailed on to Haifa and then back to Alexandria on the 17th.[3]

The picture then turned very dark for the Mediterranean Fleet. On the night of 19 December, Force K from Malta ran onto an Italian minefield off Tripoli and lost the light cruiser *Neptune* and the destroyer *Kandahar*. Back at Alexandria that night, the *Abdiel* was tied up along the seaward wall[4] when Italian frogmen riding manned torpedoes from the submarine *Scire* sneaked into the harbour. Before being captured, the frogmen attached explosives to the battleships *Queen Elizabeth* and *Valiant* and a tanker, badly damaging all of them, as well as the destroyer *Jervis*. In one stroke, the shortage of destroyers was not as important as it once was, as the Fleet had no battleships left for them to screen.

By then, war had broken out in the Far East on 7/8 December 1941. On the 10th Japanese Navy bombers sank the *Prince of Wales* and *Repulse* off the east coast of Malaya. The Royal Navy needed to reform its Eastern Fleet. On 28 December the *Abdiel* was ordered to sail to Haifa to embark mines and then to join the Eastern Fleet.[5]

She would be missed. On the 31st, Admiral Cunningham made a signal, 'Goodbye and good luck. You leave the Mediterranean Station with a fine record of arduous and hazardous service well performed, of which you may all be proud'.[6] Perhaps he was glad he had not sent her away after all.

On 3 January 1942, on the ship's entering the Indian Ocean, Lieutenant-Commander Chavasse posted an order about dress.

> The sun in the Indian Ocean is considerably stronger than in the Mediterranean. 1. Hats or helmets (as ordered) are to be worn at all times when exposed to the sun. 2. Ratings are not to sit about in the sun in a half-naked condition. 3. Between sunset and sunrise warm clothing is to be worn when on the upper deck. It is extremely easy to catch a chill in this part of the world.

The *Abdiel* arrived at Colombo during the forenoon on 10 January 10. On entering the harbour, Midshipman Goodwin recalled that 'we could hardly believe our eyes. There lay the Eastern Fleet with smart white awnings set and guns smartly laid fore and aft . . . the guns had brightly polished tompions in place and all the brass work on the quarter deck and the gangways was brightly polished . . . Here was a peacetime fleet!'

The Captain was surprised to learn that the *Abdiel* had been allocated to the 'Singapore Defence Force'. Fortunately for her, the situation in the Far East had deteriorated so rapidly – by then the Imperial Japanese Army was well on its way down the Malay Peninsula towards Singapore – that it became obvious that no useful purpose could be served by sending her to Singapore. It was then suggested that she might be useful in the Dutch East Indies, but just as fortunately for her that did not come to pass either.

Instead, the *Abdiel* became a unit of the British Eastern Fleet in the Indian Ocean and was soon tasked with carrying out a series of minelaying operations in the Andaman Islands with the object of blocking the harbours in the islands so the Japanese could not use them. The operations were to be carried out from the base at Trincomalee. In order to carry out the missions, it was necessary to run the *Abdiel* to the limit of her endurance, even burning diesel

The *Abdiel* at Colombo in 1942. (Imperial War Museum A 9688)

oil as well as fuel oil and on one occasion suction on her oil fuel tanks was lost as she came alongside the oil fuel jetty.[7]

On 28 January she completed her first minelaying operation off the Andaman Islands,[8] which lie in a line from north to south to the west of the Dutch East Indies and south of Burma. In the first series of operations, Port Blair, Elphinstone Harbour, Port Meadows and Kotara were mined. The Captain recalled that there was no difficulty from the minelaying point of view, but that the navigational hazards were reported as acute, since all the available charts were from old surveys and most of the navigational marks on the charts had ceased to exist.[9] Orders were orders and the operations continued.

On what was to be her last minelaying operation in the Andamans, the *Abdiel* sailed to lay mines in the MacPherson Strait, Port Mouat and Port Anson on 1 February. At Port Anson, she was to lay mines in waters that were charted at eight fathoms.[10] But the charts were wrong. Midshipman Goodwin witnessed what happened.

In the final day of operations we were laying mines at the northern island. The Pilot was a bit worried because there had been no chart corrections in that area for decades. Meanwhile there had been some volcanic activity. As we approached the anchorage to be mined, I was sent up to the crow's nest to look out for shoal water. This was the first time I had done anything like that. Certainly the sea around was of all different colours, mostly blue, but sometimes white. Just as I was making up my mind which was deep water and which was not, the ship gave three shudders and the engines stopped.[11]

The *Abdiel*'s starboard propeller had touched either a sand bank or a pinnacle of rock,[12] but in either case the damage was very real. As if that were not bad enough, the ship was in a very awkward position.

We were stopped at the mouth of the bay. On the shore close by, surely well within blow dart range, emerged a group of pygmies, about a dozen in all with a

The *Abdiel*'s officers at Colombo. (Norman Goodwin via Tim Goodwin)

mangy looking pie dog. They just stood and stared as we, gingerly on one engine, felt out way out to deeper water. This was not as easy as it sounds because a certain amount of haste was in order. We had touched bottom as the last of the mines had gone overboard. We had then been stopped for a while to assess the damage. There was but a thirty-minute interval between the mines being laid and them becoming armed. If we were not quick enough, we could mine ourselves into the bay.[13]

Fortunately they were quick enough and the *Abdiel* escaped from Port Anson without the further embarrassment of testing her own mines. Unfortunately, the Japanese did not test the mines either when they occupied the Andamans on 23 March. Worse, before the Japanese arrived the Royal Indian Navy tug *Sophie Marie* took shelter in those waters on 1 March and inadvertently 'tested' one of the mines. Upon finding that the mine worked, she sank.

After the *Abdiel* grounded, the 'buzz' consisting of 'Now we'll go to Durban for a refit' immediately began going around the ship.[14] For the moment, however, the *Abdiel* returned to Trincomalee on one shaft with without much difficulty and then proceeded to Colombo for docking, where she arrived on 5 February.[15] According to Midshipman Goodwin, 'We did not exactly limp back, because we could still do quite a turn of speed with one engine braked on'.[16] Docking revealed severe damage to the propeller shaft and the 'A' bracket holding it to the hull.[17] Repairs could not be completed locally, so she had to make the voyage all the way to Durban in South Africa.

She departed Colombo on 10 March, stopping at Addu Atoll on the 11th[18] and then at Kilindini on the way, all the while with the damaged propeller stowed on deck. On the way to Addu Atoll, she uncomfortably carried a cargo of high-octane petrol in four-gallon tins, with orders to throw any leaking tins overboard at once.[19] She departed Kilindini on 16 March[20] and arrived at Durban on the 20th,[21] where she docked on the 29th.[22] On this voyage she was able to make 24 knots on one shaft with revolutions for 29 knots and with $2^{1}/_{2}°$ of wheel to keep the ship on course.[23]

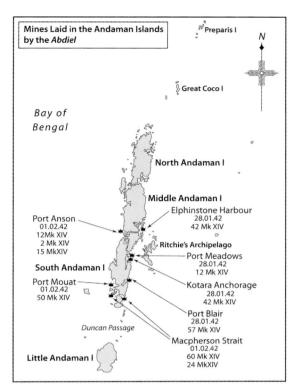

It was just as well that the *Abdiel* had left the Indian Ocean, as just a few days later a Japanese striking force of five of the fleet carriers that had attacked Pearl Harbor and four battlecruisers entered the Indian Ocean. Beginning on Easter Sunday, 5 April, the force attacked Colombo and Trincomalee, inflicting heavy losses on British warships and merchant ships but meeting some stiff resistance from Hurricane fighters over land. The British Eastern Fleet and the Japanese striking force never found each other, a fortunate outcome for the Eastern Fleet, and the Japanese never found the *Abdiel*.

Once in Durban, the *Abdiel* was put into drydock and work began. The starboard propeller shaft was withdrawn and then began the long process of straightening the 'A' bracket through which the shaft passed. This work required considerable precision, which was not made easier by the ship moving in response to changes in day night temperatures. Three weeks later, the work was completed and the *Abdiel* was ready for sea.[24]

On 6 June, the *Abdiel* was sent out to rescue survivors from the ss *Elysia*, which had been attacked the previous day in the Indian Ocean about 360 miles east-northeast of Durban[25] near the southern entrance to the Mozambique

An alert rating aboard the *Abdiel*. (Robin Pleydell-Bouverie)

Channel between Africa and Madagascar. The *Abdiel*'s normally ineffective radar, 'for the first time in its life',[26] picked up an echo, which turned out to be a lifeboat from the *Elysia*. The boat's occupants were brought aboard and the *Abdiel* learned and reported that the *Elysia* had been sunk not by a submarine but by a Japanese

surface raider.[27] There being no sign of the raider, the *Abdiel* returned to Durban the next day.

This was probably just as well for the *Abdiel*; there were actually two raiders, the armed merchant cruisers *Aikoku Maru* and *Hokoku Maru*, converted passenger ships armed with eight 5.5in guns,[28] much heavier than the *Abdiel*'s six 4in. On the other hand, the *Abdiel* might have done at least as well as the Dutch tanker *Ondina* and the minesweeping sloop HMIS *Bengal*, which encountered the same two raiders in November 1942. The *Ondina* and *Bengal* between them sported only a 4in gun and a 12pdr gun, but they survived their damage and even sank the *Hokoku Maru*[29] with a hit that set her torpedo tubes afire and blew off her stern.

Once back at Durban, the *Abdiel* was ordered home. While at Durban, her men were royally treated, the city even throwing a dinner dance for the whole crew. Lieutenant-Commander Chavasse was invited to stay with some people from Johannesburg. He had a good time, but was embarrassed when, on entering a restaurant in his uniform, the orchestra struck up 'All the nice girls love a sailor'.[30] Midshipman Goodwin and a second midshipman were invited to stay at a dairy farm south of Pietermartitzburg and were given ponies to explore the countryside. Several of the other men told Goodwin they had been put under pressure to return to South Africa and

The *Abdiel*'s crew. (Robin Pleydell-Bouverie)

at least one was given implicit permission to marry someone's daughter. While leaving on 7 June the *Abdiel* was treated to the traditional serenade by the famous singer Perla Siedle Gibson.[31]

The next stop was Simonstown, near Cape Town, and again the crew received royal treatment by the local population. The *Abdiel* also received an unusual cargo, even for a fast minelayer. As she was preparing to leave, all of a sudden police cars drove on to the quay, following by several black vans. The vans' back doors opened and out leapt several armed police, who took up defensive positions around the vans. The officer in charge asked Lieutenant-Commander Chavasse if they were ready to take over 'the bullion', which was the first he had heard of it. Two sailors were duly dressed up in gaiters and given rifles, the mining deck was cleared, a working party was went ashore and the task of loading the gold bars started.

A steady procession then began of men laden with one gold bar per wooden box, one box per man, coming up one gangway and then going back down to the quay empty-handed until almost the whole of the mining deck was covered by gold bar boxes one layer thick. Chavasse had to sign for each box of gold, the total value of which was said to be £5.5 million. A Royal Marine sergeant and a corporal, each armed with a revolver, were detailed to keep a constant guard on the gold.[32]

Thus laden, the *Abdiel* left Simonstown for Britain on 10 June, the Captain intending to make the voyage in record time. She made good time in spite of trouble with her condensers much of the way. On the way, the ship stopped at Pointe-Noire in the Congo, Tokoradi in Ghana, Freetown in Sierra Leone, Bathurst (now Banjul) in Gambia and then at Gibraltar, where she refuelled.

At Gibraltar, Midshipman Goodwin was allowed to visit his brother Ian aboard the aircraft carrier *Eagle*. After an enjoyable visit, the midshipman went to rejoin his ship only to see it leaving harbour. He began running and yelled to the quarterdeck working party to throw him a heaving line, which he caught and used to leap from dockside to the quarter fender, from which he was hauled on board.[33]

After a 'brush' with an enemy aircraft in the Channel, the *Abdiel* arrived at Greenock. There

the drill was a bit different from South Africa. A drifter came alongside and a young man from the Bank of England came aboard and asked if they had the bullion. When told they did, he replied, 'Jolly good show. Will you please send it ashore and give me a receipt', without even seeing it. The bullion boxes were loaded into cargo nets, hoisted out by the ship's mine cranes and dumped 'any old how' on the foc'sle of the drifter.[34] According to the receipt the Captain accepted from the Bank of England, she delivered 442 boxes containing 356,024.61 ounces of gold on 29 June 1942.[35]

The *Abdiel* docked on the River Tyne on 3 July to begin a well-earned refit.[36] As it was decided to replace one shaft and it was discovered that there was considerable distortion in a large number of boiler tubes, the refit was

The *Abdiel*'s receipt for the gold she brought from South Africa. (Robin Pleydell-Bouverie)

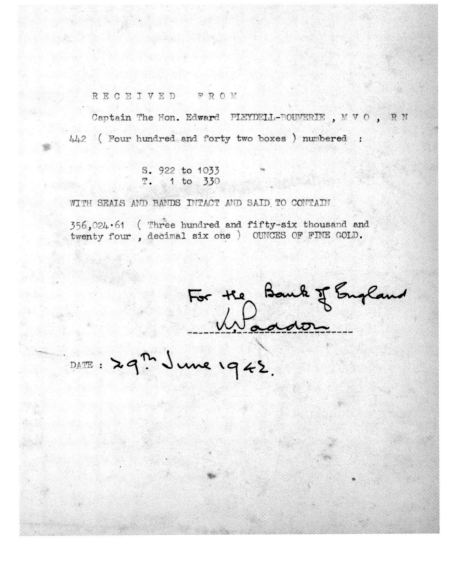

clearly going to take longer than originally thought. Accordingly, Captain Pleydell-Bouverie and most of the crew left the ship, the Captain bearing oranges and bananas from South Africa for his son.

So ended the *Abdiel*'s first commission. By all accounts – at least those of Lieutenant Austen and Midshipman Goodwin – the *Abdiel* had been a happy ship during the commission. Months later, the *Abdiel* would emerge from the refit to begin a new commission with a much different crew.

* * *

In April 1942, the Admiralty decided to transfer the *Manxman* to the Indian Ocean for service with the British Eastern Fleet to replace the *Abdiel* after she grounded. Captain Dickson learned of this momentous decision in a shoreside telephone call from Captain Cowie at the Admiralty. On 9 April, the *Manxman* sailed from the Kyle of Lochalsh for Plymouth,[37] whence she departed for the Indian Ocean on the 18th.[38]

Like the *Latona* before her, the *Manxman* had a long journey ahead of her. She called at Gibraltar on 21 April at 08.00 and departed the next day at 11.30 for Durban, South Africa, via Freetown, Tokoradi and Simonstown.[39] Such was the Axis surveillance of Gibraltar that the German naval staff learned both her arrival and her departure.[40] The *Manxman* arrived at Freetown on 27 April and at Durban on 9 May. There Captain Dickson called on the *Abdiel*,

The *Manxman* at Addu Atoll disguised as an island in the Indian Ocean in July 1942. (Elizabeth K Dickson)

which was still repairing there and sharing a graving dock with the battleship *Valiant*. As the *Abdiel* was to return to the UK, Captain Pleydell-Bouverie was most generous. From Durban the *Manxman* reached Kilindini in Kenya on 15 May.[41]

The *Manxman* arrived in the Indian Ocean just a few days after the successful conclusion of Operation 'Ironclad', the British attack on Diego Suarez, the Vichy French naval base on the northern tip of the island of Madagascar. The operation, which was jointly led by Admiral Syfret and General Sturges of the Royal Marines, had been launched on 5 May and was completed by the 7th.

The operation had been designed to deny Diego Suarez to the Japanese, who might have pressured the Vichy French into letting them use it to close the Mozambique Channel between Madagascar and mainland Africa and thereby deny the British a vital shipping route for reinforcements to the Middle East. For the time being, the British did not plan to occupy the remainder of Madagascar, which remained under the control of officials loyal to the government at Vichy, though General Smuts in South Africa urged them to do so as early as possible.[42]

In June, the *Manxman* travelled to Delhi and then Bombay, where she embarked gear required to camouflage her as a tropical island, a concept that made disguising her as the *Léopard* look simple. She returned to Colombo, where coir netting for the camouflage was being made and began to plan Operation 'Cobra', which was to involve minelaying in the Andaman Islands and off the coast of Malaya, with the *Manxman* lying up in camouflage by day. She sailed to Addu Atoll to practice rigging and un-rigging the camouflage and then rejoined the Eastern Fleet at Colombo. Alas, but perhaps fortunately for *Manxman*, 'Cobra' was abandoned and the *Manxman* sailed to Trincomalee to store the camouflage gear.[43] It is not known if the disguise included coconut trees or grass skirts.

In July, the *Manxman* visited Madras, where Captain Dickson was given a mongoose as a pet. The mongoose – named Rikki, Tikki or Tavi – was at first confined to his bathroom, but was later released to general service in the ship. As the ship left Madras, the wardroom cat, Figaro, fell into the water and had to be rescued with great difficulty and 'general panic'.

In August the *Manxman* took part in Operation 'Stab', a series of convoys using spoof signals to get the attention of the Japanese and to take the pressure off the Americans in the Pacific. Captain Dickson was the Senior Officer of the Madras convoy and at one point the *Manxman* sent signals pretending to be a merchantman in distress after a collision.

She was then detailed to assist in the conquest of the remainder of Madagascar. After Operation 'Ironclad', British forces had not attempted to take the rest of that rather large island, the fourth largest in the world, but negotiations with the French colonial government brought only delay. Perhaps not incidentally, Madagascar was a valuable prize, with substantial minerals such as mica. The British Government decided on 11 August that it was necessary to occupy the rest of the island,[44] as they had finally had sufficient forces available and the rainy season was imminent.

The second British Madagascar expedition, Operation 'Stream-Line-Jane', began in September 1942. To support the first phase, Operation 'Stream', the assault on Majunga on the west coast of Madagascar on 10 September, the *Manxman* was to carry out a diversionary operation called 'Esme (B)', which was to attack and capture the port of Hellville on Nossi Be, a sugar-growing Island about ten miles by ten lying seven miles off the far northwest coast of Madagascar. Simultaneously, but quite separately, the 7th South African Brigade, under the command of Lieutenant-Colonel N B Gettliffe, was to advance southward from Diego Suarez in Operation 'Esme (A)'.

To carry out 'Esme (B)', the *Manxman* left Kilindini on 1 September, with a cutter from the battleship *Royal Sovereign* partially suspended from the starboard mining crane. She embarked fifty Royal Marines from the old light cruiser *Caradoc* and two platoons of the South African Pretoria Highlanders. This unimposing force was then divided in two, with one part assigned to capture the town of Hellville and the other to capture the sugar factory at Dzamandzar and the nearby wharf.

Early on 10 September the *Manxman* entered the harbour at Hellville, moored and at 03.00 began bombarding suspected machine-gun

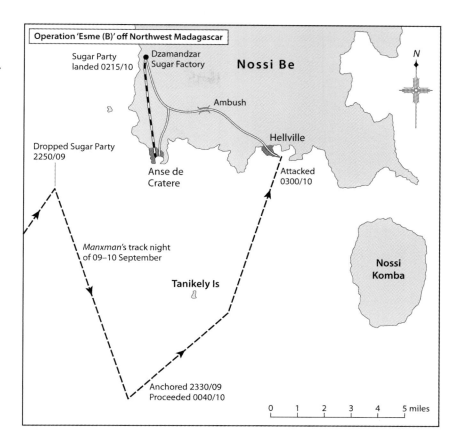

positions at a range of 500 yards with 172 HE rounds from her 4in guns, and then swept the pier with short-range weapons and mortars. Meanwhile, naval boarding parties under the *Manxman*'s Lieutenant-Commander R S Hopper captured tugs and powerboats. Under cover of fire from the *Manxman*, cutters pulled by Royal Marines – nicknamed 'the Galley Slaves' – and crewed by the Royal Navy delivered the Pretoria Highlanders to the pierhead, and they then proceeded to capture Hellville without a single casualty. The 'Galley Slaves' were then embarked and landed at 'Machine Gun Point' on the north side of the harbour to clean up some snipers. The local *Chef de District* surrendered on board the *Manxman* at noon and agreed to carry on. French casualties at Hellville were at least seven dead and eight wounded. That evening, Captain Dickson landed and drove around on a tour of inspection and found everything 'smoothed out' and the French 'beginning to play'.

The night before, the *Manxman* landed a party of Royal Marines under Captain Burton to capture the sugar factory at Dzamandzar and naval parties were to take the loading wharf and

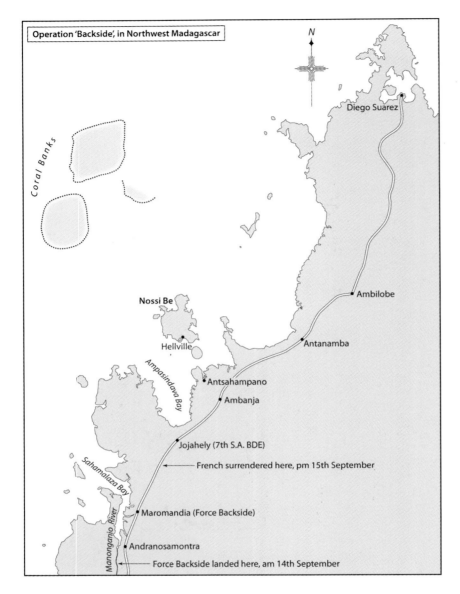

Operation 'Backside', in Northwest Madagascar

N

Diego Suarez

Coral Banks

Ambilobe

Nossi Be

Hellville

Antanamba

Ampasindava Bay

Antsahampano

Ambanja

Jojahely (7th S.A. BDE)

French surrendered here, pm 15th September

Sahamalaza Bay

Maromandia (Force Backside)

Manongario River

Andranosamontra

Force Backside landed here, am 14th September

tugs at Anse de Cratere and then to come to Hellville. Together, the two were known as 'the Sugar Party'. Commencing their attack at 02.10 on the 10th, they captured the sugar factory and the wharf without a casualty and then set off for Hellville in a commandeered car and lorry. On their way, they ran into a French ambush and the Royal Marines suffered three men wounded. With the help of a Royal Marine with a Bren gun, they moved out of the ambush and, after South African troops took the ambush in the rear, the French surrendered.

The next day, the 11th, the men of 'Esme (B)' repaired and sent off tugs to Majunga and turned their attention to recovering a ferry steamer up

a river on the mainland. Captain Dickson sent Lieutenant-Commander Hopper and an armed party in a commandeered tug to recover the steamer, but on its first try it returned empty-handed. On the 12th, 'Esme (A)'s' Sea Column ('SeaCol'), consisting of the trawler *Shapinsay* and the *R.39*, arrived with the latest news of 'Esme (A)'.

Late in the afternoon of the 12th, the party from the *Manxman* charged with recovering the ferry succeeded in its mission and also made contact with 'Esme (A)' and Colonel Gettliffe, who commanded the leading column, 'GetCol'. The advance of the South African brigade was being held up by French forces, which were retreating behind burned bridges. The Colonel asked that 'Esme (B)' land a force behind the French in the Miromandia area 50 miles south of him. The party returned to Hellville at 08.00 on the 13th with the ferry and the Colonel's request. Captain Dickson believed the stopping of 'Esme (A)' would be the sort of 'knock from any kind of Frenchman' the commanders had said they could not take. He quickly agreed to the request and sent Colonel Gettliffe the message, 'This will be done'. Thus the chance meeting with Colonel Getliffe thus led to the *Manxman*'s participation in a very *ad hoc* operation, to be rather colourfully called 'Backside'.

Planning for Operation 'Backside' began almost at once at 09.00. To execute the operation, Captain Dickson appropriated the ships and men of 'SeaCol' and formed 'Force Backside', a mixed force of eighty-five officers and men from the Royal Marines, the Royal Navy and a South African brigade, complete with eleven machine guns and two mortars. The force was conveyed in the *Manxman* and the corvette *Shapinsay*, which departed Hellville at 17.00 on the 13th.

The *Manxman* and her force sailed up the estuary of Sahamalaza Bay and at 02.45 on 14 September the *Manxman* anchored and transferred Force Backside to the *Shapinsay* and some small boats. Things then did not quite go according to plan. The force was landed in the wrong place and had to cross a mangrove swamp and then march a gruelling 25 miles to Maromandia. Captain Dickson could not contact the force and set off in a motorboat to locate it. He went ashore, braved the mangrove swamp and the mosquitos and eventually caught a ride in a car at 09.00 of the 15th to chase Force Backside through 25 miles of beautiful country, everything 'a lush green, lovely birds and tufted cranes and huge blue water lilies'.

That morning, Force Backside had taken up positions across the river from the town, which the mayor surrendered. After Captain Dickson caught up to it, it spent the rest of the day and the following day fortifying its positions and getting boats through to the *Manxman*, ten miles away. Meanwhile, GetCol engaged French troops near Jojahely at 11.00 on the 15th. Trapped between GetCol and Force Backside, the French surrendered that afternoon after a short engagement. GetCol took 114 prisoners and continued on to Maromandia.

Rumours of the surrender reached Captain Dickson on the morning of the 16th, and he therefore decided to re-embark Force Backside as soon as possible with the morning tide on the 17th. On the evening of the 16th he and the men of Operation Backside were treated to a 'high revel' by the local natives, which included chickens, vegetables, rice and plenty of coconuts, huts to sleep in, a visit by a native queen and her retainers, a huge bonfire and a sing-song. The Captain thought that 'Baden-Powell was watching from Valhalla and that he approved'.

At 09.00 on the 17th Captain Dickson and Force Backside headed for the *Manxman*. Once they and various stray boats reached the *Manxman*, she weighed anchor and began to move gingerly down the river. Just before sunset, she crossed the 100-fathom line and increased to 30 knots. The *Manxman* stopped at Nosse Be to conclude Operation 'Esme (B)' and arrived back at Diego Suarez the morning of the 18th to return the *Caradoc*'s Marines and to await further orders.[45]

Meanwhile, Operation 'Stream' was successful and was followed by Operation 'Line', an Army advance inland from Majunga and then, on 18 September, Operation 'Jane', a landing at Tamatave on the east coast of Madagascar. The 29th Brigade marched inland from Tamatave towards Tananarive, the capital of Madagascar, which was taken on 23 September. The Vichy governor refused to concede and moved south. After further landings in the southern part of the island, he was finally cornered and surrendered to the British on 6 November.[46]

As the main drama in the conquest of Madagascar was playing out, the *Manxman* was to play one last part. On 27 September, she departed Diego Suarez for Tamatave, where she dropped off some passengers and proceeded to Fort Dauphin, on the far southeast coast of the island, to see if there were an ocean-going ship was there and if so to 'cut her out'. The *Manxman* arrived at Fort Dauphin the morning of the 29th, to find a small, exposed bay, a town with a seventeenth-century fort and a sheltered boat harbour with no ships or dhows and only three boats.

Disappointed that there was nothing to 'cut out', Captain Dickson decided to put Fort Dauphin, the last port of consequence the British had not yet taken, 'into the bag' by getting the French authorities to agree to work with the British, without embarking on a 'military adventure' or getting a snub, i.e., a forbidden 'knock from any kind of Frenchman'. The Captain was taking a risk in more ways than one, as his orders forbade him to land and before sailing he was shown a signal stating 'in spite of *Manxman*'s recent success as a Brigadier it is preferred that he confine his activities to naval, repeat, naval operations'.

To achieve his end, Captain Dickson anchored the *Manxman* 300 yards offshore with all guns trained on the town and sat there silently for several hours. He then communicated with the local signal station his intention to send a boat and concluded the signal with 'Intention peaceful. If boat is attacked I shall have to attack town'. The Captain then sent an armed party ashore under the ship's First Lieutenant, Lieutenant-Commander Hopper, with instructions to request that the local chief come out to the ship under a promise of safe conduct so the Captain could communicate with him personally. Captain Dickson's report stated with some understatement that he was relieved to see the armed party reach the pier and march safely into the town; his diary stated, 'I was nearly sick, watching that boat go in'.

All went well after that. The First Lieutenant conducted his mission with what the Captain described as 'great good humour and common sense' and shortly the local *Chef de District* came aboard the *Manxman* and 'made himself very civil' over a beer. The Captain accepted his invitation to come ashore under similar safe

conduct to meet his boss, the *Chef de Région*.
Captain Dickson went ashore unarmed and in
No. 10 Dress uniform and M. Raoul met him in
full dress. The two walked together into town,
with the local population smiling and taking off
their hats as they passed.

The Captain and the *Chef de Région* then had
a very productive meeting, the latter giving
Captain Dickson a declaration 'with both hands'
that the local government would work with the
British. Nothing was put in writing. The Captain
saw very few troops or weapons, but there must
have been an artillery piece somewhere, as
earlier the *Chef de Région* had asked the First
Lieutenant to excuse him for a few minutes so
he could 'go and tell them to take the projectile
out', to which the Captain added an '!' in his
report.

The *affair de Fort-Dauphin* ended well. The
Chef de Région saw the Captain and crew off with

presents of poultry and eggs. At 14.05 the
Manxman signalled, 'Good bye. Thank you for
the way you have received our ship' and she
sailed ten minutes later. After investigating
some other harbours along the coast, she
planned to sail back to Tamatave and then to
Diego Suarez. At Tamatave, the *Manxman* went
alongside an oiler and the wardroom cat Figaro
and a recently-acquired white Persian cat went
for a walk and did not return.

With that, the *Manxman* completed her role
in the occupation of Madagascar. The *Manxman*
had once again shown her versatility in a role
not envisaged for her class, but leading a
diversion in the occupation of an island not held
by the Germans, Italians or Japanese hardly
seems fitting employment for a unit of her
importance, the only fast minelayer not already
sunk or under refit.

Indeed, her presence was already required
elsewhere. On 29 September, the Admiralty
informed the C-in-C of the Eastern Fleet that it
might be necessary to use the *Manxman* to run
urgently needed special foodstuffs to Malta. On
10 October, the Admiralty requested Admiral
Somerville to sail the *Manxman* to Aden to
operate under the orders of the C-in-C
Mediterranean.[47]

The *Manxman* had of course sailed to Malta
twice in 1941 and in 1942, during the *Manxman*'s
sojourn in the Indian Ocean, the *Welshman* had
answered the call to come to Malta's rescue.

CHAPTER 10

THE *WELSHMAN* AND THEN THE *MANXMAN* TO MALTA'S RESCUE, 1942

IN May 1942 the *Welshman* was assigned to make her first run to Malta. The island was then undergoing the ordeal of a siege by devastating aerial bombardment by the Germans and Italians and a strangling naval blockade. The island's most immediate need was Spitfires, without which convoys would be sunk before they reached the island or before they could be unloaded. A British-American operation, codenamed 'Bowery', was planned and would use the American carrier *Wasp* and the British carrier *Eagle* to fly off a total of sixty-four Spitfires to Malta.

This would be the *Wasp*'s second operation into the Mediterranean. On 31 March, Prime Minister Churchill had asked President Franklin Roosevelt for the loan of the carrier to fly off Spitfires to Malta in place of the *Eagle*, which was having defects in her rudder repaired. Her first voyage into the Mediterranean, Operation 'Calendar', went off without a hitch until the fighters landed on Malta, where most were destroyed or damaged on the ground within a few days.

Undaunted, Churchill had asked for a second loan of the *Wasp*, which was based at Scapa Flow with other American units so that British fleet units could take part in Operation 'Ironclad', the invasion of Diego Suarez in Madagascar. Once again, the President agreed and the *Wasp* once more sailed to the Clyde to load Spitfires for Malta. Operation 'Bowery' would have to be different in a number of ways and the *Welshman* was to be one of the differences.

The plan was for the *Welshman* to arrive at Malta the day after the Spitfires with supplies and personnel, disguised, as the *Manxman* had been the year before, as the French super-destroyer *Léopard*. The *Welshman*'s main cargo was to be anti-aircraft ammunition, which was in such short supply on the island that its use had to be drastically restricted. As a gunner on the island recalled, 'very often, having fired our quota . . . we have to watch formations of bombers dive on their targets and fly low over the gun site without firing a round at them. The world's most formidable barrage has been reduced to a feeble sputter!'[1] The *Welshman* could not feed the island of Malta, but she could carry enough anti-aircraft ammunition to make a difference to the island's survival.

The possibility of using a fast minelayer to run supplies to Malta was raised by Churchill's chief military adviser, General Hastings Ismay, in a minute on 3 April, but the idea was dismissed in a minute by Royal Marine Colonel Leslie Hollis on the 7th, writing that, 'Fast ships of the *Abdiel* type cannot be used now as they require refuelling on arrival and no fuel is available on the island'.[2] At some point, someone rethought the matter, whether because someone realised there was some fuel on Malta or because it was thought one could refuel on the voyage. In any case, the decision was made to send a fast minelayer.

The decision prompted a discussion of the matter between First Sea Lord Dudley Pound and the Prime Minister. On 28 April Churchill sent Pound a minute asking him to explain the procedure for sending a fast minelayer to Malta and 'how it is that speed is such an assistance'. The First Sea Lord replied the next day.

> One of the so called fast minelayers (WELSHMAN) has been selected to run A.A. ammunition through, not so much on account of her speed, but on account of her carrying capacity. She can stow about ten times as much between decks as a destroyer can. She will have to do about five hours in daylight to the southward of Sardinia within range of J.U.87 dive bombers based in Sardinia. Even here she will not be able to make full use of her speed on account of fuel endurance, but will probably do about 28 knots, weather permitting.

After explaining the course she would sail to Malta and the need for her to arrive the day after the Spitfires from the *Wasp*, he returned to the question of endurance: 'In order to avoid taking any fuel out of Malta WELSHMAN will probably have to re-fuel from an oiler south of the westernmost Balearic Islands on the return passage.' Then the First Sea Lord added a chilling conclusion to his reply: 'We are quite likely to lose this ship, but in view of the urgency of getting A.A. ammunition through to Malta there appears no alternative.'[3] Thus it was that the *Welshman*, that 'so-called fast minelayer', was deemed expendable for the greater good of saving Malta.

The *Welshman* had just received a short refit at Hawthorn Leslie when Captain Friedberger was told, 'Hush Most Secret', to load 40mm Bofors ammunition at Devonport. Knowing that Malta was then having a bad time from the Luftwaffe, he thought, 'I had no doubt of our destination'.[4] In time, he was to learn that his task was to deliver 123 men, mostly RAF but also Army, Royal Navy and civilians, and about 340 tons of cargo.[5]

One of the *Welshman*'s crewmen,

Welshman Telegraphist and diarist Robert Ferry. (Jackie Whiting née Ferry)

Telegraphist Robert Ferry, kept a diary of the voyage in a 'W/T Operators Log'. Ferry was born at home on 6 December 1922, in Poplar, East London, the seventh child of a French Huguenot family. He won a place at grammar school, but was unable to take it up because his parents couldn't afford the uniform. After finishing a technical school, he worked as a clerk before joining the Royal Navy at the age of eighteen, having learned Morse Code as a Sea Cadet. After training at Portsmouth and Chatham, he was drafted as a Telegraphist to the *Welshman*, which was then in Scotland. He began his diary on 1 May 1942.

From Devonport the *Welshman* then proceeded to Plymouth. On 25 April the C-in-C Plymouth received a special signal from the Admiralty. 'HUSH. IMMEDIATE. Request you will arrange for WELSHMAN to be disguised to represent French destroyer LEOPARD as rapidly as practicable. 2. Description of method used previously for MANXMAN are being sent by Courier, arriving Plymouth by train 18.57 today Saturday.' The *Manxman* had been disguised as the *Léopard* in 1941 for Operation 'Mincemeat', but, while she was able to sail into Italian waters and lay her mines, her disguise was never seriously tested. Disguising a fast minelayer as the *Léopard* was enough of a challenge, but by May 1942 the *Léopard* herself was manned by the Free French and had just emerged from a refit at Hull with *two* funnels, the fore funnel having been removed. Her three remaining sisters, the *Panthère*, *Lynx* and *Tigre*, had been laid up inactive in Toulon in southern Vichy France for some months.[6] The sight of any of the four in the Central Mediterranean would be considered at least unusual by any informed observer.

At 16.30 on 1 May, the *Welshman* raised anchor and set sail from Plymouth for Gibraltar. Her crew observed that the ship had been prepared for camouflage as 'a French cruiser'.[7] Two days later, Telegraphist Ferry had the Forenoon watch and spent the rest of the day on the upper deck, 'basking in glorious sunshine, getting quite sunburnt', for the first time but not for the last on the *Welshman*'s first voyage into more southerly climes. The *Welshman* arrived at Gibraltar that night. The next morning, Ferry observed that there were quite a number of ships present there, including *Renown*, *Eagle*, *Argus* and the cruiser *Charybdis*.[8] Word of the *Welshman*'s arrival reached the ears of the German naval staff.[9]

Another ship present at Gibraltar that day was the light cruiser *Penelope*, which had arrived there on 10 April after escaping from Malta on the 8th.[10] Her tale was an epic one. In March, she had escorted a convoy to Malta, but after her arrival at Grand Harbour she was damaged by a near miss off her port bow on 26 March. She had spent fifteen very long days in the No. 4 Dock in Malta undergoing repairs in between a succession of intense bombing attacks. Ju 88s and Ju 87s had dropped bombs all around her, but they somehow missed, perhaps distracted by the fierce anti-aircraft barrage thrown up by the *Penelope* and the guns around the dockyard. Instead, though, splinters from near misses had punched so many holes in her that she won her the nickname 'HMS *Pepperpot*'.[11] In Gibraltar, Captain Friedberger noticed the *Penelope* and her sad condition and thought it 'not an encouraging sight for our outward voyage'.[12]

Signs of what was to come began to accumulate. On the evening of 6 May, everybody on board the *Welshman* drew a steel helmet, and the next day they had their gas masks inspected. Bob Ferry thought, 'what with those and steel helmets, it looks as though we are getting prepared for trouble'. Later, he wrote, 'There is an indication that we are going into dangerous waters, as most of our code books have been removed and taken ashore'.

After sunset on 7 May, the *Welshman* began to assume the disguise of the *Léopard*.[13] As with the *Manxman*'s disguise, black paint was used to give the impression the ship had a break in the foc'sle instead of a flush deck and various materials were used to give the appearance of black funnel caps atop the *Welshman*'s three funnels. Captain Cowie later noted that, with more time and the resources of the Devonport Dockyard, the *Welshman*'s funnel caps were made more convincing than the *Manxman*'s. The latter's caps consisted of flat steel plates that gave the correct illusion only when viewed from the beam, but the *Welshman*'s were fitted completely 'in the round'.[14] Every little bit might help . . .

The disguise and the use of the French flag was a recognised kind of *ruse de guerre* known as 'false colours' and the Royal Navy specifically recognised it as an acceptable tactic in Clause 490 of its 1939 *Fighting Instructions*.[15] There were, however, rules limiting the ruse,[16] which Captain Friedberger well knew. 'To disguise a ship is a recognised stratagem as long as she does not open fire without first breaking out the White Ensign.'[17] In theory, and occasionally in practice, there could be consequences for violating the rule. In July 1945, the Japanese executed the British and Australian survivors of Operation 'Rimau', a commando raid to attack shipping in Singapore, in part because they had opened fire on Japanese policemen approaching their junk, the *Mustika*, without first lowering a Japanese flag and raising the White Ensign.[18] The Japanese were hardly known for their observance of international law and were guilty of a number of violations during the Pacific War, but in that instance they had the law on their side and the Allies could not have – and did not have – any complaint.

The *Welshman* departed Gibraltar at 02.00 on 8 May and passed Europa Point one hour after Operation 'Bowery's' Force W,[19] comprising the American carrier *Wasp*, the carrier *Eagle*, the battlecruiser *Renown* and the anti-aircraft light cruiser *Charybdis*, escorted by a number of British and two American destroyers. The Germans quickly learned that the *Welshman* as well as the *Renown*, the *Eagle*, the *Charybdis* and nine destroyers had departed Gibraltar, but fog prevented exact observation and their destination was unknown.[20]

In the planning for Operation 'Bowery' and the *Welshman*'s run to Malta, the minelayer was never to be part of or even to be within sight of, Force W. From the beginning, it was understood that the *Welshman* would need to arrive the day after the Spitfires were to be flown off by the *Wasp* and *Eagle*. In case this requirement and the reason for it was not clear to everyone, as early as 28 April Admiral Leatham in Malta signalled to the Admiralty and to Gibraltar, 'Request H.M.S. WELSHMAN should not arrive before completion of BOWERY as at present we cannot provide adequate fighter cover',[21] a lesson learned the hard way on the arrival of the last convoy in March. The final plan provided for the Spitfires to be flown off on the morning of 9 May and for the *Welshman* to arrive early on the 10th.

Shortly after the *Welshman* sailed from Gibraltar on the 8th, her planned visit to Malta faced a new challenge when the submarine *Olympus* struck a German mine and sank off Malta. She had arrived there on 5 May with a load of aviation fuel and stores,[22] and had departed at 04.00 on the 8th. She was carrying about ninety-eight men, many more than normal because she was also carrying six officers and thirty ratings who were survivors from the submarines *Pandora*, *P.36* and *P.39*, which had been bombed and sunk at Malta in March and April. The *Olympus* struck a mine just an hour after her departure. All efforts to inform Malta of her plight, by hand torches, distress flares and an Aldis lamp, failed; even her 4in deck gun could not be fired. Many men were able to come up from below before the *Olympus* took her last dive and each of them had to swim for it all the way Malta, seven miles away. Only twelve made it and the commanding officers of the *Olympus*, the *P.36* and the *P.39* were not among them.[23] Captain Friedberger had been the commanding officer of the *Olympus*'s sister-ship *Odin* in Hong Kong before the war.[24]

From Malta, Admiral Leatham reported the sinking of the *Olympus* to the Admiralty at 11.11 on 8 May and that afternoon Vice Admiral Frederick Edward-Collins, Flag Officer Commanding North Atlantic Station at Gibraltar, pointedly asked Vice Admiral Leatham at Malta, 'Will you be able to receive H.M.S. WELSHMAN'. Within the hour, Admiral Leatham tersely replied, 'Yes repetition Yes'.[25] The *Welshman*'s voyage to Malta was still on, but the sinking of the *Olympus* highlighted the dangers of the mission.

The rest of 8 May was uneventful for the *Welshman*. At first she was escorted by a Lockheed Hudson reconnaissance bomber of Coastal Command, which was joined by a Short Sunderland flying boat that afternoon.[26] She zig-zagged at an economical speed and altered course at one point to keep her distance from a merchant ship. She was reported by a British civil aircraft that day as a '3 funnelled cruiser steering east at 25 knots'.[27] She passed Oran at about 14.00.[28]

At dawn on Saturday, 9 May, the *Welshman* increased speed to 25 knots when she was just east of Algiers and raised the French ensign. This came as a shock to many of the crew,[29] who would nevertheless come to see its value in the days ahead.

Shortly after dawn on the 9th, Operation

'Bowery' was executed. Force W reached its designated launching point in the Western Mediterranean and the *Wasp* and the *Eagle* flew off sixty-four Spitfires, the most in any operation, forty-seven from the *Wasp* and seventeen from the *Eagle*. In what must have been a heartening sight, at 07.15 Captain Friedberger sighted two 'coveys' of Spitfires from Operation 'Bowery' making for the African coast.[30]

That day all but four of the 'Bowery' Spitfires reached Malta. This time, the island was ready for them. Fresh pilots manned them and took off to meet the inevitable air raids and the Germans were disappointed to find them in the air and not on the ground. This time they were not destroyed on the ground and made it hot for the German and Italian planes that hoped to replicate the carnage of April.

The effect on Malta's defenders and her people was palpable. Gunner Stan Fraser wrote in his diary, 'At last it seems we are in a position to meet Jerry on even terms in the air and it is difficult to convey the ecstasy which was felt throughout the island's people, having endured more than any other people in other parts of Europe.'[31] There would be plenty of Spitfires and plenty of inspired defenders and islanders, to protect the *Welshman* should she successfully arrive the next day.

The *Welshman* spent the rest of the day trying to be as invisible as possible. At 07.45, a Coastal Command Catalina flying boat was sighted in the distance. At 09.40 came the first test of the French disguise. A Ju 88 circled the ship once at four miles range, once at 1500 yards and again close enough for her crosses to be seen[32] and her numbers to be read; guns were kept fore and aft and she flew off to the eastward. At 10.15 the ship was circled by the Catalina, which was asked to proceed well clear, since it would be quite out of keeping for a Vichy French vessel to have such an escort. At 11.15 another Ju 88 made an all-round inspection at five miles range. Course was then altered to pass through Galita Channel, to appear as if the ship were making for a Tunisian port.

That afternoon, at 15.38 Vice Admiral Leatham signalled the *Welshman* with the arrangements for her arrival off Malta. He designated a new 'position Z' at 35° 56' N, 14° 37' E, from which the *Welshman* was to sail on a course of 245° to St Elmo. Position Z would be marked by a dan buoy and the trawler *Beryl* and the drifter *Trusty Star* would be on patrol at that position. Once requested by the *Welshman*, the *Beryl* would flash the letter 'BEER' in a 320° direction every five minutes. The *Welshman* was also informed that the Gozo light would be 'exhibited' in the northwest sector from 03.00 till dawn and the St Elmo light from 05.00 till dawn. Lastly, the *Welshman* was told that the submarine *P.35* would be departing Malta at 04.00 that morning and would be diving through Position Z before heading to the northeast.[33]

The *Beryl* and *Trusty Star* were the best escorts Malta could offer the *Welshman* at the time, a pale shadow of the naval striking forces that once operated from the island. Completed in 1934, the *Beryl* displaced just 615 tons and mounted a 4in gun and a .303in machine gun,[34] while the *Trusty Star* was completed in 1919, displaced just 199 tons and carried a 6pdr gun. The *Beryl* could make only 11.5 knots and the *Trusty Star* just 9 knots, but they would be good enough for the job ahead. Each ship had already risen from the dead. The *Beryl* had been sunk in French Creek in Malta by a German bombing attack that missed the *Illustrious* on January 19, 1941, and was not refloated and repaired until October of that year.[35] On 30 April 1941, the *Trusty Star* was sunk in a heavy bombing raid, but she too was raised and repaired in time to play her part.[36]

On the evening of the 9th, the *Welshman* sighted a Vichy floatplane escorting a convoy off Bizerta, but it made only a cursory inspection. When passing the African coast no notice was taken of the demand to show signal letters made by a French shore station, as Captain Friedberger thought a French warship would probably act similarly – just as well, since the *Welshman* couldn't reply anyway. At last light, the ship entered Tunisian waters and increased speed to 28 knots, which she maintained until she was close off Malta at 04.50 the next morning.[37]

This part of the voyage, at high speed close to the shore, posed the supreme navigational challenge of the voyage and was ably handled by the *Welshman*'s Navigator, Lieutenant-Commander Lindsay Gellatly, Royal Australian Navy, who was born in Sydney, New South Wales, in 1908. He was educated at the Royal

Australian Naval College at Jervis Bay and qualified in navigation in 1935. As he had just served as navigator in the *Menestheus*,[38] Captain Friedberger's last command, it seems likely the Captain was happy to bring him along to the *Welshman*.

Telegraphist Ferry recalled of that part of the voyage,

> All day we hug the French African Coast and by evening we sail peacefully along in full view of all and sundry, as at times we are between the mainland and small French islands and we could practically lean over and touch both sides. Towards the end of the day, as darkness began to draw in, we were again inspected – this time by a Dornier flying boat, so it looks as though we have not gone unnoticed and the relief will be great when it is all over and we get in the comparative safety of Malta harbour. We eventually pass into the safety of darkness, though even that is disturbed by lighthouses, one of which had a revolving beam, which lit us up every few seconds for some time.[39]

During the day, the *Welshman* may have fooled the German and Vichy French aircraft, but she had not fooled an Italian submarine. That afternoon the *Welshman* received a signal informing her that she had been reported at 11.00. Telegraphist Ferry penned, 'It looked as though we would be lucky to get away with it'.[40]

The Germans and Italians did not identify the *Welshman* until sundown on the 9th. The Italians sent two submarines and some torpedo boats to search for her. At 21.15, the submarine *Onice* sighted her and moved to attack, but claimed, rather imaginatively, that she was attacked by night fighters escorting the *Welshman* before she could launch her torpedoes. An hour later, the *Welshman* was sighted by an Italian torpedo boat, which gave chase but could not launch an attack because of the minelayer's high speed.[41]

The Axis force in the best position to stop the *Welshman* was the German 3rd S-Boat Flotilla, which was informed of the impending arrival of the *Welshman* at its base in Augusta, Sicily. The flotilla was commanded by

Kapitänleutnant Friedrich Kemnade and had been transferred to the Mediterranean from Germany via the Rhine-Rhône canal system in the Netherlands and France.[42] The S-boats (*Schnellboote* or 'fast boats'), were similar in concept to British MTBs and American PT boats and were formidable opponents.

Kemnade's S-boats were of the *S 30* class, which were built by the Lürssen firm in Vegesack. They displaced about 82 tons, were 107ft in length overall, could make 36 knots on their three Daimler-Benz diesel engines and carried a crew of sixteen officers and men. They were equipped with one or two 20mm cannon and two torpedo tubes, which could be loaded with a combination of 21in torpedoes or mines.[43] The first seven boats of the class were to go to China, but at the outset of the war the Kriegsmarine decided it needed them more than the Chinese.

For the *Welshman*'s expected arrival, Kemnade organised a welcoming committee of no less than seven S-boats. At 21.30 on 9 May, he departed Augusta with the *S 61*, *S 31* and *S 34*, which were loaded with torpedoes and mines, and at around 22.00 the remaining four boats, the *S 56*, *S 54*, *S 58* and *S 57*, sailed with just torpedoes loaded in their tubes.[44]

The S-boats were not to be running the only welcoming committee that night. The Royal Navy had hardly anything still floating at Malta, but, as promised, that night it sent out what it could, the *Beryl* and the *Trusty Star*. The *Beryl* had come to be called 'the flagship of Malta' because she was at this low ebb the largest naval vessel based there. The *Beryl* and *Trusty Star* would soon welcome Kemnade's seven S-boats to Malta. To confuse matters, that night they would also encounter the British submarine *P.35*, which shortly after leaving Malta opened fire on them when they didn't answer her challenge. 'The situation was resolved without further ado',[45] no blood was shd and the *P.35* continued on her way to Alexandria.

In the *Welshman*, Telegraphist Ferry was on watch at midnight that night. He scribbled in his diary, 'I see by our position at 00.01 that we have about 120 miles to go to Malta, which we should easily reach by 06.00 – at 28 knots'.

As the *Welshman* neared Malta, the boats of the Third S-Boat Flotilla were already there. Just after midnight, at 00.30, the lead boat, *S 61*, became aware of two vessels north of Grand Harbour, almost certainly the *Beryl* and the *Trusty Star*. By 02.00, the torpedo-armed S-boats had taken up their positions. At 04.14, the boats equipped with torpedoes and mines began to lay the mines off Grand Harbour. At 04.22, right after the last one had been laid, one of the boats, *S 31*, hit a mine abreast her engine room and broke apart amidships. The nearby *S 61* stopped to rescue her crew, while Kemnade sent the *S 34* to the north. By 0437 the *S 31* was gone.[46] Up until then, *S 31*'s claim to fame had been torpedoing and nearly sinking Captain Lord Louis Mountbatten's destroyer *Kelly* in the North Sea in May 1940.[47]

Telegraphist Ferry went up on the *Welshman*'s flag-deck at 04.30 and 'the first thing I saw was streams of tracer, fired at a low angle – evidently a scrap between small surface craft'.[48] It was 04.47 and he was witnessing an engagement between the four torpedo-armed S-boats and the *Beryl* and *Trusty Star*. In spite of the expenditure of considerable ammunition and at least the three German torpedoes that were sighted by the *Beryl*,[49] neither side drew any blood, though each side believed it had sunk an enemy vessel. Shortly after this engagement, the torpedo-armed S-boats had to turn for home due to impending daybreak. The *Beryl* and *Trusty Star* had done their job well; that group of S-boats never sighted the *Welshman*,[50] which passed the action close to port and observed the silhouettes of the expected *Beryl* and *Trusty Star*.[51]

Meanwhile, *S 61* and *S 34* kept a lookout for the *Welshman* and sighted her to the northeast at 04.48, steaming south by southwest about 15 miles northeast of Valetta. The S-boats moved to find a favourable firing position, but at 04.50 the *Welshman* turned to the east, which put the S-boats behind her. The two S-boats followed at high speed, hoping to catch her in a pincer with the second group of boats. At 05.00, the *Welshman* turned to the southwest and the S-boats decided to take their best shot. At 05.02, each boat launched two torpedoes, but all missed, as the *Welshman*, by skilful seamanship or luck, had turned 40° back to a southerly course. By 05.10, it was broad daylight and time for the S-boats to leave. They joined up with the other four boats at 05.38 and at 06.30 four Me 109s showed up to escort them back to base.[52]

As the *Welshman* neared Grand Harbour, she streamed her paravanes, torpedo-shaped objects suspended from a ship's bows and designed to cut the mooring cables of mines. Just before passing the breakwater at the entrance to the harbour, the *Welshman*'s starboard paravane cut two mines adrift just as she was taking in her paravanes and they just missed her stern.[53]

The *Welshman* entered Grand Harbour at 05.30,[54] the first surface ship to reach Malta since the last convoy in March. Once inside the harbour, she had a very tricky job getting past the sunken ships. Telegraphist Ferry recalled, 'I have never seen a place so closely built together, though I am sure I did not see a complete house the whole time. Jerry certainly knows his job'.[55] Malta did not have the reputation as the most bombed place on Earth for nothing.

At 06.08, the *Welshman* secured alongside the west wall of No. 5 dock,[56] the last remaining dock or what Bob Ferry described as 'once a dry dock, but which was now just a sort of inlet big enough to house a cruiser'. Midshipman Louis Phillips observed, 'Before our mooring lines were made fast, the hatch covers were off and the ship was swarming with dockyard mates, sailors, soldiers and airmen'. Brows were quickly provided and the passengers were quickly disembarked. Unloading began briskly at 06.30, with large working parties, plenty of motor transport and sufficient lighters to unload the ship's cargo.[57] The *Welshman* had picked up plenty of smoke canisters in Gibraltar from the ss *Llanstephen Castle*,[58] and they were soon unloaded and placed strategically around the dock to hide the *Welshman* when the need arose.

Inevitably, a German reconnaissance plane sighted the *Welshman*. At 08.00, 'Take cover' was sounded, but the *Welshman*'s men continued working. The shore labour returned quickly as soon as they were permitted to. Admiral Leatham visited the ship and pronounced himself satisfied with the progress.[59]

The first air raid was not long in coming. The British were ready for the first attack, not only with smoke but with plenty of Spitfires and Hurricanes aloft and an abundance of anti-aircraft guns arrayed around Grand Harbour. The latter was no accident. The British Army had been hard at work building up the anti-aircraft capabilities of the Royal Artillery and Royal Malta Artillery units on the island ever

since the Mediterranean War began, with a multitude of 4.5in, 3.7in, 3in and 40mm Bofors guns and the necessary fire-control equipment. In the past few months, when Malta had been able to put aloft just handfuls of Hurricanes and Spitfires, the anti-aircraft guns and gunners had been Malta's main defence against the aerial blitz. This day was to be their test and this day was to be their day.

The men at the guns eagerly awaited their moment. Leave had been cancelled for several days so the gunners would be able to protect the airfields when the Spitfires arrived and then the harbour area when ships arrived.[60] Gunner Stan Fraser was in his battery's 3.7in AA gun emplacement and later recalled the scene:

> A thick pall of smoke began to rise around the harbour area and we realised that, for the first time during the war, a smokescreen was being used to hid the contents of the harbour from the prying eyes of the recce [reconnaissance] planes. About 30 bombers were reported to be approaching the island. The stage was set and gleefully we awaited the entrance of the Villain, having laid a trap for him.[61]

There was more to the trap than smoke and a historic anti-aircraft barrage; there were also the Spitfires. Per Stan Fraser,

> When a raid is approaching we have usually sent up a few fighters but we have not always had any serviceable planes. When they have been available, the report used to come through from the fighter control room: 'three

The *Welshman* in No 5 Dock at Malta on 10 May 1942. (IWM A9504)

Hurricanes, four Spitfires – airborne'. Just imagine our joy when a report began coming through 'fifteen Spitfires, twelve Hurricanes – airborne', then within a few minutes another similar report – and another, until the total in the air reached 60 planes![62]

As the enemy aircraft flew closer to Grand Harbour, Gunner Fraser recalled that:

The siren sounded at about 9:30 a.m. and everybody was keyed up with expectancy, for large formations of Spitfires and Hurricanes were airborne, a smokescreen already enveloped the harbour area and a special ship barrage had been prepared, the restriction on ammunition being cancelled. Tele-phonist reported 'Tally-ho!' which meant the fighters have sighted and are about to engage the enemy. 'Stand by for ship barrage' was the order given, as all eyes scanned the sky in the direction of the harbour. Then, before we could see the bombers, the order came; 'Ship Barrage – Fire'. The original arrangement for the barrage was five rounds rapid fire from each gun on pre-arranged co-ordinations and then, if necessary, repeated.[63]

The eagerly-awaited attack was finally at hand.

At 10.00 the *Welshman* received the signals for 'Take cover' and 'Make smoke'.[64] As the attack began, the ship was quickly and effectively enveloped with smoke, as conditions were ideal for it. The man in charge of the smoke had been the Chief Boatswain's Mate in the *Breconshire* before she was sunk in March. There were still gaps overhead and the ship's close-range weapons were kept manned. The smokescreen evidently confused the attackers, for one German history recorded, 'Thanks to fog', the German bombers 'had to bomb blind'.[65]

The 'fog' was not all the bombers had to endure. Gunner Fraser witnessed the whole scene.

Whilst we watched the sky over the harbour, within a few seconds it became clouded with anti-aircraft shell bursts, until it developed into a thick haze with

Stukas diving through one after the other, many of them never straightening out and crashing to earth with their bomb loads. For two and a half minutes the [3.7in] guns blazed away at the rate of one round every five seconds. Never had there been such a barrage fired over this island! The noise was terrific and over the entire gun positions on the island there hung a thick pall of cordite smoke. Our fighters pounced on the enemy after they came through the barrage and made quick work of those which did manage to straighten out. What a scene! What a din! What a tonic![66]

Still the bombers came for the *Welshman*. It would take only one hit to disable her and keep her in Grand Harbour at the mercy of future attacks.

At about 10.45 the ship's crew began to hear the gunfire. Much of the crew had been ordered to shelters cut from the rock. Midshipman Louis Phillips led one party. As the anti-aircraft guns began to fire, he gave the order 'Run!' and they set off at a brisk trot for the nearest shelter. The scream of a falling bomb sent them diving for cover and four of them taking cover under a lorry, 'which seemed the safest place available'. There they lay for what seemed like hours, cursing and smoking cigarettes.[67]

At 11.00, the whole ship shook with the explosion of bombs, added to by the crashes of pieces of falling masonry and stones on the deck and showers of water. No direct hits were received, but the ship was 'near missed' six times.[68] Only three holes were made by splinters, all well above the waterline, but the ship had a list of about five degrees to starboard due to the weight of the objects that had lodged aboard.[69] As Telegraphist Ferry proudly recorded, 'The skipper was struck in the leg by two bomb splinters during this raid, but he carried on magnificently and remained on the quarter-deck throughout the ensuing raids'.[70]

The jetty alongside the dock had been piled with huge pieces of ships that had been broken up and included in the debris that was blown onto the *Welshman* was four tons of steel that had once been part of HMS *Fermoy*, an old minesweeping sloop that had been bombed and sunk at Malta in 1941.[71] During the first attack, one piece crashed on to the pom-pom deck, killing one man on the pom-pom, Able Seaman Arthur Lamb.[72] Known as 'Geordie', he was thought of as a 'nice fella' and the *Welshman* had once had his children on board for a party when they were docked on the Tyne. He was buried in the Cappuccini Naval Cemetery in Kalkara in Malta. After Lamb was killed, Able Seaman Hopper was so upset he started throwing lumps of concrete at the German planes.[73]

During the same attack, two other men were thrown onto the jetty on the far side, a distance of about 20 yards. One was unhurt, but the other sustained injuries which necessitated his being left ashore in Malta.[74] In spite of the debris and mud heaped on the pom-pom mount during the attack, the remainder of her crew put her back into action.[75] The *Welshman*'s crew believed the ship's pom-pom had shot down one Stuka during the attack.

Eventually the bombs stopped falling and then the 'All clear' was sounded. Midshipman Phillips and his mates scrambled out from under the lorry, 'and turned to thank it for the shelter'. They then realised it was full of Bofors ammunition that had just been unloaded and that it was 'not quite the safe shelter we thought'.

After the first attack, the ship's company started work immediately clearing up the debris. The dockyard people, using Malta's last remaining crane, which the Germans had somehow neglected to destroy, removed the lump of iron from the *Welshman*'s pom-pom deck. Telegraphist Ferry and others began working on the *Welshman*'s main radio aerial, which had been 'blown to hell', though the receiving aerials were undamaged. 'We had only been on the job a short time when the sirens went again, so we all went down to the shelter, which by the way, had sustained a direct hit above the entrance about half an hour previously, when we had stayed on board. We were in the shelter for about 15 minutes during which another smokescreen was laid'. Eventually, after being interrupted by more air raids, they got a new main aerial rigged.

At 11.15 Lord Gort, the Governor of Malta, arrived for a visit and was assured the ship was still seaworthy,[76] no doubt to his great relief. The ship also received a visit that day from Air Marshal Sir Hugh Lloyd, Air Officer Commanding Malta, who was delighted to find

that the *Welshman*'s commanding officer was Captain Friedberger, with whom he had 'soldiered' at the Army Staff College at Camberley in the 1930s. Lloyd later recalled, 'As he had not been to bed for the previous seventy-two hours it was not surprising that he looked extremely tired'.[77]

Unloading was slow towards the end since part of the cargo had been stowed in magazines, storerooms and shaft passages, but was completed by 13.30.[78] An hour later a second bombing attack developed, but the *Welshman* was again covered by a smokescreen and no bombs fell near her.[79]

At 17.15[80] the *Welshman* shifted to a new berth at the refuelling quay at Canteen Wharf.[81] Captain Friedberger was reluctant to deplete the island's low stock of fuel, but, at the insistence of Vice Admiral Leatham, his ship took on 300 tons of fuel out of less than 2000 tons on the island so the *Welshman* could make good speed at the beginning her journey home. The Admiralty had suggested back in April that Admiral Edward-Collins at Gibraltar should consider refuelling the *Welshman* on passage, but he rejected the suggestion, signalling that it was not considered practical to refuel her on passage either way.[82]

While the *Welshman* was at the new berth, another determined air attack, the last one of the day, began at 18.30. As the ship was lying in a new position with the open water of French Creek to port, the smoke-making arrangements were not completely trusted and all guns were manned. In fact, the smoke was thin and the *Welshman* opened fire with both her 4in guns and the close-range weapons.[83] As Bob Ferry wrote, 'we got the better of it this time – all our guns opened up and one of the Oerlikons shot down a Junkers 87'. The *Welshman* had one casualty in this raid, a loader on the 'B' 4in mounting who was hit by a piece of masonry. He suffered compound fractures to an arm and a leg and had to be left ashore.[84]

The kill was later confirmed by the Admiralty and awarded to the ship on the basis of a letter from Captain Friedberger, who gave credit to the crew of the No. 3 Oerlikon gun, the one on the searchlight platform between the second and third funnels. The rating manning the gun had reported that the aircraft approached at 2000ft, range about 3000 yards and at Red 60° it came down in a shallow dive toward the ship.

At 1000ft, after a short burst hit its nose, the aircraft banked across, showing its plan view and markings. When the gun's pan had been emptied, the aircraft lost control and dived tail over nose to the opposite shore. Of course, the gunner thought it was an Me 109 . . .[85]

After that attack ended, the *Welshman* was able to load cargo for the return voyage in peace. Still at the refuelling quay, she picked up 146 passengers, naval officers and ratings, as well as much unaccompanied baggage and the external fuel tanks of the Spitfires that had arrived with Operation 'Bowery', [86] presumably well drained of their contents.

Most of the passengers were survivors of sunken ships and many of them had been on the point of departure many times when the Germans stopped them.[87] One of the fortunate passengers was Chief Engine Room Artificer W G Wright, a survivor of the sinking of the *Olympus* just two days before. His submarine, the *P.39,* had been sunk on 26 March and when the *Olympus* was sunk he was one of the few able to swim the seven miles to shore and to safety. Even though the *Welshman* thus took on many new mouths to feed, she left nearly all her ship's stores at Malta and had to return to Gibraltar on meagre 'iron rations'.[88]

As the ship prepared to go to sea, 'All ashore' was piped and the ship emptied of those not leaving Malta. Midshipman Phillips was the 'duty boy' at the head of the brow and he recalled everyone left with a cheerful word, 'Thanks mate', 'Have a safe trip' or 'Buy you a pint sometime'. Almost the last to leave was an old Maltese dockyard matey, who said, as he bent over and removed a pack of cigarettes from Phillips' pocket, 'That was a good morning for Malta'. A nearby bosun's mate heard that and exclaimed, 'Bloody hell! If that was a good morning, what is a bad one like?'

The *Welshman* cast off at 20.40.[89] Telegraphist Ferry wrote that 'everyone on the ship was on tenterhooks until darkness came, but we eventually sailed out of Grand Harbour, Malta, with half the population of Valetta on dockside walls cheering us out'. Captain Friedberger later recalled, 'This departure was most affecting. The quiet of the shattered Dockyard frontage and a circle of five burnt out or sunken merchant vessels', but then 'a ring of cheers which seemed to come from the bastions

of Valetta and Senglea and the singing of "Roll out the Barrel"'.[90]

The *Welshman*'s departure from Malta was memorable, but not completely uneventful. As she swept out of Grand Harbour at 21.30,[91] her paravanes again did good work, warding off at least three mines.[92] Early the next morning, the tug *C.308* was not so lucky, striking a mine at about 03.00 and sinking with her commanding officer and eight of her crew.[93] The gallant *Trusty Star* would succumb to the same menace on 10 June.

As the *Welshman* left, one paravane was caught in the harbour's boom defences and she started trailing a huge piece of it behind her. This went on for some time, but it eventually broke away, seemingly taking the paravane with it.[94] Free of this impediment, the *Welshman* increased speed to 34 knots on turning to the north-westward, ultimately bound for Gibraltar.

It was not actually fore-ordained that the *Welshman* would return to Gibraltar; her ultimate destination was the subject of some discussion over the course of several days between the Admiralty, Vice Admiral Leatham at Malta and Vice Admiral Henry Pridham-Wippel, the acting C-in-C of the Mediterranean Fleet.[95] The *Welshman*'s fate hung on those discussions; westward to Gibraltar meant a return trip to the UK, but eastward to Alexandria likely meant a hazardous return trip to Malta.

On 7 May, the Admiralty gave Admiral Pridham-Wippel the option of having the *Welshman* sail to Alexandria and back to Malta in the new moon period if there were 'urgent requirements for really vital stores' that could not be transported by submarine. On 9 May, Pridham-Wippel signalled that he intended the *Welshman* to make one return trip from Alexandria, but later that day he had second thoughts, informing Admiral Leatham that in view of the probability of heavy air forces in the vicinity of the *Welshman*'s route she should not leave Malta until after dark on the 11th and that if it was undesirable to keep the *Welshman* that long she should be sailed for Gibraltar.

Admiral Leatham replied at 21.25 on the 9th that the *Welshman* would be ready to sail after dark on the 10th and that it was undesirable to keep her at Malta longer than absolutely necessary. He recommended a western passage, pointing out that the enemy would expect her to be eastbound and that the disposition of enemy forces was favourable for a western passage. He also pointed out that if she sailed after dark on the 10th she would be 130 miles southeast of an Axis convoy by daylight on the 11th and that if she sailed on the 11th she was likely to be intercepted by the escort of the returning convoy. In conclusion, Admiral Leatham said he did not think the additional risk of a double journey was justified by the quantity of stores to be carried. Only at 10.00 on 10 May Pridham-Wippel did relent and he allowed the *Welshman* to sail to Gibraltar[96] instead of Alexandria.

So it was the *Welshman* set course to the west. Bob Ferry had the First Watch the night the *Welshman* departed Malta and 'by midnight it was good to feel the old engines, knocking up the knots'. He recalled, 'Everyone was greatly relieved when the ship had got under way' and 'as we reach the end of a perfect day, very tired and weary', the crew was 'for once very happy to be safely at sea again'. Ferry was sure that 'none of them, especially those who had stayed on board, wish to experience anything like it again'. As for Malta, he wrote, 'I never want to set eyes on Malta again and I was lucky to get out of it with my life'.

Captain Friedberger, well aware of what the *Welshman*'s crew had been through that day, had a reward for them. As Telegraphist Ferry recorded, he almost forgot to mention 'an important point', which was that 'at dinner time the whole crew was dished out with a tot of neat rum and it certainly made me feel much better'.

The *Welshman* had certainly had quite a day. Captain Friedberger was given to understand that the *Welshman* had been attacked by forty Ju 87s, thirteen Ju 88s and five Italian Cants and that fifteen enemy aircraft were certainly shot down and another twenty-six were probably casualties. The *Welshman*'s casualties were one man killed and two seriously enough injured to remain in Malta. The Captain understood that his ship had been protected by seventy Spitfires and the heaviest anti-aircraft gun barrage Malta had ever concentrated over one place.[97] Of that, Bob Ferry wrote, 'The anti-aircraft barrage was terrific and a dive bomber pilot must have nerves of steel to even go near it, let alone dive through it'.

The *Welshman*'s 'gift' to Malta, as her Captain saw it, was 600 Bofors rounds per gun to add to the 1600 rounds per gun on the island and the ground staff to service the newly-arrived Spitfires.[98] It also included such diverse items as four flour mills, primers, luting (cement), telephone cable and, last but not least, 159 bags (10 tons) of mail.[99]

So ended 10 May 1942, a day that became known in Malta as 'the Glorious 10th of May' or 'The Battle of Malta'. With the Spitfires from the *Wasp* and *Eagle* and the cargo and personnel delivered by the *Welshman*, Malta could and would fight on. With a little exaggeration, Admiral Leatham's war diary recorded that the very heavy barrage and a wealth of Spitfires had inflicted such casualties on the enemy that 'daylight raiding was brought to an abrupt end'.[100] Perhaps it seemed so from where he stood, but the air battle for Malta would continue. However, with the delivery of more Spitfires in coming weeks, primarily from the *Eagle*, Malta would never again lose air superiority to the Axis.

Among the people of Malta and her defenders, the day made for a whole new attitude. Stan Fraser observed, 'Everybody goes about with a new air of cheerfulness, almost as though the end of the war had been announced' and opined, 'Malta's morale has reason to be fantastically high . . .'.[101]

There was even good news from elsewhere; the island's defenders were heartened to hear about the British invasion of Madagascar, 'forestalling the enemy for once'.[102] Little did they suspect that the preparations for the invasion of that island had set in motion a chain of events that had made it possible for the *Wasp* to bring in the vital Spitfires in the first place, the Spitfires that would finally make the skies safe enough for the *Welshman* and other ships to bring in badly needed ammunition and much more.

The worst had passed for Malta and the game had changed for good, but not everyone had gotten the word. On 10 May, Field Marshal Kesselring's *Luftflotte 2* signalled to Hitler's headquarters in East Prussia, 'Enemy naval and air bases at Malta eliminated'.[103] The report of Malta's demise was indeed exaggerated . . .

As 11 May dawned, the *Welshman* continued her voyage to Gibraltar, passing through Tunisian waters at 34 knots. With the Cani Rocks abeam at dawn, she reduced speed to 25 knots for the day.

A Vichy floatplane was again sighted in the vicinity of Bizerta and this time examined the *Welshman*'s French colours more closely, circling her a half-dozen times before flying back to the convoy it was escorting.[104]

The *Welshman*'s 140-odd passengers had been told at the beginning of the voyage that they were under no circumstances to appear on the upper deck and were to make themselves as comfortable as possible on the mining deck. A number of them made themselves useful, assisting the *Welshman*'s crew with such duties as cooking and passing ammunition. Sub-Lt Wright and an ERA were asked to assist by cleaning out the pumps for the fresh water tanks, which were continually clogging due to Rosbonite inside the tanks flaking off and clogging the pumps.

Below decks, Wright and the other passengers on the ship were treated to a narration of the day's tenser moments, when two Ju 88s looked the ship over.[105]

> During the morning the loudspeakers started up with a voice that was slow and clear and without a trace of excitement in it. I take my hat off to that voice. It went on to say, 'An aircraft is approaching us, everyone to your Stations except gun crews who will be at instant readiness on the mining deck. It is a German. Stop staring up at him, you on the fo'castle and get in with your routine job. He is circling us and sending a Morse signal. Answer him, signalman, with the message given to you'. The signalman sent his message and then says that the German replies that he does not understand it. The voice says, 'Send the signal again'. The signalman sends it and after a pause says the German replies 'Received'. The voice says he has stopped circling and is heading for North Africa, [and then] 'Hands fall out and revert to normal routine'. We had remained at this slow speed and course with one or two sailors working, apparently unconcerned, on the upper deck. Whilst this performance was going on I was sitting in the bowels of the ship with my mate and a freshwater pump in bits wondering how

> we got out of this ship if we had a direct hit. During the later afternoon we had another performance when a Junkers 88 came over and took a look at us. The voice was again perfect. The Junkers 88 asked for a recognition signal, apparently got it and went away satisfied. This time my mate and I were down in the other end of the ship cleaning another fresh water pump. I thought that this time we would be caught out but again we were lucky.

The *Welshman*'s disguise and Captain Friedberger's nerve had once again proved their worth, but it was a miracle they were able to carry it off again, since the Germans and Italians knew that a British fast minelayer had visited Malta on the 10th. Indeed, they were putting two and two together; the same day an Italian flying boat observed a 'cruiser', allegedly flying the French flag, 60 miles east of Bone on a westerly course and the Italians assumed it was the *Manxman*.[106] At 17.00 the *Welshman*, having performed enough for the day, though unaware the jig was up, hoisted the White Ensign, even though she was still close to the Algerian Coast.[107]

Events elsewhere that day demonstrated that it was just as well the *Welshman* had not been ordered to Alexandria. The Axis convoy she might have run into had she made for Alexandria made port in Benghazi safely, but not so the British destroyers that had been sent out from Alexandria to intercept it. As the *Welshman* made her way westward to Gibraltar on the 11th, four of the most modern destroyers in the Mediterranean Fleet, the *Jervis, Jackal, Lively* and *Kipling*, were sighted and attacked by a crack unit of Ju 88 bombers from Heraklion in Crete. That evening and the following morning all but the *Jervis* were sent to the bottom, with the loss of seventy-seven men, 630 men being transported back to Alexandria in the overcrowded *Jervis*.[108] To reach Alexandria, the *Welshman* would have had to run the same gauntlet and her French disguise might not have protected her.

May 12th was much less exciting. Bob Ferry acquired another sunburn before clouds began to gather at 18.00. It was pouring with rain by the time the *Welshman* entered the harbour at Gibraltar at 19.35.[109] She promptly went alongside an oiler to fuel, probably with little to spare in her tanks. On entering the harbour, her crew was surprised to find that the ship had been trailing both paravanes all the way from Malta, after thinking they had gone to the bottom.

At Gibraltar there was no great welcome for the *Welshman*. The Captain had given orders for the crew to be washed and shaved and in 'number fours', but, as Bob Ferry recorded, 'nothing happened when we did get in, so it was a waste of time getting ready'.[110] The *Welshman* and her crew deserved much better, but they were not being singled out. It had been ordered that, for security reasons, that no one should 'cheer ship' when the *Penelope* had arrived at Gibraltar on 10 April. The *Penelope*, temporarily patched up, had sailed for repairs in New York at 23.00 on 10 May.[111]

After the Prime Minister learned of the *Welshman*'s successful mission to Malta, he drafted a signal to be sent to her, but decided to run it by the First Sea Lord first. The proposed signal that would read simply, 'From the Prime Minister to H.M.S. *Welshman*. Bravo *Welshman*'. Churchill wisely left unsaid, 'We never thought you'd make it!' The Prime Minister's signal was in fact sent and received, but it was not the only congratulatory signal made to the *Welshman*. In a notice likely pinned to the *Welshman*'s board at dinnertime on 14 May Captain Friedberger told the ship's crew:[112]

The [F]irst Lord of the Admiralty and First Sea Lord have sent us a joint signal worded 'Well done *Welshman*' and the Prime Minister another 'Bravo *Welshman*'.

We have therefore been more successful than they expected. [Little did he suspect they thought the ship would be lost!] We have delivered the goods and kept our ship intact.

We have carried out 14 lays of[f] the enemy coast during which the only enemy sighted was an aircraft which missed by half a mile.

Last Sunday May 10th we were attacked by 40 Ju 88 and 5 [C]ants. The only serious loss has been one of our number killed and two seriously injured.

I think you will agree that *Welshman* is a lucky ship and may her luck continue.

I think we are certain to be called upon to repeat our last enterprise before too long.

Our example is the Chief Boatswain Mate of H.M.S. *Breconshire* [now a passenger] onboard. He was in charge of the smoke floats around the ship in berth. Seeing that one was not burning properly he left his shelter relit it and so got painfully injured owing to an exploding bomb. [N]obody could have reproached him if he had not done this. It was an act in the con[s]cientious tradition of the naval service well known to the chief P.O.s and P.O.s in fact by all well trained ratings. Let us try and live up to this. We can contribute to our safety by being on the alert and by cleaning up the mess after an attack to make ready for the next. We can never think that we have done enough for the moment and can ease off for the day.

Signed,

W.H.D. Friedberger

(Captain *Welshman*)[113]

There would also be a number of awards for the *Welshman*'s men, as well as Mentions in Despatches for five officers and men on the *Beryl* and the *Trusty Star*.[114] An interesting benediction on the episode was written by First Sea Lord Dudley Pound, who, after reviewing Captain Friedberger's report, opined, 'An interesting + effective episode which someday will make an excellent story'.[115] (Amen to that!)

After her hair-raising stay in Malta, the *Welshman* was a mess. On the voyage to Gibraltar, Bob Ferry 'spent most of the morning giving the mess a good scrub-out, which it certainly needed – when we left Malta we took half of it with us either on the upper or the mess decks'.[116] The Chief Buffer, who was responsible for the general appearance of the ship, was reputed to be most upset.[117] Captain Friedberger reported that, in addition to three holes made by bomb splinters,

She obtained a severe shaking and there is much damage to structures and equipment due to falling rubble. She requires docking, since the port propeller shaft warms up at its stern gland for both increase and decrease of revolutions. As an example of concussion due to near misses in water, two turntables on the mine deck were unseated, sufficient rosbonite was shaken from the after fresh water tank to choke the pump suction and all four cast iron feet of the C.O'.s [i.e., his] bath are fractured. Two boats are smashed and a third badly holed. One Oerlikon gun mounting is severely damaged. The multiple pom-pom was covered with a fountain of mud and should be lifted for cleaning. Two barrels of a 0.5" machine gun are bent. The R.D.F. [radar] type 286 and ZAX equipments are out of action. Probably the item that will take the most time is the crane equipment; the deck has subsided under both, so that their pivotal arrangements are out of line and both jibs are slightly buckled.[118]

Repairs were eventually carried out, but not yet and not in Gibraltar. The *Welshman* quit Gibraltar at 22.30 on 13 May,[119] bound for Milford Haven.

The *Welshman*'s departure on the 13th was detected by the Axis, but the Italians assumed she was engaged in another supply mission to Malta.[120] They moved their 7th Naval Division, with the light cruisers *Eugenio di Savoia* and *Raimondo Montecuccoli*, each armed with eight 6in guns, and two destroyers, to Cagliari in Sardinia. Acting on the intelligence that the *Welshman* was heading for Malta again, the 7th Division sailed on 14 May to intercept her and searched for her until the 15th,[121] but of course found nothing.[122]

The *Welshman* was by then far away, but not for long. She reached Milford Haven on 15 May and was finally greeted with cheers.[123] On the 20th she was taken in hand for repairs by Mssrs. Barclay Curle & Co. on the Clyde and was to be ready for further service by the 24th.[124]

That 'further service' was clearly not long in coming. The *Welshman* was loaded up with twenty Spitfire Merlin engines, drums of glycol, millions of rounds of 20mm and .303in ammunition, smoke canisters, powdered milk, corned beef, three motorcycles, a case of oxygen masks, ten tons of mail and a human cargo of 114 RAF personnel. The Spitfire engines were in crates that were mounted on modified minesinkers that allowed them to be moved about on the ship's mining rails.[125] She completed loading and proceeded downriver to the Tail 'o the Bank at 10.00 on 26 May.[126]

The *Welshman* sailed from the Clyde on the 28th and made her way to Gibraltar, whence she was to make another solo run to Malta in conjunction with Operation 'Style' – another by that name – a further flyoff of Spitfires to Malta by the *Eagle*. While entering the harbour at Gibraltar at dark, however, the *Welshman* collided with the boom and the tug *Salvonia* and damaged her propellers and stem was so badly damaged she could not steam at high speed or run the paravanes necessary to her getting past minefields and into Grand Harbour. The Admiralty considered transferring her stores to the tanker *Kentucky*, which was to take part in the next convoy from Gibraltar to Malta, Operation 'Harpoon', but instead the *Welshman* was repaired at the Gibraltar dockyard in time to take part in the convoy.[127]

It was just as well she had not made another solo run, especially if she had tried to rely on her disguise. For one thing, the Italians and the Germans were on to her. On the morning of 11 May, an Italian flying boat had sighted a cruiser flying the French flag 60 miles east of Bône on a westerly course and assumed it was the 'mine-laying cruiser' that had just visited Malta. For another, the Germans realised the ship – which they believed was the *Manxman* – had passed Cape Bon in French territorial waters the night of 9 May on her way to Malta and they were not pleased. Eventually the matter was presented to Hitler and he ordered that, if British warships attempted to use French territorial waters, German forces could attack them.[128] If the *Welshman* had made another solo voyage in disguise, her bluff might well have been called.

The 'Harpoon' convoy was to run from Gibraltar to Malta at the same time another, larger convoy, codenamed 'Vigorous', was to run from Alexandria to Malta. These were the first convoys to make the attempt to reach Malta since the 'MG.1' convoy was run from Alexandria in March and resulted in the second battle of Sirte. In that epic engagement, British light forces skilfully and gallantly fought off Italian surface units, including the battleship *Littorio*, but the convoy was delayed and suffered severe losses from air attacks while nearing Malta. Malta now had plenty of Spitfires to protect the convoys if they neared Malta, thanks to deliveries from the *Wasp* and the *Eagle*, but the Italians now had two modern battleships available. By contrast, the British had no battleships to escort 'Vigorous' and only the old, unmodernised battleship *Malaya* to escort 'Harpoon' and she was not intended to sail all the way to Malta.

The 'Vigorous' convoy occupied the attentions of much of the Italian Navy and considerable numbers of Italian and German aircraft, but, without a battleship – other than the target ship *Centurion* disguised as a *King George V* class battleship – it had to turn back in the face of a threat from the two Italian battleships, the *Vittorio Veneto* and the *Littorio*. Then, when the Italian battleships finally retired, the convoy had insufficient anti-aircraft ammunition to push on to Malta. When the battle was done, the Italians had lost the heavy cruiser *Trento* to aerial and submarine torpedoes and the *Littorio* had been damaged by a bomb and an aerial torpedo. The British lost the gallant light cruiser *Hermione* to *U-205*'s torpedoes just after midnight on the night of 15/16 June, as well as three destroyers and two merchant ships, with other ships were damaged. With the failure of the 'Vigorous' convoy, the resupply of Malta – not to mention its survival – depended on the success of 'Harpoon'.[129]

The convoy originated from the River Clyde in the United Kingdom on 5 June, with some escorts joining there and others, including the *Welshman*, from Gibraltar as the convoy entered the Mediterranean. The convoy included six merchant ships, five freighters and the American tanker *Kentucky*. The convoy was supported by Force 'W', which was commanded by Vice Admiral Curteis and comprised the *Malaya*, the old carriers *Eagle* and *Argus*, the light cruisers *Kenya*, *Liverpool* and *Charybdis* and eight destroyers, and by the close escort, Force 'X', which was commanded by Captain C C Hardy and consisted of the anti-aircraft cruiser *Cairo*, nine destroyers and minesweepers. Only Force X was to accompany the convoy all the way to Malta. The convoy was deployed in two columns in line ahead, with the *Welshman* astern of the starboard column.

The convoy entered the Mediterranean the night of 11/12 June and on the 13th it was shadowed and reported by German and Italian aircraft. Aircraft based in Sardinia began to launch fierce and repeated air attacks on the convoy the morning of the 14th and were opposed by Hurricane and Fulmar fighters from the *Eagle* and *Argus*. That morning the attackers succeeding in torpedoing the light cruiser *Liverpool*, which had to limp back to Gibraltar accompanied by two destroyers, and in hitting the Dutch merchant ship *Tanimbar*.

Captain Friedberger saw the *Tanimbar* torpedoed, go up in a sheet of flames and disappear. He recalled, 'There was no trace of her by the time we passed a minute later', but he later met a naval officer who from the *Tanimbar* who said he must have been 60ft under by then, as he and thirty others were later picked up.[130] Afterwards, the *Welshman* was promoted to replace the *Liverpool* as the guide ship for the starboard column and the convoy sailed on for Malta.

On the evening of the 14th, the convoy had to contend with attacks from German and Italian aircraft from Sicily, which were first sighted at 18.20. One attack was launched shortly after that and more attacks began at 20.00. Despite a number of close calls, the ships of the convoy escaped unscathed.

Also at 20.00, the *Welshman* was detached and sent ahead to Malta at 30 knots to unload her cargo, which happened to include the smoke-making material to cover the other ships of the convoy. As the *Welshman* left the convoy, she 'got in a beautiful free shot' at the aircraft attacking the convoy and, according to Captain Friedberger, 'disturbed them so much that four or five diverted their attack to us'. Unhit, the *Welshman* continued on to Malta.

At 21.30, Force W parted company with Force X and the merchant ships of the convoy. By then, Admiral Curteis had reports that Italian cruisers and destroyers were at sea, but thought them unlikely to be a danger to the convoy and he needed his cruisers to protect his old but valuable aircraft carriers. Accordingly, he decided to keep with Force W the light cruiser *Kenya*, with her 6in guns and the *Charybdis*, with her 4.7in guns. Curteis did not have the *Liverpool* and her 6in guns to detach and the *Kenya* was his flagship. Understandable as Admiral Curteis' decision may have been, it had serious consequences for the convoy.

In fact, the Italian cruisers and destroyers were a real danger to the convoy. The 7th Division, commanded by Admiral Da Zara and built around the light cruisers *Eugenio de Savoia* and *Raimondo Montecuccoli,* had sailed the evening of the 14th from Palermo in Sicily and were lying in wait for the convoy south of the island of Pantelleria. After the convoy emerged from the Sicilian Narrows at daybreak on 15 June, a Bristol Beaufighter sighted the cruisers and their destroyers and at 06.20 reported them to Captain Hardy in the *Cairo*. Soon they were in sight, 'hull down against the brightening sky', sailing on a converging course at high speed and drawing ahead of the convoy. The convoy had to face the Italian cruisers and destroyers with a ship no larger than the old anti-aircraft cruiser *Cairo* and no gun larger than 4.7in. The action the Italians call 'the battle of Pantelleria' soon began.

The fleet destroyers of the convoy escort, led by Commander Scurfield in the *Bedouin*, launched themselves at the Italian cruisers. The cruisers' 6in guns soon disabled the *Bedouin* and the *Partridge*, though the *Partridge* later got under way and took the *Bedouin* in tow. In return, the Italian destroyer *Vivaldi* was hit and stopped by the gunfire of the British destroyers and other Italian destroyers went to her aid. While the British destroyers kept the Italian cruisers at bay, the rest of the convoy turned away to the southwest, but German bombers took the

opportunity to sink the freighter *Chant* and to disable the tanker *Kentucky*.

The action became something of a free-for-all. After hitting and slightly damaging the *Cairo*, the Italian cruisers turned away, at least for the moment. Air attacks on the convoy continued and later that morning bombers disabled the freighter *Burdwan*. During the day, Spitfires from Malta arrived to provide some protection from air attacks, but before long had to return to Malta. Torpedo bombers from Malta attacked the Italian cruisers, but only succeeded in annoying or, at most, discouraging them.

The convoy resumed an easterly course at 11.00 and minesweepers took the *Kentucky* and the *Burdwan* in tow. Progress, however, was too slow and the danger to the remaining ships too great, so Captain Hardy decided to scuttle both ships. In each case, however, Admiral Da Zara's ships most obligingly finished the job for him. The convoy pressed on toward Malta.

Meanwhile, the *Welshman* had arrived at Grand Harbour at Malta at 07.30 and commenced unloading. Captain Friedberger reported to Admiral Leatham, who told him the situation was 'most serious', as the convoy from Egypt had turned back and only two of the other convoy survived and were under attack by cruisers and destroyers. Leatham asked Friedberger if he would like to go out in support and 'on my reply that I would hate to fight two

The Italian light cruiser *Muzio Attendolo* in the summer of 1942, when she was hunting the *Welshman* and the 'Harpoon' convoy. (M Brescia Collection)

The *Welshman* arrives at Malta in disguise in June 1942. (Imperial War Museum A 10419)

cruisers he told me to fuel and proceed'. The *Welshman* finished unloading by 13.30 and at 14.00 sailed from Malta to return to the convoy.

While the *Welshman* sped back to the convoy, the Italian cruisers had returned for another shot at the convoy, but soon, perhaps upon sighting the *Cairo*, turned away at 13.55 and returned their attentions to the *Bedouin* and the *Partridge*. The tow had to be slipped and the *Partridge* laid a smokescreen to protect the *Bedouin*. It was no use. At 14.25, an Italian bomber put a torpedo into the *Bedouin*, which shot down the culprit before she sank. The *Partridge* escaped and headed for Gibraltar. The Italian force sailed to the northward, towing the *Vivaldi*. That evening, an Italian hospital ship rescued Commander Scurfield and the rest of the survivors of the *Bedouin*.

At 17.30 the *Welshman* rejoined the convoy south of Linosa.[131] She approached the convoy at 35 knots and Captain Friedberger was later told she was an imposing sight. That evening the *Welshman* helped the convoy fight off the last air attacks of the day, by Italian S.79s and German Ju 87s and Ju 88s, which nearly hit the *Welshman*, the destroyer *Matchless* and the freighter *Troilus*.

With the end of those attacks, the way to Malta seemed open. When the convoy neared Malta, a coding error in a message, along with some confusion and exhaustion, caused it to blunder into a minefield, which spared the *Welshman* but sank the Polish destroyer *Kujawiak* and damaged several other ships. The first ships of the 'Harpoon' convoy entered Grand Harbour at 02.00 on 16 June.

The *Welshman* and the remainder of Force X departed Malta at 19.30 the same day, a magnetic mine being swept in the harbour entrance just before it departed. After weathering more air attacks, by Ju 88s on the evening of the 17th, they were able to join up with the *Kenya* and the *Charybdis* at 20.17. After refuelling from the oiler *Brown Ranger*, they reached Gibraltar without further incident or loss at 18.15 on 18 June.

In the end, though, just two merchant ships from the 'Harpoon' convoy, the *Orari* and *Troilus*, reached Malta relatively intact, even then it was a near-run thing; more resolute

The *Welshman* in disguise at Malta, June 1942. (Joseph Caruana)

action by Da Zara might well have reduced the number to zero. As it was, they delivered enough supplies to tide Malta over until August 1942.[132] The *Welshman* had played an important part in this hazardous but vital business, though less obviously than in her solo runs to Malta.

After surviving the 'Harpoon' convoy, the *Welshman* sailed from Gibraltar to Milford Haven, arriving on 24 June. There she disembarked some 200 passengers and much gear. She then proceeded to Greenock and then to the Elderslie wharf at Scotstoun, where on watch was sent on five days leave. The ship was then taken in hand for repairs to damage sustained on 10 May and subsequent defects, for boiler cleaning, the change of one propeller and installation of a system for reducing the amount of unusable oil in her bunkers. There was not enough time to fit a new Type 286 PQ radar, though some preparatory work was performed. The ship was docked from 29 June to 2 July, with the first watch returning from leave on 1 July and the second watch sent on leave the next day at noon, to return on 7 July.[133]

On the 7th, the *Welshman* left for the King George V dock, where she began loading cargo for her third run to Malta. This time her cargo included 150 tons of powdered milk in cases, 100 tons of cooking oil in drums, cased soap, mail and minesweeping stores, altogether totalling about 373 tons. At 10.00 on 9 July, she proceeded down the river and oiled at Greenock, were she also took on her human cargo, which included fourteen Fleet Air Arm and RAF officers, fourteen naval ratings, eight Army personnel and eighty-four airmen. The *Welshman* departed for Gibraltar at 20.00 on 9 July,[134] this time without her French disguise, but still painted in light gray.

The *Welshman* approached Gibraltar in the dark and at 01.00 on 14 July she secured along a small oiler in the bay. Some cargo was discharged to make room for some aircraft stores and 20mm ammunition and the ship sailed for Malta at 04.15. The first day of the *Welshman*'s outbound voyage was uneventful.

The *Welshman* was as usual sailing alone, but not far off was Force H, composed of the carrier *Eagle,* the anti-aircraft cruisers *Cairo* and *Charybdis* and five destroyers, which had also departed Gibraltar on the 14th. Their job was to execute Operation 'Pinpoint', yet another delivery of Spitfires to Malta. On the 15th the *Eagle* flew off thirty-two Spitfires, a record for the ship, and thirty-one of them arrived at Malta.[135]

Meanwhile the *Welshman* continued her solo voyage. At 12.15 on 15 July, she was sighted by a lone Ju 88, which flew around the ship and continued shadowing. At 15.30 an Italian Cant 506B floatplane joined in, followed by another Ju 88 and another floatplane. Inevitably, much more was to come. From Malta Admiral Leatham warned the *Welshman*, 'A large number of aircraft have taken off from Sicily, probably to attack you'.[136]

There were an estimated twenty-eight aircraft looking to attack the *Welshman*, including S.79 bombers, Fiat CR.42 single-engined biplanes, Ju 88s and Ju 87s.[137] The first attack was delivered at 17.40, when the ship was in the Galita channel, by six CR.42s, each diving individually and dropping one bomb each. One of the bombs fell very close to the ship's stem. The next attack was delivered by six S.79s in two groups, whose high-level pattern bombing did no damage.

Then it was the Germans' turn to try their hand. At 18.45 eight Ju 88s attacked in succession, diving out of the sun. One stick of four bombs entered the water close abreast the gearing room and exploded under the stern. Captain Friedberger recalled later, 'I thought we were done once because the explosion of a bomb must have flexed the boiler fronts, causing clouds of black smoke from all three funnels for a few seconds'.[138] At 20.05 eight Stukas dived out of the sun, but their bombs were not close. Finally, at 21.00 a shadowing Ju 88 glided in at last light and dropped one bomb that landed four cables away,[139] before, according to a sardonic Captain Friedberger, 'returning to base to claim his Iron Cross'.[140]

The *Welshman* had survived attacks by twenty-eight aircraft, but it had been 'very trying', as Captain Friedberger reported, especially since the sun was brilliant and the aircraft were not always seen until they were in their dives. The *Welshman* still had her original Type 286 radar set and with aircraft attacking out of the sun, the lack of more modern radar was very much felt. The *Welshman*'s guns kept up a brisk fire, shooting the undercarriage off a Ju 87, but no other damage was observed, as often her forward guns could not be brought to bear on the attackers.

The *Welshman*'s enemies had more than just plenty of aircraft to throw at her. Three Italian destroyers sortied from Palermo and Cagliari to intercept her, but when the aircraft failed to reduce her speed they could not catch her. Lastly, the Italian submarine *Axum* attempted to intercept her off Bizerta, but also failed.[141] The following month, the *Axum* would have better luck against different targets; during the Operation 'Pedestal' convoy to Malta in August, in a single torpedo salvo the *Axum* torpedoed the tanker *Ohio*, the light cruiser *Nigeria* and the anti-aircraft cruiser *Cairo*, damaging the first two and sinking the latter.

The *Welshman* reached the Malta swept channel at first light, 05.15, the next day, 16 July. As she entered Grand Harbour, Captain Friedberger signalled to Admiral Leatham, 'We have delivered the milk, what "can" do we take back?' Admiral Leatham replied at once, '40

Luftwaffe prisoners'.[142] The *Welshman* secured to her usual No. 5 dock at 07.00 and was given a list to simulate damage.[143]

Her precious cargo was unloaded by 12.30. Unfavourable weather that would have kept her from getting far enough to the west by dawn prevented her sailing that day and the next. Such a long stay would have been unimaginable in May, but in July it passed without incident, thanks in large part to the steady stream of Spitfires delivered by the *Wasp* and then by the *Eagle*.

Meanwhile, word got around to Malta's defenders that the *Welshman* was back. Instead

The *Welshman* arrives at Malta at sunrise, 16 July 1942. (Imperial War Museum GM 1368)

The *Welshman* passes the boom at Malta, July 1942. (Imperial War Museum GM 1369)

The *Welshman* unloads at Malta, July 1942. (Frederick Galea)

of the usual preliminary rumours, the first sign to Gunner Stan Fraser that a ship must have arrived was a smokescreen over the harbour. The rumour mill at first had it that a cruiser and a couple of destroyers had arrived, but then Fraser saw for himself that it was a ship that looked like the *Welshman*.

Finally, on the afternoon of 18 July the *Welshman* took on 400 tons of oil from a lighter and embarked ten wardroom passengers and 164 ratings, including a proportion of the crews from the merchant ships in the June 'Harpoon' convoy. The ship left the No. 5 dock at 18.00, but returned immediately owing to a suspected air attack. The attack did not develop after all and the *Welshman* was finally able to sail. She passed the breakwater of Grand Harbour at 19.42 and cleared the swept channel at 21.00, bound for Gibraltar. Gunner Fraser saw her leave at dusk and wrote, 'Perhaps that is why we received a very special treat today from the N.A.A.F.I. [canteen] – six caramels each!' The heading in his diary read, 'HMS *Welshman* to our Rescue – Again!'[144]

That night was uneventful for the *Welshman*, though not because the Italians were not out in force looking for her. No less than seven submarines were ordered to assemble north of Tunis and MAS boat patrols were sent to cover the lanes along Cape Bon. Last but not least, Admiral Alberto Da Zara's Seventh Naval Division, consisting of the light cruisers *Eugenio di Savioa* and *Montecuccoli* and the 10th

Destroyer Squadron, with the destroyers *Maestrale, Oriani, Gioberti* and *Fuciliere*,[145] each with 4.7in guns, were dispatched from Naples to cruise south of Sardinia to lie in wait for the *Welshman*. In the end, it was all wasted effort and fuel; none of the submarines sighted the *Welshman*, the MAS boats were forced to return to port by heavy seas and the cruisers and destroyers, having cruised off Sardinia the whole night, decided that the *Welshman* had not left Malta after all and packed it in for Cagliari at 07.00, thus missing their intended prey.[146]

Continuing her charmed life, the *Welshman* sailed on untouched through the night and passed the Fratelli rocks at first light on the 19th, with favourable weather for high speed. At 09.10 that morning, a Ju 88 sighted her and was joined by an Italian Caproni Ca.135 at 13.00. Once again, more was to come and the *Welshman* would have to run an aerial gauntlet.

At 14.15, a concerted attack by eleven S.79 torpedo bombers and five Ju 88 bombers developed.[147] The S.79s approached from both beams and from ahead and the Ju 88s from behind cloud in the direction of the sun. One torpedo passed close ahead and one stick of two bombs was close enough to douse the *Welshman*'s bridge and the pom-pom. The Italian torpedo bombers impressed Midshipman Phillips as 'nasty people', who 'pressed their attack home with some vigour', but who must have grossly underestimated the ship's speed, 'otherwise we would have had a very wet bed that night'. The *Welshman* claimed to have hit four aircraft, but not to have brought any of them down.

No matter. What was important was that the *Welshman*, as on her inbound voyage to Malta, had again avoided disaster. That she had done so again was particularly frustrating to the Italians, whose naval historian Commander Marc'Antonio Bragadin has written, 'It cannot be denied that this "damned" minelayer had "what it takes", but it must also be said that she was extremely lucky'.[148]

The rest of the passage was uneventful and the *Welshman* reached Gibraltar at 14.30 on 20 July. Her crew commenced inspection of her hull and machinery for damage from near misses and this process continued into the next day. She finally sailed from Gibraltar for the UK at 10.00 on the 22nd, arrived at Milford Haven at

The *Welshman* in dock at Malta, July 1942. (Imperial War Museum A 10839)

09.45 on the 25th,[149] and finally made the Kyle of Lochalsh on the 27th.[150]

After the July run, the *Welshman* was the subject of considerable praise. On 20 July, Lord Gort, the Governor of Malta, wrote to the Prime Minister, 'The arrival of *Welshman* and her cargo of milk, etc. was most acceptable as a gesture to Maltese people who remain for present in good spirits'. Vice Admiral Leatham was unstinting in his praise. He wrote to the Admiralty, 'I wish to bring specially to your notice the debt which Malta owes H.M.S. *Welshman*, for the three voyages she has made for the purpose of bringing vital supplies to the island'. As for her crew, 'I have the highest opinion of the manner in which the ship was handled by her Commanding Officer (Captain W.H.D. Friedberger, R.N.) and the conduct of her officers and Ship's Company throughout these arduous

and hazardous operations'.[151] Last but not least, on 23 July the Admiralty signalled, 'Personally [*sic*] from First Lord of Admiralty and First Sea Lord. The Prime Minister wishes to be included in the congratulations we now send you on having successfully overcome the difficulties of the passage to and from Malta. Well done!'[152]

The *Welshman* was a major part of the efforts to save and then reinvigorate Malta, along with the aircraft carrier *Eagle* and supply submarines. Those efforts paid a major dividend shortly afterwards, when the 10th Submarine Flotilla returned to the island. The submarine *P.42* arrived on 20 July and then two days later Captain Simpson arrived to command the flotilla from Malta.[153] The flotilla could once again use Malta for its depredations against Axis ships bound for North Africa and Rommel's army.

After her July run to Malta, the *Welshman*

was absent from the hazardous Mediterranean for several months, but with good reason – she would finally receive a real refit and repair period. On 28 July, she departed Port ZA for repairs on the River Tyne.[154] She would not emerge until 14 October when she left the Tyne for trials. She had received a complement of seven 20mm guns and her after deckhouse was extended forward to the third funnel. She had shed her light gray paint and donned a multi-colour camouflage scheme. She worked up at Scapa Flow from 15 to 27 October.[155]

The yard period on the Tyne caused the *Welshman* to miss the penultimate Malta convoy, Operation 'Pedestal', which sailed in the middle of August 1942. At great cost, including the sinking of the venerable *Eagle* by *U-73*, the tanker *Ohio* and five storeships made it to Malta, enabling it to hold out for months more. The *Welshman* had done her part; she had enabled Malta to hold out until the 'Pedestal' convoy could arrive.

Before returning to the fray, Captain Friedberger took advantage of the quiet time to send a letter to the former mayor of Wrexham remembering his gratitude how good the people of Wrexham had been when the ship was first commissioned. He also enclosed a copy of the recent notice in the London Gazette announcing awards to men of the *Welshman*, which was his way of letting the town know that, while the operations the *Welshman* had participated in were secret, the ship had not disgraced either herself or the Red Banner she had received from Wrexham.[156]

By October, another run to Malta was in the works for the *Welshman*. The *Welshman* visited the Kyle of Lochalsh on the 28th and departed the same day.[157] She arrived at Plymouth on the 30th to take on a load of 110 tons of corned beef, 110 tons of powdered milk, 50 tons of dried beans and peas, fifteen 18in torpedoes and 113 passengers. Then it was off to Gibraltar yet again.

The *Welshman* arrived at Gibraltar on 4 November. just in time for the execution of Operation 'Torch', the Allied invasion of French North Africa on the 7th. While she was marking time at Gibraltar, another mission was found for her. During a delicate moment in the negotiations between the Allies and the French commanders in North Africa, the Allied commanders were having difficulty getting information form Admiral Kent Hewitt's Western Task Force at Casablanca. Admiral Andrew Cunningham suggested to General Eisenhower that he send a fast ship to clear up the situation and, not surprisingly, the *Welshman* was chosen for the job.

After embarking American Rear Admiral Bernhard Bieri from General Eisenhower's staff, she left for Casablanca at 13.00 on 12 November and steamed at high speed to make contact with Admiral Hewitt at Casablanca.[158] At dusk she passed through a collection of US transports and destroyers off Fdala, in time to see one of the transports torpedoed and set on fire five miles off her port beam. She reached the entrance to Casablanca at 19.45 that night and disembarked her American passengers to travel by boat to the cruiser *Augusta*. The party was re-embarked the next morning and the *Welshman* regained Gibraltar at 10.45 on the 13th.

Her errand completed, the *Welshman* was free to make her next run to Malta, which she commenced at 11.20 on 14 November. That night an enemy aircraft passed over her several times and accurately reported her as a 'three-funnelled cruiser of the *Abdiel* class'. To make matters worse, fair seas were not on the cards for this run and by 23.00 she was bumping badly at 25 knots in a head sea with the wind at Force 8. Realising his ship would be delayed and would not be clear of Sicilian coast by dawn, Captain Friedberger decided to return to Gibraltar, which the *Welshman* reached on the 16th at 11.00.

At 10.00 on the 17th the *Welshman* sailed for another attempt. As she was approaching Sicily, the wind again increased to Force 8, but this time it was from her port beam, allowing her to make the necessary progress, at the cost of 'most uncomfortable rolling' at 30 knots. A fighter escort appeared soon after dawn the next day and the *Welshman* arrived at Malta at 08.45 on the 18th. The *Welshman* berthed at her home-away-from-home, Dock No. 5, and within five hours she had unloaded her passengers and cargo.[159]

The *Welshman*'s former stable-mate, the *Manxman*, was already there. In October, after her adventures in Madagascar, the *Manxman* had been lent, repeat, lent, by the C-in-C of the Eastern Fleet to the C-in-C Mediterranean for a run to Malta. After sailing from Kilindini, she headed for Suez, along the way overhauling her damage control organisation, anticipating some difficult days ahead. The Captain also let the men in on the upcoming trip to Malta.

The *Manxman* docked for four days at Suez, where she had her bottom scraped and her propellers and shafts cleaned. Captain Dickson wrote, perhaps tongue-in-cheek, that she was repainted in three shades of gray instead of three of green and that she received a Type 86 W/T set for directing fighters. He also wrote that she received a sixth 20mm Oerlikon gun, but as she already had six he may have meant a seventh, which was becoming the normal outfit for the *Abdiel*s.

At Suez the ship also acquired a new cat, of the black and white variety, who walked on board and domesticated herself in the Captain's cabin. She was quite welcome and in his diary the Captain reflected, 'a captain's life being what it is, I am often very lonely in the evenings'.

The *Manxman* sailed for the Mediterranean, arriving at Port Said on 30 October. There she loaded 357 tons of foodstuffs, 325 tons on the minedeck, including butter, preserved meat, dehydrated potatoes, peas, lentils and sugar. She then proceeded to Alexandria, where she was held for a few days as the Eighth Army advanced farther and farther along the coast. On 11 November, she quit Alexandria at 05.00 with an unheard-of escort of six 'Hunt' class destroyers, *Dulverton, Beaufort, Croome, Aldenham, Hurworth* and *Beauvoir*.[160] She did not get very far at first, grounding outside the boom, but with the assistance of a tug she was refloated and got underway without any damage.[161] The force started off towards Port Said and then doubled back towards Malta. At 14.10 two Italian torpedo bombers dropped their torpedoes on the *Croome* and barely missed her, before being chased off by Beaufighters.

The *Manxman* dropped her escort at nightfall,[162] and she sailed on alone at 31.5 knots. Met by fighters 200 miles out, the *Manxman* increased to 34 knots and arrived at Malta 'running like a train' at sunset on 12 November after a 36-hour voyage.[163] To Captain Dickson, there were cheering crowds, as there had been when the *Manxman* arrived there the previous year, 'but with a difference. I don't think I'm an emotional person, but when you see women kneeling on the shore and holding out their children to you in their arms it gets you'.[164] The

The *Manxman*'s officers in November 1942. On the far right of the front row is Lieutenant J C Cherry, RNVR, who was lost in the *Welshman*. (Elizabeth K Dickson)

Captain Dickson and Lieutenant Brayne-Nicholls on the bridge of the *Manxman*, November 1942. (Imperial War Museum A 13031)

The *Manxman*'s mine deck with passengers. (Imperial War Museum A 13025)

Manxman was the first surface ship to arrive with supplies in twelve weeks,[165] i.e., since the arrival of the 'Pedestal' convoy in August 1942. She moved into Dock No. 5, specially reserved for fast minelayers and her cargo was unloaded by 03.00 the next morning.

The *Manxman* stayed on at Malta for a few days and on the 14th her officers and crew threw a tea party for 100 of Malta's children in the Corradino Tunnel. The *Manxman* had thoughtfully brought food and sweets from Kilindini for the party. The children enjoyed

themselves and when they started singing the noise in the tunnel was deafening. Governor Lord Gort and Vice Admiral Leatham even joined the festivities. The *Manxman*'s football team also put its winning record on the line against a battalion from the Cheshires, the 22nd (Cheshire) Regiment of the Malta garrison. They were soundly defeated, in spite of the Cheshires having been on siege rations for some time, as noted by Captain Dickson.

The *Manxman* was joined at Malta a few days later, on the 18th, by her sister-ship *Welshman*, which had arrived from Gibraltar.[166] The two minelayers were still there when the four merchant ships and the escort destroyers of Convoy MW13, part of Operation 'Stoneage', arrived at Malta shortly after midnight on 20 November,[167] the first convoy to arrive at Malta since 'Pedestal'. While the light cruiser *Arethusa* had been badly damaged by an aerial torpedo on the voyage, not a single merchantman was damaged on the way. An American Associated Press (AP) war correspondent, Harry Crockett, took passage in one of the convoy escorts and filed a story on the arrival of the convoy, which

could not be published until the Admiralty got around to confirming the arrival of the convoy.

The two ships were kept on at Malta awaiting the decision whether to execute Operation 'Breastplate', a sortie by one battalion of the Malta garrison in the *Manxman* and *Welshman* and the escort destroyers *Tetcott* and *Croome* to capture the port of Sousse in Tunisia. Preparations for the operation were made on 21 and 22 November, but the captains of the fast minelayers were against it, Dickson believing it a 'political stunt'. In the end, 'Breastplate' was cancelled, due to the 'unloading of the recent convoy and lack of suitable assault craft',[168] most likely a fortunate decision for the *Manxman* and the *Welshman*. All of the Army guns, stores and extra boats that had been loaded were disembarked.

The *Manxman* loaded mines at Malta and on 25 November proceeded to Algiers to operate under the orders of the Naval Commander, Expeditionary Force, i.e., Admiral Andrew Cunningham. Before leaving Malta, Captain Dickson wrote to the Vice Admiral Malta, 'I hope this month sees the end of your worst troubles.

If so, we shall always be proud to remember that we were the spear-point of the relief and that we had the honour of being the first ship in when the siege was raised'.[169]

The *Welshman* spent a few more days in Malta, but sailed for Alexandria on the 27th with some Allied passengers, POWs and unaccompanied baggage, before another operation could be dreamed up for her and *Manxman*. This was the *Welshman*'s first voyage to Alexandria and it was a measure of how the war in the Mediterranean had changed that she was able to make the eastbound passage unaccompanied and unattacked. On the way, she sighted but a single Ju 88, at dawn on 28 November. Much of the voyage was made with fighter cover, a heretofore unheard-of luxury.

The *Welshman*'s crew was not allowed much time to ponder the significance of this. Upon arriving at Alexandria on the 29th,[170] she discharged her passengers and cargo, oiled and that evening was packed off to Haifa in Palestine. Arriving at dawn on the 30th, she spent the next few days loading an esoteric cargo of fifteen torpedoes, 30 tons of sugar, 30 tons of cheese, 80 tons of urgent stores, an unspecified number of cigarettes and a human cargo of one officer and thirteen submarine ratings. So loaded, she sailed for Alexandria on 1 December.

Upon the *Welshman*'s arrival on 2 December, more cargo for Malta – where else? – was embarked, together with fifteen officers, sixty-five airmen and some naval ratings and Army enlisted men. The *Welshman* was even thoughtfully provided with a month's provisions for the ship. The ship sailed for Malta at 16.30 the same day,[171] completing the striking-down of the recently loaded stores while underway.

For a change, this was not to be a completely solo run to Malta. At dawn on 3 December, the *Welshman* overtook a westbound Malta convoy, MW 14, the mercantile component of Operation 'Portcullis',[172] and came under the orders of the light cruiser *Orion*. The convoy was shadowed by enemy aircraft until the afternoon, but was under fighter escort and no enemy aircraft were actually sighted.

After dark, the *Welshman* headed for Malta on her own at 30 knots. After reaching the outer end of the swept channel at first light, she entered Grand Harbour at 07.40 on 4 December. Her cargo was not disembarked until 20.30, perhaps because she was, also for a change, not the only ship that needed to be unloaded; the four merchant ships of the 'Portcullis' convoy arrived on the 5th,[173] and other ships needed to be unloaded. After oiling, she embarked more Allied passengers and some POWs and set sail for Alexandria with the fleet destroyer *Paladin* at 16.00 on 5 December.[174] Although one of the ubiquitous Ju 88s was sighted the next day, the rest of the passage was uneventful and Alexandria was reached at 11.00 on the 7th. So ended the *Welshman*'s fifth and last supply run to Malta. She would see Malta again, but not as a desperately-needed supply ship.

The *Welshman* at Malta on 18 November 1942. (Imperial War Museum A 13681)

CHAPTER 11

THE *MANXMAN*, *WELSHMAN* AND *ABDIEL* WREAK HAVOC IN THE MEDITERRANEAN, 1942–1943

B Y the end of 1942, the situation in the Mediterranean had changed completely from just a few months before. The British victory at El Alamein and the Anglo-American landings in French North Africa had put the Axis armies on the defensive and relieved the pressure on Malta. The Germans and Italians retreated to Tunisia and had to be supplied by ships plying the Sicilian Channel. Enter the fast minelayers and the submarine *Rorqual*.

The *Manxman* loaded mines at Malta and on 25 November 1942 proceeded to Algiers to operate under the orders of the Naval Commander, Expeditionary Force, i.e., Admiral Andrew Cunningham. On the night of 29

November, she laid her first minefield in many months, this one off the Cani Rocks near Bizerta,[1] which proved to be a very worthwhile operation.

Weeks later, on 18 January 1943, mines from the field sank the 4768-ton German motorship *Ankara*[2] forty-five miles east of Cani. She had sailed from Palermo to Bizerta at 23.30 the previous night, with the destroyer *Saetta* and the escort torpedo boat *Uragano* as escorts. The *Uragano* was one of a new class of ships, roughly equivalent to an American destroyer escort, which displaced 925 tons[3] and was armed with two 3.9in guns. At 14.15 on the 18th the *Ankara* struck two mines on her starboard side opposite

An aerial view of the *Welshman* from off the port bow, November 1942. (IWM FL 4485)

the No. 4 hold and went down, of course with all her cargo.

The loss of the *Ankara* was a heavy blow to the Axis. She had made twenty-one runs to North Africa and with her especially powerful derricks she was the only ship capable of lifting and transporting Tiger tanks to Tunisia. As if that were not enough, on her last voyage the *Ankara* was carrying 1505 tons of stores, including 700 tons of sorely-needed ammunition and numerous vehicles. Furthermore, 'Her loss had a considerable morale effect, as she was regarded as an emblem of German endurance and reliability'. [4]

The *Manxman*'s minefield was not quite done. On 23 March, the same minefield damaged the Italian motorship *Ombrina*, a large ship of 6015 GRT. The field's final victim was the tug *Cervantes*, of just 300 GRT. [5]

* * *

The *Manxman*'s minelaying days in the Mediterranean were soon to be put to an

An aerial view of the *Welshman* from off the port quarter, November 1942. (IWM FL 4486)

involuntary end, but the *Welshman*'s were just beginning. Indeed, when the *Welshman* arrived at Alexandria on 7 December, she was ordered to convert to minelaying by removing certain fittings that were originally installed for the carriage of aviation spirit on the mine deck. So 'converted', the *Welshman* was to remain in the Mediterranean to ply her true trade.

After a boiler clean at Alexandria, the *Welshman* took on a half load of mines at Haifa for Malta, as well as all the equipment needed to set up a motor torpedo boat base at Bône in Algeria. When Captain Friedberger told the Commander Coastal Forces that he seemed to have 'everything bar the kitchen stove', he was told that the kitchen stove was in case no. 300. On the way to Bône, the ship had to pass within six miles of the island of Pantelleria, but Captain Friedberger thought there was little chance of an Italian radar watch keeper being alert on a Saturday night.

Pantelleria was indeed passed in peace, but Bône was a different matter. The *Welshman* arrived there at dawn on New Year's Day 1943 and at 10.00 German planes came over and dropped a bomb down the funnel of the cruiser *Ajax*. During the attack, a French floating crane driver 'headed for the foothills but returned just as one of our stoker petty officers was getting the hang of crane driving'. The ship was unloaded in record time and left for Algiers at 16.00.

At Algiers, there was evidence that old habits died hard. The *Welshman* was again loaded with supplies for Malta, this time 175 tons of seed potatoes. On the way to Malta, the ship rolled 42° each way at 30 knots in a heavy stern sea, but nevertheless arrived there on 4 January.[6] Captain Friedberger later learned the seed potatoes produced the best crop Malta had ever had.

On 7 January, the *Welshman* embarked mines at Malta and finally resumed her minelaying career. Sailing at 14.45 that day, she increased speed to 28 knots and headed for the Sicilian Narrows to lay her mines. The taut wire measuring gear broke twice, but she was still able to lay her mines accurately. She retired at 29 knots, passed to the north of the island of Pantelleria and arrived at Malta at 08.13 on the 8th, having completed her first minelay since February 1942.

Next the *Welshman* was sent to the Eastern Mediterranean to transport troops between Beirut and Famagusta, Cyprus, as part of an effort to mislead the enemy into thinking the Allies' next target was Crete or the Aegean islands, instead of Sicily.[7] According to Captain Friedberger, 'By leaving Beirut at dusk, steaming 32 knots and allowing two hours at Famagusta, to disembark 700 soldiers and embark 700 others, we could make Beirut at dawn after safe passage without escort'. This the *Welshman* did for six nights running and left Famagusta on 23 January after having completed the movement of 4300 troops in and out of Cyprus. She arrived at Malta on the 28th.

The *Welshman* departed Malta two days later for another minelaying operation in the Sicilian

The *Welshman* close up. (Maritime Photo Library 2471)

Narrows. Beginning just before midnight on the 30th, she laid 158 mines. The same day, her minefield sank the unwary Italian escorts *Generale Marcello Prestinari* and *Procellaria*.[8] The *Procellaria* was a new 670-ton corvette and the *Prestinari* was a very old 635-ton torpedo boat. The *Prestinari* sank with fifty-four men and the *Procellaria* with twenty-three.[9]

The *Welshman*'s minelaying days in the Mediterranean had been productive, in spite of interruptions for some of the usual non-minelaying duties foisted upon the ships of this class, but those days were about to be cut short. It would fall to the *Abdiel* to take up the minelaying mantle.

* * *

After her gold-laden voyage from South Africa in June 1942, the *Abdiel* completed her first and last refit in November of that year, emerging with a striking multi-coloured camouflage scheme. She also received seven single 20mm Oerlikon guns to replace her ineffective 0.5in Vickers machine guns and an advanced Type 291 radar set atop her foremast to replace her nearly useless Type 286. All bright and shiny, she began working up at Scapa Flow on 19 November.[10]

The *Abdiel* re-commissioned under the command of Captain David Orr-Ewing. He was born in 1900 and grew to be tall and slim and a very good all-round athlete. He gained a rugby blue while at Cambridge, played for the Navy and the Combined Services and was a trialist for

The Italian corvette *Procellaria* sinking on 31 January 1943 after striking one of the *Welshman*'s mines. (E Bagnasco Collection)

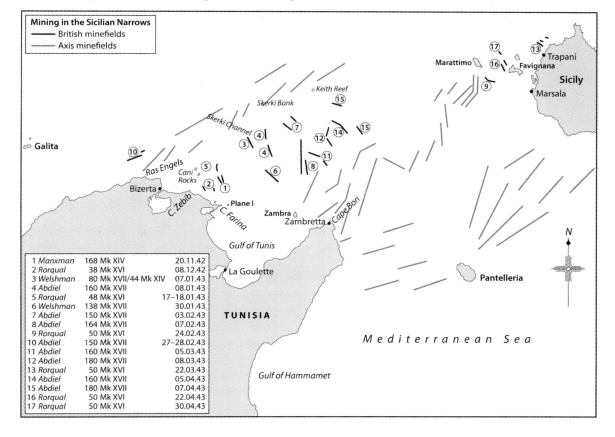

| Mining in the Sicilian Narrows |
| British minefields |
| Axis minefields |

1 *Manxman*	168 Mk XIV		20.11.42
2 *Rorqual*	38 Mk XVI		08.12.42
3 *Welshman*	80 Mk XVII/44 Mk XIV		07.01.43
4 *Abdiel*	160 Mk XVII		08.01.43
5 *Rorqual*	48 Mk XVI		17–18.01.43
6 *Welshman*	138 Mk XVII		30.01.43
7 *Abdiel*	150 Mk XVII		03.02.43
8 *Abdiel*	164 Mk XVII		07.02.43
9 *Rorqual*	50 Mk XVI		24.02.43
10 *Abdiel*	150 Mk XVII		27–28.02.43
11 *Abdiel*	160 Mk XVII		05.03.43
12 *Abdiel*	180 Mk XVII		08.03.43
13 *Rorqual*	50 Mk XVI		22.03.43
14 *Abdiel*	160 Mk XVII		05.04.43
15 *Abdiel*	180 Mk XVII		07.04.43
16 *Rorqual*	50 Mk XVI		22.04.43
17 *Rorqual*	50 Mk XVI		30.04.43

The *Abdiel* as refitted in 1942, starboard side. (The National Archives Adm 176/684-2)

The *Abdiel* as refitted, port side. (The National Archives Adm 176/784-3)

Captain David Orr-Ewing, RN. (Charles Orr Ewing)

Scotland at a time when Scotland were very strong. He boxed for the Navy and shot at the National Rifle Association at Bisley. He was very outgoing, had a tremendous sense of humour and was quite a tease.[11]

As for his naval career, he entered Osborne in 1913 and during the Great War he was in the thick of things in the battlecruiser *Princess Royal* at Jutland. After the war, he specialised in gunnery and shortly before the next war he had two stints in the battlecruiser *Hood*, as Executive Officer from 1936 to 1939 and as Staff Captain for a short time in 1941, the latter stint ending shortly before the *Hood* left Scapa Flow on 22 May to meet her fate at the hands of the *Bismarck*. History records that, while in the *Hood*, some of Orr-Ewing's notable accomplishments were commanding the winning boat in a sailing regatta at Gibraltar in March 1938 and demonstrating how to drink

beer while standing on one's head.[12] Promoted to Captain on 31 December 1940,[13] he became the commanding officer of the old light cruiser *Diomede* after he left the *Hood* and just before he took command of the *Abdiel*. He would ably command her during a commission that was, for much of the time, extremely gruelling and dangerous.

The *Abdiel*'s new crew also included her Navigating Officer, Lieutenant William Alastair Robertson, RN, who was born in 1915 in Edinburgh and went to the Royal Naval College at Dartmouth in 1928. In December 1937 he won his Fleet Air Arm wings and flew from several carriers. In January 1939, his Blackburn Skua fighter-dive bomber went into the water on take-off but he survived. At the beginning of the war, he was flying a Skua off the *Ark Royal*, when, with two other Skua crews, he had the distinction of taking part in the destruction of the first German plane shot down by the British in the Second World War, a Dornier Do 18 floatplane, on 26 September 1939.[14] Robertson returned to sea service late in 1939 and, after taking a navigator's course, he won a DSC in the minesweeper *Fitzroy* in 1941–2. In August 1942 he took part in the raid on Dieppe in the minesweeper *Blythe,* which just escaped sinking by a Focke Wulf Fw 190 on her way home.

The *Abdiel*'s new Torpedo Lieutenant was Lieutenant Geoffrey Hodges, RNR, GM. Born in 1908, he was educated at Winchester College and joined the Royal Naval Volunteer Reserve in 1939 just before the war began. He was soon posted to the Mining Department of the Royal Navy's torpedo and mine shore establishment, HMS *Vernon,* specifically to its Depth Charge and Explosives Section and the 'Rendering Mines Safe' section. He was soon involved in extremely hazardous work countering and rendering German sea and parachute mines safe. He was awarded the George Medal in 1940 for his bravery and success in these pursuits, but after being wounded by an exploding parachute mine that year he was ready for some sea duty,[15] which took him first to the slow minelayer *Teviot Bank* and then to the *Abdiel.*

Taking advantage of the *Abdiel*'s rare presence in home waters, the Admiralty ordered her to pick up mines at Milford Haven on Christmas Eve and to lay a minefield off the Île Vierge off the coast of Brittany on 30 December. After Navigator Alastair Robertson reported to Captain Orr-Ewing that they were in the proper place, the Captain passed the word to Lieutenant Geoffrey Hodges on the mining deck to get started. The *Abdiel* laid 160 mines in four lines and at a depth of 6ft, her job made easier by the light burning in the lighthouse on the island.

The main excitement of the operation was after the first two lines were laid, when a light was flashed from the shore in the *Abdiel*'s direction. The Chief Yeoman of Signals on the bridge turned to his signalman and, as Alastair Robertson explained, 'as is the practice of a Chief Yeoman on seeing a light apparently flashing Morse code' ordered 'Answer him'. As the ship was off an enemy-held coast, that was hardly prudent, so the Captain and Robertson simultaneously shouted, 'No, don't!' The next few minutes were edgy until the bridge personnel heard Geoffrey Hodges' report 'All

Lieutenant Geoffrey Hodges, GM, RNVR, in 1943. (Harley Hodges)

mines laid'. Immediately the *Abdiel* turned to the northward and increased from her laying speed of 18 knots to 35 knots and 'got the hell out of it'. Robertson thought there was a general feeling of satisfaction that they had successfully accomplished their first minelaying operation, but he privately hoped they would not be called on to do another quite so near a hostile coast.[16]

With the torpedoing of the *Manxman* by a U-boat on 1 December 1942 (see Chapter 12), the Royal Navy was short a fast minelayer in the Mediterranean. On 2 January 1943, the *Abdiel* left Milford Haven and set off once again for the Mediterranean. She passed through the Straits of Gibraltar on 5 January and anchored at Algiers the following day.[17]

The situation in the Mediterranean had changed dramatically since the *Abdiel* had left a year ago. The Allies were doing all they could to deny supplies and reinforcements to the German and Italian troops in Tunisia and the fast minelayers *Welshman* and *Abdiel* were an important part of their plan.

An aerial port quarter view of the *Abdiel*. (Imperial War Museum FL 22)

The *Abdiel* at Malta in 1943. (Joseph Caruana)

Once back in the Mediterranean, the *Abdiel* was ordered to resume her minelaying duties and to carry out operations off the coast of Tunisia and in the Sicilian Narrows.[18] The arrival of the *Abdiel* in the Mediterranean became known to the German Flag Officer Italy, Admiral Eberhard Weichold, and the prospect of a large-scale Allied mining campaign in the Mediterranean caused him considerable concern,[19] which was to prove well founded.

On the *Abdiel*'s first minelaying operation of the new year, she left Algiers at 07.15 on 8 January, bound for the Sicilian Narrows via the waters off Bône. Just after midnight, she laid 160 mines in two separate lines in spite of the very rough seas. Because the weather would have delayed her return trip, she headed instead for Malta, arriving there at 10.00 on the 9th. Her stay at Malta was short – the authorities there were not keen for her to stay for long, as she was likely to attract an air raid[20] – and she left Malta with ten passengers for Gibraltar on 11 January, arriving on the 13th.[21] The first night out, Lieutenant Robertson went to the wardroom to have dinner and found the passengers, no doubt still used to siege rations, wolfing down anything they could get their hands on. 'It was the first time I had seen what really hungry men can do to food when it is freely offered'.[22]

The *Abdiel*'s new minefield drew blood almost immediately, sinking the Italian destroyer *Corsaro* and seriously damaging the

The Italian escort *Uragano*, sunk by one of the *Abdiel*'s mines. (G Parodi Collection via M Brescia)

destroyer *Maestrale* on 9 January.[23] The *Maestrale* was built in the early 1930s, but the *Corsaro*, at about 1830 tons and with five 4.7in guns, was one of the newest and best destroyers in the *Regia Marina*.

The same minefield continued to lay in wait for more victims. On 3 February, it accounted for two very experienced escorts, the Italian destroyer *Saetta* and the new escort torpedo boat *Uragano*,[24] which had just sailed from Bizerta to Naples as part of the escort for the tanker *Thorsheimer*. The *Uragano* hit the first mine, followed by the *Saetta* as she approached her stricken companion. The loss in lives was heavy; 114 officers and men from the *Saetta* and 170 from the *Uragano*.[25]

The *Abdiel*'s next operation was to lay a minefield off the Skerki Bank, but the first attempt on 31 January didn't quite work out. First, she was shadowed by an enemy aircraft, which dropped flares in her vicinity and then four or five possible German S-boats – E-boats to the British – were sighted off the port quarter. The *Abdiel* altered course away at 32 knots and fired one salvo from her 4in guns when the boats appeared on her starboard quarter. After this incident, Captain Orr-Ewing decided to call it a day. On 3 February the operation was carried out successfully and the *Abdiel* laid 150 mines, beginning at 01.24. This field accounted for two German ferry barges on 5 March.[26]

The *Abdiel* began another minelaying operation in the Narrows on 6 February, this time escorted at first by the destroyers *Lightning* and *Loyal*. After the destroyers left to carry out a sweep, the night was interrupted by a bright flare about 3000 yards off the *Abdiel*'s starboard quarter, followed a few seconds later by the sounds of an aircraft, which then passed over her at a height of just 1500ft. The *Abdiel* opened fire, but the aircraft disappeared into the night without further ado. The *Abdiel* then laid her 164 mines in the planned position from 01.03 to 01.20 on 7 February and then returned to Bône.

After retrieving her starboard anchor there, she sailed for Algiers at 19.00 that day. As she was zig-zagging at 24 knots, her radar picked up a small echo one mile on the starboard bow. On the bridge, Lieutenant Robertson was talking to the duty signalman, who suddenly said, 'Do you see them porpoises: they are doing a good speed'. Robertson and the Officer of the Watch looked and saw two phosphorescent tracks approaching from abaft the starboard quarter and instantly realised what they were. 'Hard a port' was ordered, but to Robertson the *Abdiel* seemed to take an unconscionable time to turn. She finally did and the torpedoes passed clear of the ship by 30 yards or so and exploded at the end of their run. The *Abdiel* continued her turn a full 360° and then steadied. After this excitement, caused by the Italian submarine *Acciaio*, she arrived at Algiers at 06.30 the next morning, and then sailed for Milford Haven.[27]

After returning to Algiers, she began another lay on 27 February. Once again, the Sicilian Narrows proved to be a crowded place. Shortly before midnight, the wash of four German S-boats was sighted on the port bow. The *Abdiel*

The *Abdiel* at speed off the North African coast, 1943. (Harley Hodges)

altered course towards them and opened fire, but the relative speeds were so great that in a matter of seconds the S-boats were abeam and turned to disappear into the night.

It was probably on this occasion that Navigator, Lieutenant Alastair Robertson, experienced the firing of the 4in guns most acutely. He recalled that

> by the time our guns were laid with the correct range and bearing, the target was well abaft the beam which meant that the muzzle of B gun was only a foot or so outside the bulkhead of the charthouse where I was enjoying a cup of cocoa, with a wary eye on the echo sounder since we were fairly near the shallows of

the Skerki Bank. When the gun opened fire the effect in the charthouse was catastrophic: the lights went out, the echo sounder came clean off the bulkhead and lay wrecked on the deck and the cocoa was spilt all over the chart, all this havoc being revealed by the flickering 'secondary lighting'. As for the navigator [Robertson], he staggered on to the bridge wondering what on earth was happening: to his relief he found that we were still afloat and intact and returned to clean up the mess. In fact the whole incident was over in less than 30 seconds. No damage was done to the ship, apart from an echo sounder strewn over the charthouse, nor to the

Axis powers come to that, but nerves were a bit frayed.[28]

The *Abdiel* then proceeded to begin to lay her 160 mines just before midnight and finished the minefield off Bizerta just after midnight on the 28th. On completion of the lay, she retired at high speed and set sail for Mers-el-Kebir.[29] The same day, the new minefield sank the S-boat *S 35* – perhaps one of the S-boats the *Abdiel* had sighted the night before – and a Siebel ferry.[30]

The *Abdiel* carried out an uneventful minelaying operation on 5 March, again assisted by a diversionary sweep carried out by the destroyers *Lightning* and *Loyal*.[31] Her pace not slackening a bit, she began another operation on the 7th, only to sight a group of six German self-propelled lighters 1500 yards on her port bow and on an opposite course. She opened fire with all of her guns and in a 60-second engagement damaged two of the lighters before continuing on her way and laying her minefield just after midnight on 8 March.[32] The *Abdiel* was then assigned some less exciting duty, making three trips carrying mines and stores between Haifa and Malta.

Meanwhile, her mines remained armed and ready. On 7 March mines from the *Abdiel*'s 5 March field fouled the route of a small convoy and accounted for the escort torpedo boat *Ciclone* and a merchant ship, the *Henry Estier*.[33] The *Ciclone* was the first ship of the class to which the unfortunate *Uragano* belonged. The *Estier* was the first to hit a mine, at 12.32 and caught fire and sank. The *Ciclone* was ordered to her assistance, but at 12.40 American Liberator bombers put in an appearance and hit the merchant ship *Balzac*, which promptly disappeared. The *Ciclone* was then sent to the *Balzac*'s assistance, but hit one mine at 13.10 and another at 13.50. Before she could hit another, she was ordered abandoned at 14.05. The tough *Ciclone* survived the night, but succumbed at 13.25 on 8 March after a vain attempt by the torpedo boat *Groppo* to tow her. Her resting place is at 37° 40' N, 10° 59' E. Only fifteen of her men were lost,[34] but the *Regia Marina* had lost a very valuable escort.

Weeks later, on 24 March the mines from the *Abdiel*'s 7 March field sank the Italian destroyers *Ascari* and *Lanzerotto Malocello*, which were carrying German troops to Tunisia. The *Ascari* was one of the newer Italian destroyers, of the 'Soldati' class, and the *Malocello* was one of the larger but older destroyers of the 'Navigatori' class. The loss of life was extremely heavy; 199 men from the crew of the *Malocello*, including all of her officers, 194 officers and men from the *Ascari*, and 550 German soldiers. Italian minesweepers had swept four mines from this field the day before, but the existence of the field was not passed on in time.[35] The minefield was not quite done, claiming the *KT.13*, a 700-ton German *Kriegstransporter* or 'war transport', on the day before the field was supposed to flood.[36]

By the beginning of April, the *Abdiel* was nearing the end of her minelaying days in the Sicilian Narrows. After departing Malta, she made her seventh minelay there just after midnight on 5 April, returning to Malta that morning. Each way she attracted the attention of searchlights on the Italian-held island of Pantelleria, but drew no fire. Finally, the next day she left Malta to lay her eighth and final field in the Narrows, this one again off the Skerki Bank, just after midnight on 7 April and returned to Malta at 08.30 that morning.[37]

On one of the return voyages to Malta from a dangerous offensive minelay, the *Abdiel* demonstrated that that the sea has other dangers, especially when one gets too enamoured of one's own speed. Alastair Robertson described what happened:

With Malta in sight and keeping well clear of the alleged enemy minefield to the north of Gozo, we pushed on to 34 knots aided by a not inconsiderable following sea. In my usual place on the bridge, knowing that the operation was over, I felt quite exhilarated by the throb and power of the ship, the huge bow wave and the seas breaking on either side. It was a fine sight, set against the backdrop of the sun rising behind Malta silhouetting the island, its cliffs and promontories and the some of its multitudinous churches. But something is always happening at sea and it happened now. We seemed to be picked up by a larger than usual wave and the bow of the ship simply dived into the next wave ahead so that for a moment we put up a fair imitation of a diving submarine. Solid water shot up through both hawse pipes and it really looked as if we were going to go under. The Officer of the Watch, Sub-Lieutenant de Pass and I exchanged apprehensive glances and I said, 'You had better come down a couple of knots': he ordered 230 revolutions (for 32 knots) and at that moment David Orr Ewing appeared and asked what was going on. I explained and he said 'This class of ship is not designed to submerge: you had better make it 30'.

The *Abdiel* then continued at that rather safer speed up the Valetta mineswept channel.

Alas, the *Abdiel*'s last two minefields took no toll of the enemy, but all in all her minefields in the Sicilian Narrows had inflicted great losses. It had been very hard duty for the *Abdiel*'s men. Geoffrey Hodges recalled that

Throughout much of the greater part of this sustained effort we were in danger

areas and so were in watch-and-watch routine and became very tired. I know that my Captain never slept aft in his own quarters or indeed in pajamas, for 36 days in succession during one hard spell. Certainly some of us became desperately tired by the time the minelaying campaign was completed.[38]

For her service in this very hazardous series of operations, the *Abdiel* was specially commended by the First Sea Lord.[39]

Her minelaying duties in the Mediterranean completed, the *Abdiel* was ordered to take her

The *Abdiel* at anchor. (National Museum of the Royal Navy 1983/15.1)

mines to Milford Haven in Wales so they could be used in European waters. Then it was once again back to the Mediterranean, past the Irish coast and into the Bay of Biscay, then clear of the U-boat danger area, when the Luftwaffe broke the monotony of her voyage on a glorious afternoon 50 miles off the coast of Portugal.

Lieutenant Robertson was on the bridge that day 'relishing the southern sun' and engaged in a mundane conversation about peacetime pursuits when:

> To our amazement we heard, yes *heard*, an aircraft apparently quite near. At that moment the port lookout shouted 'Aircraft bearing Red 90' and there it was, a huge four-engined machine only a few hundred yards away and coming straight at us. Luckily it must have been as surprised as we were and had failed to identify us as a warship for it flew across the ship at masthead height, its black crosses far too close for comfort. I pressed the 'Action' alarm bell and shouted at B gun (the gun just for'ard of the bridge and permanently manned at sea) to open fire. The crew trained it round in double quick time and let off a couple of rounds at the retreating Focke-Wulf but they were hopelessly off target . . . We felt slightly ashamed of ourselves, albeit we were unharmed. Meanwhile summoned by the Alarm we were at 'Action Stations' and David [Orr-Ewing] decided that we had better stay like that in case the great bird came back. Eventually we stood down and I went aft for a cup of tea. George Brown was in the wardroom and couldn't resist pulling my leg about the 'failure of you chaps on the bridge to see an enormous aircraft like that'. I remember saying, 'Don't worry Chief; Any moment now it will come back and we'll get it for you'. My reader must believe this for it is a fact that the words were no sooner out of my mouth when there was a series of terrific explosions near enough to shake the ship. Never did Brown and I move more quickly: we were up the ladder in a trice, he to his engine room, I to the bridge when a diligent search of the cloudless

sky revealed the Focke-Wulf at an immense height heading eastwards far out of range. Its stick of bombs had missed us astern by about a hundred yards but for all that it was a remarkably accurate shot considering its height and the ship's speed and zig-zag course. It was a nasty moment which proved once again that war is 99 per cent boredom and 1 per cent fright.

The *Abdiel* must have tangled with a huge Fw 200 Condor on patrol far out to sea. Aside from an uncertain moment when Navigator Robertson worried they were about to run onto the Spanish coast, the rest of the voyage to Gibraltar was uneventful.

The *Abdiel* stopped at Gibraltar to fuel and to pick up, according to Alastair Robertson, 'believe it or not, girls – ten [members of the] WRNS who had to be transported to Algiers for some reason or another'. Robertson thought they enjoyed their trip and the *Abdiel*'s crew enjoyed having them on board. 'Certainly we enjoyed having them on board. There was a good deal of laughter and silly jokes such as "Don't look back: there's a torpedo following us".' The Wrens were eventually landed at Algiers, yet another unique 'cargo' carried by a fast minelayer.

The long North African campaign, which began with an abortive Italian offensive into Egypt in 1940, was finally coming to an end. British and American armies continued to press the Germans and Italians from the west and the east into a corner of Tunisia, where they finally surrendered on 13 May 1943. After the surrender, the *Abdiel* resumed her trooping duties, transporting troops to and from Beirut and Famagusta and between Algiers and Malta in preparation for Operation 'Husky', the invasion of Sicily.[40]

On 10 July 1943, the Allies invaded Sicily, the first time the war had been taken directly to Axis soil. The massive effort was under the Supreme Command of General Dwight Eisenhower, with the naval forces under Admiral Andrew Cunningham, the air forces under Air Marshal Tedder and the land forces, the Fifteenth Army Group, under General Harold Alexander. The British Eighth Army under General Bernard Montgomery landed mainly to the east of Cape Passero, at the southern tip of the island and the American Seventh Army under General George S Patton landed to the west of it. The *Abdiel*'s first contribution to the invasion was to ferry several thousand gallons of waterproofing for Army vehicles to Malta.

She then embarked Admiral Andrew Cunningham at Malta and transported him and his staff to Sicily, joining a veritable armada of ships and landing craft off the Sicilian coast. The *Abdiel* spent the day off the invasion beaches, lowering boats as needed to take staff members to conferences ashore. The day was so quiet and peaceful that Admiral Cunningham asked Captain Orr-Ewing if he wanted to send part of his crew to bathe (which he did). The *Abdiel* was so close inshore her men could see the Army rounding up hundreds of Italian prisoners and putting them behind wire. The *Abdiel* left for Malta that evening and with the *Abdiel* sprinting at 35 knots Admiral Cunningham was only just a little late for his dinner and more conferences.[41]

As the battle for Sicily continued, the *Abdiel* became something of a VIP transport, with such passengers as Admiral Lord Louis Mountbatten, Admiral Bertram Ramsay, Air Marshal Arthur Tedder, Admiral Stuart Bonham-Carter,[42] and, last but not least, General Bernard Montgomery. This duty was a real treat for the *Abdiel*'s crew, who were fascinated to hear all about the Sicilian operation and the progress of the war in general from the top brass. Most of the passengers were very approachable and forthcoming, but Montgomery was in a class by himself. On the *Abdiel*'s return to Malta, he handed Captain Orr-Ewing a slim brown paper parcel with the words 'Thank you Captain; you might like this'. It was a signed photograph of himself.[43]

A much more favoured guest was General Harold Alexander. On 13 July the *Abdiel* conveyed General Alexander to the beachhead at Gela. Later the *Abdiel* ferried him from Malta to Algiers. The *Abdiel* left Malta at dusk, sailing on a 'millpond calm sea' and Navigator Robertson went to the bridge shortly after midnight and found General Alexander there hunched beside the chart table gazing out ahead. Robertson recalled,

It was a very dark night though the stars were bright and the ship was surging along, zig-zagging at 32 knots, throwing up her usual phosphorescent bow wave and broad white wake, while amidships the boiler room fans kept up their unremitting roar. It was a majestic scene, the very epitome of power and deeply impressive.

Robertson took up a position near the General in case he wanted to know where they were and after a few minutes Alexander turned to him and said, 'What a magnificent night'. Robertson agreed and Alexander asked Robertson to show him where they were. Robertson threw back the canvas cover of the chart table, restoring it after General Alexander joined him and with a shaded light he showed Alexander their midnight position on the chart. Alexander was fascinated and Robertson remembered him saying, 'Good heavens, this is the first decent map [*sic*: chart] of Sicily that I have seen'. The general then gave Lieutenant Robertson a summary of the Sicilian campaign to date and a forecast of how he hoped it would develop. Robertson thought Alexander 'a charming man: if he had commandeered *Abdiel* as his private yacht we would all have been delighted'.[44]

Sicily finally fell with the capture of Messina on 17 August, after substantial numbers of German and Italian troops had escaped across to the mainland of Italy. The *Abdiel* had played a useful role in the campaign for Sicily, without firing a single shot. Nor did she lay a single mine; most importantly, she was never ordered to lay mines across the Strait of Messina to impede the withdrawal of German and Italian troops, though it would have been a hazardous operation, with heavy guns on both sides of the straits.

After her service in the invasion of Sicily, the *Abdiel* enjoyed a rest period of about three weeks at Malta at the torpedo factory at Gregale for general training and some make-and-mend.[45] Then her unique abilitis were required again.

CHAPTER 12

HARD TIMES FOR FAST MINELAYERS IN THE MEDITERRANEAN, 1942–1943

THE fast minelayers found their duties in the Mediterranean to be not only gruelling, but positively hazardous, first for the *Manxman*, then for the *Welshman* and finally for the *Abdiel*. In spite of the turn of the tide in favour of the Allies, the Mediterranean was no *Mare Pacificus*.

The *Manxman*'s luck finally ran out on the evening of 1 December 1942, when she was sighted by the prowling *U-375* while she on a voyage from Algiers to Gibraltar. At the time, she was sailing at a speed of 21 knots and zig-zagging on a mean course of 284°. Commanded by *Kapitänleutnant* Jürgen Könenkamp, *U-375* was a Type VIIC U-boat that had entered the Mediterranean on 9 December 1941.[1] Könenkamp thought he had a *London* class heavy cruiser in his sights.

The U-boat drew a bead on the *Manxman* and launched her torpedoes. Captain Dickson was on the bridge and heard the trainer in the director above the bridge sing out, 'Torpedo coming'. They watched the torpedo pass close astern from port to starboard. Telegraphist Ron Checketts spied another torpedo approaching the ship and thought to himself, 'No, not after all this'.

Three seconds later, at 17.02, just as the Captain was putting his head to the voicepipe to give orders to the wheel and engines, a second torpedo struck the ship on the port side abreast the engine room. More exactly, it struck at about Station 119, 15ft from the bulkhead separating the engine room from the gearing room and under the pom-pom. The explosion lifted the after end of the ship violently and caused Telegraphist Checketts to lose his lighter over the side. The ship limped on for three cables, then lay stopped.

Officers having tea in the wardroom when the torpedo hit just had time to escape before the

The *Manxman* listing to starboard after the torpedo hit on her port side, 2 December 1942. (Ray Moore)

top hatch was closed. Three ratings were killed outright and a fourth died after he was blown out of the engine room and recovered from the sea. Two of the four men, Heather and Ragg, were Engine Room Artificers and the other two, Watson and Seaman, were Stokers. The Captain later arranged for their next-of-kin to receive £20 from the Isle of Man fund.

If the torpedo was the standard U-boat one, a G7e, it had an explosive charge of 300kg. The torpedo tore a 28ft by 14ft hole in the ship's side plating, which opened two of the largest compartments in the ship up to the sea, the engine room and the gearing room aft of it, which immediately flooded up to the starboard side of the main deck. Despite being torpedoed on her port side, the ship soon listed 16° to starboard because of the machinery that was blown toward the starboard side of the ship. The ship trimmed aft and the draught on the starboard side aft reached 27ft. There was some progressive flooding, into the wardroom and cabins aft of it, the pom-pom magazine, the starboard side of the mine deck and a few other spaces. Eventually more than 1500 tons of water entered the ship. At first the ship's lights failed, but within a half an hour essential power had been restored with the help of a supply of emergency leads. Damage control efforts began right away.

On the bright side, the *Manxman* was carrying no cargo, passengers or mines and the sea was calm. On the other hand, she was alone and dead in the water, 27 miles from the nearest land and 71 miles north of Oran, in position 36° 39' N, 00° 15' E. Realising that she was vulnerable to another attack from the U-boat, the ship's crew did everything possible to keep the submarine down, from firing the ship's guns into the water at 1000 yards range whenever anything was heard on the Asdic, to having the ship's fast motor boat dropping depth charges around the ship for three hours to make the U-boat think that destroyers had joined up.

All of the noise and concussion created by the *Manxman* may have worked as intended. The culpable U-boat actually recorded that it fired two torpedoes to finish off the *Manxman*,[2] but, if it did, they missed. *U-375*'s captain reported in by radio the following evening, claiming 'Two hits on a "London" class cruiser yesterday in [grid] CH 8198, wreckage and boats

found, probably sunk'.[3] It must not have inspected the boats and wreckage very closely.

Captain Dickson ordered a report sent immediately after the torpedo hit, but that was easier said than done. Telegraphist Ron Checketts had to run a lead from a generator to the No. 2 W/T office before he could send it off.[4] The signal was evidently received, as the destroyer *Pathfinder* reached the *Manxman* at 23.15 and was soon joined by the destroyer *Eskimo*. The tow commenced at 00.15 at a speed of 6 knots. The tug *Restive* joined them at 05.20 and the escort destroyer *Puckeridge* joined at 07.00. The *Manxman*'s draught was still too great for her to pass over the wrecks at Oran, so she was towed to the naval base at Mers-el-Kebir. She arrived at 13.00 the next day, the 2nd, and berthed alongside the repair ship *Vindictive*.[5] By then, the list had been reduced to 9°, with the assistance of portable 30-ton pumps, which were made, as Captain Dickson pointed out in his report, by the Northern Pump Company in Minneapolis, Minnesota.

As the *Manxman* was still on loan from the Eastern Fleet, that night Captain Dickson

The *Manxman*'s torpedo hole. (The National Archives Adm 267/32)

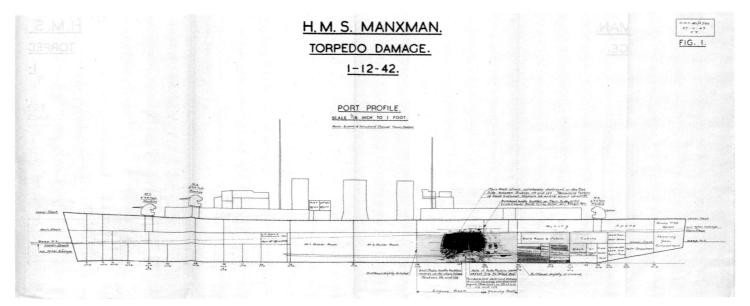

A diagram of torpedo damage to the *Manxman*. (The National Archives Adm 267/32)

informed Admiral Somerville, the C-in-C of the Eastern Fleet, of the ship's situation and 'much regret no prospects now of rejoining you' on 2 December. Admiral Somerville had had plans for her, starting with a refit at Durban and then minelaying operations, but now it was to be a long time before the *Manxman* would again sail east of Suez.

After some temporary repairs at Mers-el-Kebir, the *Manxman* was towed by the tugs *Nimble* and *Salvonia* to Gibraltar, where she arrived on 20 December.[6] Once safely in dock, the *Manxman*'s damage could be examined at leisure. There was a long list of machinery that had been damaged or destroyed or was only good for scrap. The port cruising turbine was blown onto the starting platform and the port high-power turbine was blown up to the level of the main deck. The port low-power turbine was shifted bodily three feet toward the centre of the engine room and the port main gearing was displaced about six inches to starboard. The main deck was almost completely destroyed on the port side between Stations 119 and 127 and the port bilge keel was destroyed between Stations 115 and 126.

A subsequent report by the Department of Naval Construction concluded that

> The heel *away* from the damaged side (i.e., to starboard) can only be satisfactorily accounted for by the transference of weight due to the displaced machinery . . .

This is of first importance as it is clear that the ship could hardly have been saved if she had heeled to port. The fact that the pumping operations carried out to reduce free surface. . . were so effective, demonstrates the prime importance of keeping water off the mining deck in this class of ship.[7]

More repairs were carried out at Gibraltar, including the patching of the hole and the addition of iron ballast on the port side of the engine room. The officers and men celebrated Christmas and then Captain Dickson left the ship to sail to Britain in the aircraft carrier *Argus*. He had been with the ship and most of the crew since before the *Manxman*'s completion and wrote in his diary, 'never in my service have I left a ship with such a heavy heart'.

On 23 June 1943, the *Manxman* left Gibraltar under the tow of the fleet tug *Bustler* bound for the United Kingdom. She then began extensive – and extended – repairs at a shipyard on the River Tyne. She would not emerge until May of 1945. For her, the war in Europe was over.

Soon afterwards, the *Manxman*'s hunter became the hunted. On the night of 30 July 1943, *U-375* attacked a convoy of landing craft off the island of Pantelleria in the central Mediterranean. One of the escorts was a diminutive 284-ton American submarine chaser, *PC-624*, under the command of Lieutenant-Commander Robert D Lowther. At 02.30, the sub chaser picked up a radar contact 8000 yards away and altered course to investigate. After the contact failed to respond to a challenge, she fired a star shell from her 3in gun and in the light saw a surfaced U-boat. The submarine dived, but the sub chaser's sonar immediately made contact. After a torpedo passed close down her side, she dropped a full pattern of depth charges. After losing contact with the U-boat in the roiling waters, the *PC-624* had to return to her convoy and later reported 'possible damage' to a U-boat. That single pattern was sufficient to sink *U-375* with all hands.[8] The *Manxman* was avenged.

*   *   *

Just two months after the *Manxman*'s unfortunate incident, it was the *Welshman*'s turn to run into trouble. She returned to Malta for the last time on the morning of 31 January and departed for Alexandria at 17.00.[9] She was due at Alexandria on 2 February.[10] She carried thirty-seven passengers, including seven badly wounded RAF crewmen. One famous passenger was Captain G W G 'Shrimp' Simpson, who had just handed over command of the legendary 10th Submarine Flotilla at Malta.

Simpson had asked his 'ex-submarine friend Denis Friedberger for a passage' to Alexandria and the Captain replied, 'Here's my after cabin, Shrimp, make yourself at home. My steward will look after you. Come and have a chat on the bridge any time you like'. Captain Simpson spent his newfound spare time sleeping, perusing the books in Captain Friedberger's bookshelf (eventually choosing a novel, *Juan in America* – as in Don Juan – over a volume of Byron's poems) and visiting the bridge, as the *Welshman* 'cut through the water at an exhilarating speed'.

Another *Welshman* passenger who was a bit less well known was Edward H 'Harry' Crockett, a 31-year-old AP war correspondent. Crockett was from Lowell, Massachusetts and 'got his feet wet' reporting on the accidental sinking of the submarine uss *Squalus* in 1939. He had been reporting from the Middle East since April 1942, after a gruelling flight across Equatorial Africa, first in the North African desert with the Eighth Army. In May, he reported on Rommel's tanks advancing on Bir Hacheim. In June, he told the story of the fall of Tobruk and dove under a truck to escape a strafing attack.

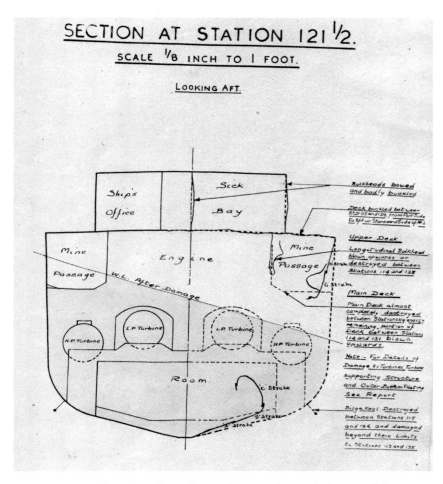

A diagram of the flooding in the *Manxman*. (The National Archives Adm 267/32)

In September, he happily took on the Mediterranean Fleet beat after AP correspondent Larry Allen was captured following the sinking of the destroyer *Sikh* in a raid off Tobruk. He witnessed a night battle from a British warship and from Malta he told of the destruction there and of the people's spirit. Reporting on cabaret singing and dancing girls working in war offices in Malta, he told of an official pointing to a scoreboard and asking, 'How do you like our figures?' Before the *Welshman* sailed on the 31st, Crockett cabled his Cairo office to let them know he was returning for a brief visit.[11]

On the evening of 1 February, the *Welshman* was sailing in an easterly direction about 45 miles east of Tobruk[12] when she crossed paths with *U-617*, which was commanded by *Kapitänleutnant* Albrecht Brandi. The Type VIIC U-boat had entered the Mediterranean on 8 November 1942,[13] and had begun her most recent patrol, her third, from Salamis on 23 January. Brandi sighted the *Welshman* at 18.35,

at a range of 3000m. The U-boat was moving at just 4.5 knots and was submerged at a depth of 13m. The *Welshman* was sailing at 25 knots and was, as usual, traveling alone. The anti-submarine air patrols that had covered her route earlier in the day were no longer about.

At 18.45, when the range had closed to 1200m, the U-boat fired a spread of four G7e electrically-powered torpedoes, which were set to run at a depth of 4m (per Brandi's report) on a course of 213° at the *Welshman*'s port side. Each torpedo was 21in in diameter, carried an explosive charge of 300kg and was equipped with a G7H exploder pistol, which could be set to detonate on contact with a ship or by a ship's magnetic field.[14]

Just 88 seconds later, the German submariners heard two explosions in quick succession, followed by a third particularly heavy explosion, 'like a boiler exploding'. Brandi, who during the war earned a notorious reputation for exaggerating his claims, stated in his war diary that he surfaced at 18.55 and saw his victim capsize and sink by the stern.[15] Brandi then withdrew to report his success, claiming two hits on a *Dido* class light cruiser, though he could not be sure of the identification. His signal was DF'd – detected by a British direction finding team ashore – at 20.30 that night.

The *Welshman* had been carrying out a standard zig-zag pattern on a course of about 85°. Captain Friedberger was on the bridge having a discussion with his executive officer and the navigating officer. The sea was calm, with light airs from the northwest and a completely overcast sky. That day the nautical twilight ended at 18.40 and there was a faint afterglow to the west. Two minutes later, when the ship was halfway through a four-minute leg on her mean course, the crew of the *Welshman* heard explosions, which one seaman described as 'sickening thuds'.[16] From the bridge, Lieutenant I N V Cox could see water and debris blown up into the air from both sides of the quarterdeck. The ship's engines stopped and she swung to the northward, losing headway with an initial list of 5° to starboard. Two of the ship's officers, seven ratings and at least one passenger were killed immediately and several men were injured and taken to the sick bay.

There was hardly any agreement aboard the *Welshman* as to the number of explosions or

The *Welshman* from overhead. (Imperial War Museum FL 4487)

their relative intensity, though in general they were thought to be relatively mild. Captain Friedberger thought there were two explosions and they did not affect his stance at all. Captain Simpson thought there were three, the first two explosions separated by three or four seconds and then a much more intense one after eight seconds. Lieutenant Cox, the ship's executive officer, heard one large explosion followed by two that were not as large. Captain Simpson thought the sound of the propellers stopped after the first explosion and after the third one all was quiet.

Fortunately, some of Captain Friedberger's first and worst fears were not realised. Foremost was his concern that the U-boat might return to finish the job and as a result he kept a watch at the guns and an all-round Asdic (sonar) sweep. Soon his Asdic operator detected a 'hydrophone effect' on 'Red Ten', which was indeed the approximate direction of *U-617* off the *Welshman*'s port side. This effect was thought to be consistent with a U-boat retiring from the scene, which was exactly what Brandi did; he had evidently believed his own report and the *Welshman* was left alone. Just over a year later, the cruiser *Penelope* would not be so fortunate; sailing alone near Anzio on 18 February 1944, she was hit by a single torpedo from *U-410*, which stuck around and finished her off with a second torpedo about 18 minutes later.[17]

At the end of this patrol, Brandi's boat reached port safely. In addition to the *Welshman*, *U-617* had also accounted for two Norwegian freighters and Brandi was awarded Oak Leaves to his Knight's Cross.[18] *U-617*'s luck ran out on the night of 11 September 1943, when she was attacked off Alborán Island by one and then another Vickers Wellington bombers of No. 179 Squadron and was so badly damaged she could not dive. The next day, pursued by the British corvette *Hyacinth*, the trawler *Haarlem* and the Australian sloop *Wollongon*, Brandi drove his boat ashore off the coast of Spanish Morocco. He and his crew abandoned ship and were able to reach shore. They were duly interned by the Spanish, but later returned to occupied France, Brandi after escaping from an internment camp.[19]

In addition to a returning U-boat, Captain Friedberger was worried about the fires spreading to oil on the water, but that did not come to pass either. Instead, almost immediately he received the good news that, although one shaft would not turn and the other propeller was gone, the boilers were intact and lighting and power were available.

At 18.45 the Captain sent the signal, 'Have been hit, require assistance' and giving the ship's positon, which was transmitted by Telegraphist Ferry on a frequency that could be read by any British warship in the area.[20] At 19.17, he signalled, 'My 18.45. Hit aft probably by two torpedoes from submarines. Main engines [are] out of action. Ship flooded as far as after bulkhead of gearing room'. The closest British ships were the 'Hunt' class escort destroyers *Tetcott* and *Belvoir* (pronounced 'BEE-ver'), which were carrying out anti-submarine operations between Benghazi and Derna. The *Tetcott* replied to the *Welshman* at 19.55, 'Am coming to your assistance now, ETA 00.30'. Captain Friedberger sent a final signal on the ship's situation at 20.00, but it was received ashore in a very corrupt state. No matter; help was on the way.

The ship's crew commenced damage control work immediately, with the ship's Engineer Officer, Commander (E) H E C Hims, in charge. The list gradually increased to 8–10° to starboard and while the order was given to transfer oil from starboard tanks to port tanks to put the ship back on an even keel, Captain Friedberger was told that the process would be slow. Extensive damage had been done to the hull aft of Station 150 and the Wardroom Flat and all compartments aft of this Station on the main (mining) deck and the lower deck had been flooded, including the storeroom and the after 4in magazine, which obligingly did not explode. There were large rents in the mining deck and a cut or step in the upper deck near the after funnel. The stern was sagging from aft of the after 4in gun mount to the sea. Fires and sparks from calcium flares that had been stowed in the wrecked storeroom were at first visible to port and starboard and a small calcium fire in the flooded storeroom was being extinguished.

An attempt was made to establish a flooding boundary at Station 150, but the bulkhead at that Station had been damaged and, despite shoring and plugging, some water continued to enter the wardroom flat forward of it, along with some oil from damaged tanks below. After a time, a small amount of water appeared on the mining deck.

Commander Hims ordered the portable submersible pumps transferred there from the wardroom flat and he thought the pumps were competing satisfactorily with the water. The sea was calm and the ship was rolling two or three degrees.

The ship's officers thought the situation seemed well in hand. Still, they ordered the boats turned out on their davits, the ship's Carley floats, rafts and floatanets unlashed and the ship's depth charges set to safe. Preparations were being made to tow forward. The port watch was ordered to supper and with 'trust born by confidence in their superiors, shipmates of the "off-duty" watch made their way below', according to Able Seaman Jim Burgess.

The ship's officer may have been confident, but some of the men were nervous. Jim Burgess recalled that during this time there was a

general buzz of conversation, although unfamiliar voices issued from familiar faces – the result of trying to appear calm when feeling bloody terrified. Corny 'cracks' brought laughter that was hollow but humourless. The whole thing seemed like a bad dream. After all, the worst of the 'Mediterranean' war was over; that this should happen to us after survival of those earlier peak-time attacks made no sense . . . Now, here we were drifting helplessly in this, fortunately, almost tideless sea.

As time wore on, his thoughts wandered to the RAF bomber crew in the sick bay, 'bandaged mummy-like from head to feet – out of the Maltese frying pan, into this lot, poor sods'.

As it turned out, the men's nervousness was well-founded. All seemed well enough, but it wasn't. At about 20.35, the list began to increase, almost imperceptibly, and then the ship suddenly lurched and took an increased list to starboard. Captains Friedberger and Simpson

The *Welshman* alone on the open sea. (Author's collection)

were in the charthouse, where the lurch caused the parallel rulers to slide from one end of the chart desk to the other. As the captains climbed up to the bridge, the list continued to increase without pause until the ship was lying on her beam ends – that is, 90° to starboard. The two then walked down the side of the bridge and then sat on the ship's side, where Captain Friedberger blew up his life belt. As the ship began to sink by the stern, she uprighted and threw the two captains into the water.

Some of the men made it into the water after some very tense moments. As the list increased, men had a more and more difficult time making their way up a deck that was quickly becoming vertical. Leading Seaman Jack Lemon was using any handhold or foothold he could find to make his way to the port side, when the door to the ship's bread store opened and dozens of loaves rained down on him. After surviving that onslaught, he lent a hand to a man behind him before making it to the deck edge and the port side of the ship. Telegraphist Reg Cook found himself on the ship's port side, unable to swim and wondering what to do next, when a 'kindly' wave swept him overboard and he found something to hold on to.[21] Just before reaching the water, some men had painful encounters with the portside bilge keel, causing Jack Lemon to lose the feeling in his legs. Although supposedly set to 'safe', one depth charge exploded as the ship was sinking, possibly killing some men already in the water, but pushing Stoker Les Payne away from the sinking ship and its deadly suction.[22]

Within about three minutes, the *Welshman* was gone. She sank stern first at about 20.40, in position 32° 12' N, 24° 52' E. Captain Friedberger recalled, 'I shall never forget the last 50 feet of that beautiful Hawthorn Leslie ship disappearing from close alongside me into three hundred fathoms'.[23]

Not everyone could make it into the water. Most likely the ship's doctor, the sick berth attendants and the wounded RAF men could not get out of the sick bay in time and some men could not get up from down below. One man likely caught below was Petty Officer John Norman Evennett, an Engine Room Artificer. An engineer in peacetime, he joined the Royal Navy and in June 1940 helped man a Dutch fishing boat, the *Doggersbank*, which was sailed to St

Malo and Cherbourg to pick up troops and then to Jersey and Guernsey in the Channel Islands to pick up British civilians in advance of the Germans. He then served in the destroyer *Bedouin* – with which the *Welshman* had served the previous June – before he was drafted to the *Welshman*.

Many men did make it into the water, some without hearing an order to abandon ship, though the need to do so became glaringly evident, in Leading Seaman Lemon's case when the batteries in his compartment showed signs of leaking sulphuric acid. The *Welshman*'s boats could not be lowered in time, but a number of Carley floats, a copper punt and floatanets made it into the water and were soon filled. Some men had to make do as best they could, Able Seaman Lionel Purdie by grabbing onto a passing side of frozen beef and holding on to it for dear life.[24]

Captain Friedberger gave up his seat in a Carley float for an injured man,[25] and swam around on a plank visiting other floats and the punt,[26] and exhorting the men to keep together.[27] The survivors kept up their spirits by singing, continuously for the first few hours, then more spasmodically, while the men waited for the arrival of their rescuers. Some of the men were unaware of the ship's distress signals and became despondent. A bearded New Zealander named Killick refused to be dispirited and led singing of 'Roll Out the Barrel', 'Tipperary' and 'Salome'.[28]

While no fuel oil had leaked into the sea and the sea was calm, Captain Friedberger felt that hours in the water at 56°F was probably too much for the older men. To make matters worse, after several hours there was a squall and a slight sea came up at 23.00 and exhausted many men. According to the Captain, 'Many of these that I talked to on rafts had disappeared' by the time the rescue ships arrived to pick them up.

The survivors cheered when the *Tetcott* and the *Belvoir* loomed out of the darkness at 00.20.[29] The ships arrived with towropes at the ready, but, instead of finding the *Welshman*, they sighted the red lights of life belts bobbing up and down in the water. They quickly lowered their boats to pick up survivors, 'gently pushing the dead away from the whaler and hauling up the living'.[30]

After hours in the water, Telegraphist Ferry was beginning to lose consciousness, but

remembers being helped up the netting on the side of what turned out to be the *Belvoir* and hearing a voice saying, 'OK, Sparks, you're all right now'. Survivors were quickly provided with warm clothing and medication in the form of neat rum.[31] Having picked up all the survivors they could find, the rescue ships then set course for Alexandria. Some of the survivors then slept until awakened in the morning to 'char' and breakfast.

At 10.00 that morning, Captain Friedberger read the burial service for two ratings and for war correspondent Harry Crockett, who had died during the night. Five men in the *Tetcott* had taken turns working on him, but they could not revive him.[32] Telegraphist Robert Ferry witnessed Crockett's burial at sea and recalled that he was buried in an American flag. Crockett left behind a wife, Sally and a daughter and a son, in Kew Gardens, New York. The Admiralty announced his death on 5 February.

The *Tetcott* and *Belvoir* arrived at Alexandria at 15.00 that day,[33] 2 February, and a number of men were taken straight to the 64th General Hospital. The Admiralty announced the loss of the *Welshman* on 5 March 1943,[34] and also confirmed that Harry Crockett had died taking passage in her. When reporting on his death, the Associated Press emphasised that 'he never lost his enthusiasm for a good story'.

It is not clear how many men were aboard the *Welshman* when she was torpedoed or how many were picked up, but, all told, the casualties were nine officers and 144 men, at least seven RAF personnel and two civilian passengers, Harry Crockett and an Admiralty Foreman of Works, Richard H Tall.[35] One of the officers lost was Lieutenant (T) John C Cherry, RNVR, who had served in the *Manxman*. Some of the dead later washed ashore on the North African coast and thirteen are buried in the great cemetery at El Alamein in Egypt.

The parents, widows and orphans of the dead and missing were eventually informed of their loss. Norman Evennett's family was not informed for six weeks that he was missing and presumed dead. The families were left with only mementoes and memories – a last visit, a final

The escort destroyer HMS *Tetcott*, a rescuer of *Welshman* survivors. (IWM A 8216)

Edward 'Harry' Crockett, the AP war correspondent who died after the sinking of the *Welshman*. (Associated Press No. 421115046)

wave goodbye – and some widows and orphans would face a hard future, with little or no assistance.

As tragic as the loss of life was, at least there were friendly ships nearby to pick up some survivors. If the *Welshman* had been similarly torpedoed (or mined) during her solo runs to Malta in May or July or even in November, friendly rescuers would not have been close at hand. The submarine *Olympus* had suffered grievous losses and she sank just a few miles off the coast of Malta. Fortunately, the naval situation in the Mediterranean had changed dramatically by February 1943 and help for the *Welshman* was at hand.

Shortly after the loss of the *Welshman*, a Board of Enquiry to investigate the circumstances of her loss was held at Alexandria aboard the light cruiser *Cleopatra*, with her commanding officer, Captain John F Stevens, presiding.[36] After taking evidence from Captain Friedberger, Captain Simpson, Commander Hims and other survivors, the Board issued its report on 14 February. The Board found that the *Welshman* had been damaged by submarine torpedoes fitted with non-contact pistols, one of which exploded under the stern, while the others were more distant. The Board concluded that the ship was in a dangerous state as regards stability immediately after the initial damage and that during the whole period that she was afloat she was settling lower in the water, resulting in the eventual flooding of the mining deck and a condition of critical instability. The Board thought it was clear that the ship's officers had believed their ship to be in no danger until she capsized and that they were misled by the ship's design, as they did not appreciate that, in the absence of any sub-division between the mining and upper decks over a large portion of the ship's length, the mining deck was in effect the upper deck for purposes of stability and were also misled by the calm sea, as there was little or no motion to enable them to sense the ship's lack of stability.

The Board found that mistakes had been made in (1) not ascertaining the condition of Nos. 13 and 14 oil fuel tanks, (2) in abandoning the attempt to pump out the wardroom flat in favour of pumping out water from the mining deck and (3) in not jettisoning all possible top weight and lowering the boats. The Board also found that all possible measures to save life were taken, except for (1) not lowering boats or getting floats out and (2) not keeping the ship's company who were not employed on vital work elsewhere on the upper deck.

The Board considered that the ship's officers had a made grave error of judgment in believing the ship was in a safe condition, placing responsibility primarily on Commander Hims but finding that Captain Friedberger shared responsibility, as he had arrived at the same conclusion as Commander Hims after an independent appreciation of the situation. Captain Friedberger and the ship's officers were exonerated from responsibility both for the damage to the ship and for the loss of their ship, as it was improbable she could have been saved; nor were they held to bear moral responsibility for the heavy loss of life, as their failure to lower boats or keep most of the ship's company on the upper deck was due to their belief that the ship was absolutely safe and that they would soon be taken in tow. The report of the board was passed along to the Admiralty and elicited a number of comments, including the observation that similar damage would not have had that effect on a destroyer, as the water would have run off the upper deck and that the absence of light would have contributed to the difficulty of appreciating the situation.

After receiving the report of the Board of Enquiry, the Admiralty issued some the findings to the commanding officers of the *Abdiel* and the *Manxman*, with a letter giving guidance on special steps to the be taken to prevent flooding of the mining deck in the event of damage,[37] such as counterflooding compartments low down in the ship to correct trim and jettisoning top weight. Separately, the Admiralty also approved an increase in the complements of certain ships, including the *Abdiel*s, to augment their damage control parties.

In July of 1943, an Admiralty officer with an undecipherable signature took the trouble to write to Captain Friedberger about the loss of his ship. After opening with 'You probably thought I forgot all about this. I hadn't but it has taken a long time to get the information', he enclosed a report on the loss of the *Welshman* and went on to explain the difference between the loss of the *Welshman* and the survival of the *Manxman* a few months before. The *Manxman* had suffered more flooding but little loss of waterplane area, while the *Welshman* had suffered little flooding but much loss of waterplane area. (The 'waterplane' is the horizontal plane that passes through a floating ship on a level with the waterline.) The *Manxman* had actually gained stability because she listed away from the torpedo damage. The writer evidently thought he had done enough and unceremoniously ended the letter. He might have gone further and pointed out that Admiralty's conclusion that the *Manxman* had only heeled to starboard because of shifted machinery and could hardly have been saved if she had heeled to port, the side of the torpedo hit, a conclusion Captain Friedberger was probably not aware of.

The findings of the Board of Inquiry could have been harsher on the *Welshman*'s officers, but the conclusion of grave errors was harsh enough. It also smacks of being wise after the event. It is easy to conclude after a ship has sunk that she was always in danger of sinking and in fact the Board held that the ship's officers' 'grave error of judgment' in thinking their ship safe was proved by the foundering of the ship. Surely it is of some importance that it did not seem so to the men on the spot, to the ship's Commanding Officer, to Captain Simpson, an experienced mariner, or to the ship's Engineering Officer.

Some aspects of the *Welshman*'s loss are a mystery, such as which of the four torpedoes caused her damage, which type of torpedo exploder pistol was in use and what caused the other two torpedoes to explode. With the information at hand, it is almost impossible to resolve those questions. In the end, however, what mattered was that one of *U-617*'s torpedoes exploded under the *Welshman*'s stern and caused her very serious damage.

It is more difficult to explain exactly how the torpedo damage caused the loss of the ship, especially when she seemed to all to be in a seaworthy condition. Only two witnesses at the inquiry reported hearing sounds before the lurch to starboard; an RAF passenger told Commander Hims he heard a large rush of air just as the ship started to move over and a leading seaman heard a noise 'like two waves breaking on a beach and it came from aft. It sounded as though it was running completely along the mining deck from aft'. The question is what those noises signified.

There were several theories. The board of inquiry concluded that during the whole time

the ship was afloat the stern was getting lower in the water due to gradual flooding of the compartments forward of Station 150, evidently referring to the wardroom flat and the gearing compartment, even though the testimony they had heard minimised the amount of flooding in those compartments.

Captain Friedberger did not offer a theory, but in his report he mentioned that after the survivors reached Alexandria, he saw Commander Hims and asked for this theory regarding the suddenness of the lurch and the sinking and whether bulkheads had given away. Hims replied that 'unfortunately the stern had sunk sufficiently to allow water to run from the riven storerooms on the to the mining deck on the starboard side; nothing could prevent this'. Captain Friedberger continued, 'The result was the worst situation as regards stability since a large quantity of fresh water was thus enclosed between the ship's side and the engine and boiler-room casings'.

At the board of inquiry, Commander Hims was asked what theory he had to account for the sudden increase in heel and he elaborated on what he had told Captain Friedberger.

> I think it must have been something of this nature. The after bulk head [*sic*] of the pom-pom magazine was water-tight to begin with, but finally split or failed in some manner, causing the magazine to flood and the aft end of the ship to settle lower in the water, thus allowing water to flow through the hole in the Mining Deck and accumulate on the Starboard side. The very slight movement on the surface could have been sufficient to cause the water to lop over and every drop that went over increased the list and the draught and consequently the amount flowing.

Nothing can be proven either way, but Commander Hims' theory seems more plausible than the Board's, as the sudden failing of the bulkhead by the pom-pom magazine seems the sort of event that would account for the sudden lurch to starboard and the consequent sinking of the ship. The ship's officers had no reason to think that the bulkhead next to the pom-pom magazine was in danger and in any event could have done little to prevent its failing. Thus they

The *Abdiel* off Sicily, July 1943. (Author's collection)

The *Abdiel* in a rare moment at rest. (Imperial War Museum FL 19)

were hardly guilty of a 'grave error in judgment'.

What is not in doubt is that the *Welshman* was the victim of a well-executed attack. Captain Simpson, a professional but not necessarily impartial observer, gave his opinion that the attack was 'certainly a good one, but under the conditions of light not exceptional'. He believed the U-boat might have been assisted by sighting the *Welshman* against the western sunset and noted the U-boat would have been guided by the ship's bow wave. The Admiralty Anti-Submarine Warfare department was more generous, noting that the *Welshman* was a difficult target, zig-

zagging at 25 knots and that it was very rare for a U-boat to succeed in hitting such a difficult target so effectively.

* * *

Finally, it was the turn of the *Abdiel* to fall on hard times and that at the time of the Allies' seeming triumph in the Mediterranean. After the surrender of Sicily, Mussolini's government fell and was replaced by the King with Marshal Badoglio, who began secretly negotiating terms with the Allies. Once terms were agreed upon,

the Allies planned Operation 'Slapstick' to secure the Italian naval base at Taranto, hoping it would be unopposed, if not assisted, by the Italians.

The *Abdiel* was ordered to Bizerta to pick up paratroopers from the British First Airborne Division, including the 6th (Royal Welch) Battalion of the Parachute Regiment, along with 6pdr anti-tank guns, jeeps, motorcycles, bicycles and ammunition. She became part of Force Z, which included the battleships *Howe* and *King George V*, the cruisers *Aurora*, *Penelope*, *Sirius* and *Dido*, the American cruiser *Boise* and the 14th Destroyer Flotilla.

Informed that their destination was Taranto, some in the *Abdiel* were sceptical. Lieutenant Robertson recalled, 'As far as we simple sailors knew, Taranto was deep in enemy territory and the whole operation seemed to be absolutely suicidal, but when you are ordered to go you go, like the Charge of the Light Brigade'. In the event, they had an easy passage in a calm sea with no enemy interference.[38]

Force Z reached Taranto on the afternoon of 9 September, just as an Italian force consisting of the battleships *Andrea Doria* and *Caio Duilio*, the light cruisers *Luigi Cadorna* and *Scipione Africano* and the destroyer *Nicoloso Da Recco*[39] sailed from Taranto. The *Scipione Africano* sailed on its own on a special mission, while the rest sailed for Malta, accompanied by the *King George V*. Attacked unsuccessfully by German bombers at 18.56,[40] they made it to Malta safely. The main Italian fleet was not so fortunate. After sailing from La Spezia, German bombers sank its flagship, the battleship *Roma*, with radio-controlled bombs, but the rest made it to Malta.

After passing the Italian force, Force Z proceeded up the Taranto swept channel and

arrived safely at Taranto at 19.45 on the 9th. Still loaded with paratroopers and their gear, the *Abdiel* anchored near the Castel San Angelo in the Mar Grande, the large outer harbour at Taranto, in 12 fathoms of water. Unsure of Italian intentions, Captain Orr-Ewing posted six lookouts to watch for human torpedoes.[41] Later that night, a signal was received from the *Howe* ordering the *Abdiel* to move at 05.00 and proceed alongside a jetty close to the Castel to disembark her military cargo.[42] She would never make that move.

Shortly after midnight, at 00.15 on 10 September 1943, a tremendous explosion occurred under the *Abdiel*, followed by a violent whipping of the ship. The force of the explosion lifted the 2pdr pom-pom off its mounting, to disappear in the direction of the quarterdeck. The ship quickly listed to port and broke in two, about by the wardroom aft of the third funnel. The lights went out and then the emergency lights went on briefly before going out. The *Abdiel* sank within just two minutes, though her two ends stayed afloat, each at a steep angle, a little longer before they disappeared.

Many British and Italian boats quickly came to rescue survivors in the water. Captain Orr-Ewing was a survivor, but six officers (fully half the ship's officers) and forty-two ratings were lost from the *Abdiel*'s company. Worse still, Colonel Goodwin and about 120 paratroopers were lost out of the 435 embarked, some of whom may have been in full gear. All of their anti-tank guns, jeeps and bicycles went to the bottom.

Every survivor would have had quite a tale. Captain Orr-Ewing probably owed his life to his sleeping in his sea cabin, having given his usual cabin to the commanding officer of the paratroopers.[43] It was nearly midnight when

The *Abdiel* on the way to Taranto. (Imperial War Museum Film ADM 465)

The Italian fast light cruiser *Scipione Africano* in April 1943. (E Bagnasco Collection via M Brescia)

Lieutenant William Alastair Robertson. (Catherine Hamilton née Robertson)

Lieutenant Robertson was about to go aft to the wardroom when he noticed his pillow and blanket on the settee in the charthouse. With sleep so pressing, he thought,

'Why go all the way aft, I'd better stay here'. So I did just that, though I had never before slept in the charthouse with the ship at anchor and almost as soon as I had lain down I was wrapped in the arms of Morpheus. The next thing I knew was that I was halfway off the settee sliding on to the deck and the ship was shaking violently with an increasing list to port: then the lights went out. I thought 'what the hell now' and dashed up to the bridge. Looking aft it seemed to me that the whole after part of the ship beyond the third funnel had disappeared. The funnels themselves, now leaning at an acute angle, were shrouded in a pall of white steam and the list to port was rapidly increasing. Obviously we were finished though by what means was a mystery. Through the steam I saw some men on the upper deck and shouted to them to abandon ship, then it occurred to me that I had

better do the same. I was determined though not to go over the side without my old Fleet Air Arm 'Mae West' which I kept in the charthouse, acting as a second pillow, for just such a purpose. Back to the charthouse then but just as I was grabbing the Mae West the sliding door, helped by the heavy list, slammed shut. For a moment I had difficulty opening it and thought 'God, this is the end', but then it yielded to an extra heavy push and I was out in double quick time and over the high side of the bridge where it was a gentle slide down the normally vertical plating to the water's edge. I fastened on Mae West and swam away, apparently the last to leave the bridge. Looking back in the dim starlight I could see poor *Abdiel* broken in two and heeled right over, the bottom plating visible through occasional gaps in the cloud of steam rising from the hull. Having plenty of buoyancy, thanks to Mae, I had no difficulty in getting some distance from the wreck in case the boilers should explode.

Lieutenant Robertson had made it safely into the water, but his night was far from over.

Lieutenant Hodges had just finished duty as the Office of the Watch and was on the ship's main deck when 'there was an ominous roar and a heaving and shaking under my feet'. He recalled remembering his duty and 'called to all and sundry to inflate life belts and get to the ship's side'. He had no lifebelt, but 'always wore a seaman's knife and was able to cut loose some Carley floats; then a minute later the ship rolled over and sank'. Once in the water, he recalled, 'It was dreadful. I tried to pull myself together, being full of terror lest the Carley float indicators burning in the oil-covered water should set the fuel alight and engulf us. Indeed this time was full of horror, with men struggling to stay alive and the scene stayed with me for a very long time afterwards'.[44]

Alastair Robertson was one of those men in the water and after helping a struggling junior signalman was picked up by one of the Carley floats. Once on board, he noticed one of the ship's men 'moaning and nearly unconscious and, as I could see, badly injured. By sheer good luck I still had my morphia phial, issued only to officers, in my breast pocket and I promptly gave him the full dose. It worked miraculously: almost at once his groans ceased and he went to sleep'. The men in the float had no sooner started paddling for shore when 'an Italian hospital boat or rather a boat with an Italian flag and a red cross on its funnel, came towards us'. Robertson was amazed to see such an improbable craft, the 127-ton *Marechiaro*, but was relieved to put the wounded man on board her. Robertson later learned that the man made a good recovery in an Italian hospital though he had had a foot amputated.

Both Hodges and Robertson were picked up and were put aboard the battleship *Howe*. They were given a chance to scrub off the oil they had encountered in the water and were provided with some makeshift clothing and then were given an opportunity to sleep. It took Robertson a while to fall asleep; he was worried about the man who had been put aboard the Italian hospital ship and wondered who else could have survived the sinking, especially from the after part of the ship. Then,

> inevitably I wondered by what mysterious chance had I decided to sleep in the charthouse and not in my cabin . . . never before had I slept in the charthouse with the ship at anchor. Why did I choose to do it on this one occasion and so undoubtedly save my life? Is there really 'a Divinity that shapes our ends, rough-hew them how we will?' Those sombre thoughts kept me awake for a long time, but eventually I must have dozed off because I awoke to find *Howe* underway.

When Robertson awoke, he was delighted to discover Geoffrey Hodges. Some of the *Abdiel*'s survivors held an emotional farewell on the *Howe* before they had to go their separate ways. Hodges recalled that they were intensely proud of the splendid record of *Abdiel* and at the same time broken-hearted at the loss of shipmates and friends.[45]

The *Howe* delivered Hodges and Robertson to Malta the next day. From the cable office in Valletta, they sent cables home. Alastair Robertson's cable to his mother read simply,

'Have been sunk. Am all right. Love Al'. He thought that anything more would have infringed censorship.

Robertson and Hodges and the rest of the survivors had lost just about everything they had. When divers were sent down to the *Abdiel* to recover her confidential materials, they recovered Captain Orr-Ewing's binoculars as well as the ship's bell. Lieutenant Hodges had lost a superb olive-wood walking stick with a carved lion's head handle that had been given to him by an Arab friend named Menassa who was the foreman at the Armament Depot at Haifa. When Menassa learned that Hodges had survived the sinking of the *Abdiel*, he procured a similar walking stick and had it sent to Hodges.[46] It survives to this day.

While it was clear enough that the *Abdiel* had detonated a mine, the reason for the presence of the mine in the harbour did not become clear for some time. The Germans had correctly suspected that the Italians were negotiating with the Allies and prepared Operation 'Achse' (Axis) to deal with an Italian surrender. As part of the plan, S-boats *S 61* and *S 54* and the ferry barge *F 478* were sent to lay mines at the naval base at Taranto to prevent Italian warships from surrendering to the Allies. The *S 54* was under the command of *Oberleutnant zur See* Klaus-Degenhard Schmidt, *S–61* under *Bootsmaat* Friedel Blomber and *F–478* under *Kapitänleutnant* Winkler.[47]

The *S 61* and *S 54* were *Schnellboote* of the *S 30* class and both had taken part in the unsuccessful stalking of the *Welshman* off Malta on 10 May 1942. The *F 478* was a heavily-armed, 155-ton Type C2 ferry barge, a *Marinefährprahm* or 'MFP' for short. She was built in 1942 by the Cantieri Navali Riuniti at Palermo and, powered by diesel engines, could make 10.5 knots.[48]

At 01.15 on 9 September, the three units received the code word *Ernte* – 'harvest' – to execute their part of Operation Achse and at 03.00 the little German flotilla formed up in the Mar Piccolo at Taranto and transited the canal into the Mar Grande.[49] Once in the Mar Grande, the *F 478* laid twenty-two TMB mines – called 'GS' by the British[50] – each one fitted with 24-hour arming delays and set for two to four actuations. The S-boats laid four mines each at the entrance to the harbour.[51]

This minelaying operation was not as easy

The German ferry barge *MFP 478,* whose mines sank the *Abdiel.* (E Bagnasco Collection)

as it might sound, as each unit had an Italian officer on board. To hide the minelaying from Italian eyes, each time a mine was dropped a German seaman ducked down on all fours under a sack in order to impersonate the contours of a mine in the darkness.[52] The ruse worked and the German flotilla passed through the harbour's outer defences at 04.30. Their mission and their escape from Taranto complete, the German craft sailed into the Gulf of Taranto. What happened to their Italian passengers is unclear.

The little flotilla had not gotten far when, on the afternoon of the 10th, they sighted the cruiser *Scipione Africano.* The Germans could not know that this particular cruiser had some experience with small torpedo boats, having dispatched the British *MTB 316* in the Strait of Messina on 17 July 1943. To make a quick getaway from the well-armed cruiser, at 14.30 the Germans scuttled the slow *F 478*[53] after taking its crew off. The *Scipione Africano* took no notice of them and sailed on to rendezvous with the corvette *Baionetta,* which was on a rather important errand to Pescara, to transport King Victor Emmanuel III and Marshal Badoglio away from the Germans to Brindisi.[54]

Relieved of the *F 478,* the two S-boats continued their adventure, no doubt unaware of their unintended success at Taranto. They were supposed to have received orders by radio to try to head for Patras in Greece, but instead they sailed up the Adriatic. Taking advantage of the chaos of the moment, they went on something of a rampage, first sinking the Italian gunboat *Aurora* off Ancona on 11 September, then capturing the transport *Leopardi,* with 700 troops aboard and finally sinking the destroyer *Quintino Sella,* before continuing on to Venice.[55] Once there, through bluff and threat Schmidt and the little *S 54* forced the city to surrender. After their epic voyage, their war continued. The *S 54* met a violent end similar to the *Abdiel*'s, striking a mine and sinking off Salonika on 31 October 1944,[56] but *S 61* survived to surrender at the end of the war.[57]

Meanwhile, Schmidt's intended target, the Italian fleet, indeed sailed from Taranto to surrender, but it eluded the as-yet unarmed mines. The mines must have armed themselves just after midnight on the 10th and just a few minutes later the *Abdiel* must have swung across one of them the requisite number of times before it exploded, with its monstrous charge of 1220lbs.[58] Whether the mine that sank her was set as a magnetic mine or as an acoustic one is not clear, but the *Abdiel* had switched off her degaussing gear some four hours before,[59] depriving her of any protection against magnetic mines. If the mine was an acoustic one, the degaussing gear would have been useless even if it had been turned on.

With tragic irony, the first real fast minelayer was done in by a mine, her own stock in trade. The Admiralty officially announced the loss of the *Abdiel* on 12 October 1943,[60] and the names of her dead and those missing and presumed killed were listed in *The Times* on 26 October 1943, their next-of-kin having already been notified that the ship in which their men were serving had been lost through enemy action.[61]

CHAPTER 13

THE REPEAT *ABDIELS* TAKE SHAPE, 1941–1943

ON 11 September 1943, the Royal Navy was fresh out of operational fast minelayers. More, however, were on the way. Before the first *Abdiel* had even been completed, the Admiralty considered the possibility of building more of them. The ships would be formally known as the 'Repeat *Abdiel*s'. Two more ships were to be built and both were ordered under the 1941 shipbuilding programme, the *Ariadne* on 19 April 1941 and the *Apollo* on 28 May,[1] just as the first four ships of the class approaching completion.

After the third and fourth *Abdiel*s had been named after the Isle of Man and Wales, there was no more of this business of naming the ships after places where British subjects actually lived. Instead, the Admiralty reverted to naming fast minelayers after Great War minelayers, which had been named after mythological figures.

As part of the design process for the Repeat *Abdiel*s, in late 1941 and early 1942 the opinions of the commanding officers of the *Abdiel*, *Manxman* and *Welshman* were sought and received, though only the comments and suggestions of Captains Dickson and Friedberger and the Director of Naval Construction's responses have survived. Those comments and suggestions reveal the complexity of a warship of the day, covering such subjects as the adequacy of ventilation, blackout arrangements and light-tightness of the superstructure, the uselessness of the pom-pom director, the placement of bollards for berthing, the subdivision of the potato locker for stowing other vegetables, the location of flour storage and many more.

The comments and suggestions also reveal that the first four ships were not quite perfect and that the three commanding officers were not quite unanimous in their opinions of their ships. Some of the suggestions were incorporated into the Repeat *Abdiel*s, but many were not, either because the existing design was thought adequate, the suggestions had already been incorporated into the design or it was thought impossible to incorporate the suggestions because of space or weight limitations, e.g., no additional power boat. It was not even possible to mount ladders at a lesser angle even though it seemed 'Hostilities Only' seamen frequently fell off ladders at sea.

The design of the Repeat *Abdiel*s differed from the first four *Abdiel*s in several important ways. Most noticeably, the twin 4in gun 'B' mount forward of the bridge was omitted, leaving the 'A' twin forward and the 'Y' mount aft, with 250 rounds per gun. The quadruple pom-pom on the bandstand aft of the third funnel was replaced by two radar-equipped Mk IV twin 40mm mounts designed by the Dutch firm Hazemeyer, one to port and one to starboard on the after superstructure, with a normal rate of fire of 120 rounds per minute.

A legend in the ships' cover shows a third Hazemeyer mount in place of 'B' twin 4in mount in the first four *Abdiel*s and seven single 20mm guns, but, in the end, just the two Hazemeyer mounts were fitted, no single 20mm guns were fitted and five twin Mk V powered 20mm Oerlikon gun mounts were fitted, one in place of 'B' 4in mount, two in the bridge wings, two on what had been in the first four ships a searchlight platform between the second and third funnels and one on the aft end of the after superstructure.

The new ships were equipped with more advanced radar sets, Types 291 and 272 in the *Ariadne* and Types 291 and 276 in the *Apollo* to augment the Type 285 on the main director.[2] The searchlights amidships were omitted, perhaps because radar had made them unnecessary and perhaps because in the first four ships they were constantly covered by spray and were very unreliable.[3] The pom-pom director was deleted, either because it was useless or because the Hazemeyer mounts had no need of it.

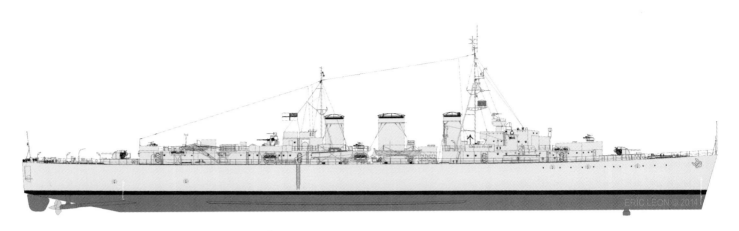

Somewhat noticeably, the mainmast was
stepped closer to the third funnel. Many changes
were not so noticeable. A second set of taut wire
measuring gear was to be fitted. The after
deckhouse was extended forward to the third
funnel. The locations of the surface and aircraft
lookouts positions were improved. Some scuttles
were deleted and escape scuttles added forward.
The two diesel dynamos were resited into
different compartments. The protective plating
on the bridge screen was increased from 10lbs to
15lbs. Additional pillars and girders were fitted to
strengthen the forecastle deck. The bakery was
enlarged, but, alas, there was no space for a
dough mixer.

Most importantly, the Repeat *Abdiel*s were
fitted with wing tanks in the boiler rooms to
store an additional 239 tons of oil fuel (for a total
of 830 tons) to increase their range to 5800 miles
at 15 knots. The storage of diesel fuel was
reduced by 6 tons, to 52 tons.[4] Their standard
displacement was designed to increase to 2810
tons and their deep displacement to 3960 tons,
giving them a designed speed of 39 knots in
standard condition and 34 knots in deep
condition. On trials, the *Ariadne* achieved a
mean speed of 34.7 knots and the *Apollo* 35.3
knots.[5]

Fortuitously for the Royal Navy, the Repeat
*Abdiel*s began to complete shortly after the loss
of the *Abdiel*, the last of the first four fast
minelayers to be sunk or damaged and put out of
action. By then, the tide of war had turned and
the nature of the war had changed dramatically
and the Repeat *Abdiel*s would have very different
wars from the first four.

CHAPTER 14

THE *ARIADNE* COMPLETES AND SHOWS THE FLAG IN THE PACIFIC, 1943–1945

THE *Ariadne,* the fifth ship of the class to complete and the first Repeat *Abdiel*, operated in European waters at the beginning and end of her career but should be best remembered for being the sole representative of the Royal Navy in the Pacific Theatre in 1944. She was the ninth Royal Navy warship to bear the name of the daughter of King Minos of Crete and the wife of Dionysus (Bacchus), who provided her with a crown that was later set among the stars. Ariadne was known for providing Theseus with a thread to guide him through the Cretan Labyrinth. The fast minelayer was also named after a large protected cruiser of that name that was converted into a minelayer in 1917. That did not last long, as she was torpedoed and sunk by the German submarine *UC-65* off Beachy Head on 26 July of the same year.[1]

The *Ariadne* was built by Alexander Stephen & Sons on the River Clyde, at the same yard where the *Manxman* was built. She was laid down on 15 November 1941, launched by her future commanding officer's wife, Reta, Lady Ashbourne, on 16 February 1943 and completed on 9 October 1943.[2] She was manned out of Devonport and was allotted the pennant number M 65. Her crest bore a garland of vines with a crown and stars and her motto was 'Swift and fearless', not translated into Latin.[3] Upon completion, she was painted up in a three-colour camouflage scheme.

The *Ariadne*'s first commanding officer was Captain Lord Ashbourne, who was born Edward Russell Gibson on 1 June 1901 and later took the title of the 3rd Baron Ashbourne, of Ashbourne, County Meath. He has been described as tall, good-looking, imperturbable, conscientious and hardworking. In his youth, he was keen on rowing and water polo.[4] He was educated at the Royal Naval College, Osborne, at the Royal Naval College, Dartmouth and at Gonville and Caius College, Cambridge University. In 1917–18, he served as a midshipman in the dreadnought battleships *Superb*, *Dreadnought* and *Monarch*. After the war, he switched to submarines and commanded the *H48* and the *Pandora*. When the Second World War broke out, he was on the staff of Admiral Andrew Cunningham, the C-in-C of the Mediterranean Fleet. He was promoted to Captain in 1939. Before becoming the commanding officer of the *Ariadne*, he took part in the invasion of Sicily in 1943 as a sector commander and that year was awarded the Distinguished Service Order.

On 6 December 1943, the *Ariadne* left Liverpool after completing some repairs, carrying Christmas mail for service personnel in the Mediterranean and the Middle East. She proceeded to cruise the Mediterranean on her appointed errands, departing Algiers on 12 December, arrived at Naples on the 15th and then proceeded to Malta. She then spent

The *Ariadne* as completed. (Barry Gibson)

Christmas Day at Gibraltar and departed the next day for the UK.[5]

While homeward-bound from the Mediterranean, on 27 December the *Ariadne* joined the hunt to intercept the German blockade-runner *Alstarufer*, which in the end was sunk by Coastal Command aircraft off Cape Finisterre the same day.[6] The next day the cruisers *Enterprise* and *Glasgow* chased down the German destroyers and torpedo boats that had sortied to escort the *Alstarufer* in and sank several of them. The *Ariadne* arrived at Plymouth without further ado on 30 December.[7]

While the *Ariadne* was innocently delivering mail to the Mediterranean and chasing German blockade runners, a very different kind of employment for her was being discussed elsewhere, in Washington, London and even Cairo. The idea seems to have originated with the British Admiralty Delegation in Washington[8] – which, yes, went by the unfortunate acronym 'BAD' – in response to an American inquiry about British mine equipment, 'sprockets' and 'grapnels', devices that were used to thwart enemy sweeping of their mines.[9]

The American inquiry may have been prompted by their recent experience with minelaying in the Solomon Islands. In May 1943, a minefield laid by three old American flush-decked destroyer-minelayers off the northwestern entrance to Kula Gulf had been swept up by the Japanese within 24 hours. That and a series of mishaps suffered by the covering force of cruisers and destroyers, caused Admiral Nimitz to doubt the risks were worth the results. The week before, however, a force comprised of the destroyer *Radford* and the converted flush-decked destroyer-minelayers *Gamble*, *Preble* and *Breese* laid a minefield in the Blackett Strait that snared a Japanese destroyer force. The destroyer *Kuroshio* was sunk outright and two more destroyers, the *Kagero* and *Oyashio*, were damaged by mines and were soon sunk by American bombers.[10] Prior to that, in February 1943, just as the Japanese began to evacuate Guadalcanal, three destroyer-minelayers laid mines off the island that so damaged the destroyer *Makigumo* that she had to be scuttled.[11]

American interest in offensive minelaying eventually rose, inspired by their recent successes in the Solomons and perhaps by the successes of British fast minelayers in the

Mediterranean in late 1942 and early 1943. On 16 December 1942, Lieutenant-Commander John Kremer, Jr. USN, inspected the *Manxman* at Oran to see if she could carry US mines. On mid-1944 the Americans finally ordered twelve 2200-ton *Allen M Sumner* class destroyers then under construction to be converted to fast minelayers – 'DMs' – capable of carrying 120 mines.[12] At the same time, however, the Americans must have realised they needed British help, at least on anti-sweeping devices; hence their inquiry to the BAD.

After the American inquiry, on 14 November 1943, the BAD's head, Admiral Sir Percy Noble, sent a signal to the Admiralty for Admiral Andrew Cunningham, by then the First Sea Lord and Chief of the Naval Staff, as Admiral Dudley Pound had very recently died. The signal read as follows:

1. it has come to my attention that an Officer of the Staff of C-in-C Pacific [Admiral Chester Nimitz] in whose area interest in minelaying activities is much on the increase has recently arrived in Washington and is stressing the use of moored mines that will be more difficult to sweep than the mark 6 US mine. The USA proposal is to use our sprocket and grapnel with the mark 6 mine which my advisors do not consider a satisfactory solution.

2. It is possible that since no modern US moored mine is designed to carry anti-sweeping devices they might consider using British mines.

3. I understand that it is intended to lay up the British First Minelaying Squadron in the immediate future.

4. Using the fact cited in paragraph 3 as a basis for the proposal it is suggested that an offer might be made to the Navy Department of this Squadron for use in any area they may deem desirable.

5. It is desired to emphasise that no indication should be given of our knowledge that the present USA moored mine is unsatisfactory.

6. While doubtful whether such an offer would be accepted the fact that it had been made might prove of value in the future. The advantages that might be

gained if the offer is accepted need no emphasis.

7. Our opinion is that Americans might refuse offer owing to lack of speed of First Minelaying Squadron. If a fast minelayer happened to be available they would probably jump at it.

Admiral Noble's signal incited a lively discussion within the Admiralty. Captain John Cowie, the Admiralty's mining expert, minuted a few days later at some length:

1. The US Mark 6 is a narrow-guage [*sic*] mine developed in the last war. D.T.M. [Director of Torpedoes and Mining] will no doubt confirm that the incorporation of British sprockets and grapnels would not be satisfactory.

2. American designers, in common with many of their minelaying staff officers, are convinced that they will never get a satisfactory moored mine unless they change to broad guage [*sic*] and anything which serves to point the superiority of the latter will be to the ultimate benefit of the United Nations.

3. Ships of the First Minelaying Squadron would be of no value for offensive purposes – the Americans might just as well use the Australian 'BUNGAREE' (11 knots – 480 mines). They would moreover have to be American manned and we might lose them altogether.

4. The possible alternatives are: -
'ADVENTURE'
(a) Too slow for offensive operations. [Here someone wrote in 'Also proposed for scrapping'.]
(b) Due for long refit.
'ARIADNE'
(a) Tentatively earmarked for minelaying in connection with 'OVERLORD', but 'APOLLO' should be available in time if required.
(b) Not required by C. in C. Eastern Fleet until we have gained a foothold on Eastern side of Indian Ocean.
'TEVIOT BANK'
(a) No more suitable than BUNGAREE (12 knots – 280 mines).

(b) Proposal to revert to trade has been made to C. in C. Eastern Fleet. [Someone interlineated, 'He has now agreed'.]

5. The advantages of placing 'ARIADNE' at the disposal of the Americans are:
(a) She is suitable.
(b) She can be spared.
(c) She would be usefully employed and would gain valuable experience.
(d) She would establish a liaison [on] minelaying questions and might have an influence on American minelayer design and equipment.

6. Suitable British mines are available in Australia. Sprockets and grapnels would have to be sent from Ceylon or the U.K.

A few days later the office of the Director of Torpedoes and Mining suggested that it might be too categorical to state that British grapnels and sprockets could not be used with American mines and raised another consideration, whether the endurance of the *Ariadne* was suitable for this service. In reply, Captain Robert Dickson of the Plans Department minuted on 20 November, 'The limited endurance of these ships is always their handicap, but I don't think this is an insuperable objection to the proposed employment of *Ariadne*'. Dickson would know something about this, as he had commanded the *Manxman* in the Atlantic and in the Indian Ocean. He may not have been aware that the *Ariadne* had been designed with greater endurance than the *Manxman* and her sisters.

Another hitch in the *Ariadne*'s proposed deployment to the Pacific arose from an unlikely direction, the crisis in manpower to fill the needs of the Royal Navy, a crisis caused by an island nation of only 45 million people having to fight a world war for four years. A merciless review at the end of 1943 had resulted in some drastic measures, including laying up or reduction to 'care and maintenance' status a number of older battleships, cruisers and destroyers.[13] A minute on 20 November suggested that the proposal to lend the *Ariadne* should be carefully considered from the manpower point of view and stated, 'As a result of the recent decision on the manpower to be made available to the Navy, drastic economies of many kinds will have to be made'.

The minute went on to suggest that because

the Royal Navy was asking the Canadians to provide crews for British vessels and might have to ask the Americans to allow Canadian manning of ships provided under Lend-Lease, that the offer of the *Ariadne* with a British crew seemed luxurious and might strike the Americans and Canadians as inconsistent with British representations of a manpower shortage. The minute continued:

> I understand that it has not been definitively decided whether a minelayer will be required for use in OVERLORD and that it is intended, if a crew cannot be found for APOLLO when she completes early next year, to lay her up with a care and maintenance party. As ARIADNE is said not to be required by us until towards the end of next year, it appears that if she were not lent to the Americans, she, also, might be laid up and the majority of her crew be made available for one of the urgent requirements which we shall be faced.

This minute is testimony to the gravity of the manning crisis in the Royal Navy – or at least the way it was perceived at the time in the Admiralty – and to the depths to which the perceived need for fast minelayers had fallen. Britain was desperately short of manpower after years of war and the war situation in Europe and the Mediterranean at that time – after the surrender of Italy and months before the invasion of France – did not demand their unique talents.

The same minute continued and concluded, 'If, however, it is felt that the undoubted advantages to be gained from lending the ARIADNE to the United States for a period justify the loan in spite of these considerations, it suggested that a draft signal to the BAD be amended to read' that the Royal Navy would be ready to lend the *Ariadne* for temporary service with the US Fleet under certain conditions.

The deployment to the Pacific seemed to be quashed in a minute on 21 November that agreed that the loan of the *Ariadne* is 'a luxury we cannot afford', rejected the possibility of loaning her to be manned by the Americans and recommended that the draft signal be revised to state, 'No fast minelayer can be offered in view of our acute manning situation, which will probably necessitate placing ARIADNE and, later, APOLLO, in care and maintenance [i.e., laying them up] until required to work with the Eastern Fleet'. A handwritten note below stated, 'After discussion with First Lord [i.e., A V Alexander], this question was referred to First Sea Lord for discussion at Sextant. . .'.

As it happened Admiral Cunningham was then attending the 'Sextant' Conference, the latest in a succession of conferences of Allied leaders that took place in Cairo and included President Roosevelt, Prime Minister Churchill and Generalissimo Chiang Kai-shek of the Republic of China and that was to decide Allied policy toward Japan. Cunningham was to see Admiral Ernest J King there.

The Vice Chief of the Naval Staff put the matter to Cunningham in a signal of 25 November, which recited the original BAD signal of 14 November, repeated the lack of alternatives to the *Ariadne* and the disadvantages of loaning the *Ariadne,* but also stated, 'On the other hand, it will give us experience which will be of great value later and should encourage the Americans to improve their minelaying equipment'. He went on to say that

> the decision should depend on the operational use to which ARIADNE should be put in the Pacific. If this is likely to be of great value and add appreciably to war effort against Japan I suggest you should offer ship to Admiral King. Need for fast minelayer in OVERLORD should be reviewed when APOLLO is completed. At present her use is not considered essential. With present plans unlikely ARIADNE will be required for use in S.E.A.C. [South East Asia Command] before Autumn 1944.

Finally, he mentioned that the First Lord 'is however very reluctant to loan ship to Americans since he foresees many uses to which we may put ship other than for minelaying'.

In the end, the misgivings felt by some in the Admiralty and the reluctance of the First Lord proved no obstacle to Admiral Cunningham. He went ahead and offered the *Ariadne* to Admiral King, formalising the offer in a letter of 3 December 1943. The offer was soon accepted. On

15 December, the American Admiral G B Brown, the Chief of Staff to Admiral Harold Stark, the Commander of US Naval Forces in Europe (COMNAVEU) in London, informed the Admiralty that CominCh – Admiral King – had sent a secret despatch, the substance of which was:

> Sir Andrew Cunningham, in a letter dated 3 December to CominCh, stated he would be grateful if I would let him know whether H.M.S. ARIADNE (Fast Minelayer) would be of any assistance in the Pacific. Say to the First Sea Lord that ARIADNE can be profitably employed in the South Pacific. If his decision is to place ARIADNE under US operational control resolve with the Admiralty problem of supplying British mines to SOPAC Area or alternatively adapting ARIADNE to lay US mines. Advise estimated date ship may be sailed to US and decisions reached.

The Admiralty replied the next day, informing Admiral Brown that the *Ariadne* was in the Mediterranean and that the Admiralty estimated it would be mid-February before she could sail for the Pacific.

As if the decision were not official enough, on 1 January 1944 the decision to loan the *Ariadne* to the Americans was announced to most of the Admiralty and approval was given for any defects she might have developed to be given priority to enable her to leave by mid-January. The next day, the Admiralty informed Admiral Brown that the *Ariadne* was in hand for defects and that it was hoped the she would sail before the end of January, that she would sail with a full outfit of 160 British Mk XVII mines and that British mine depots in Australia were available for use. He continued, 'She would, of course, be placed under US operational control'. Lastly, he asked which USA port he wished the *Ariadne* to be sailed. On the 7th, Admiral Brown confirmed that Admiral King had requested that she be sailed when ready in late January to Norfolk, Virginia, for further orders.

Meanwhile, on 5 January the Admiralty gave Captain Lord Ashbourne his instructions in a letter. It began, 'I am to inform you that H.M.S. ARIADNE is being placed under the command of the Commander-in-Chief, US Fleet for minelaying operations in the S.W. Pacific and you are to carry out any orders issued by him . . . You will come under [his] operational control . . . on arrival at the first US port you touch'. The letter continued with detailed instructions of what the Captain was to do 'in the event of your receiving an order which in your opinion unnecessarily risks H.M. ship under your command', perhaps revealing a certain lack of trust in the judgment of American naval leadership. The Captain was directed to forward to the Admiralty regular reports of his proceedings and was informed that while under US control the *Ariadne* was to be administered by the Admiralty in Washington. The letter concluded, 'By Command of Their Lordships'.

The letter was likely based on the one sent to Captain Mackintosh of the modern armoured aircraft carrier HMS *Victorious*, which the British had generously transferred to the South Pacific in 1943 when the US Navy was critically short of aircraft carriers. Codenamed 'USS *Robin*', she served with the American aircraft carrier *Saratoga* in the Solomon Islands and returned to Britain a few months later when the crisis had passed. The *Ariadne* was thus not the first Royal Navy warship to serve with the US Navy in the Pacific War, even apart from those that served in the ABDA command during the battle of the Java Sea in 1942, but, like the *Victorious* in 1943, she would be the only fighting ship of the Royal Navy in the Pacific in 1944.

The Admiralty intended to offer the *Ariadne* to the Americans for service in the Pacific until she was required in the British Eastern Fleet, though no actual time limit was placed on the loan. The *Ariadne* would continue to be manned by the Royal Navy and to lay British mines, of which there was a supply in Australia.[14]

Strangely enough, which part of the Pacific the *Ariadne* would serve in became an issue of some importance to the US Navy. The letter of 5 January to Captain Lord Ashbourne referred to minelaying duties in the *S.W.* Pacific. A copy of the letter was provided to the US Navy in London and Admiral Stark pointed out to the Admiralty on 31 January that Admiral King had said the *Ariadne* could be profitably employed in the *South* Pacific. Stark diplomatically but firmly stated, 'Attention is invited to the discrepancy' between King's despatch and the letter to the Captain of the *Ariadne*. The very next day

Admiral Cunningham wrote a letter to Admiral Stark thanking him for his letter and continuing, 'I much regret the error which has been made and am having the matter corrected immediately'. The same day the Admiralty informed Captain Lord Ashbourne of the discrepancy and directed him to amend the letter accordingly.

Perhaps the significance of the difference lies in the fact that, after General Douglas MacArthur's escape from the Philippines to Australia in March 1942, it became necessary to divide up command responsibilities in the Pacific between the General and Admiral Chester W Nimitz, C-in-C of the US Pacific Fleet (CINCPAC). Accordingly, in March 1942 Admiral Nimitz became Commander in Chief, Pacific Ocean Areas (CINCPOA) and General MacArthur became Commander, Southwest Pacific Area (SWPA).[15] Perhaps because under this arrangement General MacArthur had jurisdiction over the Southwest Pacific and Admiral Nimitz had jurisdiction over the South Pacific, the US Navy wanted to make sure it got the first crack at the *Ariadne*.

After all the administrative arrangements had been completed, it was finally time for the *Ariadne* to leave for the Pacific. She completed her repairs at Plymouth and departed for Milford Haven on 16 January.[16] After loading a full complement of mines there, she set sail for America on 20 January 1944. She ran into a severe storm in the North Atlantic between Britain and the Azores, where she was to stop at the port of Horta on the island of Faial to fuel. Driving hard into the storm, she sustained a considerable amount of weather damage. Bill Pye was in the crow's nest during the storm and

thought it was the most thrilling thing he had ever seen – that and seeing hundreds of German bombers attacking the London docks near where he lived on 7 September 1940.

The *Ariadne* sailed from Horta on 24 January bound for Bermuda and then for Norfolk, Virginia. To the *Ariadne*'s crew, Norfolk was like Wonderland, with its plentiful food after their three and a half years of war. After undergoing some repairs at Norfolk, the *Ariadne* picked up a Lieutenant Bailey, USN, who proved very popular with her crew, earning a cheer when he later left the ship. The fast minelayer then passed through the Panama Canal and arrived at Pearl Harbor on 4 March,[17] almost exactly a year after the *Victorious* had first arrived there.

The *Ariadne* arrived in the Pacific at a momentous time; after American forces had spent the end of 1942 and much of 1943 fighting their way up the Solomon Islands from Guadalcanal and Tulagi, at the end of 1943 they had taken most of Bougainville and were breaking into the Central Pacific. Admiral Nimitz's forces from Pearl Harbor took Tarawa and Makin in the Gilbert Islands in November 1943 and then took Kwajalein, Roi, Namur and Eniwetok in the Marshall Islands in January and February 1944. The invasion of Saipan in the Marianas Islands and the battle of the Philippine Sea in June 1944, were imminent. Meanwhile, General MacArthur's forces and his Seventh Fleet were working their way along the north coast of New Guinea and landed at Hollandia in April 1944. They were indeed momentous times, but, in the vast expanses of the Central Pacific, not necessarily the best of times for the employment of a fast minelayer, especially by a

The *Ariadne* in the Pacific from off her starboard bow. (Australian War Memorial 302306)

navy unfamiliar with its unique capabilities.

While at Pearl Harbor, further repairs to the *Ariadne*'s Atlantic weather damage were effected and the twin 20mm mount in her 'B' gun position was replaced by a vastly more powerful American-pattern twin 40mm Bofors mount, with a prominent tub for a US Mk 51 director fitted between the Bofors mount and the ship's charthouse. Less obviously, the shipwrights at Pearl Harbor also constructed a canvas bath for the ship, which was to prove a godsend to her crew in subsequent months in the South Pacific.

As ordered, the Captain began sending monthly reports to the Admiralty on his and the *Ariadne*'s activities.[18] In March and then in July, Captain Lord Ashbourne sent reports back to the Admiralty with his impressions of the United States Navy, addressing such topics as its ships (excellent, about 95 per cent of the Royal Navy's, but very numerous), its decision-making (very fast), its officers (of a lower standard than the Royal Navy's), its enlisted men (very keen, hardworking, well-educated and proud of their Navy), its gunnery (very good), its shiphandling (mediocre), its level of maintenance (very high and very efficient) and the ships' equipment (excellent radar, efficient Action Information Center or CIC and excellent internal communications) and its men's views of the war (little understanding or conception of what Britain faced in Europe or the Indian Ocean or of what it had been through).[19]

Everywhere the Captain went American sailors came aboard the ship ('unasked') simply to see a ship of the Royal Navy and to compare it with their own. The Captain conversed with many American sailors and found them easy to talk to, not in the least self-conscious and always showing the greatest respect. The Captain commented specifically on American friend-liness and hospitality. He reported, 'No one could have made me feel more at home. Anything that I ask for is immediately granted, if it is humanly possible' and that 'My ship has been received with open arms. Everyone has been more than kind and helpful'.

In his reports, Captain Lord Ashbourne may not have shared all of his impressions with the Admiralty; some in the *Ariadne*'s crew somehow formed the impression that he came to have some frustrations with the US Navy, some even sensing his belief that it lacked enough discipline and that its men were overpaid and overdecorated.[20]

The *Ariadne* spent about six weeks at Pearl,[21] at least in part because of the time it took to fit downcomers to the boilers,[22] if not also in part due to the need to figure out what to do with her. In the end, Admiral King informed the Admiralty that because there was no employment for the *Ariadne* in planned operations in the Central Pacific, he was considering transferring her to the US Seventh Fleet, but he first requested Admiralty concurrence, which was quickly given on 20 April. The Seventh Fleet was under General Douglas MacArthur's operational command and under the direct command of US Vice Admiral Thomas Kinkaid. MacArthur would get the *Ariadne* after all.

The *Ariadne* eventually departed Pearl Harbor, heading west in the direction of the shooting. After visits to Brisbane, Sydney and Jervis Bay in Australia, the *Ariadne* returned to Sydney on 1 June and her crew was allowed time ashore there. The men enjoyed the visit very much, even though the bars were closed by the time they made it ashore and they made many friends. Three of the *Ariadne*'s men enjoyed the stay in Sydney a bit too much and 'so forgot themselves', according to their Captain, that they remained there when the ship left. The Captain was informed that the 'prospects of their ultimate recovery' were high.

The *Ariadne* then proceeded back to Brisbane and there her Captain met with Admiral Kinkaid, the C-in-C of the US Seventh Fleet. He described the Admiral as 'most pleasant to me and discussed the war in the South Pacific for some time'. The Captain was astounded when the Admiral declined to visit his ship and only found out later that Admiral Kinkaid made it a policy never to visit ships. Even the Admiral's Mining Officer could not be coaxed aboard for a visit, but finally the Admiral's Flag Lieutenant came down to the ship.

While in Brisbane, the Captain discussed the details of a possible minelaying operation off Wewak, a major Japanese base on the north coast of New Guinea, which had been provisionally arranged the last time he was in Brisbane. The Captain learned that Wewak was defended by at least six coast defence guns, probably of 5in calibre, and that once their

The *Ariadne* in the Pacific from off her starboard quarter. (Australian War Memorial 134469)

locations were determined destroyers would be detailed to deal with them.

At 13.00 on 9 June, the *Ariadne* sailed for Seeadler Harbor on Manus Island in the Admiralty Islands. While *en route* the Captain learned that HMAS *Bungaree* would probably have to undergo a refit before she could be used to supply the *Ariadne* with mines and there was no word on how long the refit would last. This was not good news, as it had been planned that the *Ariadne* would rely on the *Bungaree* for mines since before she left the UK.

The *Ariadne* arrived at the magnificent Seeadler Harbor at 16.00 on 11 June. The *Ariadne* was berthed opposite the harbour entrance and the Captain noticed with some discomfort that the harbour as yet had no boom defence against submarines. He soon moved his ship to a more landlocked location. The Captain also saw that there was no blackout there, evidently better ventilation and cinema on the upper deck outweighing the danger of enemy attack.

The Captain could not help but notice the prodigious work going on ashore and reported,

> [I]t is amazing to see what has been done during the three months [since Manus was occupied] this work has been in progress. Roads and piers are being made; there is a good signal station and there are dozens of Nissen huts and hundreds (if not thousands) of tents around the harbour. The harbour itself has been well charted by the Australians and good beacons and buoys are in place. Air strips are in very full use and in fact everything seems to have gone

ahead well – except for defence against submarine attack.

The Captain lamented that there was nothing for his men to do ashore and even bathing was restricted due to coral and sharks, but he later arranged for his men to use a good beach, courtesy of the US 5th Cavalry Regiment. Ashore, he noted that 'anything that smacks in any way of ceremony is omitted, so that all effort may be put into getting on with the war', with Colours and Sunset the only vestige of ceremony observed there.

The Captain continued to be amazed at what he saw of the work ashore at Manus and reported,

> The extent of the construction work ashore has to be seen to be believed . . . Great clearings have been hacked out of the jungle and cocoa-nut plantations and broad, well sign-posted roads with a good surface have been laid out. Piers and dolphins have been erected and a few ships can now unload alongside . . . There must be literally thousands of jeeps, trucks, bulldozers, etc. and the traffic is so heavy that there is traffic control at cross roads. Work is still in progress and during the half hour I spent with [General Swift's] Staff, there were two considerable explosions close to the Nissen hut we were in. On looking out, palm trees, coral and sand could be seen flying in all directions and much fall on the roof of our hut. Apparently no warning is given of this blasting and I am told that if one is caught outside it is best to get behind a palm tree and duck.

The Captain completed his meeting and, having survived the blasting ashore, returned to the *Ariadne* none the worse for it.

On the afternoon of 12 June, Task Forces 74 (Rear Admiral Crutchely, RN) and 75 (Rear Admiral Berkey, USN) arrived at Seeadler Harbor. That evening the *Ariadne* hosted many Australian officers from the heavy cruiser *Australia* and the destroyers *Arunta* and *Warramunga*. The Captain thought they were all evidently very pleased to see to see a ship of the Royal Navy, even 'before drinks were served'. In the ensuing days, the Captain came to believe the Royal Navy was very popular there and that he was reaping full benefit from this popularity being the only Royal Navy ship present.

Captain Lord Ashbourne felt honoured to be invited by Major-General I P Swift, the American commander of the Admiralty Islands, to stand beside him at a medal presentation and who then invited the Captain to be a reviewing officer at a review of the US 1st Cavalry Division. On the latter occasion, the General invited the Captain to bring with him his 'Chief of Staff' and 'Flag Lieutenant', leading the Captain to report to the Admiralty, 'I have no idea what has led him to suppose I am so well staffed'.

Captain Ashbourne began to notice the state of Australian-American relations in the Pacific and wrote, 'The truth is, I think, that the Royal Australian Navy is perhaps a little tired of the United States Navy and vice versa'. In the coming months he would hear much more about that subject, at least from the Australians. After discussions with Australian naval officers in June and August, he was to report, 'All were very bitter in their views and comments, on the Americans,' and felt that they 'were being thwarted' and 'all have a very great desire to get away from the Americans and to join the Eastern Fleet'. He went on to note, 'There seems to be in general a very bitter feeling among the Australian Navy and Army, due to the fact that they are being intentionally and as far as possible kept in back areas by the Americans . . .'.

Planning went ahead for the intended minelay off Wewak and Captain Ashbourne spent weeks preparing for the operation, trying to obtain suitable depth soundings and aerial photographs of the area to be mined. On 15 June, Admiral Kinkaid gave orders setting the operation in motion. Planning conferences were held on Rear Admiral Russell Berkey's flagship, the light cruiser *Phoenix*, and on the *Ariadne* and final orders were issued. To the Captain's disappointment, it was not possible to carry out a rehearsal for the operation, but he was informed by the Americans that rehearsals were very rare as only very short notice was given for an operation. The Captain was nevertheless satisfied the operation was going to receive adequate attention and it was clear to him it should be 'well laid-on'.

For the operation off Wewak, the *Ariadne* was allotted three US fleet destroyers, the *Abner Read*, *Ammen* and *Bache* of Destroyer Division 48, which bombarded Japanese gun positions at Wewak the night before the minelay. At 06.00 on 19 June, the *Ariadne* sailed from Seeadler Harbor and at 14.00 she rendezvoused with her three destroyers, which provided information on the lack of opposition the night before at Wewak. The night was moonless, but there was no wind and incredible visibility, allowing ships to be seen five miles away and even farther during the frequent lightning flashes.

That night the *Ariadne* laid 146 Mk XVII/XVII* moored mines off Wewak, encountering no opposition, even when she passed within five cables of the shore. The mines were laid with sprockets and grapnels to foil sweeping and were set to lie at a depth of 9ft and then to sink on 29 July.[23] The *Abner Read*, *Ammen* and *Bache* again bombarded targets ashore, with the assistance of American PT boat captains who were aboard to point out targets.[24] During the operation all inter-ship communication after dark was conducted by TBS (voice radio), which the Captain thought was secure and was quicker and more convenient than W/T (Morse Code by radio) or ZAX (an infrared signalling device). The minelay successfully completed, the *Ariadne* proceeded independently to Seeadler Harbor, arriving at 11.30 on 20 June.

The *Ariadne* had originally embarked the mines she laid off Wewak at Milford Haven on 19 January and had landed them and then reloaded them successively in Norfolk, Pearl Harbor and Sydney. The *Ariadne* carried the mines 21,343 miles before they were laid, giving them the dubious title of 'the most travelled mines in the world'.[25]

After her successful minelaying operation off Wewak, the *Ariadne* was ordered to Australia again, first to Milne Bay and then to Brisbane.

On the voyage, the effects of the hot weather of the past two weeks began to tell on the crew's health, with cases of boils and prickly heat. At Brisbane, the Captain again met with Admiral Kinkaid, who instructed him to proceed to Melbourne for a boiler cleaning and to dock to have the ship's bottom cleaned. The *Ariadne* was to load mines at Geelong and then would be ordered north to Seeadler Harbor again, probably for more minelaying operations. The *Bungaree* would probably not be available to act as a mine carrier until mid-August, but the Captain thought that would be time enough.

After more travels in the Pacific, including Melbourne and Cairns in Australia, the Whitsunday Islands and Magnetic Island, the *Ariadne* arrived again at Seeadler Harbor on 7 August. While there, she went to sea to conduct exercises with the heavy cruiser *Shropshire*, which had been loaned by the Royal Navy to the Royal Australian Navy and some of the American ships there.

On 23 August, the *Ariadne* received something of a new lease of life, though not the one she was designed for, when Admiral Kinkaid ordered her to unload her mines and to report to the Commander of the 7th Amphibious Force at Hollandia for duty as a fast troop carrier. The *Ariadne* was to be put generally in charge of four four-stacker destroyer transports, APDs. To Captain Ashbourne, the Americans seemed to have a quite definite requirement for his ship in that role and he wrote that 'it is good to feel that one is really wanted again'. The *Ariadne* was to retain her mines for the present and the Captain hoped to have the chance to discuss a mining plan for the forthcoming operations with Rear Admiral Daniel Barbey, USN.

The Captain called on Admiral Barbey, who, '[i]n spite of my glowing account of mines and their value', had no use for them then and still intended to use the *Ariadne* as a fast troop carrier. Nevertheless, the same day Admiral Kinkaid ordered was arranged that the *Ariadne* would lay her mines off Wewak the night of 31 August/1 September, which still pleased the Captain.

Even though the night would be two nights short of a full moon – an almost unheard-of condition for offensive minelaying in the European or Mediterranean theatres of war – Captain Ashbourne had no misgivings, since even moonless nights in the area were very light and with a good moon 'one can at least see more easily where one is going'. This time the *Ariadne* was accompanied by another three US destroyers, the *Lang*, *Stack* and *Murray* and the *Ariadne* laid another minefield according to plan about three miles northeast of Wewak. The destroyers took the opportunity to bombard Japanese gun positions ashore.[26]

The second Wewak operation would be the *Ariadne*'s last minelaying operation in the Pacific; after that, she was involved solely in amphibious operations. On 1 October, the destroyer tender USS *Dobbin* completed the alterations necessary to fit the *Ariadne* for troop carrying. Once refitted, the *Ariadne* would become part of the massive armada of American and Australian ships for the invasion of Leyte, the opening move of the Allied return to the Philippines.

Captain Ashbourne was already well acquainted with the commanding officer of the *Dobbin*, Captain Shirley Youngs Cutler,[27] who on their first meeting the Captain described as 'an excellent guest' and whom he learned was a 'real Mormon'. Captain Cutler regaled his hosts with a

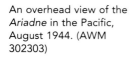

An overhead view of the *Ariadne* in the Pacific, August 1944. (AWM 302303)

story of being an engineering officer in the battleship *Maryland* at Pearl Harbor and of how his ship had kept burning oil from the battleship *Arizona* away from the *Maryland* by going ahead on the engines for several days. Captain Ashbourne would see Captain Cutler often in the coming days and would later refer to him as 'my Mormon friend'.

On 2 October, the *Ariadne* sailed from Hollandia to Aitape to embark 250 American troops with a view to spending the night at sea with troops embarked. The troops were then disembarked at Aitape and Captain Ashbourne thought the trial a great benefit in perfecting internal organisation in the ship with troops embarked. The *Ariadne* was ready for her new duties.

During this trial came the first use on a revolutionary improvement to a fast minelayer, presumably provided by the *Dobbin* at Hollandia. Two LST ventilation fans had been fitted to the forward mining hatches and the Captain described them as

> an unqualified success; a really good draught is created on the mining deck, which, in spite of high temperatures, is now perfectly habitable. These fans would be a considerable improvement and are at least very desirable for a ship of this class in the tropics, even if troops are not being carried; with the fans fitted work can be carried out on the mining deck in comfort instead of considerable discomfort.

The *Ariadne* had indeed reaped the benefits of Yankee ingenuity.

On 4 October, the *Ariadne* arrived back at Hollandia and reported to the amphibious force flagship *Wasatch*, where Rear Admiral A D Struble informed him of the part the *Ariadne* would play in the upcoming amphibious operation. She would be nominally part of Task Group 78.3, The Panaon Attack Group, commanded by Admiral Struble in the destroyer *Hughes*, which was part of Admiral Barbey's Northern Attack Force, which in turn was part of Admiral Thomas Kinkaid's Central Philippines Attack Force[28] and his Seventh Fleet. The Central Philippines Attack Force also included a Southern Attack Force, Task Force 79, and the

Captain Lord Ashbourne with Rear Admiral Daniel Barbey, USN, in 1944. (Barry Gibson)

Northern and Southern Attack Forces were both supported by escort carriers and old battleships. The entire Attack Force was also supported by Vice Admiral William Halsey's Third Fleet and its Task Force 38, which included the US Navy's fast carrier task forces, including its fast battleships,[29] which could be formed into a separate force, Task Force 34.

Before the Philippines operation, the *Ariadne* was finally joined in the Pacific by some British warships, but they were not to be in on the invasion. In September 1944, Force X, composed of seven British LSIs ('Landing Ships Infantry') under the command of Rear Admiral A G Talbot, RN, reported to the Seventh Amphibious Force for duty. They were the *Lothian* (Admiral Talbot's flagship), the *Empire Mace*, the *Empire Spearhead*, the *Glenearn*, the *Empire Battleaxe*, the *Clan Lamont* and the *Empire Arquebus*. At least according to the Americans, the design and material condition of the British LSIs made them unsuitable for use in assault operations and they were assigned to the Amphibious Training Group for duty. They carried the British type LCA landing craft and it was not practicable to alter them to accommodate the US-type LCVP. Capacity was limited to about 800 troops and cargo space was extremely limited. Captain Lord Ashbourne learned that Admiral Barbey had no use for the LSIs because he thought the ships were unsuitable for service in the tropics and because they were not allowed to roll more than 15°. To the Captain, who had presided over a court martial in the *Lothian*, it would be a sad blow if they were sent away, as 'I have much been looking forward to being in company once more with ships of the Royal Navy'. Upon completion of troop training in the New Guinea area, the British LSIs did make a lift of service troops from New Guinea to the Philippines and at the end of February 1945, they were released to the British Pacific Fleet.[30] The *Ariadne* would be the only Royal Navy warship to participate in the invasion of the Philippines.

Soon the game was on. On 8 October, the *Ariadne* embarked an advance party of one officer and twenty men from the US 21st Infantry Regiment and on the 9th she took on the balance of her charges, three officers and 274 men, with 24 tons of stores. On the 10th, the *Ariadne* took part in a rehearsal for the invasion of Panaon at Tanahmerah Bay and on the 11th she took part in a rehearsal for the invasion of Dinagat at Humboldt Bay. After a briefing the morning of the 12th, at 15.00 that day she sailed for the Philippines as part of the Dinagat Attack Group under Admiral Struble in the destroyer *Hughes*. On the 15th, the *Ariadne* joined Task Group 78.5, made up of minesweepers and fleet oilers and when that group rejoined Admiral Struble's task group the *Ariadne* became the Fleet Guide and Fleet Centre.

At daylight on 17 October, the *Ariadne* and her companions arrived off Leyte Gulf and entered the gulf in single file behind the minesweepers, as it was believed the entrance was mined. At 09.20, a landing was made on the northwest corner of Dinagat Island and half the troops the *Ariadne* was carrying were landed. The weather was already poor and then deteriorated further, with Force 8 winds, torrential rain and low visibility. Not surprisingly, no aircraft were sighted. That evening the task group left the beaches and proceeded to sea for the night.

The *Ariadne*'s task group returned to the landing beaches soon after daylight on 18 October, with much better weather. Three Japanese aircraft were sighted and one flew low over the task group and the beaches. In a draw, the plane dropped nothing and when it was fired on 'by all and sundry', including the *Ariadne,* it

flew off unscathed. That afternoon, the *Ariadne* re-embarked the troops it had landed the day before, as no opposition had been encountered ashore and the troops would be needed at Panaon.

On the 19th, the *Ariadne* entered Leyte Gulf with her task group and was detached by Admiral Struble to obtain information on tidal sets in the entrance to the gulf that were necessary for the entry of the main landing forces on D-Day. The minesweepers attempted to clear mines from the area, but the American destroyer *Ross* hit two mines and was badly damaged and the Australian heavy cruiser *Shropshire* would later cut a mine with one of her paravanes. After the *Ariadne* rejoined Admiral Struble, a Japanese Zero flew in over the mountains behind the beach and dropped one bomb on the beach and one about 200 yards from the *Ariadne*. It then made a quick getaway back over Dinagat unharmed. At dusk the *Ariadne* departed Dinagat in company with the *Hughes* and spent the night patrolling Surigao Strait. Japanese aircraft dropped several flares during the night, but none was sufficiently near to cause worry and no attacks developed. There were to be real fireworks in Surigao Strait in a few days, but the *Ariadne* would not be there for them.

October 20th was D-Day for the landings on Leyte itself. The weather was perfect, with a calm sea and a clear sky. At 03.30, the *Ariadne* and her force were joined by the Panaon Attack Force, which consisted of three Australian LSIs, the *Manoora*, *Kanimbla* and *Westralia*, and a number of American destroyers and mine-sweepers. The force arrived off the landing beaches at Panaon at 09.00, with the only sign of the Japanese on the way being one aircraft that dropped a bomb close astern of the formation at 07.15.[31] The landing began at 09.30, without any opposition at all and by 11.30 the *Ariadne* had been cleared of troops and stores.

Her mission as a troop carrier completed, the *Ariadne* was then ordered to report to Admiral Barbey. Before leaving Panaon, Admiral Struble signalled to the *Ariadne* 'My appreciation and commendation for splendid work of Ariadne on the Dinagat and Panaon venture', which the Captain found most gratifying. The *Ariadne* then sailed independently to the vicinity of Dulag on the western shore of Leyte Gulf to await orders. At 16.00 that day, the *Ariadne* was joined by two American destroyers and two destroyer transports and then by five LSDs (Landing Ships

Dock). The Captain was to command this force, to be known as Task Group 78.9, which was to proceed forthwith to Hollandia. The force was for the moment unmolested by the Japanese, but from anti-aircraft fire seen in the distance it was evident that the Southern Attack Group was being attacked.

Late on 20 October, the quiet enjoyed by the *Ariadne* and the Allied ships near her came to an abrupt end. As the *Ariadne* was waiting in the vicinity of Dulag for her task group to join her, a single Japanese torpedo plane came in from the northward and obtained a hit on the American light cruiser *Honolulu*, which suffered sixty officers and men killed or missing.[32] The Allied ships in the area put up a terrific anti-aircraft barrage, but the plane escaped the fire unscathed, only to be brought down by a fighter shortly afterwards.

The *Ariadne*'s force was ordered to Hollandia, but because the *Ariadne* and the destroyer transports lacked enough fuel to get there, other arrangements had to be made. On 22 October the *Ariadne* and her force finally departed Leyte Gulf for Palau and entered Kossol Road there on the 23rd. After a badly-needed refuelling, on 24 October the *Ariadne* sailed for Hollandia with the American APDs *Crosby* and *Kilty*. Shortly after sailing, the *Ariadne* passed the *Honolulu*, which was down by the bow as a result of the torpedo hit on the 20th, and the heavy cruiser *Australia*, which had been badly damaged by a Japanese Kamikaze aircraft, a 'Val' dive bomber, on the 21st. The damage to the *Australia* was very evident, including the missing director above her bridge and her bent foremast. She had lost her commanding officer, Captain Dechaineux and twenty-nine other officers and men, with sixty wounded.[33] Both of the ships had their colours at half-mast and while passing them the *Ariadne* lowered her colours in sympathy.

The *Ariadne* and her task group missed the battle of Leyte Gulf, but they certainly heard about it. On 25 October, while on passage from Palau to Hollandia, it became evident to Captain Ashbourne from intercepted signals that the situation in the Philippines had changed radically since the *Ariadne* had left. 'Enemy air interference had greatly increased and enemy heavy surface forces were in contact'. Indeed they were. While a Japanese battle force under

Admiral Nishimura had been nearly annihilated by American battleships and other Allied forces in Surigao Strait the night before, early on the 25th a much more powerful battle force, with the battleship *Yamato* and commanded by Admiral Kurita, had passed through the San Bernardino Strait and entered Leyte Gulf off Samar. The force came within a whisker of destroying 'Taffy Three', Task Unit 77.4.3, which consisted only of escort carriers and destroyers and destroyer escorts. With perhaps some understandable bitterness, the Captain reported to the Admiralty, 'I wonder very much if the Commander-in-Chief, Seventh Fleet [Admiral Kinkaid], does not now wish I was back in the area with a full load of mines to put down quickly in the San Bernardino Strait to catch the Japanese battleships if and when they retire from the area west of the Philippines'. Not to mention that the *Ariadne* could have been used to mine the Strait to prevent the Japanese from passing through it in the first place on the morning of the 25th, after Admiral Halsey took the battleships of Task Force 34 with him and his carriers and left the Strait unguarded to chase after Japanese aircraft carriers acting as decoys. American inattention to the possibilities of offensive minelaying had cost the Allies a chance to have the *Ariadne* re-enact the first *Abdiel*'s minelay at the battle of Jutland, with potentially considerable losses to the Japanese and the saving of many American lives.

Another, less obvious opportunity for the *Ariadne*'s offensive minelaying talents was also missed. Just after the end of the battle of Leyte Gulf, the Imperial Japanese Navy began running troops to Leyte via Ormoc, on the western coast of the island. The runs were reminiscent of the 'Tokyo Express' runs down The Slot in the Solomons to Guadalcanal in 1942 and in these runs the Japanese succeeded in bringing in about 45,000 troops – enough to double their strength on the island – and 10,000 tons of supplies. Belatedly, the Americans sent in destroyers and PT boats to intercept the runs, with mixed success and American troops landed at Ormoc Bay on 7 December 1944, but Japanese reinforcement runs did not end until 10 December.[34] The new American *Sumner* class destroyer-minelayers were not yet ready – and were never used for minelaying anyway[35] – but the *Ariadne* could have been used to mine and

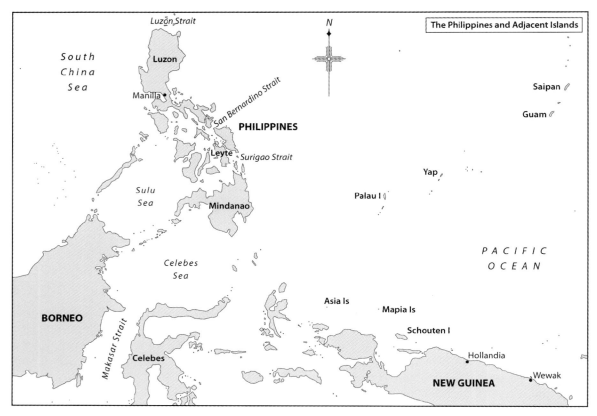

strangle the Ormoc supply route. Not that it would have been easy; there were Japanese mines about, not to mention night-flying Japanese aircraft and fearsome Kamikaze attacks by day and the occasional Japanese destroyer, but if the *Ariadne* had been used to mine the Ormoc supply route and had succeeded, the grinding battle for Leyte could have been shortened. Instead of being used for the purpose she was intended, the *Ariadne* followed her orders and continued on her way from the Philippines to Hollandia, where she arrived on 26 October to receive a large mail that included welcome news of increases in pay. Otherwise, Hollandia was, literally, no picnic; bathing had been halted because of the fouled water and there was no other recreation to be had. Furthermore, fresh provisions were hard to obtain in the crowded harbour.

The food supply situation later became worse for all the Allied ships in the area. As the sole British combat unit in the Pacific at the time, the *Ariadne*'s unique supply needs were sometimes harder to meet. In one of his reports, the Captain commented on the shortage of rum, which was causing him anxiety. Even in the

Pacific, the men's rum ration was due at 11.00. The rum had been ordered months before from Sydney, but had still not arrived and he was considering 'more drastic action'. The ship's shortage of rum was probably not made up until December, when the ship once again reached Seeadler Harbor and took on stores awaited for many weeks. Mutiny was thus averted.

Early in November, the *Ariadne* received a general signal saying that the men who had taken part in the Leyte operation could now mention that fact in private correspondence. The Captain thought that cut across all British regulations, but also thought it would be good for morale, especially with nothing to do at Hollandia and let it pass. For the same reason, he allowed his men to mention that they had visited Australia some time ago. He also reasoned that if the Japanese learned of the presence of a British fast minelayer, they would engage in some unnecessary minesweeping and would think that other British forces had arrived or were about to arrive in the Pacific.

During the lull after Leyte, the *Ariadne*'s men could not understand why they were working with the Americans if they were not required for minelaying and there were plenty of American transports to carry more troops than they could. To the Captain, 'The difficulty is that I cannot explain to them what, to my mind, is the one excellent reason for our presence with the United States Pacific Fleet, i.e., to show the White Ensign and to provide tangible evidence, albeit small, that the Royal Navy is taking [part] in the Pacific war'. Little did he suspect that the *Ariadne* was about to show the White Ensign in a very prominent way.

Just when the Captain was contemplating a change of scenery to Sydney, on 5 November he was ordered to report to Admiral Barbey's flagship, the *Blue Ridge*, for a special assignment. Admiral Barbey put him in charge of amphibious operations to take the Mapia Islands and the Asia Islands off the northwest coast of New Guinea. The islands were on the route between Biak and Mindanao and had little strategic importance in and of themselves, but the Americans wanted to deny them to the Japanese as lookout posts and weather reporting stations and for Allied use as weather stations and as sites for the Long Range Aid to Navigation (LORAN) system.[36] This would mark the first time a British officer would command an American amphibious operation.[37] The landing troops were to be Americans, from the reinforced Second Battalion of the 167th Regiment of the 31st Infantry Division, together with other elements of the division, including a portable surgical hospital.[38] The 167th traced its history to the 4th Alabama Infantry, CSA, which fought at Antietam and Gettysburg and was part of the 42nd (Rainbow) Division in the First World War, when it fought at St Mihiel and in the Meuse-Argonne offensive.[39]

The Captain was to command Task Group 78.14, which would consist of the *Ariadne*, the destroyer escort *Willmarth*, two PC patrol boats, twelve LSMs (Landing Ship – Medium), six LCI(G)s ('Landing Craft Infantry [Gunboats]) and four LCIs (Landing Craft – Infantry). Admiral Barbey would later add to the task group two destroyers, the *Caldwell* and the *Shaw*, the latter being a resurrected veteran of Pearl Harbor, in time for D-Day of the Mapia Group invasion.

On the evening of the 6th, when the Captain was aboard the *Blue Ridge* discussing the operation plan with the staff,

I happened to meet the Admiral on deck. He at once asked me to come and have my photograph taken with him for the Press and this was accomplished outside his cabin without more ado. He was most friendly and pleasant with me and said that as I had been taking orders from American officers throughout the Leyte operation, he thought I would now like to run a show of my own. I told him how grateful I was for the opportunity. He also told me he thought it was quite time the unit of the Royal Navy under his orders received some publicity and said, if I had no objection, he would like to send some Press representatives with me on the forthcoming operation. I naturally agreed and representatives were embarked in due course; they included a man from Reuters, the *Daily Telegraph*, an artist, [and] a cameraman.

On 7 November, the *Ariadne* and her task group sailed from Hollandia for Morotai and on the 9th the *Ariadne* passed the 50,000-mile mark since her commissioning. On the 11th she and her task group arrived at Morotai after an uneventful passage – uneventful, that is, other than a fire in the engine room of an LSM and an LCI(G) damaging a propeller on a waterlogged tree trunk. As preparations for the operation continued, Morotai was the object of Japanese air raids the next day and then the following one.

On 13 November, the Captain learned that the day before the Americans had carried out an air strike on Pegun Island, his first objective in the Mapia Islands. The aircraft had encountered moderate anti-aircraft fire and one of them had been shot down. At 11.00 that day, Task Group 78.14 sailed from Morotai for Pegun Island.

Early on 15 November, the American destroyers *Caldwell* and *Shaw* joined the *Ariadne*'s task group and, after a heavy bombardment, at dawn the task group landed American troops on Pegun Island, about 130 miles north of Manokwar in Dutch New Guinea.[40] By the evening, all troops and stores had been landed and the island was completely occupied. The troops found the wreckage of the B-25 Mitchell bomber that had been shot down over Pegun a few days before, with three dead crewmen inside it.[41]

The Japanese who chose not to fight on Pegun demonstrated to the men of the *Ariadne* that the Pacific War was very different from anything they had ever experienced. The Captain reported:

> The first assault wave reached the northern tip of Pegun Island at 11.15 without having seen a single Japanese, but at 11.30 there were a series of dull explosions behind our troops and upon investigation, these proved to be the remains of thirteen Japanese soldiers, who had decimated themselves for the Glory of the Emperor by holding hand grenades to their stomachs. Prior to committing suicide the Japanese had destroyed a wireless set and all their rifles. For some inexplicable reason they had discarded their uniforms and for the ritual of self-destruction had attired themselves in pajamas. I was amazed at the size of the enemy who had killed themselves in this fashion; they were all between 5' 10' and 6' 0'. They looked remarkably fit and did not appear in the slightest degree emaciated.
>
> It is difficult to understand the mentality of the enemy on Pegun Island. These thirteen men had committed suicide when there was an excellent opportunity of their occasioning our troops many casualties after the latter had passed by. In addition, three Japanese guns – a 37mm anti-tank gun and two 75mm mountain guns – had been found intact, loaded and without a shot being fired through them on D-Day.[42]

As strange as this incident was, it was preferable to the usual Imperial Japanese Army practice of

Captain Lord Ashbourne on the bridge of the *Ariadne* during the Mapia Landings. (US National Archives and Record Administration II 80-G-301545)

contesting every yard of ground and fighting to the very last man. The rest of the Japanese troops on Pegun had fled to nearby Bras Island just before the invasion to escape the bombing and they would soon demonstrate the customary way the Imperial Japanese Army fought.

The invasion of Pegun Island was well covered by the press, including the BBC and there were headlines in British newspapers back home. The *Ariadne* was not named in any of the reports, but was instead referred to as 'the British warship *Ether*'. The *Daily Express* reported,

> A war despatch received in London last night reported that an officer of the Royal Navy, Captain Lord Ashbourne, commanded an American amphibious operation for the first time in the Pacific war when US troops swarmed ashore and occupied Pegun, largest island of the Mapia group, lying between Dutch New Guinea and the Philippines, last week. Sailors from the Midlands, the North and West Country had their first crack at the Japanese – and enjoyed it. As gun crews aboard the flagship, they helped blast a way for the American jungle fighting infantry.
>
> Petty Officer Alfred Edward Joyney, of Cleethorpes, fired the first shell. Captaining the forward turret, he remembered Singapore and Japanese atrocities at Hong Kong. He thought, too, of a brother-in-law who fought in the cruiser *Exeter* as she went down under Japanese fire in 1942. 'That's for you, Joe', he said, as the shell fired the coconut groves in which the Japanese had dug defences.
>
> When the American amphibious tanks and tractors rolled up the beach the island was a furnace.[43]

While the *Ariadne*'s name was not mentioned in press accounts, Captain Lord Ashbourne was prominently mentioned in several of the accounts, allowing anyone who knew he was the commanding officer of the *Ariadne* to figure out the true identity of HMS '*Ether*'.

The occupation of Pegun Island accomplished, the *Ariadne* then sailed for Morotai with most of the task group, leaving US Army troops on Pegun five days to take the other two islands in the Mapia Group, Bras and Fanildo, before the *Ariadne* returned with the LORAN gear and to pick them up. On the morning of the 16th, American troops landed on Bras Island, but this time the beach was defended and resistance was stubborn and prolonged. The landing force eventually encircled the Japanese on the island and then had to destroy them, position by position. The occupation of Bras was finally completed on the 18th and a landing was made on Fanildo Island, the third island in the Mapias, the same day.[44]

Meanwhile, the *Ariadne* and her charges arrived at Morotai on the 17th. The task group then embarked 400 troops and vehicles from Company F of the 124th Infantry Regiment and other elements of the 31st Division[45] for the assault on Igi Island in the Asia Group. The Captain also met with the commanding officer of the 31st Infantry Division, Major General Clarence Martin.

At 07.30 on the 18th, the task group sailed for Igi. After a preliminary bombardment, at dawn on the 19th troops were landed on Igi Island in good weather and with no opposition. This operation went even more quickly than the one on Pegun Island; by 07.00 all troops had been landed, by 10.30 the island was fully occupied and by 12.00 the *Ariadne* and much of the task group had sailed for Pegun Island in the Mapias, 190 miles away.[46] A few landing craft were left behind to assist in the capture of the other two islands in the group and to land the LORAN gear after a suitable site for it had been found.

The *Ariadne*'s task group arrived back at Pegun Island at 06.30 on 20 November and soon learned from the US Army there that the whole of the Mapia Group had been occupied. The Japanese soldiers in the Mapia Islands who chose to fight, presumably the ones on Bras Island, had inflicted casualties of seventeen dead and thirty wounded on the American troops. The Japanese had lost 160 men killed in the fighting and eight by the bombing: none were taken prisoner.

The rest of 20 November was spent landing the LORAN gear and re-embarking the troops there. This did not go as expeditiously as the Captain would have liked and he noted a certain lack of urgency ashore. To make matters worse, 'a fair number of the crews of the L.C.I. (G) got

ashore for Church Services and souvenir hunting, before I could stop it; all these men had, of course, to be re-embarked later in the day'. Many years later, an *Ariadne* crewman still recalled the Captain's signalling as to why the men were going ashore and his considerable frustration with the Americans over the incident.

As a result of all this, the disembarkation of the LORAN gear and the re-embarkation of everyone and everything else was not completed until well after nightfall. Finally, at 20.00 the task group departed Pegun Island to continue the shuttle to Igi Island to re-embark the troops there.

On arrival at Igi at 13.00 on the 21st, the Captain learned that the entire Asia Group had been occupied without any opposition (or for that matter, any Japanese). The LORAN gear had already been landed there and no time was lost in re-embarking the troops and sailing at 16.30 for Morotai. The task group arrived at Morotai at 12.00 on 22 November and all men and vehicles were unloaded immediately. On 27 November, the task group reached Hollandia and the Captain reported directly to Admiral Barbey on the operation.

The operation was thus successfully completed. No one suggested it was another Guadalcanal or Tarawa, but amphibious operations are notoriously difficult and complicated and this one was well led and executed by Captain Lord Ashbourne, perhaps helped by his experience in the Allied landing on Sicily in 1943.

Even with the successful conclusion of the operation, there was still the necessary paperwork. The Captain's report on the operation was dated 27 November,[47] and was endorsed and kudos on the operation were transmitted all the way up to Admiral King, by Admiral Barbey and by Admiral Kinkaid. Admiral Barbey reported that, 'The tasks assigned Task Group 78.14 were executed in a most able manner by the Task Group Commander, Captain Lord Ashbourne, D.S.O., RN' and Admiral Kinkaid reported, 'The Task Group Commander, Captain Lord Ashbourne, D.S.C., R.N., is congratulated on his able handling of this combined British-American group'. Such praise of a Royal Navy officer could not have hurt the Royal Navy's cause, even in Admiral King's rather Anglophobic eyes.

At the beginning of December, the *Ariadne* sailed for Seeadler Harbor and then to Madang in

New Guinea to collect stores she had been awaiting for weeks (including, one would hope, an adequate supply of rum). While at Seeadler Harbor, she witnessed the arrival of the heavy cruiser *Australia*, fresh from expeditious repairs at the US base at Espiritu Santo. At peaceful Madang, the *Ariadne* could complete boiler cleaning and her crew could take advantage of opportunities for bathing and playing cricket ashore, consuming very welcome fresh fruit and vegetables and enjoying Australian hospitality.

The respite at Madang could not last forever, however, and on 15 December the *Ariadne* left Madang and rendezvoused with the USS *PC 1131* and the British LSIs *Empire Spearhead* and *Clan Lamont* bound for Morotai. The *PC 1131* was detached and after the arrival of the *Ariadne* and her two charges at Morotai, the Japanese radio – 'Tokyo Rose', perhaps? – announced that the three ships had been sunk while approaching Morotai. Miraculously still afloat, they then sailed for Hollandia.

The *Ariadne* had been away from the UK a very long time and the news from home was not always good. Britain was then being subjected to attack by Hitler's V-weapons and one *Ariadne* sailor, a bo'sun's mate, learned while he was in the Pacific that his mother had caught a virus and died while visiting a sister whose home had been

the target of a V-2 rocket. He received this sad news while thousands of miles away and with little prospect of returning home any time soon.

Indeed, developments in the Far East did not seem to portend an early return home for the *Ariadne*. On 22 November 1944, the British Pacific Fleet was formed at Trincomalee under Admiral Sir Bruce Fraser as the C-in-C.[48] This news of the formation of the British Pacific Fleet did not reach the *Ariadne*'s captain until 5 December and he described it as very welcome news. 'It will indeed be a Red Letter Day for Australia, the United States Pacific Fleet and for my own ship when our fleet arrives in this area and I am certain that a very warm welcome awaits them'. On 2 December, Admiral Fraser hoisted his flag in the battleship *Howe* and with four destroyers sailed for Fremantle, Australia.[49] The news that the *Howe* had reached Melbourne reached the Captain on 12 December and he described it as 'great news indeed'.

To the Captain the day of liberation from American control seemed close at hand. He had by then lost faith in American intentions for his ship. He reported to the Admiralty, 'As long as the war in the Pacific is under United States control, I see no future in surface minelaying and with the amphibious forces adequately provided with Destroyer Escorts converted to fast troop carriers, there seems to be no future requirement in that respect either'. He was referring to American 'APDs', which he learned from Admiral Barbey could carry four LCVP landing craft, 140 troops and 70 tons of stores. The future for his ship under American control seemed bleak.

It took a while to assemble the British Pacific Fleet and it was natural for Admiral Fraser to want the *Ariadne* to be included. Indeed, at least as early as October 1944 it was planned that the *Ariadne,* as well as the *Apollo* and *Manxman,* would form part of the British Pacific Fleet. The *Apollo* was working up and the *Manxman* was supposedly about to complete repairs, they were to leave the UK in March 1945.

Weighing in on the future employment of the *Ariadne,* Captain Cowie minuted on New Year's Eve 1943 that there was nothing to be gained by bringing the *Ariadne* back to the U.K. and that while she may not have been extensively employed in her proper role in the Pacific, worthwhile opportunities had been few. 'These opportunities will however increase', he said and noted hopefully that he understood that the Americans were appointing or had appointed a Flag Officer to co-ordinate minelaying activities in the Pacific. He continued, 'On the other hand, the presence of "ARIADNE" in the Pacific has been of political value and her commanding officer and ship's company have gained valuable experience in that theatre'. He concluded, 'As the advance-guard of the British Navy in the Pacific, it seems wholly logical that "ARIADNE" should now join the British Pacific Fleet . . .'.

It remained for the *Ariadne* to be transferred back to British control. Prodded by the Plans Department, the Admiralty suggested to Admiral Fraser on 10 January 1945, that with the formation of the British Pacific Fleet as a balanced force it seemed inappropriate that the only British fast minelayer in the Pacific should continue on loan to the Americans and proposed seeking the concurrence of COMINCH – Admiral King – to the *Ariadne* being transferred to British operational control and becoming part of the British Pacific Fleet.

In reply, Admiral Fraser estimated the fast minelayers should be ready to move into forward areas by 1 June and that Admiral Nimitz had stated that there would be no difficulty transferring the *Ariadne* from the Seventh Fleet to the British Pacific Fleet. However, the *Ariadne* was not Nimitz's ship and Admiral Kinkaid, C-in-C of the Seventh Fleet, does not seem to have received the memo. Admiral Fraser signalled the Admiralty that 'Having seen Admiral Kinkaid I do not advise altering the status of ARIADNE repetition ARIADNE until necessary to carry out the plans' for the fast minelayers given in his earlier signal.

Before a week had passed, however, these best-laid plans suddenly came to naught. On 18 January 1945, the Admiralty informed Admiral Fraser that the necessity of embarking on an extensive anti-submarine minelaying campaign in the coastal waters of the British Isles called not only for the retention of the *Apollo* and *Manxman* in Home Waters but the return of the *Ariadne* to the UK and expressed regret that the employment of the fast minelayers in the Pacific in an offensive role had to be deferred. On 27 January, the BAD in Washington informed the Admiralty that the commander of the task force under which the *Ariadne* had been serving had agreed to release her forthwith. On 3 February, Admiral Barbey signalled to the *Ariadne*'s Captain, 'To you and your ship's company a most pleasant trip home. It has been a pleasure to have the always ready ARIADNE in the 7th Amphibious Force'. The same day Admiral Kinkaid signalled, 'Your hearty co-operation and the efficient manner in which you have carried out all assignments here with the Seventh Fleet are sincerely appreciated. Good luck and Bon Voyage'. The *Ariadne* was finally free to go home.

The BAD had requested that Admiral King route the *Ariadne* to the UK via the Panama Canal. She exited the Pacific the way she had come, via Pearl Harbor. On 23 February, Admiral Nimitz signalled, 'We are happy to welcome an old friend back to Pearl. Congratulations on a splendid tour of duty'. From Pearl, she proceeded to the Panama Canal and then back into the Atlantic.

The *Ariadne* had served well in the Pacific, even though her talents were not put to the fullest use, in part because the vast expanses of the Pacific did not lend themselves well to offensive minelaying and in part because of the US Navy's lack of interest in minelaying, much less offensive minelaying. It is a shame that a fast minelayer – such as the *Manxman* in the autumn of 1942 – could not have been sent to serve alongside the US Navy during the long battle for Guadalcanal from August 1942 to February 1943, when a fast minelayer's offensive minelaying and cargo-carrying abilities would have been ideal for hindering the Tokyo Express coming down 'The Slot' in the Solomons, as the Americans finally discovered in February 1943, and for bringing supplies to the beleaguered Marines on the island.

Captain Lord Ashbourne and the *Ariadne* did accomplish the important but less tangible benefit of proudly and competently showing the Royal Navy's White Ensign to the Americans and Australians in the Pacific in 1944. While she was on her way home, an Admiralty office in Washington informed the Secretary of the Admiralty that

> On completion of H.M.S. 'ARIADNE's' period of duty with the United States Pacific Fleet and her withdrawal from my administration I desire to call attention to the good and able service performed by Captain Lord Ashbourne, who appears to have established most cordial relations with United States Flag

and Commanding Officers and to have earned their respect and consideration for the Royal Navy, of which he was, for an appreciable period, the only representative in those waters.

With the British Pacific Fleet about to join the fight against the Japanese, that was not an unimportant accomplishment. As a final symbol of American esteem for the Captain and the *Ariadne*, on reaching London he was awarded the Legion of Merit by Admiral Harold 'Betty' Stark.

The deployment to the Pacific of the *Ariadne,* of a type unknown to the Americans, and of her diplomatic and competent commanding officer, had been a success and was well worth the effort. The objections to the deployment based on manning concerns seem petty in comparison to the returns.

The *Ariadne* finally arrived at Plymouth on 31 March 1945.[50] She was put to work very soon. After giving leave and cleaning boilers, on 8 April the *Ariadne* proceeded to Milford Haven to assist the *Apollo*.[51]

A painting of the *Ariadne* transiting the Panama Canal. (Ian Marshall)

CHAPTER 15

THE *APOLLO* ROUNDS OUT THE SIX AND BECOMES A YEOMAN MINELAYER, 1944–1945

WHILE the *Ariadne* was away in the Pacific, the *Apollo*, the sixth and last of her class, was completed and began to make her mark as a hard-working minelayer.

The *Apollo* was built by Hawthorn Leslie & Company, at the same yard on the River Tyne where the *Welshman* was built. Her keel was laid on 10 October 1941, she was launched on 5 April 1943 and she was completed on 12 February 1944.[1] The *Apollo* cost £807,000, excluding guns, ammunition and a few other items.[2] She was a Chatham-manned ship and took the pennant number M 01.

The eighth Royal Navy warship to bear the name Apollo, the last fast minelayer was named after the Greek sun god, the son of Zeus and brother of Diana and after the small protected cruiser that was completed in 1892 and converted to a minelayer in 1909.[3] That *Apollo* served in the First World War and in 1914–15 comprised part of a minelaying squadron that operated out of the Nore and Dover. The seventh *Apollo* was unceremoniously sold in 1920 to be broken up.[4] Apropos of her name, the *Apollo*'s crest wore a gold sun and her mottos were *Arcu*

semper intento – 'With bow always bent' – and *Fortis et benignus* – 'Strong and merciful'.[5]

The *Apollo*'s first commanding officer was Captain John Annesley Grindle, who joined the *Apollo* in November 1943 when she was fitting out at Hawthorn Leslie.[6] Captain Grindle was born on 17 September 1900 and joined the Navy as a cadet in 1913. After attending Osborne and Dartmouth, his first ship as a midshipman was the battleship *Orion* in 1917, after the battle of Jutland had been fought. After the First World War, the Admiralty sent him to university at Pembroke College, Cambridge. He specialised in gunnery and in peacetime served as the Gunnery Officer of the battleship *Revenge* and of several cruisers and as the Executive Officer of the battleship *Warspite*.

Once the war started, he took part in the destruction of harbour facilities at Cherbourg in 1940 and received his first Mention in Despatches. He was the Executive Officer of the battleship *Rodney* when she helped sink the German battleship *Bismarck* on 27 May 1941. While serving under Admiral Cunningham at Director of Landing Craft (Mediterranean), he

The *Apollo* as completed. (Tyne & Wear Archive)

Captain John A Grindle.
(Jeremy Grindle)

drove his landing craft crews hard and after the invasion of Sicily he was appointed CBE.

Captain Grindle has been described as a good and fair captain and a 'decent chap'.[7] One of the *Apollo*'s midshipmen wrote to his widow:

> As a very green Midshipman RNVR, fresh from King Alfred, HMS *Apollo* was my first appointment and I was the first of two Mids appointed for her trials and commissioning . . . I was then a very lowly officer in what can be described as a very august wardroom. Nevertheless Captain Grindle dined the two midshipman on more than one occasion and showed much kindness and understanding . . . Notwithstanding our lowly rank and his overwhelming responsibilities, the Captain always saw to it that we were fairly treated. We had the highest admiration and respect for him.[8]

While commanding the *Apollo*, Captain Grindle kept a pet terrier named Thoruna, supposedly after a glamorous model in a wall calendar of the time. Sadly, Thoruna did not survive the war.[9]

The *Apollo* acquired as its Torpedo Lieutenant an experienced mining hand, Lieutenant Geoffrey Hodges, RNVR, GM, a survivor of the *Abdiel*. He felt warmly accepted at once, finding that having served in the *Abdiel* was a special recommendation.[10]

The *Apollo* spent a short time working up at the Home Fleet's base at Scapa Flow and she was then ordered to the mine depot at Milford Haven to begin Operation 'Maple', a series of minelaying operations off the French coast in preparation for the Normandy landings. The minefields she and other ships laid were intended to create a barrier to keep the German Navy from interfering with the D-Day landings[11] in June.

On 11 April, the *Apollo* arrived at Milford Haven to load mines and on the 16th she sailed from Plymouth, accompanied by one British and two Canadian destroyers, to complete her first minelay in Operation 'Hostile 28'.[12]

Most of the *Apollo*'s subsequent lays were routine, but the one that began on 15 May, Operation 'Hostile 32', was definitely not. On this operation, she was to be supported

The *Apollo* with a bone in her teeth. (Jeremy Grindle)

independently by the light cruiser *Bellona* and the destroyers *Tartar*, *Huron* and *Haida*. Things began to go wrong at 00.30 on the 16th when the *Apollo*'s radar burst into flames and was put out of action. After sighting lights from unknown vessels, Captain Grindle decided to abandon the operation, but his signal to the *Bellona* was not received. At 0.140 the *Apollo* encountered her erstwhile escorts and was illuminated by starshell and then hotly engaged by one of the destroyers. The *Apollo* switched on her IFF, signalled 'Cease firing' and zig-zagged to avoid damage. At 02.10 the *Bellona* finally suspected that all was not well and asked the *Apollo* to report her position, course and speed. The 'engagement' then ended. No harm was done and the operation was successfully executed two days later by the same cast of characters.[13]

Slightly less exciting was the lay on 20 May, when just before 01.53 the *Apollo* was illuminated by a Leigh Light from a Wellington on anti-submarine patrol. Recognising the *Apollo* was not a submarine and taking a photograph to prove it, the Wellington went off to find something else to do. The *Apollo* shrugged off the intrusion and completed the lay without further incident.[14] The ship was illuminated once again on 22 May, when a Halifax flew over her and dropped a 'photoflash'.[15]

The *Apollo*'s last lay during the lead-up to the Normandy invasion was on 25 May. Captain Grindle reported that she had laid 1200 mines at 20 knots without a hitch on the mining deck. He also reported that her maximum speed was 34 knots fully loaded and 35.5 knots without mines and that on three lays her average speed had exceeded 34 knots. Even at those speeds, her smoke could be controlled and she was remarkably steady.[16]

On 7 June, D-Day +1, the *Apollo* was given the special mission of conveying the D-Day Allied Naval Commander Expeditionary Force, a long title for Admiral Sir Bertram Ramsey and General Dwight D. Eisenhower, the Supreme Commander of the Allied Expeditionary Force, to the Western Assault Area, where British and Canadian troops had landed. Flying Eisenhower's personal flag, with four white stars on a red field, the *Apollo* carried Ramsey and Eisenhower to confer with the military and naval commanders for the area, both British –

General Bernard Montgomery and Vice Admiral Sir Phillip Vian[17] – and American, General Omar Bradley and Admirals Alan Kirk and John Hall.[18] At times the *Apollo*'s bridge became very crowded and General Eisenhower found that the most comfortable place to sit was at the bridge chart table, where he was provided with hot soup laced with sherry.[19]

All went well until, at 16.12,[20] the *Apollo* went too close ashore and encountered a sand bar. Admiral Ramsay had just commented on how shallow the water seemed to be ('Johnny, aren't your tailfeathers a bit high?'), but Captain Grindle had just called through to the navigator below for the depth of water and had been told there were six fathoms under her bottom.[21] Captain Harry Butcher, General Eisenhower's naval aide, witnessed what happened next.

Captain Grindle quickly elected to try to force her across and accordingly did not reduce power. With the mast swaying violently, the entire ship jerking, grinding and even bouncing like a Flexi-Flier suddenly hitting bare gravel, we eventually swung off the bar and floated free. However the propellers were bent and possibly also the drive shafts.[22]

The ship's engines were stopped and when she was clear of the sand bar she resumed on her port shaft at 100 revolutions.[23] The *Apollo*'s esteemed passengers had to be transferred to the destroyer *Undaunted*,[24] and the ship was given an escort of the sloops *Lark* and *Crane* back to Plymouth.[25]

As for the cause of this unfortunate incident, one story has it that the *Apollo*'s bridge became so crowded with visitors that Captain Grindle sent the Navigator to the wheelhouse below.[26] Another story has it that the Navigator was working with a series of charts of the landing area that were not all on the same scale and had transferred the ship's position from one chart to another by using dividers and had thereby started with the ship in the wrong place on the new chart.[27]

General Eisenhower felt badly for Captain Grindle and later put in a good word for him with his old friend, First Sea Lord Admiral Sir Cunningham. After the incident, General Eisenhower called on Captain Grindle, who was

Allied Top Brass (from left, Admiral Sir Bertram Ramsay, General Eisenhower and General Montgomery) by a mine hatch on the *Apollo*, D-Day + 1. (Jeremy Grindle)

taking it hard. The *Apollo* was then in drydock, 'with both propellers looking like three-petalled flowers which had been serrated at the edges by a cruel hand'. Both propellers had to be replaced and in addition one of her struts had been broken. General Eisenhower informed Captain Grindle that Montgomery's destroyer had run aground the same day and the news cheered him up a bit.[28]

While the ship was being repaired, Captain Grindle had to undergo the obligatory court martial for grounding his ship. He was found guilty of hazarding his ship by not having the largest available chart on the bridge, but was found not guilty of stranding her because the Navigator had the largest chart in the wheelhouse, one deck below. Captain Grindle was severely reprimanded, but the president of the court is said to have told him after the trial, 'Don't worry, Johnny, I grounded a battleship within five miles of here'[29] or 'Join the club; we've all been reprimanded'.[30] Indeed, the Captain's command of the *Apollo* and his immediate career survived the incident.

The grounding off Normandy inspired a bit of doggerel from a talented member of the ship's crew. It read,

HMS Apollo

MISHAPS AT SEA

By Geoffrey A. Hodges
June 1945

Apollo: Captain Johnny G.
Was famous for Velocity
With Tedder, Ramsay, Eisenhower,
He reached the French Coast in an hour!
But with his eyes toward the land
He steamed too fast upon the sand
The Ship and Admiral got a shock
The former going into Dock.
The latter's Thanks fell very short
And later he convened a Court
To look into the Matter!

The *Apollo* underwent temporary repairs at Sheerness and more repairs on the Tyne that lasted until the end of September.[31] Once repaired and refitted and her dignity restored, the *Apollo* was needed for less showy but still vital minelaying duties. From late October 1944, she was engaged in laying defensive minefields to protect coastal shipping around the UK from U-boats equipped with the 'Schnorkel' breathing apparatus. In the middle of November, she had to take a break to repair some turbine joints.[32] Then, from January to April 1945, she laid offensive minefields off the coast of Norway to disrupt German coastal shipping.[33] There were occasionally problems with the mines laid, one sort called 'surface failures' and another called 'married failures'.

During the night of 11/12 January, the *Apollo* took part in Operation 'Spellbinder' off the port of Egersund in southwestern Norway. While a force under Rear Admiral McGrigor, consisting of the heavy cruiser *Norfolk*, the light cruiser *Bellona* and three destroyers, attacked an enemy

The *Apollo* at 30 knots off the Pembroke coast on 30 January 1945. (Harley Hodges)

The *Apollo* also on 30 January 1945, off her port quarter. (Harley Hodges)

convoy, the *Apollo* laid mines across the shipping routes. In this endeavour she was screened by the destroyers *Zealous* and *Carron.* At one time she closed to within seven cables of the enemy-held shore, but encountered no opposition and returned to port safely. The enemy convoy attacked by Admiral McGrigor's force was protected by shore batteries, which made things lively for the attackers, but the convoy still lost two ships and an escorting German minesweeper.[34]

On 20 February 1945, the *Apollo* was involved in a collision with the corvette *Clarkia* at Milford Haven and naturally Geoffrey Hodges was inspired to more doggerel:

Apollo: Captain Johnny G.
Was once again upon the sea
But lost in fog he had a try
Relying on his P.P.I. [Point Position Indicator]
To guide his ship past wrecks and buoys
Up to a pier called 'Newton Noyes'
Another ship was on the move
Which after all could only prove
That when you cleave a ship in two
Their Lordships take a gloomy view
And look into the Matter!

Repairs were carried out at Pembroke Dock and were completed on 4 March. The time was not totally wasted as she cleaned her boilers at the same time.[35]

On 10 April, the *Ariadne*, newly arrived from the Pacific, began taking turns with the *Apollo* in laying mines in the North West Approaches in the vicinity of Oversay. The *Ariadne*'s first lay was on the Nymph Bank. On the 11th, the *Apollo* laid two minefields in one day, likely a record

but an accomplishment that was against Admiralty policy as too risky.[36]

For a real change of pace, the *Apollo*'s next duties took her to the Soviet Union. When German U-boats started making a considerable nuisance of themselves off the Kola Inlet leading to Murmansk, the Admiralty ordered the *Apollo,* the minelaying destroyers *Opportune, Obedient* and *Orwell* and the light cruiser *Dido* to execute Operation 'Trammell' under the designation 'Force 5'. On 17 April Force 5 left Scapa Flow, its crews supplied with a special issue of warm clothing. They circuitously rounded Norway's North Cape and on the 21st arrived at the Soviet naval base at Polyarno on the Kola Inlet. There they found the arrangements for refuelling woefully inadequate.

The *Apollo*'s taut wire measuring gear, January 1945. (Imperial War Museum A 27052)

Captain Grindle in his cabin on the *Apollo*. (Jeremy Grindle)

The *Apollo* in a gale. (Ron Thake)

The *Apollo*'s mining control room. (Imperial War Museum A 27057)

The *Apollo* with an open mine door and mines ready to go. (IWM A 27056)

That evening Captain Grindle sallied forth with two officers, including Lieutenant Hodges, to a dinner hosted by the Russians. There was plenty of food and even more vodka with which to drink the many toasts that were offered that evening. The visitors kept their heads anyway, except when Hodges accepted an invitation to play chess with 'the Russian Admiral', who beat him twice in five minutes.[37] They then withdrew as gracefully as they could to the *Apollo*.

Finally topped off with fuel, the next day the *Apollo* and *Obedient* laid mines in the eastern

area and the *Orwell* and *Opportune* laid mines in the western area, the *Apollo* laying 156 mines and the destroyers laying forty each. The lay went off without a hitch, but it had been necessary to run up the minelaying machinery on the mine deck to move the trains of mines forward and aft to make sure that nothing would freeze up in the intense cold.

The mines were set to lie ten fathoms down in order to catch prowling U-boats, but the Soviet naval officers who witnessed the lay from the *Apollo* were highly sceptical that the mines would take their depth as set. Captain Grindle dealt with the situation by having the Russian officers check their position on the chart with the Navigator and then directed the pilot to take them back to Polyarno directly across the minefield they had just laid. The *Apollo* and her guests survived this demonstration and the Russians later signalled the promise of a special dinner with whole roast piglet if the field caught a U-boat. Mission accomplished, Force 5 left for Scapa Flow on 23 April.[38] Most of the members of the *Apollo*'s crew thus qualified for 'Blue Nose' certificates for their first crossing of the Arctic Circle.[39]

On the *Apollo*'s trip to Russia, she carried an unusual additional passenger, one Midshipman John Robin Grindle, the Captain's eldest son. Before the *Apollo* sailed for Operation 'Trammell', Midshipman Grindle and his mother and younger brother Jeremy had learned, despite the censorship of the day, that if they went to Haverfordwest in Wales they would see a lot of Captain Grindle, who was with the *Apollo* at Milford Haven, for the first time since 1938. When the Russians agreed to the lay off Kola Inlet and the *Apollo* had to sail, the Captain suggested that Midshipman Grindle, who was then on leave, take passage in the *Apollo* to Scapa Flow. There, permission was granted by the C-in-C of the Home Fleet for him to continue on with the *Apollo* to Kola Inlet. While Captain Grindle used his sea cabin, Midshipman Grindle luxuriated in the Captain's normal sleeping cabin and was only responsible for plotting the weather map twice a day.

After the *Apollo* laid the deep trap field, Force 5 was sailing for home at 20 knots when it passed Bear Island and the *Apollo* was told to detach from her escorts and proceed forthwith. Midshipman Grindle recalled, 'Pa made a bit of a show of this . . . He rang on 40 knots and passed very close to the cruiser escort and put me on his bridge chair as he accelerated – it felt like a full foot down in a fast car!' Afterwards, Midshipman Grindle could claim to have been the only man in the Royal Navy to have gone on leave to North Russia during the war.

When the *Apollo* was away far above the Arctic Circle, the *Ariadne* carried on in Home Waters the rest of April and in May. Captain F B Lloyd took command of the *Ariadne* on 25 April 1945, just as the *Ariadne*'s minelaying days were ending.

They weren't quite over, though. On 1 May the *Ariadne* had a bit of excitement when Allied aircraft twice illuminated her with a powerful Leigh Light, the second time within fifteen minutes of commencing the lay, even though her IFF was switched on and was working properly. Luckily the Allied aircraft didn't fire on her or drop anything lethal.[40] One may assume a complaint was lodged.

On 6 May, without further incident, the *Ariadne* carried out her last minelaying operation, off Tory Island off the coast of Donegal, Ireland.[41] With the surrender of Germany, the *Ariadne*'s and *Apollo*'s minelaying duties finally came to an end. From April 1944 to the surrender of Germany on 8 May 1945, the *Apollo* had steamed 30,000 miles and had laid 8355 mines in fifty-six separate operations,[42] more than any of her sisters.

Lieutenant Geoffrey Hodges' 'Blue Nose' certificate, received for crossing the Arctic Circle in the *Apollo*. (Harley Hodges)

The *Ariadne* on 28 March 1945, on the way to Plymouth. (Author's collection)

CHAPTER 16

WAR'S END

Wᴴᴱɴ the war in Europe ended on 8 May 1945, VE Day, the *Apollo* and *Ariadne* was required for happier duties than minelaying. On the 11th, they took part in the aptly named Operation 'Kingdom'[1] and departed Rosyth with the heavy cruiser *Devonshire* and four destroyers for Norway carrying Prince Olav, the Norwegian Crown Prince, the rest of the Royal Family and Cabinet Ministers. The *Devonshire* had spirited the Royal Family away from the Germans in June 1940.

On the way, the Norwegians in the *Ariadne* discovered that their luggage had been put aboard the *Apollo* and the luggage was duly transferred using the fast minelayers' loading cranes, to the interest and delight of the passengers.

After taking on a German pilot – the maritime kind, not the Luftwaffe kind – they arrived in Oslo on 13 May[2] to a tumultuous welcome, first by small boats and then by cheering crowds ashore, who repeatedly sang the Norwegian national anthem.

The Norwegian Crown Prince Olav aboard the *Apollo*, May 1945. (Jeremy Grindle)

Captain Grindle later described the voyage to Norway in a letter to his wife. At 15.30 on 12 May Crown Prince Olav joined the *Apollo* at Rosyth and was met by a guard of honour. He was introduced to the ship's officers and inspected the ship's company at divisions. 'HRH of course had my cabin . . . The passage over was very peaceful – nearly flat calm and fine. We were, of course, swept over [i.e., by minesweepers] so could not go at any decent speed', no doubt to the intense disappointment of the Captain, who like any fast minelayer captain must have wanted to show off her speed to HRH.

By 08.00 the next day the flotilla was in the approaches to Oslo Fjord.

It was a lovely day and the whole countryside was covered in the Norwegian flag . . . boat after boat came out and cheered HRH. At 09.30 I held a Victory Sunday service in the mining deck attended by HRH and the whole staff – we went into committee and chose hymns whose tunes were used in Norway and I think it went down very well. It was recorded by the Norwegian BBC and I heard it played over afterwards . . . By the end of the service we were in the narrowest part of the fjord and it simply became a Royal procession, with the ship barging her way through a massed crowd of boats. HRH ran from side to side of the bridge trying to show himself to everyone and he usually succeeded. . . . At about [13.30] we stopped to pick up a harbour pilot and were simply swamped by boats whose occupants sang the National Anthem about 3 times – it was actually quite effective tho we could not have stood for a 4th time . . . Then at [15.50] we fell everyone in, paraded a guard and he landed in my boat . . . Naturally I did not see the landing except at a distance of $^1/_2$ mile or less, but it was quite terrific. HRH is extremely popular and obviously deserves to be.

Just a few days later, Prince Olav wrote a letter to Captain Grindle thanking him, his officers and crew for a 'safe and happy passage'.[3]

The *Apollo*'s official duties were over for the time being, except that she hosted a party for the children of Oslo. As Captain Grindle recalled, 'I arranged for the children to come to tea the next day and we had a tremendous time – & did they eat white bread and butter!'

Captain Grindle saw the signs that, after five years of German occupation, times were rapidly changing in Norway. He wrote to his wife:

Our Airborne troops had been here since Thursday and everything was quiet both politically and militarily. They have an enormous number of Germans still in the country – I have heard the figure of 3 hundred thousand mentioned and they are scattered in small defence posts everywhere. So, as they are acting quite correctly, they are marching in to selected concentration areas and are being disarmed on arrival – for example yesterday. . . I passed a complete and fully armed German cyclist battalion on the march.

At the same time, loyal Norwegians were being released from detention camps, which were being filled with Quislings awaiting investigation

Norwegian children on the *Apollo*, May 1945. (Jeremy Grindle)

into their activities during the occupation.

Leave was granted to the *Apollo*'s crew, which quickly experienced the warm hospitality of a liberated population. Lieutenant Hodges' red beard brought him many hugs from Norwegian girls. Alas, all good things had to come to an end. After a few extraordinary days in Oslo, the *Apollo* departed for Rosyth. In mid-May, the *Apollo* and *Ariadne* and were both taken in hand for refits prior to their joining the Pacific Fleet.

After a short refit, in June 1945 the *Apollo*, by now commanded by Captain L N Brownfield, left to join in the British Pacific Fleet in its operations against Japan, but she arrived too late

The *Ariadne* entering Grand Harbour at Malta, c. 1945–6. (Bill Pye)

A view of *Manxman's* twin 4in mounts from forward. (IWM HU 12964)

to take part in any combat operations. She did, however, arrive in time to transport stores from Sydney to an unnamed Australian cruiser in Tokyo Bay. The stores included crates of beer, which the Middle Watch found one night and many bottles ended up empty. The empty bottles were filled with water and the beer was then unloaded onto the cruiser in quick time before the *Apollo* quickly sped away.[4] Having avoided retribution, the *Apollo* returned to the United Kingdom in 1946.

In August, the *Ariadne* headed back to the Pacific, this time bound for Australia carrying urgent radar stores required at Sydney. Her travels included a sobering visit to Nagasaki. She did not return to the United Kingdom until April 1946.[5]

*   *   *

At long last, the *Manxman* re-commissioned for further service on 9 April 1945, under Captain G Thistleton-Smith. The ship's single 20mm Oerlikon guns had been replaced by four twins and she had been given a largely new suite of radars, including a Type 291 set for air search and a Type 276 set for surface search. The *Manxman* had also been fitted with a modified form of Action Information Centre, the lack of which having been noted by Captain Lord Ashbourne in 1944.[6] She sported a standard Admiralty paint scheme, an overall light gray with a large blue panel amidships.

Much of the *Manxman's* machinery must have been new. Spherical fronts were fitted to the ship's boilers, but the higher temperatures

The *Manxman* after completion of repairs in June 1945. (Imperial War Museum FL 4437)

Mines alongside the
Manxman, 1945.
(Imperial War Museum
HU 16144)

they generated restricted the ship's speed except in an emergency. Her new commanding officer reported that, probably because of additional displacement, the ship's endurance was considerably less than before,[7] news that was surely unwelcome.

Because of boiler defects, the *Manxman* did not sail from Sheerness for the Pacific until June 16th. As a result the delay, she missed her chance at any more action in the War, including the possibility of meeting any Kamikazes. She did not arrive at Colombo until 14 July and, when the Japanese surrendered on 14 August, she was at Melbourne, Australia. The *Manxman* remained with the British Pacific Fleet until June 1946 and then returned to the UK. After a refit, she returned to the Pacific Fleet in 1947. On her homeward journey in December of that year, her crew helped quell riots in Aden. On her arrival in the UK she paid off into reserve.[8]

A mine being loaded aboard the *Manxman*, 1945. (Imperial War Museum HU 129653)

CHAPTER 17

PEACETIME

OF the six fast minelayers, only the *Manxman*, *Ariadne* and *Apollo* survived to know the quiet of peacetime service.

The *Ariadne* returned to Britain from the Pacific in April 1946 and was reduced to reserve at Plymouth. She remained there until 1958, when consideration was given to refitting her as a 'fast despatch vessel'. The idea was abandoned in 1963 and she was sold for scrap and towed off to Dalmuir in 1965.[1]

In contrast, the *Apollo* enjoyed a more interesting post-war career. After she returned to the UK in 1946, she was reduced to reserve status and was laid up at Sheerness in the Thames estuary. She remained there for five years, until a shortage of vessels during the Korean War resulted in her leaving reserve status in the summer of 1951. After some modernisation, she rejoined the Home Fleet on 1 August. At the end of that month, she was sent to Jamaica to help the victims of Hurricane Charlie and returned to the UK on 1 October.

After her return, the *Apollo* was still not needed for minelaying and was instead designated a 'Despatch Vessel', which has been described as 'an anachronistic title, dating back to the pre-wireless days, when Commanders-in-Chief needed a fast vessel to carry signals back and forth'.[2] The role nevertheless made her virtually the flagship of the Home Fleet and the C-in-C made full use of her accommodations spaces, which were equal to those of a cruiser, except during exercises, when he would transfer to a more appropriate unit.[3]

From 1951 to 1961, the *Apollo* visited many Atlantic and European ports, including Leningrad in 1955 and 1960. She was present at the 1960 International Trade Fair at Helsinki, but by then her days were nearing an end. She was withdrawn for disposal in 1961 and was finally sold for scrapping in November of 1962.

The *Manxman* soldiered on for many more years.[4] In the spring of 1951 she recommissioned and in September she arrived at Malta to join the Mediterranean Fleet. On 24 October she transported 3rd Battalion Grenadier Guards to Tripoli to protect King Idris from an Egyptian coup. In June 1953, she returned to the UK for the Coronation Review and could be seen near the *Apollo* at the same occasion.

In 1953, the *Manxman* made her film debut as the German raider *Essen* in the film *Sailor of the King*, also known as *Single-Handed*. Disguised with makeshift turrets, she took part in filming off the coast of Gozo, Malta.[5] Film glory behind her, she reposed in operational reserve in Malta

The *Apollo* in 1952.
(Marius Bar)

The *Manxman* in 1952. (Imperial War Museum FL 4444)

from August of that year to February 1956. Then her after 4in guns were removed to make way for more accommodation.

Early in 1956, the *Manxman* was once again able to make use of her unique talents. After the devastating Chim earthquake in southern Lebanon on 16 March, she left Malta for Beirut loaded with 4000 blankets, 2000 camp beds, bully beef and condensed milk. She covered the 1026-mile voyage at a speed of 26 knots and arrived on 21 March.[6]

In October and November of 1956, she took part in the abortive Suez operation. For a few days in November, she was flagship of the Mediterranean Fleet. There is a story that she shadowed the US Sixth Fleet, which could not outrun her. When the Suez Canal was cleared, the *Manxman* was sent up and down the Canal to make sure. After spell in reserve, she recommissioned at Chatham as a Forward Ship for Coastal Minesweepers in the Far East and then served in Borneo from 1963 to 1966. After a

refit in Singapore, she left for the UK in October 1968. In November 1968, she took part in the Beira Patrol, which was designed to keep oil for the regime in Rhodesia from reaching it via the port of Beira in Mozambique. On 18 December 1968, she arrived in Spithead.

The last of the fast minelayers, she ended her days in 1972 in the scrapyard at Newport, Monmouthshire. CPO John Hordless served in her in 1956–7, and described her as 'a proper warship'.

The *Manxman* delivering supplies to Beirut after the 1956 earthquake. (IWM HU 101338)

The *Manxman* in the 1960s with her twin 4in mounts removed. (National Museum of the Royal Navy 1984.15)

CHAPTER 18

EPILOGUE AND HONOURS

THE fast minelayers of the *Abdiel* class served in every ocean and every theatre of operations in the Second World War. They and their design were highly successful and more than fulfilled the hopes of their designers and the Admiralty.

The success of their design is all the more remarkable because there had been nothing like them before, the design process was a very short one and the designers were operating in an environment in which rearmament had been delayed for years and there was tremendous pressure to complete designs so that necessary ships could be built. Their faults were few and were no different than other warships of the Royal Navy of their day; less endurance than expected and indifferent directors to control their 4in guns and the pom-pom.

They and their talents were ideal for the war the Royal Navy had to fight, especially in the

The *Manxman*'s bell, now in the Malta War Museum. (Author's collection)

critical years of 1941 and 1942. As the war progressed and the tide turned in favour the Allies, there was less need for their speed or their spacious mine decks, but they carried on to the end.

The fast minelayers proved their worth in the battle for Crete, on the run to Tobruk, in many hazardous runs to Malta, in convoy or sailing alone, in assaults on Madagascar and on Pacific islands and, yes, even in offensive mine laying runs off heavily defended enemy coasts or in their shipping lanes. Their runs played a vital role in the salvation of Malta and their mines directly accounted for a respectable number of Axis ships, both warships and supply ships and restricted the movements of others.

The toll inflicted by the fast minelayers includes the Italian destroyers *Ascari*, *Saetta*, *Corsaro*, *Lanzerotto Malocello* and *Carlo Mirabello*, the escort torpedo boats *Ciclone* and *Uragano*, the corvette *Procellaria*, the torpedo boat *Prestinari*, the minesweepers *Carmelo Noli* and *M 1208*, the gunboat *Pellegrino Matteuci*, the merchant ships *Marburg*, *Kybfels*, *Ankara* and *Henry Estier*, the war transport *KT.13*, a Siebel ferry, two ferry barges and the S-boat *S 35*.

The men who sailed in the fast minelayers experienced everything other men serving in the Royal Navy experienced. There was the terror of being under air attack, sudden explosion and death from torpedoes or mines, boredom, exhaustion from long hours at sea and at Action Stations, 'chokker', homesickness and loneliness.

But for the men of the fast minelayers there was more; much more than other men in the Royal Navy, their ships often sailed alone, often at night and in enemy waters. The many solo voyages put tremendous pressure and responsibility on their captains, one of whom admitted to a brief case of 'pure schoolboy woe'. Sometimes their men knew immediately that they had accomplished something, such as when greeted enthusiastically by the populace of Malta on their arrival there, but at other times, after laying a minefield in enemy waters, the men of the fast minelayers could only wonder if they had done the enemy any harm. Such is the nature of offensive minelaying.

There were plenty of battle and campaign honours for the fast minelayers, as well as awards, honours and decorations for the men who served in them, notices for which were periodically published in the *London Gazette*.

The *Abdiel* herself earned four Battle Honours, for 'Biscay 1941', 'Crete 1941', 'Libya 1941' and 'Sicily 1943'.[1] She had 'sunk a Panzer division' and Axis ships bound for North Africa, ferried troops to and from Crete, Cyprus and Tobruk, survived angry bombers in the Mediterranean and the Bay of Biscay, dodged 'porpoises', transported VIPs and Wrens and even carried gold. The first fast minelayer had served well and had thoroughly vindicated her unique design.

During her splendid career, the *Abdiel*'s men won many decorations, though the King and the Admiralty were strangely ungenerous to her first commission, handing out seven Mentions in Despatches, three to officers (including Captain Pleydell-Bouverie) and four to petty officers and ratings.[2] The second commission fared rather better, with Captain Orr-Ewing becoming a Companion of the Distinguished Service Order and the Bar to the Distinguished Service Cross was awarded to Lieutenant Robertson, the Distinguished Service Medal was awarded to petty officers and ratings and Mentions in Despatches were awarded to three officers (including Lieutenant Hodges) and five petty officers and ratings.[3]

As for Captain Pleydell-Bouverie, after sailing the *Abdiel* back to Britain, he went on to command HMS *Hornet*, a Coastal Forces base at Gosport in Hampshire. Judging by one of his photo albums, he witnessed the surrender of German S-boats there in 1945. He was invalided out of the Navy in 1946 and he retired to the New Forest in Hampshire, where he was chairman of the New Forest Rural District Council. In 1951, he died on the operating table at the Lymington Hospital from a perforated ulcer.

After the sinking of the *Abdiel*, Captain Orr-Ewing became the Captain of the Gunnery School at Devonport. After the war he was appointed Commodore Superintendent of the Malta Dockyard and then Commanding Officer of the battleship *Anson*. He retired to farming at the family home in Scotland and passed away in 1964.[4]

During her short career, the *Latona* received one Battle Honour, for 'Libya 1941'. The *Latona* has been given a fitting epitaph by Tom Burton, the author of the Warship Profile on the *Abdiel*s. 'So perished this fine ship, without having laid a single mine, the victim of her own versatility'.[5] And, one might add, the victim of the 'obduracy' of General Blamey and the Australian Governments of the day.

A number of men from the *Latona* won awards for 'courage and resolution when H.M.S. *Latona* was sunk'. Chief among them, Acting Sub-Lieutenant William Barrett received the Distinguished Service Cross. He would go on to serve in the Royal Navy for twenty-three years, but would never reveal what he did to win the DSC to Gertrude, his wife of many years, just as he would never explain to her how he acquired the burn wounds on his legs. Another *Latona* crewman, Writer Geoffrey Peters, received the Distinguished Service Medal and three petty officers and ratings received Mentions in Despatches.[6]

After commanding the *Latona*, Captain Bateson was able to return to sea and commanded the light cruiser *Ajax* and then, after a spell at the Admiralty, the heavy cruiser *London*. After the war, he served as the Director of the Naval Electrical Department at the Admiralty, was promoted to Rear Admiral (L) while there and was awarded a CB and a CBE. After his retirement, he served as the Sheriff of Rutland in 1958.[7] After his first wife passed away, he married Marie, whose first husband was wounded in the disaster at Bari in 1943 and had died prematurely.

For her efforts, the *Manxman* received one Battle Honour, 'Malta Convoys 1941-42'. The *Manxman* missed much of the war with repairs for torpedo damage, but she was in the middle of the fray in 1941 and 1942 when it really counted. She contributed much to minelaying operations off the coast of France and especially to the survival of Malta and executed a very hazardous minelaying operation right off the coast of Italy. Hers was a record to be proud of.

While in command of the *Manxman*, Captain

Dickson received a Distinguished Service Order and three Mentions in Despatches.[8] Executive Officer Lieutenant-Commander Hopper and Navigator Lieutenant Brayne-Nicholls won the DSC, seven petty officers and ratings won Distinguished Service Medals and several other men won Mentions in Despatches.[9] Telegraphist Ron Checketts was later awarded an MBE for his diplomatic service after the War.

As the *Manxman*'s repairs would not be completed for some time, Captain Dickson left the *Manxman* for an appointment at the Admiralty. Later in 1943, he was treated to an audience with the Prime Minister, but, alas, it was Mr Churchill who did almost all the talking. Dickson was soon promoted to Rear Admiral and became the Director of Naval Information from 1944 to 1946. In that post, he gave a number of radio broadcasts, one of which dealt with a typical night-time operation by a fast minelayer in enemy waters, while another dealt with the disguise of the *Manxman*.[10] Admiral Dickson died in an accident in 1952 and his death was duly noted in the *Times of Malta*.[11]

The *Welshman* won one Battle Honour, 'Malta Convoys 1942', which was appropriate enough, but hardly does her service to Malta justice. Years later, Ronald Walford, a Boy Scout in Malta during the War, said of the *Welshman*, 'As one of the many, many thousands of people from babies to the most elderly, who lived on the food brought by *Welshman* and who were defended by the fuel and ammunition she carried, I must emphasise most strongly the sense of gratitude towards her for our survival'.[12]

Shortly after the *Welshman*'s loss, Ian Hay wrote an epitaph for her in his *The Unconquerable Isle*. The *Welshman* had become 'an object of adoration to the Maltese. They regarded her, perhaps rightly, as their mascot. To-day the *Welshman*'s task is done: she lies at the bottom of the Mediterranean, somewhere off the North African coast and her story is ended. But it is still told in the Island and always will be'.[13]

The *Welshman* had an extraordinary though short career as a true 'jack of all trades, master of all', leading her ship's company to wonder at one point, 'What the Hell are we, a minelayer, a Bank or a grocer's shop?'[14] She was all of those and more.

There was plenty of recognition for the officers and men of the *Welshman*. In September of 1942, Captain Friedberger won the Distinguished Service Order, Lieutenant-Commander Lindsay Gellatly, RAN, won the Distinguished Service Cross. Five petty officers and ratings received the Distinguished Service Medal, and thirteen officers, petty officers and ratings received Mentions in Despatches, including a posthumous one for Able Seaman Arthur Lamb.[15] In May 1943, more officers, petty officers and ratings were gazetted for Mentions in Despatches, including Commander (E) Hims, Lieutenant-Commander Gellatly, Lieutenant I N V Cox and Paymaster Lieutenant Basil Kenneth Freedman,[16] but some men had been lost with the ship before they could receive their awards.

After commanding the *Welshman*, Captain Friedberger returned to the Plans Division of the Admiralty. After the end of the war in the Pacific, he became the Commodore Superintendent of HM Dockyard in Singapore. He retired in 1949. At the age of 66, he became ill with cancer and died on 5 January 1963. The death notice in the *Daily Telegraph* prompted a letter to his widow from Able Seaman John Owen. On 10 January he wrote to her of how Captain Friedberger was greatly respected by all the members of the crew, that Owen had 'never known a more courageous and competent sailor' and that 'I owe my life at least a dozen times to his seamanship and coolness'.

There was little demand for a 'Pacific 1944' Battle Honour, but the *Ariadne* would have qualified. She served honourably in the Mediterranean before and in Home Waters after her stint in the Pacific, but it was her time in the Pacific that truly set her apart. The *Ariadne* showed what British constructors and shipbuilders could achieve and she and her Captain and crew ably represented the Royal Navy in the Pacific before the British Pacific Fleet could arrive.

After commanding the *Ariadne*, Lord Ashbourne returned to submarines and commanded the 3rd Submarine Flotilla. After the war, he was awarded the Companion Order of the Bath (CB) and rose to the rank of Vice Admiral. He was finally able to serve in the House of Lords. He passed the final bar on 3 September 1983.[17]

During the war, the *Apollo* earned one Battle Honour, 'Normandy 1944'. Evidently there was no Battle Honour for 'Norwegian Coast, 1944-45', much less for 'Kola Inlet, 1945'. The *Apollo* had had a relatively short but arduous war and laid more mines than any other fast minelayer. While commanding the *Apollo*, Captain Grindle twice received Mentions in Despatches to add to his CBE. The ship's Torpedo Officer, Lieutenant John Stevens, RNVR, was awarded the

not one was preserved. Nothing like them has been built since and may never be built again.

Those who served in them were proud of their unique design. In 1949, Captain Dickson, by then a Rear Admiral, objected to a description of the *Manxman* in a press release as 'one of four new minelayers' and said it should more properly read, 'one of the four new Fast

Distinguished Service Cross, three petty officers received the Distinguished Service Medal and no less than thirteen other officers, petty officers and ratings received Mentions in Despatches.

After commanding the *Apollo*, Captain Grindle went to the Far East as the war was ending and afterwards was the senior British naval officer in Japan. When the *Apollo* visited Japan, he made sure her crew was able to visit Hiroshima. Captain Grindle retired from the Navy in 1950 and among other pursuits served as a magistrate in Fareham for nineteen years. He passed away in 1991.[18]

The fast minelayers are no more today. The hazardous duties they were assigned resulted in the loss of three of their number during the war, two with heavy loss of life. The three surviving ships soldiered on in war and then in peace, but

Minelayers'. He went on to point out that they were 'an entirely new type in any Navy – a most successful venture by the British Admiralty'.[19]

Tangible reminders of the fast minelayers are now few. The *Manxman*'s bell lies behind glass at the National War Museum at Fort St Elmo in Malta. There are also several memorials. One of them is a memorial to the fast minelayers, the port of Milford Haven and the minelayer *Adventure* at the site of the old Mining Depot in Milford Haven, in the form of a plaque affixed to a mine on a platform overlooking the sea. The same mine also carries plaques to the workforce at the Mining Depot at Milford Haven, which supplied mines to the fast minelayers and to the paratroopers who were lost in the *Abdiel* on the night of 9/10 September 1943.

Less prominently, but more conveniently to

most, the memorial to the Siege of Malta in London, near All Hallows by the Tower church, mentions 'single-ship deliveries by fast warship', which can only mean the fast minelayers.

The *Welshman* has been well remembered. The Welshman Association was started by George and Angela Evennett in the 1990s to remember George's brother John Norman Evennett, who was lost when the *Welshman* went down. The Association commissioned a stained glass window with an image of the ship, the word 'Malta', an image of a Welsh dragon and a plaque listing all the men who were lost in the *Welshman*, all at the St George's Centre in Chatham. For years, the Association held commemorations in honour of the *Welshman* and her men on the anniversary of her loss on 1 February, with as many survivors as possible attending, but it has held its last.

The *Abdiel*'s name has been used again, with the minelayer and mine countermeasures support ship *Abdiel*, which was completed in 1967 and could make all of 16 knots.[20] The *Ariadne*'s name was revived for a modern *Leander* class frigate, which was built by Yarrow in Scotstoun, laid down in 1969 and put into service in 1973. This most recent *Ariadne* was almost as large as her predecessor, but was designed for a mere 27 knots.[21] Like the *Ariadne*, the *Apollo*'s name was revived for a *Leander*, which was built by Yarrow in Scotstoun, laid down in 1969 and put into service in 1972.[22] Not so the *Latona*, *Manxman* or *Welshman*.

The *Welshman* has even been remembered in celluloid or whatever passes for it these days. In the 1953 film *The Malta Story*, with Alec Guinness, Jack Hawkins and Muriel Pavlow, there is a reference to the arrival of 'the unescorted fast minelayer *Welshman*', followed by a scene purporting to show someone boarding the *Welshman,* which is actually played by a *Dido* class cruiser.

The number of men who braved so much and who accomplished so much in the fast minelayers is rapidly dwindling and they should never be forgotten. Nor should the unique and very special ships they served in, a triumph of British warship design and construction, of which Britain can be justly proud.

The *Manxman*'s wash, November 1942. (Imperial War Museum A 13028)

APPENDIX
Plans, Camouflage and Models

Plans

The official plans for the *Abdiel* class are held in the National Maritime Museum's Brass Foundry at Woolwich Arsenal, where there are sets of as-fitted plans for the *Abdiel* and for the *Ariadne*. There are no official plans of the first four as refitted in 1942. A set of plans of the *Ariadne* by A&A Plans was available for purchase and was reproduced in a book called *British Warships of the Second World War* and in the Warship Profile on the *Abdiel*s, which also featured a foldout colour plan of the *Abdiel* in 1942–3.

Camouflage

The subject of Royal Navy warship camouflage in the Second World War is a complex one, with many colours and many different patterns in use from 1939 to 1945, no less for fast minelayers than any other class of ship. Documentation is often sparse, non-existent or contradictory, and one often has to guess at the colours used in a particular scheme or pattern. The beautiful colour artwork by Eric Leon in this book is offered as a well-educated guess. It is not helpful that some photographs of the fast minelayers have been labelled as the wrong ship.

The Profile's beautiful colour centerspread of the *Abdiel* in her 1942–3 pattern provides no information on which colours were used. There was likely an official pattern but it has not survived.

Abdiel

When nearing completion and once completed, she was painted up in a medium gray, probably one known as 507B.

In the Mediterranean, she was repainted into a scheme of light gray overall with black shapes from her waterline almost but not quite up to her upper deck and on her funnels and upperworks.

She emerged from her 1942 refit with a new and striking 'disruptive' camouflage scheme, seemingly of four colours and seems to have remained in that scheme until her loss. The colours may be 507A, a dark gray, MS3, a medium gray-green, 507C, a light gray, and white.

Latona

When new, the *Latona* was painted up in a layer-cake camouflage scheme of three tones, with the darkest one lowest and the lightest one highest in the ship. The three tones may have been dark and medium shades of Mountbatten Pink and white or may instead have been dark and medium grays – 507A and 507B, perhaps, and white. She seems to have remained in that scheme, but with the light colour on the funnels painted out, as shown in film of her in the Mediterranean at the Australian War Memorial under F03526.

Manxman

Upon completion, she was painted up in an overall medium gray, probably one called 507B and seems to have carried that scheme until she was torpedoed, except presumably when she was disguised as the *Léopard* in 1941.

In November 1941, when orders arrived for the *Manxman* to paint up in the same Admiralty 'disruptive' design as *Welshman* at the next repainting, Captain Dickson wrote that he hated the prospect of it and 'Give me plain gray every time'. He seems to have gotten his way, perhaps by avoiding repainting before the *Manxman* left for the Indian Ocean.

A photograph of the *Abdiel* at Colombo in 1942, which can be found at the Imperial War Museum under A9688, was mislabelled in the Warship Profile as the *Manxman*, leading some to think the *Manxman* wore the *Abdiel*'s 1941–2 pattern of light gray with black geometric black shapes. Captain Dickson would have been horrified.

When the *Manxman* had a docking in Suez in

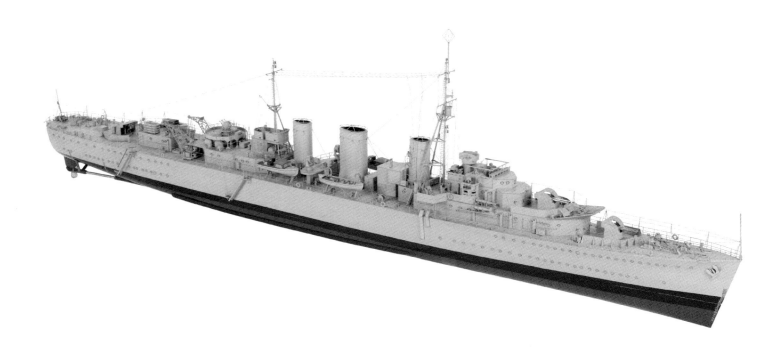

October 1942, her Captain wrote that she was repainted in three grays instead of three greens, which would at least suggest she was painted in green in the Indian Ocean, perhaps when she was testing her 'island' disguise.

When the ship emerged from repairs in May 1945, she wore an Admiralty Standard scheme with a dark panel amidships and a lighter overall colour.

Welshman

Upon completion, the *Welshman* wore a striking disruptive-style four-colour scheme, which was similar to the one worn by the *Abdiel* in her second commission, but with less contrast between some of the colours. Two of the colours were MS4A, a light gray-green, and white, which was replaced by 507C by December 1941.

When the *Welshman* was disguised as the *Léopard* in May 1942, she was painted in a light gray of unknown hue, though it may have been 507C. During the 'Harpoon' convoy in June, she retained the disguise and the light gray paint and by her July voyage to Malta she had doffed the disguise but retained the light gray paint.

When the *Welshman* completed her refit in October 1942, she had shed her light gray paint

and donned a multi-colour disruptive camouflage scheme similar to the one she carried when she completed, but quite possibly with different colours and even less contrast between some of them.

Ariadne

Upon completion, she was painted up in a camouflage scheme of three colours, which was much less 'disruptive' than the ones carried by the *Abdiel* in her second commission and by the *Welshman* twice during her short career. By the time she was back in Home Waters, she was painted in an unusual scheme of a very dark panel carried up to her upper deck and a medium shade overall. Perhaps after the war ended, she wore a scheme with her hull painted in a medium colour and her upperworks in a lighter colour.

Apollo

Upon completion, she was painted up in a wavy camouflage scheme of two colours, which seems to have morphed into the same pattern but with three colours. By January 1945, she wore a very unusual scheme of a light-to-medium panel amidships but a very dark colour overall. She

was later painted in an Admiralty Standard scheme with a medium shade of panel amidships and a lighter colour overall.

Models

There are no 1:1 scale fast minelayers left, so anyone wanting a 3D representation of them must be content with a scale model. There are several very fine, large-scale models of the *Abdiel* class, one in 1/48 scale of *Abdiel* herself at Chatham at the National Maritime Museum location there and one of the *Latona* at the SeaCity Museum in Southampton. Both are available for viewing by appointment.

In a much smaller scale, an exquisite, pre-painted and built-up model of the *Abdiel* in 1/1250 scale in white metal was produced by the German firm Neptun and can still be found for purchase. Other members of the class have been produced over the years in metal by other German firms in 1/1250 or 1/1200 scale. Finally, there is a 1/2400 scale model of the *Manxman* from GHQ.

Model kits of the *Abdiel*s have been produced by various firms over the years, including one of the *Manxman* in 1/96 scale by Dean's Marine, one in resin, brass and white metal of the *Abdiel* in 1/350 by White Ensign Models, a plastic one of the *Manxman* in 1/600 by Airfix, ones in resin and white metal of the *Abdiel* and *Ariadne* in 1/700 by the Japanese firm Waveline, a plastic one of the *Ariadne* in 1/700 by Matchbox and a resin one of the *Abdiel* in 1/700 by B-Resina.

Model of *Abdiel*, stern. (National Maritime Museum L2724-02)

NOTES

Introduction
[1] Courtesy of Captain Pleydell-Bouverie's son, Robin Pleydell-Bouverie.
[2] F N Goodwin, *Midshipman Royal Naval Reserve* (Spennymoor: The Memoir Club, 2001).

Chapter 1: Mines, Minelaying and Minelayers: Origins to the Eve of the Second World War
[1] Jack Sweetman, *American Naval History: An Illustrated Chronology* (Annapolis: Naval Institute Press, 1984), pp 2–3; Thomas J Cutler, 'Courage and Innovation Combined', *US Naval Institute Proceedings* (November 2013), p 93.
[2] Harry Barnard, *Armsmear: The Home, the Arm, and the Armory of Samuel Colt, A Memorial* (New York: 1866), pp 275–92; Martin Rywell, *Samuel Colt: A Man and An Epoch* (Harriman, Tennessee: Pioneer Press, 1955), pp 70–3.
[3] D K Brown, *Before the Ironclad: Development of Ship Design, Propulsion, and Armament in the Royal Navy, 1815-60* (London: Conway Maritime Press, 1960), pp 152–3; Our Special Correspondent, 'Russian Infernal Machines', *The Illustrated London News* (23 June 1855), pp 623–4.
[4] Encyclopaedia Britannica Online, accessed 22 January 2014.
[5] Naval Staff History, *British Mining Operations 1939-1945*, BR 1736 (56)(1) (London: HMSO, 1973), p 2.
[6] H Jentschura, D Jung and P Mickel, *Warships of the Imperial Japanese Navy 1869-1945* (Annapolis: Naval Institute Press, 1977), p 204.
[7] Paul H Silverstone, *Directory of the World's Capital Ships* (New York: Hippocrene Books, 1984), pp 328, 339 and 382.
[8] Jentschura, Jung and Mickel, *Warships of the Imperial Japanese Navy*, p 17.
[9] Naval Staff History, *British Mining Operations*, pp 3–4.
[10] M P Crocker, *Mine Warfare Vessels of the Royal Navy – 1908 To Date* (Shrewsbury: Airlife Publishing Ltd., 1993), pp 26–8; Naval Staff History, *British Mining Operations*, p 4.
[11] F J Dittmar and J J Colledge, *British Warships 1914-1919* (London: Ian Allen Ltd., 1972), p 45.
[12] Naval Staff History, *British Mining Operations*, p 6.
[13] Sir Julian S Corbett, *History of the Great War, Naval Operations, Vol. I, To the Battle of the Falklands December 1914* (London: Longmans, Green & Co., 1920), pp 239–46.
[14] Arthur J Marder, *From the Dreadnought to Scapa Flow, Volume II, The War Years: To the Eve of Jutland* (London: Oxford University Press, 1965), pp 246–7.
[15] Silverstone, *Directory of the World's Capital Ships*, p 195.
[16] Norman Friedman, *British Destroyers From Earliest Days to the Second World War* (Annapolis: Naval Institute Press, 2009), pp 154, 296 and 307.
[17] Admiral Viscount Jellicoe, *The Grand Fleet 1914-1916: Its Creation, Development & Work* (New York: George H Doran Co., 1919), p 373.
[18] V E Tarrant, *Jutland: The German Perspective* (London: Arms & Armour Press, 1995), p 234.
[19] Reinhard Scheer, *Germany's High Seas Fleet in the World War* (London: Cassell & Co., 1920), p 166.
[20] Captain J S Cowie, CBE, RN, *Mines, Minelayers and Minelaying* (London: Oxford University Press, 1949), p 56; Arthur Marder, *From the Dreadnought to Scapa Flow; Jutland and After, May 1916 to December 1916*, 2d ed. (Oxford: Oxford University Press, 1978), pp 159 and 251; Sir Julian S Corbett, *History of the Great War: Naval Operations, Vol. III*, 2d ed. (London: Longmans, 1940), pp 418–21.
[21] Jellicoe, *The Grand Fleet*, pp 373 and 482.
[22] Gerhard Koop and Klaus-Peter Schmolke, *Kleine Kreuzer 1903 – 1918 (Bremen bis Cöln Klasse)* (Bonn: Bernard & Graefe Verlag, 2004), p 217.
[23] Ibid, pp 215–18; Anton Novik, 'The Story of the Cruisers *Bremse* and *Brummer*,' *Warship International*, Vol. VI, No 3 (Summer 1969), pp 185–9; H M Le Fleming, *Warships of World War I* (London: Ian Allen, 1961).
[24] Norman Friedman, *British Cruisers: Two World Wars and After* (Annapolis: Naval Institute Press, 2010), p 325.
[25] Naval Staff History, *British Mining Operations*, p 44.
[26] Ibid, p 45.
[27] H T Lenton, *British and Empire Warships of the Second World War* (London: Greenhill Books, 1998), pp 306 and 308.
[28] Australian War Memorial FO1549.
[29] Captain J S Cowie, RN, 'Minelayers', *Journal of the Royal United Service Institution*, Vol. C (February–November 1955), p 605.
[30] Friedman, *British Cruisers*, p 328.
[31] See TNA Adm 226/38, pp 300–1.

Chapter 2: Getting It Just Right – Designing the *Abdiel* Class
[1] *Abdiel* Class Ships Covers, No 594, National Maritime Museum, Woolwich Arsenal.
[2] TNA Kew Adm 1/9435.
[3] Friedman, *British Cruisers*, p 400.
[4] D K Brown, *The Design and Construction of British*

Warships 1939-1945, The Official Record: Major Surface Vessels (London: Conway Maritime Press, 1995), p 123.

[5] E-mail from Harley Hodges, citing a letter from Admiral Sir Morgan-Giles to Geoffrey Hodges of 1 July 1993.

[6] Samuel Eliot Morison, *Leyte: June 1944 –January 1945* (Boston: Little, Brown & Co., 1958), p 117.

[7] John Campbell, *Naval Weapons of World War Two* (London: Conway Maritime Press, 1985), p 56.

[8] Revised Legend, May 1942, Ship's Cover, National Martime Museum, Woolwich Arsenal.

[9] Campbell, *Naval Weapons of World War Two*, pp 56, 71–4, 75–6 and 78.

[10] Cowie, *Mines, Minelayers and Minelaying*, p 55.

[11] Brown, *The Design and Construction of British Warships*, p 124.

[12] TNA Adm 1/12350.

[13] Captain Dennis Friedberger, 'Fast Minelayer', in Hawthorn & Leslie, *Our Ships at War* (1946), p 13.

[14] John English, *Afridi to Nizam: British Fleet Destroyers 1937-43* (Gravesend: World Ship Society, 2001), p 12.

[15] *Abdiel* Class Ships Covers, National Maritime Museum.

[16] Maurice Northcott, *Hood Design and Construction: An Ensign Special* (London: Bivouac Books, Ltd., 1975), p 52.

[17] Friedberger, 'Fast Minelayer', p 13.

[18] Brown, *The Design and Development of British Warships*, p 123.

[19] D K Brown, 'On Trial . . .,' *Warship World*, Vol V, No 5 (Winter 1995), pp 19–21.

[20] Pleydell-Bouverie, 'HMS *Abdiel*'; F N Goodwin, Letter to J V Calcraft of 21 January 2001.

[21] Henri Le Masson, *Navies of the Second World War: The French Navy I* (London: MacDonald & Co., 1969), pp 116 and 118.

[22] Jürg Meister, *Soviet Warships of the Second World War* (New York: Arco Publishing Co., 1977), p 50.

[23] Aldo Fraccaroli, *Italian Warships of World War II* (London: Ian Allen, 1968), p 37.

[24] A J Watts, *Japanese Warships of World War II* (London: Ian Allen, 1966), p 153.

[25] Meister, *Soviet Warships of the Second World War*, p 49.

[26] Brown, *The Design and Construction of British Warships*, p 123.

[27] Signal from FOCNA to VA(M) at 1024B on May 1, 1942. TNA Kew Adm 223/553.

[28] Brown, *The Design and Construction of British Warships*, p 11.

[29] Ibid, p 27 n18.

[30] 'History of the U.S. Navy's Minelayer *Terror*,' *Warship International* Vol VI, No.3 (Summer 1969), pp 190–8.

[31] Hans Lengerer, 'Imperial Japanese Minelayers *Itsukushima*, *Okinoshima*, and *Tsuguru*,' in John Jordan (ed) *Warship 2008* (London: Conway Maritime Press, 2008), pp 52–66.

[32] Meister, *Soviet Warships of the Second World War*, pp 79–81.

[33] Siegfried Breyer, *Marine-Arsenal Special Band 5, Der Z-Plan: Streben zur Weltmachtflotte* (Friedberg: Podzun-Pallas-Verlag, 1996), p 44.

[34] Le Masson, *Navies of the Second World War: The French Navy I*, pp 96–7.

[35] Jürgen Rohwer, *Chronology of the War at Sea 1939-1945* (London: Chatham Publishing, 2005), p 77.

[36] Pierre Hervieux, 'German Destroyer Minelaying Operations off the English Coast (1940–41 [*sic*: 1939–40]), in John Roberts, (ed), *Warship* Vol IV (London: Conway Maritime Press, 1980), pp 110–16.

[37] George Moore, *Building for Victory* (Gravesend: World Ship Society, 2003), pp 11, 12.

[38] TNA Kew Adm 1/10161, Courtesy of David Davies; T D Manning and C F Walker, *British Warship Names* (London: Putman, 1959), p 47.

Chapter 3: The Royal Navy Readies for Mine Warfare in the Second World War

[1] Campbell, *Naval Weapons of World War Two*, p 96; Cowie, *Mines, Minelayers and Minelaying*, pp 92–93, 111, 113.

[2] Naval Staff History, *British Mining Operations*, pp 46, 574.

[3] Ibid, p 123.

[4] Cowie, *Mines, Minelayers and Minelaying*, p x.

[5] Ibid, pp vii–viii.

[6] Ibid, p 100.

Chapter 4: The *Abdiel* Completes and Proves Her Worth: Home Waters and the Mediterranean, 1941

[1] Manning and Walker, *British Warship Names*, p 67; T P Stopford, *Admiralty Ships Badges: Original Patterns, 1919-1994* (Strood: Stone Frigate, 1996), Vol 1, p 2.

[2] TNA Kew Adm 1/12247.

[3] Moore, *Building for Victory*, p 145.

[4] See Supplement to the *London Gazette*, 13 October 1942, p 4449.

[5] TNA Kew Adm 1/12247.

[6] Stopford, *Admiralty Ships Badges*, Vol 1, p 2.

[7] See Alan Coles, *Three Before Breakfast* (Havant: Kenneth Mason, 1979) for a full account of the loss of these ships.

[8] Memoir of Captain P M B Chavasse, CBE, DSC, RN. Documents 9064, Imperial War Museum.

[9] Naval Staff History, *British Mining Operations*, p 296.

[10] N H G Austen, Memoir. Imperial War Museum No 19689.

[11] TNA Kew Adm 1/12247.

[12] Captain P M B Chavasse, CBE, DSC, RN, Memoir.

[13] Naval Staff History, *British Mining Operations*, p 298.

[14] Ibid, p 298. Pleydell-Bouverie, 'HMS *Abdiel*'.

[15] Viscount Cunningham of Hyndhope, *A Sailor's Odyssey* (New York: E P Dutton & Co, Inc., 1951), p 360.

[16] Goodwin, *Midshipman RNR*, p 24.

[17] TNA Kew Adm 199/413.

[18] Pleydell-Bouverie, 'HMS *Abdiel*'.

19 Ibid.

20 Michael Simpson (ed.), *The Cunningham Papers: Volume I The Mediterranean Fleet, 1939-1942* (Aldershot: Ashgate Publishing Limited for the Naval Records Society, 1999), p 400.

21 Ibid, p 405, citing TNA Cab 106/722.

22 TNA Kew Adm 199/414, p 241.

23 Admiralty Historical Section, *The Royal Navy and the Mediterranean, Volume II: November 1940 – December 1941* (London: Routledge 2002), pp 94–100.

24 Pleydell-Bouverie, 'HMS *Abdiel*'.

25 TNA Kew Adm 199/414.

26 Ibid.

27 Ibid.

28 Pleydell-Bouverie, 'HMS *Abdiel*'.

29 Maurizio Brescia, *Mussolini's Navy: A Reference Guide to the Regia Marina 1930-1945* (Barnsley: Seaforth Publishing, 2012), pp 107, 175.

30 Fraccaroli, *Italian Warships of World War II*, p 42.

31 Franz Steinzer, *Die 2. Panzer-Division 1935-1945* (Friedberg: Podzun-Pallas-Verlag, 1977), pp 69–70.

32 Post by Hans Weber on January 24, 2004, on Jason Pipes' site, Feldgrau.net. Accessed 3 November 2014.

33 C.F. Gian Carlo Pagano, *La Guerra di Mine*, 2nd Edition (Rome: Ufficio Storico della Marina Militare, 1988), p 458.

34 Admiralty Historical Section, *The Royal Navy and the Mediterranean* II, p 105; Naval Staff History, *British Mining Operations*, pp 572–3.

35 Franz Halder, *Kriegstagebuch* II (Stuttgart: W Kohlhammer Verlag, 1963), pp 426–7.

36 Steinzer, *Die 2. Panzer-Division*, p 69.

37 Halder, *Kriegstagebuch* II, p 427.

38 Steinzer, *Die 2. Panzer-Division*, pp 70, 107, 111.

39 Memoir of Captain P M B Chavasse, p 9.

40 Gavin Long, *Australia in the War of 1939-1945, Series One, Army, Vol. II, Greece, Crete and Syria* (Canberra: Australian War Memorial, 1953), p 243.

41 Memoir of Captain P M B Chavasse, p 8.

42 Long, *Australia in the War of 1939-1945: Greece, Crete & Syria*, pp 244, 251.

43 Antony Beevor, *Crete: The Battle and the Resistance* (London: John Murray (Publishers), 1991), p 194.

44 Michael Davie (ed.), *The Diaries of Evelyn Waugh* (London: Weidenfeld & Nicolson, 1976), pp 498–9.

45 Long, *Australia in the War of 1939-1945: Greece, Crete and Syria*, p 251.

46 Cunningham, Despatch, 'The battle of Crete'. Supplement to the *London Gazette* of 24 May 1948.

47 David A Thomas, *Nazi Victory: Crete 1941* (New York: Stein & Day Publishers, 1972), p 221.

48 Cunningham, Despatch, 'The battle of Crete'. Supplement to the *London Gazette* of 24 May 1948.

49 Goodwin, *Midshipman RNR*, p 26.

50 Long, *Australia in the War of 1939-1945: Greece, Crete and Syria*, p 305.

51 Goodwin, *Midshipman RNR*, pp 26–7.

52 Memoir of Captain P M B Chavasse, p 9.

53 J F Cody, *The Official History of New Zealand in the Second World War 1939-1945: 28 (Maori) Battalion* (Wellington: Historical Publications Branch, 1956), p 27.

54 *50th Golden Jubilee N.Z. 28 Maori Battalion, 1940-1990, Seventeenth Reunion* (Auckland, NZ: The Battalion, 1990), pp 75–6.

55 R J M Loughnan, *Official History of New Zealand in the Second World War: Divisional Cavalry* (Wellington: War History Branch, 1963), p 109.

56 Angus Ross, *Official History of New Zealand in the Second World War: 23 Battalion* (Wellington: War History Branch, 1959), p 93.

57 G G Connell, *Valiant Quartet* (London: William Kimber, 1979), pp 200–3.

58 Goodwin, *Midshipman RNR*, p 27.

59 National Museum of the Royal Navy

60 Pleydell-Bouverie, 'HMS *Abdiel*'.

Chapter 5: The *Latona* Takes to the Water and Sails around the Cape, 1941

1 Trevor Piper, *Vosper Thornycroft Built Warships* (Liskeard, Cornwall: Maritime Books, 2006), p 47.

2 Naval Historical Branch, HMS *Latona* Summary of Service May – October 1941 (February 1985).

3 See service numbers in Supplement to *London Gazette* of 20 January 1942, p 340.

4 Translation courtesy of Eric Bateson via Diana Porter; Stopford, *Admiralty Ships Badges*, Vol 1, p 23.

5 Manning and Walker, *British Warship Names*, pp 263–4; Crocker, *Mine Warfare Vessels*, p 27.

6 Le Fleming, *Warships of World War I*, pp 82, 127.

7 Admiralty Press Notice No 1353, Promotions and Retirements, 7 January 1949. Papers of Rear Admiral Robert K Dickson. National Library of Scotland.

8 Sidney Albert Banner, 'Episodes From My Life (1921-1993)'. Copy in the National Museum of the Royal Navy.

9 Southampton Arts & Heritage, Thornycroft Woolston Archive, Box 40.

10 Donovan, 'HMS *Latona*', unpublished narrative. Courtesy of Ray Moore.

11 Ibid

12 Osborne, 'My Diary of Naval Life', p 19.

13 Letter from Charles F Simmons to Mrs Bateman, Easter 1980.

14 Banner, 'Episodes from My Life', Book 3, p 1.

15 Ibid.

16 Ibid, p 2.

17 Donovan, 'HMS *Latona*'.

18 Banner, 'Episodes from My Life', Book 3, pp 2–3.

Chapter 6: Pawns of Coalition War – The *Abdiel* and *Latona* on the Tobruk Run, 1941

1 David Coombes, *Morshead: Here of Tobruk and El Alamein* (Oxford University Press, 2001), p 121.

2 TNA Kew Adm 199/415.

3 HMS *Abdiel* Summary of Service; TNA Kew Adm 199/415.

4 HMS *Latona* Summary of Service.

5 Admiralty Historical Section, *The Royal Navy in the Mediterranean*, Vol II, pp 143–4; TNA Kew Adm 199/415.

6 HMS *Latona* Summary of Service.

7 Admiralty Historical Section, *The Royal Navy and the*

Mediterranean II, p 144.

[8] See the text of the letter in Barton Maughan, *Australia in the War of 1939-1945, Series I, Army, Vol. III, Tobruk & El Alamein* (Canberra: Australian War Memorial, 1966), pp 310–11, and see Auchinleck's Despatch of 8 March 1942, Operations in the Middle East, 5 July 1941–31 October 1941, Supplement to the *London Gazette*, 20 August 1946, Section 28.

[9] Paul Hasluck, *Australia in the War of 1939-1945: The Government and the People, 1939-1945* (Canberra: Australian War Memorial, 1952 & 1965), p 616.

[10] Coombes, *Morshead*, p 119.

[11] Auchinleck Despatch, Section 28.

[12] W J Hudson and H J W Stokes, *Documents on Australian Foreign Policy 1937-49, Vol. V, July 1941-June 1942* (Canberra: Australian Government Publishing Service, 1982), No 10, p 17.

[13] Maughan, *Australia in the War of 1939-1945, Series I, Army, Vol. III*, p 311; see Auchinleck Despatch, Section 28.

[14] Hasluck, *Australia in the War of 1939-1945*, p 618.

[15] Hudson and Stokes, *Documents on Australian Foreign Policy, Vol. V*, No 37, p 65. See also Auchinleck, Despatch, Section 28.

[16] Winston S Churchill, *The Second World War III: The Grand Alliance* (Boston: Houghton Mifflin Co., 1950), p 415.

[17] Auchinleck Despatch, Section 29.

[18] Maughan, *Australia in the War of 1939-1945, Series I, Army, Vol. III*, p 339.

[19] Ibid, p 332.

[20] Michael Simpson, *The Cunningham Papers* I, p 502.

[21] Donovan, 'HMS *Latona*'.

[22] TNA Kew Adm 199/415.

[23] Copy courtesy of Robin Pleydell-Bouverie.

[24] Pleydell-Bouverie, 'HMS *Abdiel*.'

[25] Cunningham, *A Sailor's Odyssey*, p 415.

[26] Memoir of Captain P M B Chavasse, p 10.

[27] Banner, 'Episodes from My Life', Book 3, p 5.

[28] Goodwin, *Midshipman RNR*, p 33.

[29] Sidney Banner, 'The Loss of HMS *Latona*: 25 October 1941,' *Warship World*, Vol 4, No 2 (Spring 1992), pp 14–15; Banner, 'Episodes from My Life', Book 3, p 5.

[30] National Museum of the Royal Navy.

[31] Ibid.

[32] Banner, 'Episodes from My Life,' Book 3, p 5.

[33] TNA Kew Adm 199/415; Alberto Santoni and Francesco Mattessini, *La Partecipazione tedesca alla guerra aeronavale nel Mediterraneo: 1940-1945* (Rome: Edizioni dell'Ateneo e Bizzarri, 1980), p 107.

[34] Admiralty Historical Section, *The Royal Navy in the Mediterranean*, Vol II, p 160; A Raven and H T Lenton, *Ensign 2: Dido Class Cruisers* (London: Bivouac Books Ltd., 1973).

[35] TNA Adm 199/415.

[36] G Santoro, *L'aeronautica Italiana nella seconda Guerra mondiale*, Vol. I (2d ed.) (Milan-Rome: 1957), p 560.

[37] Admiralty Historical Section, *The Royal Navy and the Mediterranean*, Vol II, p 160. Slightly different figures appear in the Mediterranean Fleet war diary.

TNA Kew Adm 199/415.

[38] Churchill, *The Grand Alliance*, p 410; Hasluck, *Australia in the War of 1939-1945*, p 618.

[39] Auchinleck Despatch, Section 29.

[40] Hudson and Stokes, *Documents on Australian Foreign Policy 1937-49, Vol. V* , No 58, p 96.

[41] Ibid, No 59, p 98.

[42] Hasluck, *Australia in the War of 1939-1945*, pp 619–20.

[43] Hudson and Stokes, *Documents on Australian Foreign Policy 1937-49, Vol. V*, No 64, pp 105–6.

[44] Ibid, No 68, p 111.

[45] Churchill, *The Grand Alliance*, p 413.

[46] Auchinleck Despatch, Section 29.

[47] Martin Gilbert, *Winston S. Churchill, Vol VI, Finest Hour* (Boston: Houghton Mifflin Co., 1983), p 1191 n1.

[48] Churchill to Oliver Lyttleton, September 18, 1941, Churchill, *The Grand Alliance*, pp 414–15; Martin Gilbert, *Churchill, Vol VI*, p 1191 n2, citing Churchill Papers, 20/42.

[49] Churchill, *The Grand Alliance*, p 413; Gilbert, *Churchill, Vol. VI*, p 1191 & nn1, 2.

[50] Churchill, *The Grand Alliance*, p 414.

[51] Lord Tedder, *With Prejudice* (Boston: Little Brown & Company, 1966), pp 145–6.

[52] Michael Simpson, *The Cunningham Papers* I, p 509.

[53] TNA Kew Adm 199/415.

[54] Admiralty Historical Section, *The Royal Navy in the Mediterranean*, Vol II, p 184.

[55] Cunningham, *A Sailor's Odyssey*, p 414.

[56] Hudson and Stokes, *Documents on Australian Foreign Policy 1937-49, Vol. V*, No 73, p 120.

[57] Maughan, *Australia in the War of 1939-1945, Series I, Army, Vol. III*, p 380.

[58] Churchill, *The Grand Alliance*, p 415.

[59] Hudson and Stokes, *Documents on Australian Foreign Policy 1937-49, Vol. V*, No 77, p 127.

[60] Churchill Papers, Char 20/43/87 & 125, Churchill Archive Centre.

[61] Churchill Papers 20/43/134, Churchill Archive Centre; Churchill, *The Grand Alliance*, p 416.

[62] Hasluck, *Australia in the War of 1939-1945*, p 623.

[63] Hudson and Stokes, *Documents on Australian Foreign Policy 1937-49, Vol. V*, No 91, p 153; Hasluck, *Australia in the War of 1939-1945*, p 623.

[54] Maughan, *Australia in the War of 1939-1945, Series I, Army, Vol. III*, p 395.

[65] Sir Sam Falle, *My Lucky Life: In War, Revolution, Peace & Diplom*acy (Lewes, Sussex: The Book Guild Ltd., 1996), p 28.

[66] Recollections of Corporal John Lovegrove and Lance-Corporal Allan Jones, both in 1988, Courtesy of author Mark Johnson; Interview with Private Bill Mitchell, 2001, Imperial War Museum No 22083.

[67] Maughan, *Australia in the War of 1939-1945, Series I, Army, Vol. III*, p 400.

[68] TNA Kew Adm 199/415.

[69] Admiralty Press Notice, Biography of Rear Admiral Stuart Latham Bateson.

[70] TNA Adm 199/415.

[71] Michael Simpson, *The Cunningham Papers* I, p 335.

[72] Falle, *My Lucky Life*, p 28.

[73] Maughan, *Australia in the War of 1939-1945, Series I, Army, Vol III*, p 398.

[74] Georg Brütting, *Das waren die deutschen Stuka-Asse 1939-1945* (Stuttgart: 1985), pp 267–9, courtesy of Obertst Bormann of the Zentrum für Militärgeschichte und Sozialwissenschaften der Bundeswehr in Potsdam.

[75] Christopher Shores, Giovanni Massimello, and Russell Guest, *A History of the Mediterranean Air War, 1940-1945, Vol. I: North Africa June 1940 – January 1942* (London: Grub Street, 2012), p 280.

[76] Marco Mattioli, *Savoia-Marchetti S.79 Sparviero Torpedo-Bomber Units* (Oxford: Osprey Publishing, 2014), p 23.

[77] Paddy Donovan, 'The Life of Paddy Donovan'. Courtesy of Gertrude Barrett.

[78] Shores, Massimello, and Guest, *A History of the Mediterranean Air War, Vol I*, p 280; Peter C Smith, *The Junkers Ju 87 Stuka* (Manchester: Crecy Publishing Ltd., 2011), p 272; Santoni and Mattessini, *La Partecipazione Tedesca*, p 109. Sources cannot agree on the size of the bomb.

[79] Smith, *The Junkers Ju 87 Stuka*, p 272.

[80] While it has been stated by some otherwise reputable sources that she was hit in the 'after' engine room, that is not so; the *Abdiel*s had only one engine room. Also, contrary to some sources, her magazine(s) did not blow up.

[81] Paddy Donovan, 'The Life of Paddy Donovan'.

[82] Rohwer, *Chronology of the War at Sea*, p 108.

[83] Fast Minelayer Association Newsletter. Courtesy of Gertrude Barrett.

[84] Admiralty Historical Section, *The Royal Navy in the Mediterranean*, Vol II, p 184.

[85] TNA Kew Adm 199/415.

[86] 'Loss of HMS *Latona*', TNA Kew Adm 267/120.

[87] Goodwin, *Midshipman RNR*, p 29.

[88] A Heckstall-Smith, *Tobruk: The Story of a Siege* (London: Anthony Blond, 1959), pp 147–8.

[89] Churchill, *The Grand Alliance*, p 417.

[90] Churchill Papers, Char 20/44/76; Churchill, *The Grand Alliance*, p 418.

[91] Churchill Papers, Char 44/86, Churchill Archive Centre.

[92] Maughan, *Australia in the War of 1939-1945, Series I, Army, Vol III*, p 400.

[93] Churchill Papers, Char20/44/102, Churchill Archive Centre.

[94] TNA Kew Adm 199/415.

[95] Admiralty Historical Section, *The Royal Navy in the Mediterranean*, Vol II, p 187.

[96] Pleydell-Bouverie, 'HMS *Abdiel*'; Austen, Memoir, Imperial War Museum.

[97] TNA Kew, Adm 1/12247.

[98] Pleydell-Bouverie, 'HMS *Abdiel*'.

[99] Michael Simpson, *The Cunningham Papers I*, p 537.

[100] Shores, Massimello and Guest, *A History of the Mediterranean Air War, Vol I*, p 280.

[101] Maughan, *Australia in the War of 1939-1945, Series I, Army, Vol III*, p 409. For this, Maughan credits the Inshore Squadron and the garrison's 4th Anti-Aircraft Brigade.

[102] Telegram of September 11, 1941. Churchill Papers, Char 20/42B/134. Churchill Archive Centre, Cambridge University.

[103] Hasluck, *Australia in the War of 1939-1945*, pp 623–4.

[104] Maughan, *Australia in the War of 1939-1945, Series I, Army, Vol III*, Chapter 10, 'Ed Duda'.

[105] But see Hasluck, *Australia in the War of 1939-1945*, p 624.

[106] Telegram to Prime Minister of 11 September 1941, Churchill Papers, Char 20/42B/134. Churchill Archive Centre, Cambridge University.

[107] Maughan, *Australia in the War of 1939-1945, Series I, Army, Vol III*, p 348.

[108] Churchill, *The Grand Alliance*, p 411.

[109] Churchill to Oliver Lyttleton, September 18, 1941, quoted in Churchill, *The Grand Alliance*, p 414.

[110] Maughan, *Australia in the War of 1939-1945, Series I, Army, Vol III*, p 305.

[111] Hudson and Stokes, *Documents on Australian Foreign Policy 1937-49, Vol. V*, No 449, p 691.

[112] Ibid, No 131, p 233.

[113] Churchill, *The Grand Alliance*, p 418.

[114] Maughan, *Australia in the War of 1939-1945, Series I, Army, Vol III*, p 348.

[115] 'Naval Diary of the War', *The Naval Review*, Vol XXX, No 1 (February 1942), p 65.

Chapter 7: The *Manxman* Enters the Fray: Malta Runs and a Disguise, 1941

[1] HMS *Manxman*, Fast Minelayer, Summary of Service.

[2] Stopford, *Admiralty Ships Badges*, Vol 2, p 240.

[3] David Hobbs, *Aircraft Carriers of the Royal and Commonwealth Navies* (London: Greenhill Books, 1996), pp 221–2.

[4] TNA Kew HO 45/17738.

[5] Papers of Robert Kirk Dickson, National Library of Scotland.

[6] Obituary, *The Times*, 20 September 1952; Admiralty Press Notice No 1353; Autobiographical Details, February 1949, Dickson Papers, National Library of Scotland.

[7] TNA Adm 1/12304.

[8] National Maritime Museum, Woolwich Arsenal.

[9] Admiralty Historical Section, *The Royal Navy and the Mediterranean Convoys: A Naval Staff History*, (London: Routledge, 2007), pp 13–15; Richard Woodman, *Malta Convoys* (London: John Murray Ltd., 2000), pp 184-209.

[10] Woodman, *Malta Convoys*, pp 208–9.

[11] Stan Fraser, *The Guns of Hagar Qim* (Malta: Wise Owl Publications, 2005).

[12] Brescia, *Mussolini's Navy*, pp 47, 190, 195.

[13] TNA Kew Adm 199/415.

[14] Cowie, *Mines, Minelayers and Minelaying*, p 148.

[15] Admiralty Historical Section, *The Royal Navy and the Mediterranean II*, p 152.

[16] TNA Kew Adm 205/11, p 353.

[17] David A. Thomas, *Malta Convoys, 1940-42*

(Barnsley: Leo Cooper, 1999), p 104.
[18] Ibid.
[19] TNA Kew Adm 199/413.
[20] Admiralty Historical Section, *The Royal Navy and the Mediterranean* II, p 153.
[21] S R Roskill, *The War at Sea II: The Period of Balance* (London: HMSO, 1956), p 369; Woodman, *Malta Convoys*, p 212.
[22] Woodman, *Malta Convoys*, p 212.
[23] Joseph Caruana, *The Battle of Grand Harbour: July 26, 1941* (Malta: Wise Owl Publication, 2004), p 46 n17.
[24] Diary of Captain R K Dickson for 7 June to 29 November 1941. R K Dickson Papers, National Library of Scotland. Dickson, 'First Commission of HMS *Manxman*'.
[25] Cowie, *Mines, Minelayers, and Minelaying*, p 148.
[26] Ibid, p 149.
[27] Naval Staff History, *British Mining Operations*, p 574.
[28] Rear Admiral Robert K Dickson, DSO, *Naval Broadcasts* (London: George Allen & Unwin, Ltd., 1946), p 34.
[29] Admiralty Historical Section, *The Royal Navy and the Mediterranean* Vol II, p 163.
[30] Naval Staff History, *British Mining Operations*, p 57; Dickson, Autobiographical Details; HMS *Manxman* Summary of Service.
[31] HMS *Manxman* Summary of Service.

Chapter 8: The *Welshman* Joins the *Manxman*: Laying Mines for the *Scharnhorst* and *Gneisenau*, 1941–1942

[1] HMS *Welshman* Summary of Service.
[2] Letters of September 1940, File on HMS *Welshman*, Papers of R H Hawthorn & Leslie, Tyne & Wear Archives.
[3] National Maritime Museum, Woolwich Arsenal.
[4] Ibid.
[5] Interview with Jack Cornwall, in George & Angela Evennett, *That Gallant Little Ship HMS 'Welshman'* (n.d.), p 58.
[6] HMS *Welshman* Summary of Service.
[7] Naval Staff History, *British Mining Operations*, p 435.
[8] Evennett, *That Gallant Little Ship HMS 'Welshman'*, p 64.
[9] Dickson, *Naval Broadcasts*, p 9.
[10] TNA Kew Adm 1/12304.
[11] Naval Staff History, *British Mining Operations*, p 309.
[12] HMS *Manxman* Summary of Service; First Commission of HMS *Manxman*.
[13] First Commission of HMS *Manxman*; Naval Staff History, *British Mining Operations*, p 310.
[14] War Diary RA(M), TNA Kew Adm 199/421.
[15] TNA Kew Adm 199/662.
[16] Evennett, *That Gallant Little Ship HMS 'Welshman'*, p 70.
[17] TNA Kew Adm 199/662.
[18] HMS *Welshman* Summary of Service; Naval Staff History, *British Mining Operations*, p 310.
[19] Evennett, *That Gallant Little Ship HMS 'Welshman'*, p 70.
[20] Roskill, *The War at Sea, II: The Period of Balance*, p 151.
[21] Naval Staff History, *British Mining Operations*, p 313.
[22] Ibid, p 319.
[23] German Naval Staff Operations Division War Diary, February 1942, p 102.
[24] Naval Staff History, *British Mining Operations*, p 317.
[25] Ibid, pp 319–20.
[26] Roskill, *The War at Sea, II: The Period of Balance*, p 154.
[27] Letter from Captain Cowie to Patrick Beesly of February 1, 1976. Churchill Archive Centre, MBLE.
[28] William H Garzke, Jr, and Robert O Dulin, Jr, *Battleships: Axis and Neutral Battleships in World War II* (Annapolis: Naval Institute Press, 1985), pp 149–50; Naval Staff History, *British Mining Operations*, p 319.
[29] Naval Staff History, *British Mining Operations*, p 317.
[30] Ibid, pp 324–5.
[31] War Diary, RA(M), TNA Kew, Adm 199/421 and Adm 187/18.
[32] Ibid.

Chapter 9: The *Abdiel* and then the *Manxman* to the Indian Ocean, 1941–1942

[1] TNA Adm 199/415.
[2] Admiralty Historical Section, *The Royal Navy and the Mediterranean* II, pp 218–19; Donald Macintyre, *The Battle for the Mediterranean* (London: BT Batsford, 1964), p 117; Pleydell-Bouverie, HMS *Abdiel*.
[3] TNA Adm 199/415.
[4] Andrew Murray, 'The First Commission of HMS *Abdiel*, 1941-42.' Courtesy of Gertrude Barrett.
[5] TNA Kew Adm 199/415
[6] TNA Kew Adm 1/12247.
[7] Pleydell-Bouverie, 'HMS *Abdiel*'; Memoir of Captain P M B Chavasse, p 12.
[8] HMS *Abdiel* Summary of Service.
[9] Pleydell-Bouverie, 'HMS *Abdiel*'.
[10] Naval Staff History, *British Mining Operations*, p 680.
[11] Goodwin, *Midshipman RNR*, p 41.
[12] Compare ibid with Pleydell-Bouverie.
[13] Goodwin, *Midshipman RNR*, pp 41–2.
[14] Andrew Murray, 'The First Commission of HMS *Abdiel*, 1941-42'.
[15] Naval Staff History, *British Mining Operations*, p 680.
[16] Goodwin, *Midshipman RNR*, p 42.
[17] Pleydell-Bouverie, 'HMS *Abdiel*.'
[18] TNA Kew Adm 187/18.
[19] Goodwin, *Midshipman RNR*, p 42.
[20] TNA Kew Adm 187/18.
[21] Ibid.
[22] Pleydell-Bouverie, 'HMS *Abdiel*'; HMS *Abdiel* Summary of Service.
[23] Pleydell-Bouverie, 'HMS *Abdiel*.'

[24] Goodwin, *Midshipman RNR*, p 44.
[25] HMS *Abdiel* Summary of Service.
[26] Goodwin, *Midshipman RNR*, p 45.
[27] Naval Historical Branch, *War With Japan III: The Campaigns in the Solomons and New Guinea* (London: HMSO, 1995), pp 6–7.
[28] Jentschura, Jung and Mickel, *Warships of the Imperial Japanese Navy*, p 235.
[29] Naval Historical Branch, *War With Japan III*, pp 109–10.
[30] Memoir of Captain P M B Chavasse, p 12.
[31] Goodwin, *Midshipman RNR*, p 45.
[32] Ibid, p 46.
[33] Ibid, p 47.
[34] Memoir of Captain P M B Chavasse; Goodwin, *Midshipman RNR*, p 47.
[35] Copy courtesy of Robin Pleydell-Bouverie.
[36] TNA Kew Adm 199/421.
[37] War Diary, RA(M), TNA Kew Adm 199/421.
[38] Naval Staff History, *British Mining Operations*, p 682.
[39] War Diary, North Atlantic Command, Gibraltar, TNA Kew Adm 199/662.
[40] German Naval Staff Operations Division War Diary for April 1942, pp 221, 234.
[41] North Atlantic Command War Diary, TNA Kew Adm 199/662; Admiralty War Diary, TNA Kew Adm 199/2239; HMS *Manxman* Summary of Service.
[42] Winston S Churchill, *The Second World War IV: The Hinge of Fate* (Boston: Houghton Mifflin Co., 1950), pp 235–6.
[43] Dickson, 'First Commission of HMS Manxman.'
[44] Naval Historical Branch, *War with Japan III*, p 25.
[45] Report by Captain Dickson in National Library of Scotland; Summary of Service, HMS *Manxman*; Naval Historical Branch, *War with Japan III*, p 27.
[46] Naval Historical Branch, *The War Against Japan III*, pp 143–4; Warren Tute, *The Reluctant Enemies: The Story of the Last War Between Britain and France 1940-42* (London: Collins, 1990), p 208.
[47] TNA Kew Adm 223/571.

Chapter 10: The *Welshman* and the *Manxman* to Malta's Rescue, 1942

[1] Fraser, *The Guns of Hagar Qim*, p 146.
[2] TNA Kew Prem 3/266/2.
[3] Adm 205/13.
[4] Friedberger, 'Fast Minelayer', p 13.
[5] Report, TNA Kew Adm 1/12350.
[6] Jean Lassaque, *Les C.T. de 2 400 tonnes du type Jaguar* (Bourg en Bresse: Marines éditions, 1994), pp 73, 76.
[7] Ferry Diary.
[8] Ibid.
[9] German Naval Staff Operations Division War Diary for May 1942, p 65.
[10] War Diary VA Malta for April 1942; TNA Kew, Adm 199/424.
[11] Ed Gordon, HMS *Pepperpot! The Penelope in World War Two* (London: Robert Hale, 1985).
[12] Friedberger, 'Fast Minelayer', p 13.
[13] Adm 1/12350.
[14] TNA Kew Adm 199/678.
[15] *The Fighting Instructions*, C.B. 04027 (39), TNA Kew Adm 239/261.
[16] J A Hall, *The Law of Naval Warfare*, 2nd edition (London: Chapman & Hall, 1921), pp 84–5.
[17] Friedberger, 'Fast Minelayer', p 13.
[18] Ronald McKie, *The Heroes* (New York: Harcourt, Brace, & Co., 1960).
[19] Report, TNA Kew Adm 1/12350.
[20] German Naval Staff Operations Division War Diary for May 1942, p 105.
[21] TNA Kew Adm 223/553.
[22] John Wingate, DSC, *The Fighting Tenth: The Tenth Submarine Flotilla and the Siege of Malta* (London: Leo Cooper, 1991), pp 188–9.
[23] Wingate, *The Fighting Tenth*, p 188; Rear-Admiral G W G Simpson, *Periscope View* (London: MacMillan London Ltd., 1972), p 228; TNA Kew Adm 199/424.
[24] E-mail from Mark Friedberger to the Author of 11 January 2012.
[25] TNA Kew Adm 223/553.
[26] Ferry Diary.
[27] Report, TNA Kew Adm 1/12350.
[28] Ferry Diary.
[29] Ibid.
[30] Report, TNA Kew Adm 1/12350.
[31] Fraser, *The Guns of Hagar Qim*, p 146.
[32] Ferry Diary.
[33] TNA Kew Adm 223/553.
[34] Gerald Toghill, *Admiralty Trawlers I* (Liskeard: Maritime Books, 2003), p 203; Lenton, *British & Empire Warships of the Second World War*, p 413.
[35] Rex Needle, 'Salvaging HMS Beryl,' in *Malta at War* II (2002), p 471.
[36] Vice Admiral (Malta) War Diary for April 1942. TNA Adm 199/413.
[37] Report, TNA Kew Adm 1/12350; Ferry Diary.
[38] Not the '*Menisthem.*' Who's Who in Australia 1921-1950, via ancestry.com, accessed 8 April 2012.
[39] Ferry Diary.
[40] Ibid.
[41] Marc'Antonio Bragadin, *The Italian Navy in World War II* (Annapolis: U.S. Naval Institute, 1957), p 170.
[42] Hans Frank, *German S-Boats in Action in the Second World War* (Barnsley: Seaforth Publishing, 2007), p 76.
[43] Roger Chesneau (ed.), Conway's *All the World's Fighting Ships 1922-1946* (London: Conway Maritime Press, 1980), p 249; Frank, *German S-Boats in Action*, p 151.
[44] Friedrich Kemnade, *Die Afrika-Flottille: Der Einsatz der 3. Schnellbootflotille im Zweiten Weltkrieg, Chronik und Bilanz* (Stuttgart: Motorbuch Verlag, 1978), p 237.
[45] Wingate, *The Fighting Tenth*, pp 190.
[46] Kemnade, *Afrika-Flotille*, pp 239.
[47] Rohwer, *Chronology of the War at Sea*, p 23.
[48] Ferry Diary.
[49] War Diary, TNA Adm 199/424.
[50] Kemnade, *Afrika-Flotille*, pp 241.
[51] Report, TNA Adm 1/12350.
[52] Kemnade, *Afrika-Flotille*, pp 241.
[53] Ferry Diary; Report, TNA Adm 1/12350.

[54] TNA Adm 199/424.

[55] Ferry Diary.

[56] Report, TNA Adm 1/12350.

[57] Ibid.

[58] Adm TNA Adm 223/553.

[59] Report, TNA Adm 1/12350.

[60] Fraser, *The Guns of Hagar Qim,* p 146.

[61] Ibid.

[62] Ibid.

[63] Ibid, p 147.

[64] Report, TNA Adm 1/12350.

[65] Cajus Bekker, *The Luftwaffe War Diaries* (Garden City, NY: Doubleday & Co., 1968), p 242.

[66] Fraser, *The Guns of Hagar Qim,* p 148.

[67] Vuniwai, 'A Good Morning: Malta 1942', WW2 People's War, BBC, 2003.

[68] TNA Adm 199/424.

[69] Report, TNA Adm 1/12350.

[70] Ferry Diary.

[71] Ferry Diary; Report, TNA Adm 1/12350; Lenton, *British and Empire Warships of the Second World War,* p 251.

[72] TNA Adm 1/12350; Ferry Diary; Evennett, *That Gallant Little Ship* HMS *'Welshman'*, p 45.

[73] Recollection of Cecil 'Jack' Cornwall, in Evennett, *That Gallant Little Ship* HMS *'Welshman'*, p 59.

[74] Ferry Diary.

[75] Adm TNA Adm 1/12350.

[76] Ibid.

[77] Air Marshal Sir Hugh Lloyd, *Briefed to Attack: Malta's Part in African Victory* (London: Hodder & Stoughton, 1949), p 186.

[78] Report, TNA Adm 1/12350.

[79] Ibid.

[80] Ferry's diary says it was at 14.00.

[81] Ferry Diary.

[82] TNA Adm 223/553.

[83] Report, TNA Adm 1/12350.

[84] Ferry Diary; Report, TNA Adm 1/12350.

[85] TNA Adm 199/678.

[86] Report, TNA Adm 1/12350.

[87] Ferry Diary.

[88] Ibid.

[89] Report, TNA Adm 1/12350.

[90] Ibid.

[91] TNA Adm 199/424.

[92] Ferry Diary.

[93] TNA Adm 199/424.

[94] Ferry Diary.

[95] Roskill, *The War at Sea* II, *The Period of Balance,* pp 56, 63.

[96] TNA Adm 223/553.

[97] Report, TNA Adm 1/12350.

[98] Ibid.

[99] TNA Adm 223/553.

[100] TNA Adm 199/424.

[101] Fraser, *The Guns of Hagar Qim,* p 148.

[102] Ibid.

[103] Bekker, *Luftwaffe War Diaries,* p 350.

[104] Report, TNA Adm 1/12350; Ferry Diary.

[105] TNA Kew Adm 199/662.

[106] German Naval Staff Operations Division War Diary for May 1942, p 145.

[107] Ferry Diary.

[108] Peter C Smith, 'A Needless Tragedy,' in *Warship International* No 2 (1971), pp 154–69.

[109] Report, TNA Adm 1/12350.

[110] Ferry Diary.

[111] TNA Kew Adm 199/662; Gordon, HMS *Pepperpot!,* pp 155, 158.

[112] See Ferry Diary.

[113] Original in the Library of the National Museum of the Royal Navy.

[114] Supplement to The *London Gazette*, 29 September 1942, p 4227.

[115] TNA Kew Adm 199/678.

[116] Ferry Diary.

[117] Vuniwai, 'A Good Morning: Malta 1942'.

[118] Report, TNA Kew Adm 1/12350.

[119] TNA Kew Adm 199/662.

[120] German Naval Staff Operations Division War Diary for May 1942, p 188.

[121] Ibid, pp 203–4.

[122] Bragadin, *The Italian Navy in World War II,* p 171.

[123] Jock Fison, RNVR, Wartime Experiences Episode 19, in '*Welshman*' Newsletter No 38 (December 2009).

[124] TNA Kew Adm 199/678.

[125] ACNS(F), Naval Historical Branch. Recollections of Robert Ferry, in Evennett, *That Gallant Little Ship* HMS *'Welshman'*, pp 45–6.

[126] ACNS(F), Naval Historical Branch.

[127] TNA Kew Adm 199/662; Friedberger, 'Fast Minelayer', p 14.

[128] German Naval Staff Operations Division War Diary for May 1942, pp 145 and 267.

[129] Admiralty Historical Section, *The Royal Navy and the Mediterranean Convoys,* pp 55–67; TNA Kew Adm 223/292; Woodman, *Malta Convoys,* pp 329–47.

[130] Friedberger, 'Fast Minelayer', p 14.

[131] Admiralty Historical Section, *The Royal Navy and the Mediterranean Convoys,* p 66.

[132] Ibid, p 67.

[133] Report, TNA Adm 1/12350.

[134] Ibid.

[135] Roger Nailer, 'Aircraft to Malta,' in *Warship 1990* (London: Conway Maritime Press, 1990), p 163.

[136] Friedberger, 'Fast Minelayer', p 14.

[137] Some Italian sources say there were twenty-eight Italian aircraft and sixteen Stukas. Giuseppe Fioravanzo, *La Marina Italiana nella Seconda Guerra Mondiale V, La Guerra nel Mediterraneo, Le Azioni Navali, Tomo 2, Dal 1 aprile 1941 all'8 settembre 1943* (Rome: Ufficio Storico della Marina Militare, 1960), p 354; Bragadin, *The Italian Navy in World War II,* p 204.

[138] Friedberger, 'Fast Minelayer', p 14.

[139] TNA Adm 1/12350.

[140] Friedberger, 'Fast Minelayer', p 14.

[141] Bragadin, *The Italian Navy in World War II,* p 204.

[142] Friedberger, 'Fast Minelayer', p 14.

[143] TNA Adm 199/650.

[144] Fraser, *The Guns of Hagar Qim,* p 164.

[145] Elio Ando, *Orizzonte Mare, navi italiane nella 2e Guerra mondiale, incrociatori leggeri classe condottieri gruppo duca d'aosta, parte seconda* (Rome: Edizioni Dell'Ateneo, 1985), p 55.

[146] Bragadin, *The Italian Navy in World War II*, pp 204–05.

[147] Fioravanzo, *La Marina Italiana nella Seconda Guerra Mondiale V, La Guerra nel Mediterraneo, Le Azioni Navali, Tomo 2, Dal 1 aprile 1941 all'8 settembre 1943*, p 354; TNA Kew Adm 199/662. Italian sources say there were five Stukas, not Ju 88s, and British sources say there were fifteen S.79s, not eleven.

[148] Bragadin, *The Italian Navy in World War II*, p 205.

[149] TNA Kew Adm 199/662.

[150] TNA Kew Adm 199/421.

[151] Ian Cameron, *Red Duster, White Ensign: The Story of Malta and the Malta Convoys* (Garden City: Doubleday & Co., 1960), p 182; Evennett, *That Gallant Little Ship HMS 'Welshman'*, p 19.

[152] Evennett, *That Gallant Little Ship HMS 'Welshman'*, p 18.

[153] TNA Adm 199/650.

[154] TNA Kew Adm 199/421.

[155] Ibid.

[156] Courtesy of Angela Evennett.

[157] TNA Kew, Adm 199/1039.

[158] Cunningham, *A Sailor's Odyssey*, p 494.

[159] HMS *Welshman* Summary of Service.

[160] TNA Kew Adm 199/651.

[161] Ibid.

[162] First Commission of HMS *Manxman*.

[163] TNA Kew Adm 199/651.

[164] Letter from Dickson to Leatham.

[165] HMS *Manxman* Summary of Service.

[166] TNA Kew Adm 199/651; First Commission of HMS *Manxman*.

[167] TNA Kew Adm 199/424.

[168] TNA Adm 199/651.

[169] Letter from Dickson to Leatham.

[170] TNA Kew Adm 199/651.

[171] Ibid.

[172] Woodman, *Malta Convoys*, p 461.

[173] TNA Kew Adm 199/651.

[174] Ibid.

Chapter 11: The *Manxman*, *Welshman* and *Abdiel* Wreak Havoc in the Mediterranean, 1942–1943

[1] First Commission of HMS *Manxman*; HMS *Manxman* Summary of Service.

[2] Several sources give credit to the submarine-minelayer *Rorqual*, but Naval Staff History, *British Mining Operations* gives credit to the *Manxman*.

[3] Paolo Pollina, *Le Torpediniere Italiane 1881-1964* (Rome: Ufficio Storico Marina Militare, 1964), p 290.

[4] Naval Staff History, *British Mining Operations*, p 636; I S O Playfair, C J C Molony and F C Flynn, *The Mediterranean and the Middle East, Volume IV: The Destruction of Axis Forces in Africa* (London: HMSO, 1960), pp 245–6; *Kriegstagebuch der Seekriegsleitung* [War Diary of the German Naval Operations Staff] (Herford: Verlag E. S. Mittler & Sohn, 1988) Volume 41, January 1943 (U.S. Navy Department Library, Washington, D.C.).

[5] Naval Staff History, *British Mining Operations*, p 639–40.

[6] Playfair, Molony and Flynn, *The Mediterranean and the Middle East, Volume IV*, p 200.

[7] Roskill, *The War at Sea, Vol. II, The Period of Balance*, p 438.

[8] Naval Staff History, *British Mining Operations*, p 637.

[9] Pagano, *La Guerra di Mine*, pp 479, 480.

[10] TNA Kew Adm 199/421.

[11] E-mails from Lt.-Cmdr. Charles Orr Ewing to the Author.

[12] Bruce Taylor, *The Battlecruiser HMS Hood – An Illustrated Biography 1916-1941* (London: Chatham Publishing, 2005), pp 64, 135.

[13] E-mail from Charles Orr Ewing of 8 April, 2013.

[14] Peter C Smith, *Skua! The Royal Navy's Dive Bomber* (Barnsley: Pen & Sword, 2006), p 73.

[15] Geoffrey A Hodges, *Of Mines and Men* (Winchester: John Corries, 1993), pp 36–7.

[16] Naval Staff History, *British Mining Operations*, pp 331–2; William Alastair Robertson, 'Some Recollections of World War II 1939-1945'.

[17] Naval Staff History, *British Mining Operations*, p 597.

[18] HMS *Abdiel* Summary of Service.

[19] Naval Staff History, *British Mining Operations*, p 628.

[20] Robertson, 'Some Recollections'.

[21] Naval Staff History, *British Mining Operations*, p 597.

[22] Robertson, *Some Recollections*.

[23] Naval Staff History, *British Mining Operations*, p 636 n1.

[24] Ibid, p 637.

[25] Pagano, *La Guerra di Mine*, p 482.

[26] Naval Staff History, *British Mining Operations*, p 638.

[27] Ibid, p 603; Robertson, 'Some Recollections'.

[28] Robertson, 'Some Recollections'.

[29] Naval Staff History, *British Minelaying Operations*, p 604.

[30] Ibid, p 637.

[31] Ibid, p 604.

[32] Ibid, p 605.

[33] Ibid, p 638.

[34] Pagano, *La Guerra di Mine*, p 486.

[35] Naval Staff History, *British Mining Operations*, p 639.

[36] Ibid, p 640.

[37] Ibid, pp 607–8.

[38] Hodges, *Of Mines and Men*, p 62.

[39] Naval Staff History, *British Mining Operations*, pp 607–8.

[40] Ibid, p 613.

[41] Hodges, *Of Mines and Men*, p 66.

[42] Ibid, p 67.

[43] Robertson, 'Some Recollections'.

[44] Ibid.

[45] Hodges, *Of Mines and Men*, p 67.

Chapter 12: Hard Times for Fast Minelayers in the Mediterranean, 1942–1943

[1] Lawrence Paterson, *U-Boats in the Mediterranean 1941-1944* (Annapolis: Naval Institute Press, 2007), p 186.

[2] Ibid, p 117.

[3] Translation of War Diary of Captain U-Boats, Italy, 1 July–31 December 1942, p 522, Internet Archive, archive.org, accessed 23 February 2015.

[4] Author's conversation with Mr Checketts on 7 December 2005.

[5] TNA Kew Adm 267/116.

[6] HMS *Manxman* Summary of Service.

[7] TNA Kew Adm 267/32.

[8] Edward P Stafford, *Subchaser* (Annapolis: Naval Institute Press, 1988), pp 159–60; Clay Blair, *Hitler's U-boat War: The Hunted* (New York: Random House, 1998), p 379; William J Veigle, *PC Patrol Craft of World War II* (Santa Barbara: Astral Publishing Co., 1998), pp 177–8, 293–4.

[9] Naval Staff History, *British Mining Operations,* p 599; HMS *Welshman* Summary of Service.

[10] G W G Simpson, *Periscope View,* p 283.

[11] Information and stories courtesy of the Associated Press. E-mails from Francesca Pittaro to the Author of 23 July 2014.

[12] HMS *Welshman* Summary of Service.

[13] Paterson, *U-Boats in the Mediterranean,* p 187.

[14] Campbell, *Naval Weapons of World War Two,* p 263; copy of *U-617*'s War Diary, courtesy of Telegraphist Robert Ferry.

[15] Naval Staff History, *British Mining Operations,* p 601.

[16] Evennett, *That Gallant Little Ship HMS 'Welshman',* p 40.

[17] Daniel Morgan and Bruce Taylor, *U-boat Attack Logs: A Complete Record of Warship Sinkings from Original Sources 1939-1945* (Barnsley: Seaforth Publishing, 2011), pp 377–8.

[18] Blair, *Hitler's U-boat War: The Hunted,* p 209.

[19] H T Lenton, *Navies of the Second World War: German Submarines I* (Garden City: Doubleday & Co., 1965), p 121; Morgan and Taylor, *U-boat Attack Logs,* p 323; Blair, *Hitler's U-boat War: The Hunted,* pp 413–14.

[20] Evennett, *That Gallant Little Ship HMS 'Welshman',* p 48.

[21] Ibid, pp 65–6.

[22] Ibid, p 62.

[23] Friedberger, 'Fast Minelayer', p 15.

[24] Evennett, *That Gallant Little Ship HMS 'Welshman',* p 55.

[25] Ibid , p 57.

[26] TNA Kew Adm 1/13090.

[27] Recollections of Robert Ferry, in Evennett, *That Gallant Little Ship HMS 'Welshman',* p 48.

[28] Evennett, *That Gallant Little Ship HMS 'Welshman',* p 42.

[29] Naval Staff History, *British Mining Operations,* pp 599–600.

[30] Evennett, *That Gallant Little Ship HMS 'Welshman',* p 74.

[31] Recollections of Jack Lemon, in Evennett, *That Gallant Little Ship HMS 'Welshman',* p 51.

[32] Ibid, p 75.

[33] Ibid.

[34] 'Naval Diary of the War,' *The Naval Review,* Vol. XXXI, No 2 (May 1943), p 158.

[35] HMS *Welshman* Summary of Service; Naval Historical Branch note with Summary of Service.

[36] TNA Adm 1/13090.

[37] Naval Staff History, *British Mining Operations,* p 600.

[38] Robertson, 'Some Recollections'.

[39] Erminio Bagnasco, *Corsari in Adriatico: 8-13 settembre 1943* (Milan: Ugo Mursia Editore, S.p.A., 2006), p 60.

[40] F Bargoni and F Gay, *Orizzonte Mare, Navi Italiane nella 2e Guerra Mondiale 2 Corazzate classe caio duilio* (Rome: Edizione Bizzarri, 1972), p 76.

[41] TNA Kew Adm 267/116.

[42] Robertson, 'Some Recollections'.

[43] E-mail from Charles Orr-Ewing to the Author of 19 March 2012.

[44] Hodges, *Of Mines and Men,* p 68.

[45] Ibid, p 69.

[46] Ibid, p 69.

[47] E-mail from Hans Frank to the Author of 3 July 2012.

[48] www.historisches-marinearchiv.de, accessed 11 July 2012.

[49] Bagnasco, *Corsari in Adriatico,* p 42.

[50] Campbell, *Naval Weapons of World War Two,* pp 272–3.

[51] Naval Staff History, *British Mining Operations,* pp 617–19.

[52] Gerhard Hümmelchen, *Die deutschen Schnellboote im Zweiten Weltkrieg* (Hamburg, Berlin and Bonn: Verlag E.S. Mittler & Sohn, 1996), p 103.

[53] Ando, *Incrociatori leggeri classi 'Capitani Romani',* p 87.

[54] Rohwer, *Chronology of the War at Sea,* p 272.

[55] Ibid, p 272.

[56] Jean-Philippe Dallies-Labourdette, *S-Boote: German E-Boats in action 1939-1945* (Paris: Histoire & Collections, 2003), p 92.

[57] Rohwer, *Chronology of the War at Sea,* p 414.

[58] TNA Kew Adm 267/116.

[59] Ibid.

[60] 'Naval Diary of the War,' *The Naval Review,* Vol XXXI, No 4 (November 1943), p 351.

[61] TNA Kew Adm 358/2978.

Chapter 13: The Repeat *Abdiel*s Take Shape, 1941–1943

[1] Moore, *Building for Victory,* p 145.

[2] National Archives of Australia, MP1049/5, Item 2037/7/257, courtesy of Peter Cannon; Peter Burton, *Warship Profile 38: Abdiel-Class Fast Minelayers* (Windsor: Profile Publications Ltd, 1973), p 30.

[3] Hodges, *Of Mines and Men,* p 56.

[4] Brown, *The Design and Construction of British Warships,* p 123.

[5] Burton, *Abdiel-Class Fast Minelayers*, p 30.

Chapter 14: The *Ariadne* Completes and Shows the Flag in the Pacific, 1943–1945
[1] Manring, *British Warship Names*, p 88, Stopford, *Admiralty Ships Badges*, Vol. 1, p 4, and Crocker, *Mine Warfare Vessels*, p 32.
[2] HMS *Ariadne* Summary of Service.
[3] Stopford, *Admiralty Ships Badges*, Vol. 1, p 4.
[4] E-mail from Barry Gibson, 4th Baron Ashbourne, of 17 May 2012.
[5] Undated letter from Bill Pye to the Author; TNA Kew Adm 199/767.
[6] HMS *Ariadne* Summary of Service.
[7] TNA Kew Adm 187/32.
[8] Loan of R.N. Minelayer to U.S. Navy, TNA Kew Adm 1/17224.
[9] Cowie, *Mines, Minelayers and Minelaying*, pp 44, 101.
[10] S E Morison, *History of United States Naval Operations in World War II*, Vol. 6, *Breaking the Bismarcks Barrier* (Boston: Little, Brown & Co., 1957), pp 112–16; Theodore Roscoe, *United States Destroyer Operations in World War II* (Annapolis: Naval Institute Press, 1953), pp 213, 220.
[11] S E Morison, *History of United States Naval Operations in World War II*, Vol. 5, *The Struggle for Guadalcanal August 1942 – February 1943* (Boston: Little, Brown & Co., 1948), p 367.
[12] Robert F Sumrall, *Sumner-Gearing Class Destroyers: Their Design, Weapons, and Equipment* (Annapolis: Naval Institute Press, 1995), p 53.
[13] Correlli Barnett, *Engage the Enemy More Closely: The Royal Navy in the Second World War* (New York: W W Norton & Co., 1991), pp 770–1.
[14] HMS *Ariadne* Summary of Service.
[15] Richard B Frank, *MacArthur* (New York: Palgrave MacMillan, 2007), p 56.
[16] TNA Kew Adm 187/32.
[17] HMS *Ariadne* Summary of Service; Letter from Bill Pye to the Author.
[18] TNA Kew Adm 1/15783; Adm 1/117383.
[19] TNA Kew Adm 1/16096.
[20] Undated letter from Bill Pye to the Author.
[21] Letter from Bill Pye to Author of 9 July 2012.
[22] TNA Kew Adm 1/16096.
[23] Information courtesy of Naval Historical Branch, Ministry of Defence.
[24] Robert J Bulkley, Jr., *At Close Quarters: PT Boats in the United States Navy* (Annapolis: Naval Institute Press, 1962, 2003), pp 245.
[25] HMS *Ariadne* Summary of Service.
[26] Ibid.
[27] Navsource.org, accessed 11 July 2013.
[28] G Hermon Gill, *Australia in the War of 1939-1945, Royal Australian Navy 1942-1945* (Canberra: Australian War Memorial, 1968), p 494.
[29] Ibid.
[30] Seventh Amphibious Force Command History, 10 January 1943–23 December 1945, U.S. Navy, 1945; Gill, *Australia in the War of 1939-1945, Royal Australian Navy 1942-1945*, p 495.

[31] Gill, *Australia in the War of 1939-1945, Royal Australian Navy 1942-1945*, p 495.
[32] Ibid, p 510.
[33] Ibid, p 513.
[34] Morison, *Leyte*, pp 349–54, 368–92; Samuel Elliot Morison, *The Two-Ocean War* (Boston: Little, Brown & Co., 1963), pp 470–4.
[35] Norman Friedman, *U.S. Destroyers: An Illustrated Design History* (Annapolis: Naval Institute Press, 1982), p 135.
[36] Daniel E Barbey, *MacArthur's Amphibious Navy* (Annapolis: Naval Institute Press, 1969), p 280; Captain Lord Ashbourne Report, 27 November 1944.
[37] HMS *Ariadne* Summary of Service.
[38] *History of the 31st Infantry Division in Training and Combat 1940-1945* (Nashville: The Battery Press, Inc., 1946, 1993), p 101.
[39] *31st Infantry Division in the Pacific/167th Infantry Regiment* (Baton Rouge: Army & Navy Publishing Co., 1951).
[40] HMS *Ariadne* Summary of Service.
[41] Article, Courtesy of Lord Ashbourne.
[42] Barbey, *MacArthur's Amphibious Navy*, p 280.
[43] 'And Britons have first crack at Japs,' *The Daily Express*, 20 November 1944.
[44] *History of the 31st Infantry Division in Training and Combat 1940-1945* (Nashville: The Battery Press, 1946 & 1993), p 101.
[45] *History of the 31st Infantry Division*, p 23.
[46] Morison, *Leyte*, p 54.
[47] Action Report – Mapia Islands and Asia Islands Operation, Commander Task Group 78.14, No 1073/08, U.S. National Archives & Records Administration II, College Park, Maryland.
[48] Gill, *Australia in the War of 1939-1945, Royal Australian Navy 1942-1945*, p 476.
[49] Ibid, p 477.
[50] HMS *Ariadne* Summary of Service.
[51] Naval Staff History, *British Mining Operations*, p 222.

Chapter 15: The *Apollo* Rounds Out the Six and Becomes a Yeoman Minelayer, 1944–1945
[1] Moore, *Building for Victory*, p 145.
[2] Brown, *The Design and Construction of British Warships*, p 123.
[3] Crocker, *Mine Warfare Vessels*, p 27; Manning, *British Warship Names*, pp 84–5.
[4] John Roberts, 'HMS *Apollo*,' in John Roberts (ed.), *Warship VI* (London: Conway Maritime Press, 1982), p 38.
[5] Stopford, *Admiralty Ships Badges*, Vol 1, p 3.
[6] Memoir of John Robin Grindle, 2011. Courtesy of Jeremy Grindle.
[7] Author's conversation with Ronald Thake, 14 January 2013.
[8] Letter from J. Mervyn Tommey to Mrs. Grindle of 4 March 1991. Courtesy of Jeremy Grindle.
[9] E-mail from Jeremy Grindle to the author of 10 July 2012.
[10] Hodges, *Of Mines and Men*, p 78.

[11] HMS *Apollo* Summary of Service.

[12] Naval Staff History, *British Mining Operations,* p 351.

[13] Ibid, pp 365–6.

[14] Ibid, p 369.

[15] Ibid, p 371.

[16] Ibid, p 375.

[17] HMS *Apollo* Summary of Service.

[18] Harry Butcher, *My Three Years with Eisenhower* (New York: Simon & Schuster, 1946), p 571.

[19] Letter from J Mervyn Tommey to Mrs Grindle. Courtesy of Jeremy Grindle.

[20] Ship's Log of HMS *Apollo*, June 1944, TNA Kew Adm 53/118832.

[21] Butcher, *My Three Years with Eisenhower*, p 572.

[22] Ibid. This incident somehow escaped mention in her Summary of Service.

[23] Ship's Log.

[24] Naval Staff History, *British Mining Operations,* p 383.

[25] Ship's Log.

[26] John Winton, Obituary for Captain John Annesley Grindle, 1991.

[27] Memoir of John Robin Grindle, 2011.

[28] Butcher, *My Three Years with Eisenhower*, p 577.

[29] Memoir of John Robin Grindle, 2011. Courtesy of Jeremy Grindle.

[30] John Winton, Obituary for Capt John Grindle, 1991.

[31] Naval Staff History, *British Mining Operations,* p 383.

[32] Ibid, p 207.

[33] HMS *Apollo* Summary of Service.

[34] G G Connell, *Arctic Destroyers: The 17th Flotilla* (London: William Kimber, 1982), pp 190–1.

[35] Naval Staff History, *British Mining Operations,* p 215.

[36] Ibid, p 224.

[37] Hodges, *Of Mines and Men*, p 80.

[38] Naval Staff History, *British Mining Operations,* pp 453–4.

[39] Hodges, *Of Mines and Men*, p 81.

[40] Naval Staff History, *British Mining Operations,* p 226.

[41] HMS *Ariadne* Summary of Service; Naval Staff History, *British Mining Operations*, p 227.

[42] HMS *Apollo* Summary of Service.

Chapter 16: War's End

[1] Naval Staff History, *British Mining Operations*, p 227.

[2] HMS *Ariadne* Summary of Service.

[3] Letter of 15 May 1945. Courtesy of Jeremy Grindle.

[4] Letter from Ronald Thake to the Author.

[5] HMS *Ariadne* Summary of Service.

[6] TNA Kew Adm 1/16096.

[7] Letter from Thistleton-Smith to C-in-C, British Pacific Fleet of 25 July 1945, National Maritime Museum, Woolwich Arsenal.

[8] HMS *Manxman* Summary of Service; Letter from Thistleton-Smith to C-in-C, British Pacific Fleet of 25 July 1945, National Maritime Museum.

Chapter 17: Peacetime

[1] HMS *Ariadne* Summary of Service; e-mail from Brian Hargreaves.

[2] HMS *Apollo* Summary of Service.

[3] Ibid.

[4] Letter from Rear Admiral P N Buckley, CB, DSO, Naval Historical Branch, to Lieutenant A J Bensted, RN, of 7 March 1969. Ship's Book for HMS *Manxman*, National Maritime Museum, Woolwich Arsenal.

[5] Allan George, 'The Heroines Are the Ships: RN Warships in Film', *Warship World*, Vol 13, No 9 (January/February 2014), p 21.

[6] Burton, *Warship Profile 38: Abdiel-Class Fast Minelayers*, p 44.

Chapter 18: Epilogue and Honours

[1] HMS *Abdiel* Summary of Service.

[2] Supplement to the *London Gazette*, 13 October 1942, p 4449.

[3] Supplement to the *London Gazette*, 4 May 1943, p 2007.

[4] E-mail from Charles Orr Ewing to the Author of 23 March 2012.

[5] Burton, *Warship Profile 38: Abdiel-Class Fast Minelayers*, p 30.

[6] Supplement to the *London Gazette*, 20 January 1942, p 340.

[7] *Who Was Who*, 1971-1980, p 50.

[8] Biography, Dickson Papers.

[9] Supplements to the *London Gazette* of November 1941, May 1942, February 1943 and June 1943.

[10] Dickson, *Naval Broadcasts*, pp 9 and 31.

[11] *Times of Malta*, 2 October 1952, p 4.

[12] Evennett, *That Gallant Little Ship HMS 'Welshman'*, p 38.

[13] Ian Hay, *The Unconquerable Isle: The Story of Malta G.C.* (London: Hodder & Stoughton, 1943), p 184.

[14] Evennett, *That Gallant Little Ship HMS 'Welshman'*, p 70.

[15] Supplement to the *London Gazette* of 8 September 1942, p 3917.

[16] Supplement to the *London Gazette* of 11 May 1943, p 2112.

[17] Entry in The Peerage, thepeerage.com. of 26 March 2012; Obituary, *The Times*, 8 September 1983, p 12.

[18] John Winton, 'Capt John Grindle,' in *The Daily Telegraph*, 1991.

[19] Dickson, Autobiographical Details.

[20] Crocker, *Mine Warfare Vessels*, p 25.

[21] Jean Labayle Couhat (ed.) and A D Baker III, *Combat Fleets of the World 1982/83, Their Ships, Aircraft, and Armament* (Annapolis: Naval Institute Press, 1982), pp 243–4.

[22] Ibid, p 243.

SOURCES

Articles

Banner, Sidney, 'The Loss of HMS *Latona* 25 October 1941', *Warship World*, Vol 4, No 2 (Spring 1992), pp 14–15.

Caruana, Joe, 'Emergency Victualling of Malta During WWII', *Warship International*, No 4 (2012).

Cowie, Captain John S, CBE, RN, 'The British Sea-Mining Campaign, 1939-1945,' *Journal of the United Service Institution,* Vol XCIII (February to November 1948), pp 22–39.

_____, 'Minelayers', *Journal of the United Service Institution*, Vol C (February to November 1955), pp 601–10.

Dodson, Aidan, 'The Fast Minelayers,' *Ships Monthly* (May 1992), pp 14–17.

Flemming, Ian M, 'Royal Navy Fast Minelayers', *Airfix Magazine for Modellers* (March 1979), pp 370–3 and 383.

Hargreaves, Brian, '*Abdiel* Class Fast Minelayers (UK)', *Warships* No 134 (April 1999), pp 1–15.

Johnson, Bill, 'HMS Manxman', *Warship World,* Vol 6, No 9 (Winter 1999), pp 18–20.

Williams, John F, 'Minesweeping at Malta 1940-1946, Part Two', *Warships*, No 133 (1999), pp 3–11.

Wright, Richard N J, '*Abdiel* Class Fast Minelayers At War', in Roberts, John (ed.), *Warship 1994* (London: Conway Maritime Press, 1994).

Books

Ando, Elio, *Orizzonte Mare, navi italiane nella 2e Guerra mondiale, incrociatori leggeri classe condottieri gruppo duca d'aosta, parte seconda* (Rome: Edizioni Dell'Ateneo, 1985).

Bagnasco, Erminio, *Corsari in Adriatico 8-13 settembre 1943* (Milan: Ugo Mursia Editore S.p.A., 2006).

Barbey, Daniel E, *MacArthur's Amphibious Navy* (Annapolis: Naval Institute Press, 1969).

Bekker, Cajus, *The Luftwaffe War Diaries* (Garden City, NY: Doubleday & Co., 1968).

Blair, Clay, *Hitler's U-boat War: The Hunted* (New York: Random House, 1998).

Bragadin, Marc'Antonio, *The Italian Navy in World War II* (Annapolis: US Naval Institute Press, 1957).

Brescia, Maurizio, *Mussolini's Navy: A Reference Guide to the Regia Marina 1930-1945* (Annapolis: Naval Institute Press, 2012).

Brown, D K, *The Design and Construction of British Warships 1939-1945 the Official Record: Major Surface Vessels* (London: Conway Maritime Press, 1995).

Burton, Tom, *Warship Profile 38: Abdiel-Class Fast Minelayers* (Windsor: Profile Publications Limited, 1973).

Butcher, Harry, *My Three Years with Eisenhower* (New York: Simon & Schuster, 1946).

Cameron, Ian, *Red Duster, White Ensign: The Story of Malta and the Malta Convoys* (Garden City: Doubleday & Co., 1960).

Campbell, John, *Naval Weapons of World War Two* (London: Conway Maritime Press, 1985).

Churchill, Winston S, *The Second World War III: The Grand Alliance* (Boston: Houghton Mifflin Co., 1950).

_____, *The Second World War IV: The Hinge of Fate* (Boston: Houghton Mifflin Co., 1950).

Coombes, David, *Morshead: Hero of Tobruk and El Alamein* (Oxford University Press, 2001).

Cowie, Captain J S, CBE, *Mines, Minelayers & Minelaying* (London: Oxford University Press, 1949).

Crocker, M P, *Mine Warfare Vessels of the Royal Navy – 1908 to Present* (Shrewsbury: Airlife Publishing, 1993).

Cunningham of Hyndhope, Viscount, *A Sailor's Odyssey* (New York: E P Dutton & Co, Inc., 1951).

Dickson, Rear Admiral Robert K, *Naval Broadcasts* (London: Allen & Unwin Ltd., 1946).

Evennett, George and Angela, *The Gallant Little*

Ship 'HMS Welshman' (Crayford, Kent: Privately Published, 2006).

Falle, Sir Sam, My Lucky Life: In War, Revolution, Peace & Diplomacy (Lewes, Sussex: The Book Guild Ltd., 1996).

Faulkner, Marcus, War at Sea: A Naval Atlas 1939-1945 (Annapolis: Naval Institute Press, 2012).

Fioravanzo, Giuseppe, La Marina Italiana nella Seconda Guerra Mondiale V, La Guerra nel Mediterraneo, Le Azioni Navali, Tomo 2, Dal 1 aprile 1941 all'8 settembre 1943 (Rome: Ufficio Storico della Marina Militare, 1960).

Fraccaroli, Aldo, Italian Warships of World War II (London: Ian Allen, 1968).

Frank, Hans, German S-Boats in Action in the Second World War (Barnsley: Seaforth Publishing, 2007).

Fraser, Stan, The Guns of Hagar Qim: The Diaries of Stan Fraser 1939-1946 (Malta: Wise Owl Publications, 2005).

Friedman, Norman, British Destroyers: From Earliest Days to the Second World War (Annapolis: Naval Institute Press, Barnsley: Seaforth Publishing, 2009).

_____, British Cruisers: Two World Wars and After (Annapolis: Naval Institute Press, 2010).

Martin Gilbert, Winston S. Churchill, Vol VI, Finest Hour (Boston: Houghton Mifflin Co., 1983).

Gill, G Hermon, Australia in the War of 1939-1945, Royal Australian Navy 1942-1945 (Canberra: Australian War Memorial, 1968).

Goodwin, F N, Midshipman Royal Naval Reserve (Spennymoor: The Memoir Club, 2001).

Gordon, Ed, HMS Pepperpot! The Penelope in World War Two (London: Robert Hale, 1985).

Halder, Franz, Kriegstagebuch II (Stuttgart: W Kohlhammer Verlag, 1963).

Hasluck, Paul, Australia in the War of 1939-1945: The Government and the People, 1939-1945 (Canberra: Australian War Memorial, 1952 & 1965).

Hodges, Geoffrey A, GM, Of Mines & Men (Winchester: John Corrie, 1993).

Jellicoe, Admiral Viscount, The Grand Fleet 1914-1916: Its Creation, Development & Work (New York: George H Doran Co., 1919).

Jentschura, H, Jung, D, and Mickel, P, Warships of the Imperial Japanese Navy 1869-1945 (Annapolis: Naval Institute Press, 1977).

Kemnade, Friedrich, Die Afrika-Flottille: Der Einsatz der 3. Schnellbootflotille im Zweiten Weltkrieg, Chronik und Bilanz (Stuttgart: Motorbuch Verlag, 1978).

Le Fleming, H M, Warships of World War I (London: Ian Allen, 1961).

Le Masson, Henri, Navies of the Second World War: The French Navy I (London: MacDonald & Co., 1969).

Lenton, H T, British and Empire Warships of the Second World War (London: Greenhill Books, 1998).

Long, Gavin, Australia in the War of 1939-1945, Series One, Army, Vol. II, Greece, Crete and Syria (Canberra: Australian War Memorial, 1953).

Lott, Arnold S, Most Dangerous Sea, A History of Mine Warfare, and an Account of US Mine Warfare Operations in World War II and Korea (Annapolis: U.S. Naval Institute, 1959).

Manning, Captain T D and Walker, Commander C F, British Warship Names (London: Putnam, 1959).

Maughan, Barton, Australia in the War of 1939-1945, Series I, Army, Vol. III, Tobruk & El Alamein (Canberra: Australian War Memorial, 1966).

Meister, Jürg, Soviet Warships of the Second World War (New York: Arco Publishing Co., 1977).

Moore, George, Building for Victory (Gravesend, Kent: World Ship Society, 1995).

Morgan, Daniel and Taylor, Bruce, U-Boat Attack Logs: A Complete Record of Warship Sinkings from Original Sources 1939-1945 (Barnsley: Seaforth Publishing, 2011).

Morison, Samuel Eliot, Leyte: June 1944 –January 1945 (Boston: Little, Brown & Co., 1958).

_____, The Two-Ocean War (Boston: Little, Brown & Co., 1963).

Pagano, C F Gian Carlo, La Guerra di Mine, 2nd Edition (Rome: Ufficio Storico della Marina Militare, 1988).

Paterson, Lawrence, U-Boats in the Mediterranean 1941-1944 (Annapolis: Naval Institute Press, 2007).

Playfair, I S O, Molony, C J C, and Flynn, F C, The Mediterranean and the Middle East, Volume IV: The Destruction of Axis Forces in Africa (London: HMSO, 1960).

R & W Hawthorn Leslie & Co Ltd, Our Ships at War (1946).

Rohwer, Jürgen, *Chronology of the War at Sea 1939-1945* (London: Chatham Publishing, 2005).

Roskill, S R, *The War at Sea II: The Period of Balance* (London: HMSO, 1956).

Santoni, Alberto, and Mattessini, Francesco, *La Partecipazione tedesca alla guerra aeronavale nel Mediterraneo: 1940-1945* (Rome: Edizioni dell'Ateneo e Bizzarri, 1980).

Shores, Christopher, Massimello, Giovanni, and Guest, Russell, *A History of the Mediterranean Air War, 1940-1945, Vol. I: North Africa June 1940 – January 1942* (London: Grub Street, 2012).

Silverstone, Paul H, *Directory of the World's Capital Ships* (New York: Hippocrene Books, 1984).

Simpson, Rear-Admiral G W G, *Periscope View* (London: MacMillan London Ltd., 1972).

Simpson, Michael (ed.), *The Cunningham Papers: Volume I The Mediterranean Fleet, 1939-1942* (Aldershot: Ashgate Publishing Limited for the Naval Records Society, 1999).

Smith, Peter C, *Into the Minefields: British Destroyer Minelaying 1916-1960* (Barnsley, South Yorkshire: Pen & Sword Maritime, 2005).

Steinzer, Franz, *Die 2. Panzer-Division 1935-1945* (Friedberg: Podzun-Pallas-Verlag, 1977).

Stopford, T P, *Admiralty Ships Badges: Original Patterns, 1919-1994*, two vols (Strood: Stone Frigate, 1996).

Wingate, John, DSC, *The Fighting Tenth: The Tenth Submarine Flotilla and the Siege of Malta* (London: Leo Cooper, 1991).

Woodman, Richard, *Malta Convoys* (London: John Murray Publishing Ltd, 2000).

Diaries and Private Memoirs

Austen, N H G: Documents. 19689, Imperial War Museum.

Banner, Sidney Albert: 'Episodes from My Life (1921–1993), National Museum of the Royal Navy.

Chavasse, P M B: Documents. 9064, Imperial War Museum.

Dickson, Captain Robert K: The National Library of Scotland.

Ferry, Robert: 'W/T Operator's Log of Events', The Ferry Family.

Osborne, H, 'My Diary of Naval Life': Documents, 1322. Imperial War Museum.

Robertson, William Alastair Robertson: 'Some Recollections of World War II 1939–1945' (c. 1980), The Hamilton Family.

Wright, Sub-Lt W G Wright: Documents. 17345, Imperial War Museum.

Official Sources

Hudson, W J, and W Stokes, H J, *Documents on Australian Foreign Policy 1937-49, Vol. V, July 1941-June 1942* (Canberra: Australian Government Publishing Service, 1982).

Llewellyn-Jones, Malcolm (ed), *The Royal Navy and the Mediterranean Convoys: A Naval Staff History* (Abingdon: Routledge, 2007).

Naval Historical Branch, Summaries of Service for HM Ships *Abdiel, Apollo, Ariadne, Latona, Manxman,* and *Welshman* (Imperial War Museum).

Naval Staff History, *British Mining Operations 1939-1945*, BR 1736 (56)(1) (London: HMSO, 1973).

Internet

www.naval-history.net

INDEX